DREAMS

HIDDEN MEANINGS AND SECRETS

by
Orion

A FIRESIDE BOOK
Published by Simon & Schuster
New York London Toronto Sydney Tokyo Singapore

FIRESIDE

Rockefeller Center
1230 Avenue of the Americas
New York, New York 10020

First Fireside Edition 1992

Published in 1987 by Prentice Hall Press

Previously published by Arco Publishing, Inc.

Manufactured in the United States of America

13 14 15 16 17 18 19 20

ABACUS. This ancient device for counting and figuring is, when seen in a dream, a portent of financial improvement through careful attention to details and thorough, painstaking work. Seen in operation as a child's toy, it foretells success in any business deal that may be pending. 291

ABALONE. To eat this shell fish in a dream foretells an unusual experience. Whether this will be pleasant or otherwise will depend on whether or not the abalone has a pleasing flavor. A dream of the highly colored, iridescent inside of an abalone shell is a warning to be on your guard against jealous acquaintances. 315

ABANDONMENT. There are three ways of interpreting this dream, since it may have three aspects—active, as when you abandon someone; passive, as when someone abandons you; and objective, as when you see or hear of someone else's abandonment. 601

Active. To dream of abandoning evil companions, or of ceasing from a nefarious enterprise, predicts an increase in income. If in your dream you abandon your wife, husband, children or sweetheart, it portends trouble of a serious nature. 800

Passive. If you dream of being abandoned by someone for whom you have friendship or affection, it is a prophecy of illness in your circle of near relatives. 368

Objective. If in a dream you are a witness to the abandonment of a person of either sex or any age, you will be the recipient of news that will have a profound influence on your life. 739

ABASEMENT. To dream of being abased or humiliated warns one against boasting of his physical or mental prowess. One who is shamed by a superior will profit by the dream if it stimulates him to rise above his shortcomings, but if the abasement comes from a child or a person of low degree, the import of the dream is distinctly unfavorable. 343.

ABBESS. If you see an abbess in your dream, the future will be bright, particularly so if she smiles at you. 095

ABBEY. In the sunlight, an abbey is propitious for the dreamer if seen from the outside. In gloom or at night it portends sadness and failure. 900

ABBOT. Long days of suffering are predicted if you dream of meeting and talking with the abbot of a monastery. If he speaks with a pronounced foreign accent, the augury is of having to be continually on the move. If his voice is high-pitched and he is an excitable person, you will have to make amends for a wrong you have done. 755

ABBREVIATION. To dream of seeing words abbreviated or hearing a person speak in abbreviations—such as *N.Y.* for New York, *Mass.* for Massachusetts, *mon.* for money, etc.—is to look forward to the loss of friends or income. 383

ABDICATION. Kings or queens abdicating portend achievement in social fields. 314

ABDOMEN. This is a fortunate omen in a dream when seen by itself; it predicts prosperity in every case where the abdomen is part of a living person. A pain in the abdomen foretells a long period of good health. 502

ABDUCTION. If you have a dream of being abducted, you will succeed in any new enterprise, whether business or social. 283

ABHORRENCE. To dream of feeling abhorrence or loathing of persons or things is a presage of danger from an unknown source. 958

ABILITY. A dream in which your own ability is recognized, even by yourself, points toward some achievement that will give you great happiness. If the dream is one in which you are impressed by the ability of someone else, you will receive a small sum of money. 858

ABJECTNESS. If you dream of a person who approaches you abjectly and you receive him or her with cordiality, you will be called upon to fill a new position at a much higher rate of remuneration. 017

ABLUTION. (See Bath.) 394

ABNORMALITY. To see in a dream a person or thing that is not normal—such as a man who walks on all fours, a cat with horns, a house built upside down, or the like—is an omen of a pleasant outcome to something that has worried you. 122

ABODE. (See Home.) 116

ABOMINATION. Beware of those who seek to do you ill if you dream of abominating anyone. 242

ABORIGINES. A dream of the primitive inhabitants of any country—Indians, Eskimos, African Negroes, etc.—points toward your being able to pay your debts. 133

ABORTION. You will not succeed in the project in which you are most interested at the time of this dream, whether it concerns love or money. 735

ABRASION. The scraping of skin off a finger or other part of the body, or the scratching of leather from a new pair of shoes or handbag predicts a succession of petty irritations. 610

ABROAD. Going abroad is a dream of excellent import. If you leave your own country on a ship or a train, the augury is of a trip in the near future with delightful companions. 053

ABSALOM. A dream of this Biblical character or of anyone who, like him, is caught by the hair in the limb of a tree, warns of approaching danger that may be avoided only by the greatest care. 612

ABSCESS. Do not engage in any enterprise involving real estate or securities if you dream of having an abscess. If someone else has it, such an affliction is an indication of a change of scene. 087

ABSENCE. If in a dream you notice particularly the absence of a friend or one of the family who would normally be present, you are likely to receive disquieting news from someone a long distance away. 553

ABSINTHE. Drinking this potent and demoralizing liqueur in a dream is a sure sign that someone you have trusted is seeking to ruin your reputation. 912

ABSOLUTION. Those who dream of forgiveness from a friend or absolution from a priest may look forward to a long period of peace of mind. 174

ABSTINENCE. Consciously abstaining from drink or anything else tempting in a dream is an augury of an accident. Abstaining through necessity or deprivation is a happy omen, particularly for women with child. 459.

ABSURDITY. If what happens in a dream is contrary to all reason, it foretells happiness in love affairs, particularly if there is a humorous twist to the dream. 874

ABUNDANCE. To dream of having a great plenty of one or more things is a warning to conserve your resources against lean times to come. 334

ABUSE. Strangely enough, if you dream of abusing someone, there will be an improvement shortly in your financial condition. If someone abuses you, you will have an illness. 239.

ABYSS. This is a bad dream for those engaged in either domestic service or farm work. If one falls into the abyss, he or she should wait at least a month before making a change in occupation. 748

ACACIA. The acacia tree in bloom will make any dream turn out lucky, or it will counteract any harmful omens if they are present. For lovers to dream of sitting under such a tree is an augury of marriage and a happy home. 298

ACADEMY. This institution of learning portends new experiences and new friends, but it warns against speculation. 396

ACCELERATOR. Increasing the speed of an automobile by pressing on the accelerator is an indication that by continued and sustained effort you will achieve the goal you have set for yourself. If in your dream you cannot remove your foot from the accelerator, you should regard it as a warning against vices such as gambling and drinking. 632

ACCEPTANCE. When a person hands you money or something else of value in a dream, your acceptance is an omen of success in love or business. Your refusal means exactly the opposite. If you accept counterfeit money, you are in grave danger. 109

ACCIDENT. Take warning from an accident dream, and if possible avoid the thing that figures in the accident. Thus, if you dream of an automobile crash, do not ride in a car for twenty-four hours, and be additionally careful in crossing the streets. Shun airplanes, trains or horse-drawn vehicles if the dream accident pertains to them. Avoid sharp knives or pointed instruments if you dream of cutting yourself, and if you dream of falling, watch your step. 845

ACCIDENT INSURANCE. It is an augury of a long and successful career to dream of taking out accident insurance. If the dream is of being paid an indemnity, you will probably have a setback of some kind. 695.

ACCOMPANIMENT. Whether you are a musician or not, you will be fortunate in matters pertaining to the heart if you dream of playing an accompaniment to someone's singing. 590

ACCORDION. This instrument heard in a dream is a presage of sadness, which, although inevitable, will not be bitter. For one to dream that he or she is playing an accordion points toward a satisfactory and lasting love affair, but if the instrument is out of tune, there will be many trials to bear. 056

ACCOUNTS. A woman who dreams of keeping accounts, household or otherwise, will suffer through the indifference of her lover, but a happy outcome may be expected if her accounts appear to be straight. Men or women who dream of being bookkeepers and of having difficulty in calculating and balancing will go through a period of strenuous difficulty. To dream of correctly balancing accounts at the first trial points definitely to a profitable business deal. 348.

ACCOUNTANT. For a young woman to dream that she loves an accountant means that she will not be happy in her married life, but that she will be well provided for. 462

ACCUSATION. Being accused of wrongdoing warns you to be on guard against those who will flatter you in order to obtain favors. 812

ACE. This denomination of playing cards signifies four different things, according to the suit, and in each case the portent represents the ultimate degree. An ace of hearts foretells success in love; of diamonds, good fortune in money matters; of spades, unrewarded labor; and of clubs, disgrace. 870

ACETIC ACID. The sour, vinegar-like odor of this acid portends a disagreeable experience with someone of the opposite sex. 552

ACETYLENE. To dream of seeing the intensely white light of an acetylene gas flame is a prophecy of a complete change of scene that will contribute to your contentment. If you smell the foul odor of this gas, you will be hounded by creditors. 693

ACHE. (See also Abdomen.) A dream of headache warns you against confiding in anyone regarding your business plans. If your legs or arms ache, it is a sign that you will have this effect—a night's repose; in other words, contentment. 710

ACID. A dream of acids is usually unfavorable. To dream of taking an acid internally is a forerunner of great difficulty on account of debts. If acid is thrown in your face, you will have unsatisfactory dealings with a foreigner through an interpreter. 238

ACNE. (See Pimples.) 382

ACORNS. Seen growing or lying on the ground or in baskets, acorns may be regarded as the harbinger of the successful outcome of your plans for the future. 479

ACQUAINTANCE. To dream of making a new acquaintance or of seeing an old one whom you have not met in a long time is a sign of receiving money that is owed you. 003

ACQUITTAL. Practice relaxation with all the power at your command if you dream of being acquitted by a jury, for you are to undergo a trying experience, which will lose most of its danger if it is met in a calm spirit. 533

ADAM AND EVE. Anyone who dreams of Adam and Eve in the Garden of Eden is headed for troubles of various kinds, including operations and family difficulties. 604

ADAPTABILITY. You may rest easy regarding your financial future if you dream of adapting yourself to unusual or abnormal conditions. 060

ADDER. Poisonous snakes portend trouble. This variety indicates a family row because you are paying attentions to one who is beneath you. To kill an adder is to look forward to a solution to the problem involved. 559

ADDITION. (See also Accounts.) If you dream of adding figures, you will run into difficulties of a personal nature. If you add them correctly, you will become master of the situation. 949

ADENOIDS. A dream of having you adenoids removed points toward success in community work. 841

ADJOURNMENT. If in a dream you are present when a meeting comes to an end, you should be especially careful to avoid eating anything that is difficult to digest. 839

ADJUSTMENT. The adjustment of any kind of machinery in a dream is a sign of increasing business success. 092

ADMIRAL. This highest naval rank points to your making a success of your career, both socially and in business. A maiden who dreams of marrying an admiral will be wooed by a wealthy widower. 760

ADMIRATION. A man who dreams of receiving admiration is in danger of illness and degradation. A single woman having this dream is likely to be criticized for her vanity. Honest admiration for someone else is a sign that points towards prosperity. 161

ADOBE. Houses made of this sun-dried brick are a favorable omen for seam-stresses. 148

ADOPTION. If a man or woman dreams of adopting a child, there will be a year during which speculation will bring rich returns. 182

ADORATION. Religious or otherwise, this is a dream that presages quiet contentment and a useful future. 529

ADORNMENT. Women who dream of adorning themselves for the purpose of making an impression on men will be fortunate in their love affairs. 874

ADRIFT. Being adrift in an open boat without any means of propulsion, such as sails, oars or motor, presages a situation in which you will not know what to do. 837

ADULATION. (See Admiration.) 040

ADULTERY. A dream about adultery is an omen of distress and worry. Committing it in a dream portends disputes with family, friends and business associates. To be tempted and to resist is a sign of many setbacks but eventual triumph over those who seek to defame you. If one dreams of seeking an adulterous union, he or she should go slow in making new friends. 855

ADVANCEMENT. This is really a dream of improvement, and whether it concerns you or someone else, it has a fortunate significance. 097

ADVENTURE. The nature of the adventure will govern the prediction of this dream. It will follow closely according to whether it is distressing, exciting, humorous or shameful. It is always well to exercise your best judgment and care after such a dream. 205

ADVENTURER. A woman may expect passionate wooing from a handsome, dashing man if she dreams of meeting an adventurer, but she should exercise caution in her dealings with him. 051

ADVENTURESS. A woman of this type augurs no good to the man who dreams of her. He will almost certainly have to prove himself in a situation of great delicacy. 186

ADVERSARY. If you dream of making your adversary your friend, you will have an opportunity for business advancement that you should embrace. 573

ADVERSITY. Undergoing adversity in a dream means that you will eventually overcome the difficulties that beset you. 415

ADVERTISEMENTS. Reading advertisements in a dream is a sign of prosperity if they are accompanied by pictures, but if not, the portent is of hard work and a meager living. 879

ADVICE. You will have a falling out with your best friend if you dream of giving him or her advice. To dream of being advised points toward happiness in love. 173

AEOLIAN HARP. To dream of the sound of wind blowing through strings on an instrument, or through wires indicates deep emotional attachment. 801

AERIAL. If in a dream you string an aerial, you will succeed in a plan that you had believed was next to impossible. 711

AFFECTION. Signs of affection in a dream are propitious if they are within the bounds of decency and restraint. They foretell a happy outcome to love affairs and congenial married life. 691

AFFLICTION. To dream of suffering from a physical affliction is an augury of good health. 900

AFFLUENCE. This dream points to an increase in income that will go far toward solving your immediate problems. Women having this dream may look forward to making a good marriage. 238

AFFRONT. The prediction of a dream of receiving an affront is that you will be embarrassed by criticism of the clothes you are wearing. 989

AFRICA. Being in Africa in a dream portends being called for jury duty. If you are in the Sahara Desert, you will be called for civil suits; otherwise, for criminal cases. 666

AFTERNOON. A dream of events that happen in the afternoon is likely to have a better portent than those happening in the morning or at night. 992

AGATE. To dream of wearing an agate in a ring or other jewelry is a sign that you will be called upon to arbitrate a disagreement between two of your friends. Beware of butting in where quarrels between men and their wives are concerned. 199

AGE. It is bad luck to dream of guessing a woman's age. You are likely to get into hot water with a person of the opposite sex. 635

AGENT. A woman who dreams of dealing with an agent in negotiating for a husband is in danger of being deceived. 231

AGNOSTIC. Any implication of religious disbelief in a dream is a sign of a degrading experience with regard to the opposite sex. 706

AGONY. If you dream of suffering agony, you will be likely to meet an old friend who will be in want. To see anyone else suffering is a portent of a change of scene. The agony of an animal portends grief. 554

AIR BRAKE. The sound of escaping air as brakes are applied on a railroad train or automobile is a presage of woe, foretelling the miscarriage of plans. 489

AIREDALE. Dogs are lucky dreams, particularly if they appear friendly or if their bark is not menacing, and an airedale in a dream points toward a happy home life with simple pleasures. 056

AIR-GUN. Shooting an air-gun at a target predicts failure through lack of concentration. Shooting at a person is a sign that you should guard your tongue against idle gossip. 472

AIRPLANE. If you dream of piloting an airplane, you will achieve something of outstanding merit in the arts or in your business. If a passenger, you will have your income increased. If you fall from or bail out of an airplane you may expect several months of hard luck. 621

AIRPLANE. Traveling by an airplane is a portent of a long period of indecision regarding your love affairs. 511

AISLE. An aisle in a church, theatre or other public place is a sign that you will have a decision of great importance to make. 297

ALABASTER. To see a statue or other article fashioned from alabaster, or to compare with alabaster anything seen in a dream, is to look forward to ill health or family disputes. 003

A LA CARTE. If you dream of ordering a meal a la carte in a restaurant, you will suffer a disappointment of some kind. 806

ALARM. A dream of turning in a fire-alarm portends more money in your pocketbook. To make an alarming statement in a dream is an omen of having to apologize to someone of inferior rank. To dream of hearing a clock ring an alarm predicts a profitably exciting time. 173

ALBATROSS. Seen from the deck of a ship, an albatross indicates success to those who are interested in any of the artistic pursuits. 717

ALBUM. To look at a photograph album in a dream, whether of portraits or snapshots, is a forerunner of a minor accident. 650

ALCOHOL. Dreamed of merely as a chemical, used in the arts or sciences, this is entirely favorable. As a beverage, it portends success if taken in moderation—otherwise failure. 966

ALDER. An alder tree seen in a dream is an omen of happiness for those with high ideals. 261

ALE. Drinking ale in a dream is a forerunner to a hearty enjoyment of simple pleasures. 526

ALGEBRA. Problems in algebra or formulas seen in a dream point to a misunderstanding with regard to a bill. 837

ALIBI. Any kind of an alibi given in a dream is an omen of marital discord. If you are puzzled by someone else's abili, you will be singled out for some kind of honor. 942

ALIEN. If you dream of being friendly to an alien, or foreigner, you will find a sum of money that will lead to a succession of worth-while business deals. 309

ALIMONY. This is usually a dream of either receiving or paying alimony. Of receiving portends a visit to a doctor. Of paying is a sign of careless pleasures. 612

ALLEGORY. A dream in which the people and scenes appear to have a symbolical meaning predicts a succession of surprises, some of which will be disappointing. 028

ALLEY. Going through a dark alley in a dream is a presage of the loss of a lover. To be chased by an evil person augurs disgrace. To come to the end of a blind alley predicts the failure of a well-considered plan. 252

ALLEY CAT. The yowls and moans of alley cats heard in a dream are a prediction that you will become associated with obnoxious people. To dream of missiles being thrown at them is a sign that you will find a way out of the difficulty. 660

ALLIANCE. To dream of making an alliance by marriage or otherwise with rich and influential people foretells a disagreement with someone you love. 393

ALLIGATOR. Being attacked by an alligator in a dream is a sign that you will be laughed at by people who do not like you. Seeing alligators in a zoo is a prediction of a short journey. 981

ALLOWANCE. To receive an allowance in a dream from a husband or parent portends happiness. If a man dreams of receiving an allowance from his wife or some other woman, he will quarrel with his friends and acquaintances. 120

ALLOY. A dream of combining metals in a crucible points toward a happy marriage and healthy children. 547

ALLSPICE. The flavor of allspice, or its use in a dream, points to romance that will bring both interest and happiness. 071

ALLUREMENT. If, as you dream, you are definitely conscious of the allurement of one of the opposite sex, you are likely to receive invitations that will advance you socially. 655

ALMANAC. Women who dream of consulting the almanac will be forced to break important engagements, although this may be to their advantage. A man who has this dream will be fortunate in a business transaction. 119

ALMOND. To dream of lying under an almond tree that is in bloom is to look forward with certainty to happiness in the married state. Eating almonds predicts a journey into pleasant places. 742

ALMS. To give alms cheerfully in a dream is a good sign, but if they are given with any regret, the augury is of hard luck for a long time to come. To dream of soliciting alms is a sign that there will be an upturn in your business afairs. 230

ALPACA. This South American animal whose wool is woven into cloth is an omen of discontent with your surroundings. 589

ALPEN-STOCK. If you dream of climbing mountains with an alpen-stock, you are likely to suffer a setback in family or love affairs. To break an alpen-stock is a sign that you will lose money in a business transaction. 604

ALPHABET. The letters of the alphabet, either in their regular order or jumbled, point toward success as a writer, an actor, or a librarian. 055

ALTAR. As long as this dream is one in which reverence is shown, it is propitious. To dream of praying before an altar is an omen of release from pressing worries. 449

ALTAR-BOY. Performing his duties in the chancel of a church, he is a sign of good news from an unexpected source. 194

ALTERCATION. (See also Fight, Quarrel.) For a woman to dream of having an altercation with her lover is a sign of a successful marriage. 322

ALTITUDE. To dream of looking down from a high altitude predicts danger of making a serious mistake. Shortness of breath on account of high altitude foretells an entanglement with someone who is not your equal. 752

ALUMINUM. Kitchen utensils made of this metal augur happiness to lovers if they are bright and shiny, but frustration if they are dull. 469

AMATEUR. A dream of doing things in the arts—painting, photography, literature, dramatics, and the like—merely for the love of it portends a handsome reward for something you have done for an older person. 490

AMAZEMENT. You may be sure of an exciting experience of some kind if you dream of being amazed at a sight you see or news you hear. 261

AMBASSADOR. Treachery from one you have heretofore trusted is the portent of a dream of seeing or talking with an ambassador from a foreign country. If you dream of being an ambassador from your own country to another, you should go very slowly in making any sort of an investment. 414

AMBITION. This is a favorable dream to those who are doing office work. It predicts a rise in salary and new responsibilities. 604

AMBROSIA. Dreaming of this food of the gods, or of food called by this poetic name, is a sign of misfortune through carelessness. 014

AMBULANCE. This is distinctly a warning dream. If you see one, it merely warns against being indiscreet where persons of the opposite sex are concerned. To dream of being placed in one warns against carelessness in speech or behavior. 075

AMBUSH. There is a pleasant surprise in store for you if you dream of hiding in ambush. 021

AMERICA. It is an augury of happiness in family life to dream that you have come to live in any part of America. 574

AMETHYST. This semi-precious gem prognosticates sadness through the loss of a relative or a friend. 905

AMIABILITY. You will be loved and admired by your acquaintances if you have a dream in which you display your own amiability. If others are amiable toward you, you must take care to guard your speech and actions. 917

AMMONIA. Those who are inclined to drink more than is good for them should be warned of excess by a dream in which they smell the fumes of ammonia. To dream of using it in the household is a sign of good health. 914

AMMUNITION. If you dream of buying ammunition for a hunting trip, you are likely to be called to account for something you have failed to do. To lose a quantity of ammunition is a sign that you will have a bitter quarrel with a person of the opposite sex. 959

AMOUR. Legitimate love dreams augur happiness in love, but to dream of illicit amours is a sign that you will have difficulties with a wife, husband or landlord. 269

AMPUTATION. Anyone who is dependent on legs or arms for a living may look forward with certainty to an increase of income after a dream of having one of these members cut off. 062

AMUSEMENT. (See also Games, Theatre, Movies.) If in indulging in any kind of amusement in a dream, you are conscious of enjoying yourself, the future will be a bright one. If the amusement bores you, you are almost certain to have trouble. 135

ANACONDA. This huge, dangerous snake, is a harmful augury. To dream of being attacked by one indicates a struggle to hold your position. 715

ANEMIA. To be told by a doctor that you are anemic is to look forward to a period of good health. 300

ANESTHESIA. (See Chloroform, Ether, Novocaine.) To take an anesthetic against your will points towards a painful sickness. Willingly to undergo anesthesia is a prophecy of better health. 235

ANAGRAMS. A dream of playing anagrams predicts a pleasant solution of difficulties concerned with love. 432

ANARCHIST. A man or woman who dreams of being an anarchist must beware of giving way to impulses. They should consider the possible results of any hasty actions. 339

ANCESTORS. To dream of ancestors other than parents denotes devotion to ideals that carry on tradition. You will be respected in the community where you live. 806

ANCHOR. Seen on shore, an anchor predicts a successfully completed task. On a ship, it points to an opportunity that is coming your way. To dream of being on shipboard when the anchor is dragging predicts danger from an unknown source. If you see anchors used as decorations on uniforms, clothing, or elsewhere, you have an intesesting experience in store for you. 497

ANCHOR. To dream of anchoring a boat in a harbor presages a long period of freedom from anxiety. If the dream is of raising an anchor, the portent is of adventure with a spice of danger. 593

ANCHOVY. This small fish, alive, canned or in paste form augurs a reward for conscientious effort. 215

ANCIENTS. A dream of anything old and reputable is generally a sign that you will have the respect of those with whom you are associated. 459.

ANDIRONS. In use in a fireplace holding burning logs or a grate, holding live coals, a pair of andirons is a portent of promotion to a higher position in business or the social world. Seen in a cold, empty fireplace, they are an omen of disappointment or chagrin. 509

ANECDOTE. You may look forward to attending a happy celebration if you dream of telling or hearing an anecdote. 840

ANGELS. A dream of seeing angels is none too good an omen. It betokens illness—either yours or a friend's—but it will not be fatal. 210

ANGER. The portent of a display of anger in a dream is either good or bad—good if the anger is roused by injustice; bad if merely an exhibition of temper. To dream of striking a person in anger predicts shame through an amour. 933

ANGLE-WORM. This is an omen of good luck for those who write for a living or for anyone who earns his or her daily bread in musical, dramatic or other artistic work. 981

ANGLER. (See Fisherman, Fishing.) 079

ANGORA CAT. (See Cats, Kittens.) You will be deceived or double-crossed if you dream of a friendly Angora cat, but if the cat shows signs of unfriendliness, you may expect that someone will show an honest dislike to you. 444

ANIMOSITY. For anyone to show animosity toward you in a dream means that you are likely to be surprised at someone's lack of moral sense. 137

ANKLE. To sprain an ankle in a dream, or otherwise injure it, is an omen of loss of money. For a man to dream of women's ankles predicts a love affair. 123

ANNIVERSARY. Birthday celebrations, wedding anniversaries, and similar occasions are omens of happy family reunions. 468

ANNOUNCEMENT. Usually it is a good sign to dream of receiving an announcement of a social or business event. But such an announcement portends evil if the card or letter is edged with black. 344

ANNOYANCE. A fly or mosquito buzzing around your head—a radio playing too loud—a doorbell that rings just as you are about to go to sleep. Such an annoyance experienced in a dream is a portent of a series of trials that you can overcome if you will. 502

ANNULMENT. Anyone who dreams of the annulment of his or her marriage is sure to find contentment. 808

ANT. These may be dreamed of either as examples of industry or as pests. If you dream of watching their industrious and intelligent habits, you are likely to be chastised by someone for not performing your duty. If they are pests, overrunning your living quarters or getting in your clothing, the omen is that you will be the victim of many petty irritations, from which you can escape only by radical measures. 909

ANTARCTIC. To dream of going into the South Polar regions for any or no cause is a sign that the pet project that you have had in mind for a long time will not be successful. 508

ANTELOPE. A sudden increase in income will be received by those who dream of seeing one or more antelopes in the out-of-doors. To see them in a zoo indicates a disappointment. To shoot one is a sign that someone will persecute you. 844

ANTHEM. All music in dreams is a favorable sign if it is in tune and pleasing to the ear. Hearing an anthem sung is a particularly favorable augury, especially to those with weak hearts. 155

ANTICS. Seeing children, their elders, or paid performers doing antics is a dream that points toward a change of scene that will be accompanied by great financial profit. 925

ANTIDOTE. (See also Poison.) If you dream of taking an antidote for poison, you will find yourself in a very embarrassing situation through your own lack of foresight. 231

ANTIQUES. Seen in a shop, old pieces of furniture, clocks, brass ware, china and other antiques are signs of happiness in home life. 497

ANTISEPTIC. The use of an antiseptic in a dream portends a motor accident. 039

ANVIL. Any appearance of an anvil in a dream is a forerunner of good luck in money matters to those who work with their hands. A blacksmith hammering on an anvil is a prediction of a legacy that is unexpected. 866

ANXIETY. A feeling of anxiety in a dream, even if the cause is not apparent, portends loneliness. 108

APARTMENT. A dream of living in an apartment that is too small is a sign that you will quarrel with your immediate relatives. A large luxurious apartment predicts increasing prosperity. 124

APE. Someone is likely to make fun of you if you dream of seeing an ape. If an ape chases you, the prophecy is that you are in danger of losing your position through inattention to your work. 079

APOLOGY. If you make an apology to anyone in a dream, you will receive an apology from one of your friends. If someone apologizes to you, the chances are that you will receive a minor injury. 617

APOPLEXY. It is a sign that you will travel to foreign lands if you dream of seeing a person with an attack of apoplexy. To dream that you yourself have an attack augurs criticism from your family. 434

APOTHECARY. (See Druggist.) 521

APPAREL. (See Clothes.) 022

APPARITION. Seeing an apparition in a dream is a portent of serious illness. If the apparition is of someone you know, you should write immediately to learn if the person is all right. 715

APPENDICITIS. (See also Abdomen, Ache.) To dream of an attack of this disease predicts an improvement in your financial condition if you keep your own plan of action. 487

APPETITE. One who dreams of having a good appetite may look forward with certainty to always having enough to eat. To dream of loss of appetite means a period of depression. 657

APPLAUSE. Hearing applause in a dream is a forerunner of receiving a small legacy from a distant relative. If you are a performer and the applause is meant for you, the augury is of success in an entirely new venture. For you to dream of applauding someone's performance is a prediction of good health. 037

APPLE. This popular fruit predicts happiness if it is ripe—otherwise woe. Seen on a tree, the ripe fruit is a sign that you are on the point of doing good for yourself—if green, it augurs ill. If you dream of eating a raw apple, it predicts good health and energy. Cooked apples—baked, in sauce, or in pies—are practically a promise that you will receive some merited honor. 028

APPLEJACK. A dream of this exhilarating beverage foretells embarrassment through ill-advised statements or acts. 761

APPOINTMENT. (See also Date.) To dream of making an appointment to meet a friend is a sure sign that some undercover plan of yours will be found out. 534

APPRECIATION. It is lucky to dream that you show appreciation of someone else, but if you or your acts are appreciated, you will be likely to have someone criticize your clothing. 801

APPRENTICE. It is a portent of success both in business and love to dream of being an apprentice and learning a trade of some kind. If you dream of having an apprentice under you, the augury is of having an opportunity to make a great deal of extra money. 867

APPROVAL. To express approval of a person or thing usually portends happiness but if the object of your approval is unworthy, you will have a setback of some kind. For a woman to have dresses sent to her on approval augurs deceit on the part of a friend. 892

APRICOT. Disappointment in love, but luck in money matters, will be the lot of those who dream of eating this fruit. 003

APRICOT BRANDY. If you accept a proffered drink, you will get the best of those who seek to outwit you in business. 601

APRON. A man who dreams of wearing an apron will be subject to a woman's whims and caprices. Good fortune is in store for women who dream of wearing dainty aprons. 839

AQUARIUM. (See also Fish.) Hard going is predicted by a dream of large or small aquariums. If the fish are unusual in any way—size, shape or color— you should guard against accidents. 363

AQUEDUCT. Either an overhead or underground aqueduct points toward good health and a happy love life if there is water running through it. If dry, it portends woe. 720

ARAB. A dream of Arabs in their native haunts is a presage of romance and exciting experiences. Mounted on horses going at full gallop, Arabs give warning against jealous people of the opposite sex. 272

ARBITRATION. To dream of acting as an arbitrator between two quarreling factions predicts a dangerous situation from which you will extricate yourself with difficulty. To dream of submitting your own claims to arbitration is a fortunate omen. 701

ARBOR. Young women who dream of being under an arbor with handsome men are likely to have success in artistic pursuits. They should beware of repeating confidences. 879

ARBUTUS. This beautiful little spring flower is a portent of happiness to lovers. 475

ARCADE. Walking through an arcade of any kind points toward temptations that you will find difficult to resist. 152

ARCH. You will be unjustly criticized by a number of people if you dream of passing under an arch. A broken arch signifies wasted effort. 918

ARCHBISHOP. Family quarrels are predicted by a dream of an archbishop in his ecclesiastical vestments. 221

ARCHERY. (See Arrow, bow.) 597

ARCHITECT. At work on plans for a building, the architect in a dream foretells a difficult task that will be completed successfully. 907

ARC-LIGHT. A sputtering arc-light seen in a dream predicts petty irritations arising from conditions over which you have no control. If the arc-light burns clear and white, you may look forward to peace and plenty. 752

ARCTIC. Progress through the ice-fields of the Arctic toward the North Pole augurs the achievement of a high ambition. 989

ARENA. If you dream of looking into an arena where a sporting event is being held, there is a strong chance of your being offered a new position. Consider it carefully before you make up your mind. 498

ARGUMENT. It is lucky to dream of arguing providing you do not lose your temper—otherwise the dream is a warning against hasty action in making decisions. 223

ARISTOCRAT. To dream of being snubbed or "high-hatted" by an aristocrat is an omen that you are due to receive an increase in the amount of your worldly goods. 880

ARITHMETIC. (See also Accounts, Addition.) Dreams of doing problems in arithmetic predict vexations that are difficult to understand but are possible to solve. 547

ARMCHAIR. Dreaming of a comfortable-looking armchair occupied by a person at ease points to a vacation and travel in a southern climate. An empty armchair is an omen of a minor mystery. Seeing a cat asleep in an armchair is a warning against loss of temper. If the cat wakes up and stretches, beware of scandalous tongues. 875

ARMHOLE. If you dream of putting your arms in the wrong armholes of a coat, you will find yourself in a position of great danger to your reputation. You are warned to be very discreet in your relations with the opposite sex. 326

ARMISTICE. When armies cease to fight, the prediction of such a dream is extremely favorable. A dream of celebrating an armistice augurs well for the future. 893

ARMOR. Metal armor such as worn by the Knights of old prophesies high honors if dreamed of in an ancient castle or museum, but if you dream of wearing such armor yourself, you are warned of impending financial strain. To dream of armor on a battleship, submarine or car is a warning of personal danger. 809

ARMORY. This building where arms are stored and soldiers are drilled predicts a menace to your peace of mind if seen from the outside. To be alone in an empty armory or arsenal presages disappointment—if the armory is crowded with military men, the omen is of success in a business undertaking. 927

ARMS. Men bearing arms—guns, pistols, hand-grenades, or other weapons—portend an event that will mark a turning point in your life. Whether this will be for the better or worse will depend on the courage with which you meet it. A dream in which someone of the opposite sex puts his or her arms around you prophesies a period of prosperity and happiness. 482

ARMY. (See also Arms.) If you dream of an army on the march, the portent is one of worry about a mysterious occurrence. An army in battle foretells a scandal from which you can escape only through closely guarding your tongue. 935

AROMA. (See Odor.) 557

ARREST. To dream of being arrested by an officer is a warning against taking chances such as driving too fast, going through red lights, gambling, or writing checks for more than your bank balance. If you dream that you are an officer and that you arrest someone, you will find a solution for your immediate problems. 107

ARRIVAL. Arriving at a railroad, bus or airplane terminal is a dream of the successful conclusion of a difficult task. To see others arrive is a sign of health. 470

ARROGANCE. Arrogant, overbearing people met in a dream predict an experience that will cause you both amusement and satisfaction. 621

ARROW. You should be extremely careful in your dealings with the opposite sex if you dream of arrows. To be struck by an arrow signifies disgrace. To shoot arrows at a target of any kind portends unfaithfulness. 572

ARSENAL. (See Armory.) 438

ARSON. (See also Fire, Flame.) Arson, or the willful setting of fire to a house, is a dream that warns a man against associating with women of loose morals. Women who have this dream should be on their guard with men with whom they are not well acquainted. To dream of seeing a person set fire to a building is a portent of loss of reputation. 587

ART. (See Museum, Painting, Picture, Statue.) To discuss art in a dream or to look at objects of art is an omen of advancement for those who are engaged in clerical or secretarial work. 467

ARTERY. (See Blood, Tourniquet, Vein.) It is a sign that you will be well liked for your fairness if you dream of cutting an artery. This is an expressly good dream for a woman to have. 301

ARTESIAN WELL. To dream of an artesian well with a good supply of clear cold water is to be assured of a moderate but steady income. 946

ARTHRITIS. Freedom from bodily ills is predicted by dreaming of being afflicted with this painful disease. 383

ARTICHOKE. Eating this thistle-like vegetable in a dream is an omen of doing something that will make you appear ridiculous. 537

ARTILLERY. In action, large calibered cannon are an indication of futile attempts to make an impression on the world. 969

ARTISAN. An expert worker in metals, wood or stone occupied in his calling is a dream that predicts happiness in married life. 011

ARTIST. Seen in a dream painting or drawing from a nude model, an artist is an omen of gay and not altogether worthy pleasures. To dream that you are the artist betokens ill luck in business. 013

ASBESTOS. The use of asbestos gloves or clothing as a protection against fire in a dream signifies discord within the family circle. 545

ASCENT. Dreaming of making the ascent of a mountain portends an increase in salary, but if you dream of falling while making the ascent, you will suffer reverses. 248

ASCETIC. Talking to an ascetic in a dream augurs hard times, but if you dream that you are an ascetic, you will meet someone who will become a staunch friend. 562

ASH WEDNESDAY. To observe this holy day in a dream is a forerunner of contentment. 282

ASHES. Dreaming of having ashes blown on you foretells hard times ahead. Emptying ashes from a stove or furnace predicts embarrassment. Sifting ashes for pieces of good coal is an indication that you will prosper. 573

ASP. It is very bad luck to dream of being bitten by an asp. If you find an asp in the grass, and kill it, you will fall in love with an actor or actress. 956

ASPARAGUS. To dream of eating asparagus is a sign that you will have to admit that someone with whom you disagreed was absolutely right. 783

ASPEN. This tree with the quivering leaves is an augury of loneliness. To dream of an aspen that has been cut or blown down predicts the illness of a young person. 334

ASPHALT. Men at work laying an asphalt pavement are a prediction of travel to the West Indies. 478

ASPIC. To dream of eating food in aspic jelly foretells a period of luxury. If the dream is simply of looking at beautifully arranged jellied meats, fish, etc., the augury is of an invitation to a large fashionable party. 558

ASPIRIN. Someone will seek to defame you if you dream of taking aspirin. If you give it to someone else, you must be especially careful not to repeat gossip. 302

ASS. (See also Donkey, Mule.) If you dream of "making an ass" of yourself, you are likely to make new and congenial friends. To see someone else acting similarly is a sign of business success. To show disapproval of such actions is an omen of unpopularity. 204

ASSASSIN. To dream of seeing a well-known person being killed by an assassin predicts news that will be sensational though not necessarily depressing. 384

ASSAULT. (See also Arms, Army.) Grave danger is predicted by dreaming of an assault being made on a woman. If a man is the victim, the augury is of disquieting news. If you are the victim, there will be a serious altercation in your household. An assault made by troops on an enemy stronghold is a prognostication of an attack on your character. 670

ASSEMBLY. (See also Speech.) Your presence in an assembly of people is a dream that depends for its augury on the purpose of the gathering: if peaceful, the prediction is of an improvement in your personal affairs; if warlike, the opposite may be expected. 551

ASSEMBLYMAN. A dream of having dealings with an assemblyman usually means that a pet plan is in danger of being upset. 073

ASSESSMENT. (See also Taxes.) If you dream of having an assessment made on real estate, securities, or other property, you will have to take special care to avoid dealings with business men of low credit rating. 091

ASSIGNATION. (See Adultery, Amour.) 871

ASSIGNMENT. (See also Bankruptcy, Failure.) To dream of assigning one's interest in property, predicts that you will make an important change in your plans. 519

ASSISTANCE. If you receive assistance in a dream—financial or physical— you will find that you must have help in a business deal. If you give assistance you will be successful. 231

ASTHMA. There is no significance to this if the dreamer is an asthma sufferer, as the actuality is likely to be a carryover into sleep. For others, the dream signifies distress through carelessness. 305

ASTONISHMENT. To be astonished in a dream predicts selling goods below cost. To astonish others is a sign of increasing prosperity. 294

ASTRAL FORM. If you dream of seeing the astral form of either yourself or someone else, you will receive an important letter from an old sweetheart. 353

ASTROLOGY. (See also Horoscope.) To read a book on astrology in a dream is an augury of happiness and wealth that will come by patient effort. 418

ASYLUM. Illness and misfortune are the presages of a dream of being confined in an asylum. 866

ATHEIST. If you dream of yourself or another's being an atheist, you will be disappointed in the returns or investments of time and money. 569

ATHLETICS. (See Sports.) Family, school or college reunions are predicted by a dream of engaging in athletics of all kinds. It is lucky to dream of winning in such contests. If there is any injury sustained, the augury is of commendation from your business or social superiors. 854

ATLAS. (See also Globe, Map.) Journeys, either long or short, are indicated by a dream of studying an atlas. A large atlas indicates travel by sea; a small one, travel on land; and maps in black and white, travel by air. 957

ATOM. Dreams in which you seem to see atoms predict that someone you have trusted will tell you a lie. To hear a person speak about atoms is a sign that for a time you will have to get along on a smaller income. 424

ATOMIZER. If a woman dreams that she is using a perfume atomizer, it is a sign that she will receive a proposal from an elderly man. If a man has the dream, it predicts that his sense of humor will help in his advancement. The use of a nose or throat atomizer in a dream is a warning against accidents. 877

ATONEMENT. Doing penance in a dream or atonement for a sin or a wrong you have done is a sign that you will break a precious heirloom. 651

ATROCITY. As with most horror dreams, an atrocity, even of extreme cruelty does not necessarily augur misfortune. The prediction is one of change, either of occupation or place of abode. 219

ATTACK. (See Assault.) 935

ATTAINMENT. It is an omen of the satisfactory conclusion of the task on which you are engaged if you dream of the attainment of an important object. 657

ATTIC. You have every expectation of a loving mate, healthy children and sufficient worldly goods if you dream of rummaging in trunks and boxes in an attic. To dream of being a child playing in the attic is an especially propitious dream for those who are past middle age. 509

ATTORNEY. (See Lawyer.) 234

AUCTION. It is a sign of a salary rise or money-making in some form to dream of attending an auction of any description, but to see yourself as auctioneer is unlucky. 415

AUDIENCE. To face an audience from a stage or platform predicts an intense but temporary pleasure. To sit in an audience predicts that you will be able to help out a friend. 491

AUDITOR. Going over accounts, an auditor seen in a dream is a forerunner of tangled finances. 583

AUDITORIUM. (See also Audience.) Music of any kind heard in a large auditorium is an omen of achievement unless the music is not played or sung in tune, in which case it augurs disappointment. 339

AUGER. To dream of boring a hole with an auger predicts that you will meet a tiresome acquaintance. 795

AUNT. If the aunt of whom you dream is your father's sister, the prediction is of simple pleasures in the company of old friends. An aunt on your mother's side predicts financial security. 157

AURORA BOREALIS. (See Northern Lights.) 975

AUTHOR. This dream may be one of the greatest interest. Meeting an author on terms of friendship or pleasant companionship foretells mental enjoyment and social prestige. If an author tries to borrow money from you in a dream, it predicts that you will receive a legacy. To dream that you are an author predicts financial difficulties. 881

AUTOBIOGRAPHY. You are in danger if you dream of writing your autobiography. Your wife, husband or sweetheart will suspect you if you have this dream. If you dream of reading the story that someone else has written of his life, you are likely to advance in your social or business position. 805

AUTOGRAPHS. The collecting of autographs in a dream signifies that you will profit by the example of great men and women. You should read the lives of those who have accomplished big things. If you dream that you are a celebrity and are asked for your autograph, you will make a success of your work. 550

AUTOMAT. If you dream of obtaining and eating food in one of these coin-in-the-slot restaurants, you should follow the advice of the one you consider your best friend. 720

AUTOMOBILE. In this era of gasoline transportation a dream of going places in an automobile has no particular significance. It is the exceptional use of a car that makes the dream of importance. For instance, if you dream of driving on the left-hand side of the road, the augury is of travel to foreign lands. If the dream is of not being able to get sufficient power to go over a hill, the augury is of disappointment in love. A dream of running out of gas in an unpopulated country predicts hard labor for a meager living. 546

AUTOPSY. To dream of the examination of a corpse after a murder has been committed predicts an interesting though unprofitable experience. 312

AUTUMN. If in a dream the leaves on the trees are bright colored and slowly dropping to the ground, you will receive a gift from someone you believed to be unfriendly. 992

AVALANCHE. Guard your health with special care if you dream of being caught in an avalanche. 210

AVERSION. (See also Hate.) If a person shows an aversion, or unfriendliness, toward you in a dream, the prediction is that you will be able to recognize an attempt at deception. 177

AVIARY. A cageful of many different kinds and colors of birds portends brilliant social achievements but a lessening income. It is a warning against spending too much time away from your business. 644

AVIATOR. For a woman to dream of being in love with an aviator predicts an early marriage. If she goes up with him in an airplane, there will be an elopement. If a man dreams of being an aviator, he will be singled out for high honors. To see two aviators having a fist fight is a portent of hard labor without reward. 723

AVOCATION. (See Hobby.) 148

AWAKENING. If you have the rare dream of waking up, you have much happiness to anticipate. To dream of an awakening of the spirit denotes many friends who will stand by you through thick and thin. 434

AWARD. Good fortune will come to you if you dream of receiving an award for work that is well performed. 947

AWE. You are warned against vanity and a tendency to show off if you dream someone stands in awe of you. If you are awe-struck by a personage of high rank, you must work harder if you are to keep your job. 687

AWL. This is a warning not to spend your time with loose acquaintances, either male or female. 247

AWNING. To dream of sitting under an awning is a sign that you will escape an expected injury. Raising an awning signifies many suitors to an unmarried woman, and children to the married. To a man it signifies happiness in marriage. Lowering an awning denotes a change of occupation that will mark a slight improvement. 228

AXE. Dreaming that you are handling a bright, keen axe is an augury of satisfaction and advancement in your work. A poor but honest lover is promised to a young woman having this dream. Those who dream of trying to use a dull axe should pay more attention to their dress. 864

AXLE. Disaster is predicted by a dream of breaking an axle on any kind of automobile, wagon or other vehicle. To dream of mending an axle or fitting a new one is a sign of improvement in conditions. 749

BABOON. Fortunate is the young woman who dreams of this animal. She will contract a most favorable marriage with a man of high social position. Others who dream of baboons will be lucky in business undertakings. 213

BABY. To hear a baby crying in one's dream, is a forerunner of sickness and disappointments. A sweet, clean baby, predicts a satisfied love and a host of good friends. To see a baby walking alone, foretells independence, and the will to rise above smaller spirits. A woman who dreams she is nursing a baby, receives a sign that she will be deceived by the one in whom she has the greatest confidence. To pick up a baby ill with fever is not a good sign. You will have many worries. 714

BABY CARRIAGE. To dream of a baby carriage is a sign that you will have a true friend who will plan many happy surprises for you. 922

BACCARAT. The significance of this dream is not affected by the results achieved by gambling. Win or lose, it predicts a succession of harassing experiences, one or more of which may prove to be serious. 579

BACHELOR. If a man dreams he is a bachelor, he must take warning and stay away from the ladies. If a woman dreams of a bachelor, it hints of wanton love. 302

BACK. To dream of a bare back, presages loss of power. Beware of lending money or giving advice. Sickness often follows this dream. To observe a person deliberately turn and walk away from you, points to envy and jealousy, causing unhappiness. If you dream of your own back, misfortune will befall you. 584

BACKBITING. Your fortune will change for the worse if you dream of being guilty of backbiting. If your friends indulge in backbiting, it predicts worriment from inside the home. 353

BACKBONE. You may look forward with certainty to a contented old age if you dream of seeing someone else's backbone. If you get a glimpse of your own in a mirror, it is a sign that you will make an advance in your worldly estate through your own efforts. 710

BACKGAMMON. If you dream of playing backgammon, it is a prediction that you will make a visit and encounter a lack of hospitality, but while there, you will win friendships that will be true and lasting. If you lose in the game, your affections will be unrequited, and your business will be unpredictable. 218

BACON. If you eat bacon, it is a sign of prosperity. Rancid bacon foretells dissatisfaction that will cause uneasiness. To dream of curing bacon is not a good omen; it foretells sickness. 324

BACTERIA. This dream's prediction is in the main favorable, but it should always be considered in connection with other features of the dream. 156

BADGE. Wearing a badge in a dream foretells social advancement. 483

BADGER. It is a sign of good luck to dream of a badger, especially so if you have encountered hardships. 749

BADMINTON. This game of skill played in a dream is a precursor of your having to make a decision that will have a definite influence on your future. 832

BAG. The significance of a bag depends on the material from which it is made. Of paper, it signifies danger, which can be avoided by taking ordinary precautions. Of cloth, the prediction is of success in your business. Of leather, the prophecy is of travel. Pleasant experiences are foretold by a dream of having someone carry your bag for you. 173

BAGGAGE. (See also Bag.) Trunks and other traveling luggage grouped in a home or railroad station foretell a long trip, probably to a foreign country. Seeing them handled by expressmen predicts happiness on the journey. To see a piece of baggage dropped is a bad sign. 803

BAGPIPE. To see a group in Scotch highland uniforms playing bagpipes is a generally fortunate omen. If, however, the bagpipes are being played out of tune, or if the uniforms are worn and soiled, the portent is one of misfortune. 688

BAIL. Unforeseen troubles will come to you if you dream of seeking bail; accidents may occur; and unwise alliances may be contracted. The same result is to be expected, though not as dire, if you go bail for another. 270

BAIT. Whether worms, minnows, or any other form of animal life intended for bait, the omen of such a dream is that you will be distressed at the critical illness of a dear friend. 798

BAKERY. Rows of bread loaves and pastry in a bakery, or bakers clad in white, presage an increase in the family for young married couples. 368

BAKING. A man or woman who dreams of baking bread, cake, pies or beans may look forward with confidence to a rise in their fortunes. 797

BALCONY. If sweethearts dream of an adieu on a balcony, a long separation may follow, perhaps final separation. To dream of a balcony also denotes bad news and absent friends. 653

BALDNESS. A bald-headed man seen in a dream predicts swindlers who will try to interest you in some business that will be unwise; but by keeping your eyes open you will outwit them. For a man to dream of a bald-headed woman is a sign that he will have a vixen for a wife. A bald hill or mountain foretells famine and suffering in many forms. For a woman to dream of a bald-headed man is to forewarn her to be discreet and not accept her next proposal of marriage. If new babies are bald-headed it points to a happy home, a loving mate and obedient children. 571

BALE. The solution of a pressing problem is indicated by a dream of seeing well baled material, such as cotton, paper and so on. 284

BALL. This is a good omen, if well dressed people are happily dancing to the strains of good music. If you are unhappy and distressed, a death in the family may be expected. 138

BALLET. To dream of a ballet indicates infidelity in marriage, failure in business matters, and dissension and jealousy among those you love. 672

BALLOON. Adversity and unrealized hopes are indicated by this dream. Business of every sort will suffer temporary loss. If you ascend in a balloon, it foretells an unfortunate journey. 431

BALLOT. Casting your ballot at an election points to the fulfillment of a wish you had thought impossible of accomplishment. 258

BALLROOM. Empty, this signifies pain and sorrow. Crowded with dancers, it means that fate has a pleasant surprise in store for you. 631

BALSAM. It is a sign of better health to dream of being in pine woods and smelling the scent of balsam. 002

BALUSTRADE. If you dream of sliding downstairs on a balustrade, you will find yourself beset with petty annoyances in regard to money. 257

BAMBOO. To see a clump of growing bamboo in a dream is to be assured of many delightful hours in the company of a well-loved poet. 179

BANANA. Eaten in a dream, this fruit betokens sickness. Seen growing, it predicts that one of your friends will prove to be a shallow individual. 394

BANDAGE. Seen in rolls by itself, bandages are a warning against betting on racehorses. In use, as on limbs or other parts of the body, bandages portend trouble. 040

BANDANNA. Hard work and worry will be the lot of one who wears a bandanna in a dream. To see a black woman wearing a bandanna signifies a happy family life. 724

BANDIT. To dream of being held up by a bandit in a lonely place is a forerunner of stomach disturbances. If you dream of being a bandit and holding up someone else, it is a sign that you will have to apologize for something. 518

BANDSAW. Using a bandsaw in a dream means that you will win the approval of your employer before long. 477

BANISHMENT. If one dreams that he or she is banished from home or country, there is every probability of there being danger of fire. 794

BANJO. If you dream of a banjo, you will enjoy pleasant amusements. If a negro is playing one, you will meet with slight worries. For a young woman to see negroes playing their banjos is an omen she will fail in some anticipated pleasure. She will also quarrel with her lover. 681

BANK. To see vacant tellers' windows at a bank predicts business losses. Dispensing gold money foretells carelessness; receiving it, great gain and prosperity. 098

BANKBOOK. To lose a bankbook is a warning against taking part in church, business or society politics, and against gossiping about your neighbors. 121

BANKER. Loss of money usually follows a dream about a banker, even if the dream points to a profitable deal. 416

BANKNOTES. Clean, crisp banknotes predict financial independence, but if they are soiled and wrinkled, your money will be accompanied by trouble. 840

BANKRUPTCY. Here is a dream with an opposite meaning. It foretells either an inheritance or the acquisition of money by some other means. 376

BANNER. To dream of seeing one's country's flag flying in a clear sky predicts triumphs over alien foes. To see it torn and bespattered is significant of wars and loss of military honors on land and sea. 849

BANQUET. It is a good omen to dream of a banquet. Friends will favor you. To dream of yourself, with many smartly-dressed guests, eating from a costly plate and drinking wine of a fabulous price and age, portends great gain in business of every nature, and happiness among friends. If you dream of seeing eerie faces or empty tables, in strange surroundings, it is ominous of grave misunderstandings. 975

BANTAM. If you dream of bantam chickens, your fortune will be small, but you will enjoy contentment. If the chickens appear sickly, or are exposed to wintry storms, your interest will be lessened in value. 072

BANYAN TREE. To dream of this spreading tree of India, whose branches take root as they lean to the ground, is an augury of acrimonious arguments with your relatives or in-laws. 351

BAPTISM. A dream of baptism signifies that your character needs strengthening. If you are an applicant for baptism, you will be in danger of humiliating yourself. To see John the Baptist baptizing Christ in the Jordan, indicates you will have a desperate mental struggle. 509

BAR. (See also Barroom.) Tending a bar denotes that you will stoop to some questionable way to advancement. Seeing a bar denotes community interests, good fortune and the consummation of illicit desires. 552

BARB. Catching one's clothes or a part of the body on a barb predicts that you will be disgraced unless you stop associating with evil companions. 377

BARBARIAN. To have dealings in a dream with a savage, uncivilized person is auspicious for those engaged in business but only if the dreamer seems to have the upperhand. It is unlucky for anyone to dream of being chased or captured by barbarians. 804

BARBARITY. Looking on at any barbarous act by a savage means that you must take great care in selecting the food you eat, lest you suffer from poisoning. 176

BARBECUE. To dream of seeing animals of any kind being roasted whole is a sign that your hospitality will be abused by relatives or acquaintances. If you eat at a roadside "barbecue" stand, you will suffer a disappointment. 683

BARBER. Success will come through close attention to business if you dream of a barber. For a young woman to dream of a barber suggests that her fortune will increase, though slightly. 128.

BAREFEET. If you wander in the night barefoot with torn garments, you will be disappointed in your expectations, and bad influences will hover about your efforts for advancement. 139

BARGAIN. The achievement of a pet project is assured if you dream of taking advantage of a bargain. A bargain sale in a department store is propitious for women especially. 315

BARITONE. Hearing a baritone is a lucky dream for those who are in love if the singer keeps in tune. If he sings off key, there will be an unpleasant occurrence. 821

BARK. To pick the bark off a tree or twig does not argur well for the dreamer. Gathering pieces of bark with which to make a fire is a sign that you will have an embarrassing experience with someone of the opposite sex. It is a "watch-your-step" dream (*Sailboat*.) To see a bark under full sail, in fair weather or foul, is a prophecy of a release from care and worry. 756

BARKING. A dog's bark may be joyous, warning or menacing; and the significance of this dream follows these qualities closely. When the barking has a menace in it, you are in grave danger. 981

BARLEY. A field of barley in the sunshine predicts happiness for lovers; under clouds, it points to unrequited love. 885

BARMAID. For a man to dream of a barmaid signifies his desire for low pleasures; he will scoff at purity. For a woman to dream that she is a barmaid denotes that she will be attracted to men of low repute, and that she will prefer irregular pleasures. 418

BARN. If the barn is filled with ripe, golden grain and perfect ears of corn, with goodlooking cattle in it, the omen is one of great prosperity. If empty, the reverse may be expected. 483

BARNACLES. Seen on the bottom of a boat or on driftwood, this marine growth indicates that your labors will be rewarded and you may look forward to a calm and peaceful old age. 851

BAROMETER. A barometer denotes that a change will soon take place in your affairs, which will be profitable to you. If the barometer is broken, you will encounter disturbing incidents in your business, coming unexpectedly. 688

BARREL. A full barrel seen in a dream foretells prosperity. An empty one is an omen of distress. 211

BARRIER. Walls, closed doors, fences and other barriers as a rule predict the frustration of your plans. 187

BARROOM. Your family and friends will give you their unswerving loyalty if you dream of being in a barroom. To dream of seeing women drinking at a bar is a portent of indulgence in indiscreet pleasures. If, in such a drinking place, you dream of becoming intoxicated, you will receive disappointing news. 694

BASEBALL. A baseball game in your dreams, assures you of contentment, and your cheerfulness will make you a popular companion. For a young woman to dream of playing baseball means much pleasure for her, but no profit. 862

BASEMENT. (See also Cellar.) A dream of being in a basement foretells that you will have few chances of making money. 125

BASIN. A dream of filling a basin with clean warm water augurs happy days with a loving mate. Cold water in a basin predicts family troubles. To dream of finding a basin filled with dirty water is a sign of divorce in the family of one of your relatives. Emptying a basin predicts a season of prosperity. 871

BASKET. Carrying food or packages in a basket predicts that you will have new opportunities for advancement. If you take full advantage of these, you will go far in your work. An empty basket predicts disappointment. 831

BASS DRUM. It is a sign that you will achieve a pet ambition if you dream of thumping a bass drum. To see someone in a band playing a bass is a prediction of an exasperating experience. 555

BASSOON. To dream of playing the bassoon is to look forward to wasted effort of some description. 691

BASS VIOL. A happy family life, with one or more talented children, is the augury of a dream of playing this instrument. To dream of carrying a bass viol in a crowd predicts an amusing experience. To dream of losing one predicts petty irritations. 816

BASS VOICE. If you dream you have a bass voice, it points to some irregularity in your business, brought about by the deceit of one of your employees. For the lover, this dream foretells estrangements and quarrels. 407

BASTARD. If you dream that you are a bastard, you are almost certain to receive both honors and wealth. It is a sign of impending bad luck to call a person a bastard, but if another calls you by this name, you will receive a promotion of some kind. 285

BAT. To see a bat flying about is a dream that augurs ill if you are afraid of it. But if it does not bother you, it prophesies new interests that will be profitable. 121

BATH. Young, unmarried men and women who dream of taking a bath will save themselves considerable trouble if they will constantly be on guard against overindulgence in alcohol. For a pregnant woman to dream of bathing usually means a miscarriage. To a man, the dream means a temptation from an adulteress. Those who dream of bathing in the same tub with others are warned to avoid frivolous and immoral companions. Bathing in muddy water predicts slander from your enemies. Sea bathing is a prediction of prosperity. A warm bath foretells the reverse. 974

BATHROOM. For a young woman to dream of a bathroom is a sign her inclinations will turn toward dangerous pleasures and indiscretions. To see white or yellow roses in a bathroom signifies a minor sickness that will interfere with anticipated pleasure; but something good will result from this disappointment. This dream suggests caution in making changes in one's career. A woman should guard against social errors. 126

BATON. An orchestra leader's baton is a favorable sign, signifying a realization of your chief ambition. The baton carried by a drum major at the head of a parade is an augury of family squabbles. 106

BATTERY. If you dream of the storage battery in your car going dead, there will be a grave accident to one of your friends. 711

BATTLE. Dreaming of hearing the sound of battle from a distance is a warning against infection from a slight wound. To dream of winning a battle is an omen of success in love affairs. 089

BATTLESHIP. If in your dream you see a battleship alone at sea, you will find your life becoming easier yet more productive. A battleship in action, with guns being fired, predicts business difficulties. A group or fleet of battleships is a sign of success in a business deal. 749

BAUBLE. Flashy or cheap jewelry in a dream, is a forerunner of illness. On yourself it is a prediction of skin diseases, but seen on others it betokens a loss of weight, fallen arches, or some minor ailment. 031

BAY. There is pleasure in store for those who dream of sailing in a calm bay. If the water is rough, beware of false friends. To look upon a bay from a high point predicts travel. 176

BAYONET. If you jab a person with a bayonet in a dream, you must be on your guard against indiscreet behavior with persons of the opposite sex. If you dream of being jabbed, you are in danger of losing a sum of money. 318

BAY TREE. Fortunate are those who dream of bay trees beside pleasant doorways, for this tree is a prediction of sound investments and a well-ordered life. 863

BAY WINDOW. It is an augury of pleasant hours ahead if you dream of looking out of a bay window. If one or more of the windows are broken, you will change your address. 319

BEACH. To dream of lying on a beach in a bathing suit is a sign that you will have to explain some action that your friends have not understood. If you are naked on a beach, the prophecy is of a new and unusual undertaking. If you dream of dragging a boat up on the beach, you will be likely to need financial assistnce. 654

BEACON LIGHT. (See also Lighthouse.) Fair weather is predicted to a sailor who dreams of a beacon light. A landsman having this dream may look forward to a prosperous undertaking. 371

BEADS. (See also Ornament, Rosary.) Some person of wealth and high position will single you out for attention if you dream of handling beads. If you string beads you will receive a sum of money that will surprise you. To count them is an augury of contentment. To drop a number of them portends discontent. 484

BEAGLE. (See also Barking.) A beagle hound seen on a crowded city street is a forerunner of many pleasant letters from friends. 887

BEAK. The beak of any bird seen in a dream is a portent of change. The beak of a bird of prey, such as an eagle or a vulture, foretells a change for the worse. A buzzard's beak portends a scandal that threatens you and can be avoided only by exercising the greatest care in your conduct. 163

BEAM. To dream of seeing a heavy beam of wood or steel being swung through the air by a derrick or crane foretells the successful termination of an important piece of work. A beam of light from a searchlight or spotlight is a harbinger of the solution of a problem that has been troubling you. 980

BEANS. In general, a dream of growing beans, whether limas, string, butter, soy, or other varieties, predicts financial security. To dream of eating baked beans is a warning against gossip, especially in social circles. 986

BEARS. A bear foretells competition in business pursuits. To kill a bear foretells release from social entanglements. If a young woman dreams of a bear she will be threatened with a rival or some other misfortune. 214

BEARSKIN. It is a sign that you will become discontented if you dream that you dress yourself in a bearskin. It is especially unfortunate in such a dream if you or someone else makes a pun of the words "bearskin" and "bareskin." 918

BEARD. To see a beard on a woman portends that an enemy will plot against you. There will be a battle for mastery, and you will lose some money. If the beard is gray, you may expect hard luck and fights with relatives. If some one pulls your beard, it means you will lose your property and friends. If a young woman admires a beard, it shows a desire to marry, and she will be threatened with an unfortunate alliance. 212

BEATING. Being beaten by an angry person, bodes no good for the dreamer. It points to family jars and discord. To see a child beaten, you will take unfair advantage of another. You are warned against the tendency to treat a child cruelly. 565

BEAUTY. To dream of beauty is pre-eminently good. A lovely woman brings pleasure and good business. A beautiful child indicates reciprocated love and a happy marriage. 147

BEAVER. A beaver foretells that you will obtain comfortable circumstances by patient effort. If you dream of killing one you will be accused of fraud and misconduct. 201

BECKONING. If it is a friendly person who beckons to you in a dream, the augury is one of good cheer and prosperous months ahead. If an enemy beckons, you may expect reverses. If a devil beckons, you should look to your moral conduct. 349

BED. A clean, white bed, foretells peace and freedom from worries. For a woman to dream of making a bed, is to expect a handsome lover. To dream of being in bed in a strange room is an augury of unexpected friends on a visit. If you are sleeping on a bed in the open air, you will have delightful experiences and an opportunity to make a considerable amount of money. To dream of seeing one of the opposite sex lying in bed, either asleep or awake, is a sign that your mind is too much given to thoughts of pleasure, no matter how innocent. 644

BEDBUGS. Definitely bad news may be expected if you dream of seeing bedbugs. If you are able to kill them or otherwise get rid of them, you will be able to rise above misfortune. 835

BEDCHAMBER. One that is newly furnished foretells a change for the better in health, income, and happiness. It is not unlikely that you will have a vacation trip to a pleasant resort. 593

BEDFELLOW. To dream of being in bed with a strange person of the opposite sex is an indication of having to meet new emergencies. If the bedfellow is of your own sex, the prediction is of having to explain your failure to comply with someone's request. 050

BEDPAN. A sudden rise to fortune is indicated by a dream of a bedpan in any circumstances. 723

BEDTICK. If you dream that you are wearing a dress or a suit made of bedtick, you will have an experience of an unusual nature that will have a profound influence on your future. It is an unpleasant augury to dream of sewing on bedtick. 434

BEEF. This is not a propitious dream, especially if it is raw and bloody. It predicts internal disorders for women and is a warning against carelessness that may result in cuts or bruises. Cooked beef is better, but its augury is of worry and marital disturbances. 669

BEER. It is a good portent to dream of pouring or drinking beer, especially if there is foam on the top. To have a pitcher filled with beer is a sign of happiness in the family circle. To dream of beer that is flat or stale indicates disappointment in love. 017

BEES. Good luck may be expected after a dream of bees around a hive, or swarming. Even a dream of being stung by bees is a portent of a profitable undertaking. 244

BEESWAX. Burning beeswax is a sign of want. Rubbing beeswax on a pressing iron predicts an improvement in marital relations. 157

BEETLES. If they are crawling on your person, they foretell many difficulties in money matters. If you kill them, you will solve these problems. 048

BEETS. A thriving field of growing beets signifies that you will prosper through your close attention to your work. To eat them with a meal is a sign of a welcome change. To eat them raw foretells disaster. 628

BEGGAR. No good will come of a dream in which you refuse to help a beggar, but should you grant his request, you will have exceedingly good luck. 660

BEGONIA. To wear a blossom from this plant predicts that a relative will criticize you for being extravagant. A dream of a healthy begonia plant is a presage of happy hours. 410

BEHEADING. To dream of being beheaded foretells defeat in a struggle or failure in some undertaking. To see others beheaded, if blood flows, death or exile is predicted. 730

BEHIND. (See Buttocks.) 393

BELCH. This dream indicates that you will look back on happier times rather than forward to them. To dream of belching at a refined dinner is a prediction that you will lose a good friend unless you exercise great caution. 830

BELIEF. A dream in which your own or another's belief in their God is taken away is an omen of desperate times ahead. 422

BELLOWS. To work a bellows foretells a struggle, but a triumph over poverty. If you see a bellows, it shows that friends living at a great distance are hoping to see you. An old discarded bellows means that you have wasted your time by doing unimportant things. 559

BELLS. To dream of bells tolling portends the death of a distant friend, and news of wrong will annoy you. Liberty bells denote an improvement in business. 474

BELLY. (See also Abdomen.) If one dreams of a distended belly, it is a sign that illness will follow. Humiliation is predicted if one sees anything moving on the belly. A healthy belly signifies unusual desires. 983

BELT. A new belt foretells you are soon to meet and make engagements with a total stranger, who will put a stop to your rise to wealth. If the belt is not of the latest fashion, you will be criticized for rudeness to your acquaintances. 075

BELTING. It is a sign of prosperous business conditions if you dream of seeing machinery that is kept in motion with belting. If the belting breaks or gets tangled, it portends a loss of money. 314

BENCH. If you dream of sitting on a bench, beware of trusting people who owe you money and of making confidants. If you see one, there will be happy reunions between you and the friends who have been separated from you through some disagreement. 981

BENEDICTION. To dream of a priest or other clergyman pronouncing a benediction is a most favorable sign. It carries hope for those in love and for any legal enterprise. 995

BENEFACTOR. If you are the benefactor in a dream, you will be fortunate in your investments or your job. If someone gives you money, you should look out for your reputation. 893

BENZINE. Be warned against believing idle gossip if you dream of smelling the fumes of benzine. If you dream of using it for cleaning fabrics, you will have an opportunity of changing your occupation. 302

BEQUEST. A feeling of satisfaction from the knowledge of duties well done, and the health of young people are assured by this dream. 643

BEREAVEMENT. To dream of the death of a child signifies that your plans will miscarry, and where you have hoped for success, there will be failure. To see the death of relatives or friends foretells the frustration of your plans and a gloomy outlook for the future. 775

BEST MAN. A single man will marry within a year if he dreams of being best man at a friend's wedding. 028

BET. To dream of betting on the races is a warning. Do not engage in new undertakings. Your enemies are trying to distract your attention for their own advantage. To bet at the gaming tables suggests that immoral means will be used to procure money from you. Beware of loose women. 072

BEVERAGE. To dream of drinking alcoholic beverages is a sign of thoughtful occupations ahead. Other beverages predict a vacation. 367

BEWILDERMENT. You will be puzzled by a letter that you receive if you dream of being bewildered for any reason. 911

BEWITCHMENT. For a man to dream of a bewitching young woman, is a forerunner of financial disaster. 358

BIAS. To dream of cutting cloth on the bias is a sign of receiving a message of distress from a friend. 114

BIBLE. To see a Bible denotes that a position of trust will be offered you. If you dream of casting doubt on the teachings of the Bible, it denotes that you will succumb to temptation and be led astray by a false friend. 912

BICARBONATE OF SODA. It portends that you will make a short trip to a neighboring state if you dream of taking this as medicine. 273

BICKERING. You will have a quarrel with someone you love if you dream of bickering. 097

BICYCLE. To ride a bicycle uphill indicates bright prospects. To ride it downhill, if the rider is a woman, it is a caution to her to guard her good name and her health, for misfortune is in sight. 830

BID. (See also Auction.) Making a bid at an auction or other sale is a prelude to disappointment. 163

BIER. It is a sign of calamity to see a dead person lying on a bier. A personage lying in state and a line of spectators passing is a portent of war. 709

BIG GAME. To dream of tracking or shooting big game is a prediction of success in manufacturing enterprises. 170

BIGAMY. If a man commits bigamy in a dream he will suffer loss of virility and failing mentality. To a woman, it denotes that she will suffer dishonor unless she is most discreet. 921

BIGOTRY. A dream of arguing about religion or politics without due regard for another's opinions augurs humiliation by someone who is beneath you socially. 834

BILGE-WATER. It is a prediction of an automobile or airplane accident if you dream of bilge-water in a ship. 440

BILIOUSNESS. If you dream of being bilious, you will have difficulty in making ends meet. It is a warning against extravagant living. 798

BILL. To receive bills for rent, board or merchandise in a dream is a sign of impending good fortune. 213

BILLBOARD. To hide behind a billboard portends embarrassment through no fault of your own. A dream of advertising billboards predicts that someone will nag you. 090

BILLIARDS. Billiards portend imminent disaster. There will be law-suits and controversies over property rights. The dreamer is likely to be slandered. To see a billiard table and balls idle means that false friends are plotting against you. 667

BILLYGOAT. A dream of being chased by a billygoat is an omen of being late for an appointment. To be butted by this animal augurs the loss of money by gambling. 075

BINDING. If you dream of a beautiful and rich bookbinding, you may expect to find a release from worry. One who dreams of binding books need never worry about income. To tear the binding on a garment signifies an entanglement with one of the opposite sex. 536

BINOCULARS. A dream of using binoculars for spying on people or things you have no right to see predicts scandalous reports about the dreamer. If binoculars are used at a race-track, the omen is one of good fortune. 668

BIOGRAPHY. It predicts a serious illness if you dream of reading your own biography. If you write the story of your life, you will be appointed to a high position. 770

BIRCH BARK. To dream of peeling bark off a birch tree is an omen of criticism that will cause you unrest. If you eat birch bark, you will be likely to suffer reverses of one kind or another. 988

BIRDS. It is a good omen to dream of birds with beautiful plumage. A rich husband and a happy marriage are predicted if a woman dreams thus. Moulting and songless birds signify crushing injustice to the unfortunate by people of wealth. To see a wounded bird foretells worry caused by willful and disobedient children. It is a sign of prosperity to see birds flying. Disagreeable surroundings will improve, as will health and fortune. To catch a bird is good luck. To hear it speak is a prediction that one will be called upon to perform tasks that demand clear understanding. To kill a bird with a gun means disaster, such as failure of crops or of business enterprises. 085

BIRD'S-EYE MAPLE. Women who dream of furniture made of this wood may expect a proposal of marriage before long. 751

BIRD'S NEST. To dream of seeing an empty bird's-nest presages gloom and a poor outlook for business. With eggs in the nest, good results may be expected from all engagements. If the young birds are in the nest, it denotes interesting journeys and satisfactory business dealings. If the young birds are deserted, the folly of someone in the family will cause you anxiety. 804

BIRTH. If a married woman dreams of giving birth to a child, great happiness and a large legacy are foretold. For a single woman, loss of reputation and desertion by her lover. It is a warning against careless behavior. 560

BIRTH CONTROL. This is a propitious dream for married people. The prophecy is of sturdy children who will prove a blessing to their parents. 370

BIRTHDAY. To be present at a birthday celebration predicts poverty to the young; to the old, many troubles and loneliness. 156

BIRTHDAY PRESENTS. To receive birthday surprises indicates that you will have many accomplishments. People of industry will advance in their profession. To give presents means that you will be a welcome guest at an important gathering. 875

BISCUITS. To eat or bake biscuits in a dream indicates sickness and the disruption of family peace over trivial disputes. 897

BISHOP. Teachers and authors will suffer great mental distress, caused by the study of difficult topics if they dream of a bishop. A tradesman will buy unwisely, and will incur a loss of money following this dream. To see a bishop, hard work will be required to reach the goal for which you are aiming. 818

BIT. To adjust a bit for boring either through wood or metal is a sign that you will face a problem but that you will solve it without too much trouble. 416

BITE. To dream of being bitten forebodes ill fortune. It suggests that you will wish to undo something you have done. You will suffer losses through someone who dislikes you. 244

BITTER-SWEET. The simple joys of a well-ordered home life are predicted by a dream in which bitter-sweet appears. 409

BLACKBERRIES. Blackberries foretell setbacks. To gather them is an unlucky sign. To eat them is a forerunner of great losses. 670

BLACKBIRD. You will be called upon to show a good deal of courage if you dream of blackbirds flying. If they alight, you will be fortunate. A dead blackbird is a presage of trouble. 055

BLACKBOARD. To dream of seeing a blackboard covered with writing in white chalk, means that you will receive unhappy tidings of some friend, or that your financial security will be threatened by the unsettled condition of ose who dream of black

BLACKSMITH. A blacksmith seen in your dreams, is an omen that you will embark on undertakings that will soon work out to your credit and advantage. 984

BLACKING. Good fortune at cards and other games will attend those who dream of blacking their own shoes. If the shoes are on someone else, it predicts luck at the races. 001

BLACKJACK. To dream of using a blackjack on an enemy is a warning against losing your temper, for it predicts an occasion on which you will wish to do someone bodily harm. 972

BLACKMAIL. If someone tries to blackmail you in a dream, you should be warned against free and easy conduct with members of the opposite sex. If you are the blackmailer, you will have general bad luck for a long period. 475

BLACK SHEEP. To be called a "black sheep" in a dream means that you will have a temptation which, if it is not overcome, will prove that you are. Therefore this is a warning to watch your step. To dream of seeing a sheep that is actually black predicts an experience that will be both amusing and profitable. 312

BLADDER. To see a bladder, means you will have a physical setback if you are not careful of your health and the way you exert yourself. 846

BLADE. (See also Cut, Knife, Razor, Sword.) A bright, keen blade without a handle of any kind predicts that you are in danger of being criticized for questionable conduct. A rusty blade indicates illness. 582

BLAME. (See also Praise.) If you dream of hearing a person take the blame for something, you should look out for hypocrisy among your friends. If you are blamed, you will be fortunate in business, but if you blame someone else, your peace of mind will be threatened. 923

BLANKET. To dream of soiled or ragged blankets signifies treachery. If they are snowy white and new, success will follow where you feared failure, and a fatal illness will be avoided. 920

BLARNEY. Beware of making insincere statements, for if you dream of indulging in blarney, they will certainly react on you seriously. 750

BLASPHEMY. Blasphemy predicts an enemy who under the pretense of friendship will cause you great embarrassment. If you yourself blaspheme, it denotes evil fortune. If you are cursed by others, relief from financial troubles will follow. 562

BLAST. To dream of setting off a blast is a prediction of greater ease than you have heretofore enjoyed. 698

BLAST FURNACE. This is a fortunate dream for young men or women who are just entering a business career. To dream of feeding a roaring blast furnace is a sign of rapid advancement. 623

BLAZE. (See also Fire.) In a fireplace a blaze foretells home comforts and obedient children. A blazing house is an omen that your friends will distrust you. 851

BLEACHING. (See also Hair.) For a young woman to dream of bleaching her hair is an omen of popularity among men. If a man has this dream, the prediction is one of shame. 675

BLEATING. Young bleating animals signify new duties and cares, but since they will be pleasant ones, this is a fortunate dream. 727

BLEEDING. Death by accident or malicious reports about you are the omens of the dream of bleeding. Fortune will desert you. 379

BLEEDING HEART. This old-fashioned flower augurs contentment when seen in a dream. To wear it in your buttonhole is an omen of good news. 519

BLEMISH. If a woman dreams that she has one or more blemishes on her face, she will be wooed by many lovers. If her blemishes are on her legs, she will have to use extraordinary precaution to protect her reputation. 565

BLESSING. If one of the clergy or a poor person pronounce a blessing on you, your dream will portend a happy future, but if in your dream you bless another, you will have many vexations to contend with. 200

BLIGHT. To see growing things afflicted with blight is a warning against careless behavior in the company of light-hearted companions. 867

BLIMP. This form of dirigible balloon seen in a dream soaring overhead carries a portent of impending trouble. To be a passenger in fair weather augurs promotion; in stormy weather it promises trouble. 087

BLINDFOLD. If a woman dreams of being blindfolded, a disturbing influence will arise in her life. Disappointment will be felt by others on her account. 137

BLIND MAN'S BUFF. If you dream of playing blind man's buff, you will engage in some foolish venture which will humiliate you, and from which you will suffer money losses. 548

BLINDNESS. You may expect a change from comfort to poverty, if you dream of being blind. To see others who are blind denotes that some worthy person will ask you for financial aid. 785

BLINKING. A person or animal blinking his eyes points toward a situation in which you will be required to use great tact. 368

BLOCK. If you dream of seeing or handling a block of wood, stone, metal or other hard material, you are almost certain to need financial help. 941

BLOCKADE. In time of war, it is a sign of hunger ahead if you dream of your country being the object of a blockade. If you dream of blockading the ports of an enemy country, you will be mistaken for a fool by an acquaintance. 570

BLONDE. Men who dream of blonde women are in danger. Misbehavior in such a dream predicts illness, loss of reputation or money, and business reverses through inattention to work. To dream of seeing a blonde woman putting on her hat is a sign of an automobile accident. Women who dream of being admired for their blonde hair are likely to have an illness. 587

BLOOD. To dream of blood-stained garments warns of enemies who will try to destroy the successful career that is opening up for you. Beware of strange friendships after this dream. If blood flows from a wound, beware of physical deterioration and guard against business failure from disastrous dealings with foreign concerns. If blood is on your hands, you will have a long period of bad luck, unless you are careful of your person and your personal affairs. 293

BLOODHOUND. Unless they appear to be on your trail bloodhounds are a fortunate augury in a dream. They portend faithfulness on the part of a friend. If they pursue you, the omen is one of deceitfulness from a former friend. 225

BLOOD MONEY. If you dream of taking money for the betrayal of a person, you are warned against association with people with red hair. Otherwise, violent quarrels will ensue. 324

BLOOD STONE. To see a blood stone foretells disaster in your engagements. For a young woman to receive a gift of a blood stone means that she will lose a friend, but will make a new one who will more than make up for the loss. 621

BLOOD SUCKER. (See also Leech, Vampire.) Dreaming of being attacked by a blood-sucking animal is a sign that you should choose your companions more carefully. 759

BLOSSOMS. To see trees and shrubs in bloom presages a time of great prosperity and ease, both of body and of mind. 777

BLOT. It is a forerunner of sadness to dream of making an ink blot while you are writing with a pen. 612

BLOTCH. (See also Pimple.) A young man or woman who dreams of seeing a blotch of any kind on the face, arms or legs is warned against temptations to drink alcoholic beverages to excess. 416

BLOTTING PAPER. To use blotting paper indicates that you will be in danger of betraying secrets which will involve a good friend. If you see worn blotting paper, family quarrels or disagreement with friends may be expected. 346

BLOW. Beware of injury to yourself. If you receive a blow, you will be likely to get into difficulties of a serious kind. To defend yourself means a rise in business. 862

BLOWOUT. If one of your automobile tires blows out in a dream, it is a warning to guard against accidents. 623

BLUDGEON. It is good luck to dream of hitting a person with a bludgeon, particularly if the person is misbehaving. To dream of being hit is a sign that people are gossiping about you. You should find out the cause and correct it. 098

BLUSHING. If a young woman dreams of blushing, she will be concerned in and shamed by lying reports. If she sees others blush, she will be in danger of making wisecracks that will displease her friends. 223

BOA-CONSTRICTOR. To dream of a snake is on a par with dreaming of the devil; it predicts hard times and ill fortune, as with Adam and Eve. Disillusionment will follow. To kill a boa-constrictor is good fortune. 459

BOARDING HOUSE. To see a boarding house in your dreams, predicts chaotic conditions in business, and you will probably move to a new address. 448

BOARDWALK. To dream of strolling along a seaside boardwalk in the company of an agreeable person of the opposite sex predicts an expected but long delayed legacy. 432

BOASTING. To boast in dreams presages regret for an impulsive act, which may cause trouble among your friends. To boast to a rival foretells that you will be unjust and will use questionable means to get ahead of your competitors. 505

BOAT. Signals seen from a boat forecast bright prospects, if you are upon still water. If the water is turbulent, you are threatened with many cares. If you are with a gay party aboard a sailboat, many favors will be bestowed upon you. To dream of falling overboard from a boat foretells irritations. 722

BOBBIN. A bobbin means important work for you, but your interests will be adversely affected if you neglect the proper attention to the bobbins under your care. 404

BODY. A beautiful body seen in a dream is a portent of success. A female body augurs public approval, while a male body predicts business advancement. 740

BODY SNATCHER. If you should dream of seeing anyone robbing a grave of the body buried there, you will be criticized for something that is not your fault. If you yourself are the grave robber, you are warned against taking sides in any quarrels among your friends or relatives. 096

BOGY. Good luck will attend anyone who dreams of seeing a terrifying and grotesque figure of semi-human form. It predicts relief from money troubles. 208

BOHEMIAN. If you have a dream of being with artistic or literary people known as bohemians and of living an unconventional life, you are likely to get into difficulties through being misunderstood. It is a warning against making new friends too quickly. 512

BOILER. To see a rusty boiler of any kind foretells that you will suffer from disappointment. For a woman to dream that she sees a boiler in a cellar signifies that sickness and losses will come to her. 741

BOILS. It is an augury of distasteful work ahead if you dream of having a boil lanced. If you dream of picking at a boil, you will have trouble with your near relatives. 985

BOLERO. This short, sleeveless jacket, worn by a Spaniard in a dream, points to gayety that must be kept from getting out of hand. As part of a woman's costume it predicts a hectic love affair. 189

BOLL WEEVIL. Cotton farmers who dream of this insect pest will do well to guard their reputation, for the dream is a warning against slanderous enemies. 937

BOLO. This wicked sword used by the wild Moro tribe of the Philippines is a symbol of sudden disaster when seen in a dream. In use by a savage it predicts the fulfillment of the thing you have most dreaded. 340

BOLONEY. You will be surprised by a sudden turn in your luck, either for better or for worse, if you dream of eating boloney. If you dream of hearing or using the word in a slang sense, you will have an amusing experience. 051

BOLSTER. One who dreams of putting a bolster on a bed will have an experience that he or she will wish to hide. To put a fresh pillowcase on a bolster is a sign of having a new opportunity of making good. 854

BOLTS. From this dream you may expect that formidable obstacles will oppose your progress. If the bolts are broken or old, you will not succeed in your expectations. 541

BOMBARDMENT. One may look forward with confidence to security if he or she dreams of being bombarded by the guns of an enemy. 804

BOMBERS. These airplanes, seen soaring above you in a dream, predict a menace in your life that can be averted by the decisive use of your best judgment. If bombs are dropped and do not appear to explode, you are in danger of losing your position. If they explode, you will change your place of residence. 794

BOMBPROOF. It is a sign that you need not worry about the future if you dream of going into a bombproof shelter in wartime. 462

BOMB-SHELLS. Dreams of bomb-shells foretell anger and disputes, ending in lawsuits. Many upsetting incidents are likely to follow this dream. 281

BONANZA. To dream that you are a miner and strike a bonanza is a sign that you will have to work hard for a living. 912

BONBONS. If you dream of sending bonbons to a favored friend or lover, you will be accused of duplicity by a trusted friend. 230

BONDS. To receive valuable bonds in a dream augurs well for those who are connected with the building trades. 653

BONDAGE. It is unfortunate to dream of being in bondage to another person for whatever reason. 110

BONDSMAN. A sharp-featured bondsman who, in a dream, gets bail for you if you are arrested, is an augury of success in buying and selling. 114

BONES. If you dream that bones stick out from the flesh, beware of treachery. A pile of bones predicts famine or other bad influences. 858

BONFIRE. (See also Blaze.) A large bonfire is indicative of your triumph over difficulties, unless a wind scatters sparks from it, in which case it predicts annoyances. 061

BON MOT. A bright saying—yours or another's—in a dream points toward a happy, carefree future. 704

BONUS. To dream of receiving a sum of money over and above what is due you is a sign that you are on the right track in your business career. 974

BOOBY. If there is any augury from a dream of being considered a booby, it is of an amusing experience in store for you. Altogether, it is a happy dream. 910

BOOK. To dream of books and reading denotes pleasant days and honor and riches if you study them. For an author to dream of his own manuscript going to press, means caution; he will encounter difficulties in placing it before the public. To see children at their books, predicts harmony and good behavior among young people. To dream of old books is a warning to avoid the appearance of evil. 445

BOOKCASE. To dream of a bookcase, is a sign that you will apply yourself diligently both to your work and recreation. To see an empty bookcase presages loss of position due to lack of education. 435

BOOK ENDS. The accomplishment of a favoritE project is predicted by a dream in which book ends are a feature. 886

BOOKKEEPER. (See Accountant.) 396

BOOKMARK. If you dream of using a bookmark to keep your place in a book you are reading, you will be sure to keep an appointment that will be of benefit to you. 839

BOOK PLATE. It is an augury that you will lose prestige through selfishness if you dream of pasting a book plate in one of your books. 049

BOOKSELLER. To dream that you earn a living by selling books predits that you will have many friends who are both intellectual and agreeble. It is also lucky for you to dream of talking with a bookseller. 901

BOOKSTORE. If you visit a bookstore in your dream, you will become a writer, but your literary attempts will interfere with your regular work and pleasure. 752

BOOKWORM. For someone to call you a bookworm in a dream is a presage of quiet happy hours. Loss of money is predicted if you use the name for somebody else. 859

BOOM. To be struck by a boom while dreaming of being on a sailboat is a sign that you should be wary of strangers who profess friendship. 024

BOOMERANG. If you dream of throwing a boomerang and it comes back and hits you, it is a warning against making careless or unguarded statements. 763

BOOT. If you see a pair of boots on another, your place will be usurped in the affections of your sweetheart. If you wear a new pair of boots, you will be fortunate in business. If you are working for another, you will receive a higher salary. Old or worn out boots foretell sickness and trouble. 697

BOOTJACK. Easy living is predicted by a dream of using an old-fashioned bootjack for removing one's boots. 973

BOOTY. To find booty that has been hidden by pirates or thieves is a sign of prosperity at an early date. 049

BOOZE. (See Alcohol,Beer, Whiskey, Wine.) 409

BORACIC ACID. It is a sign that you will receive a message to get in touch with an influential person, either a man or woman, who will contribute to your advancement. 491

BORAX. To dissolve borax in a tub of water before taking a bath in a dream signifies that you will live to old age in comfort and good health. 455

BORDERLAND. A dream of being on the borderland between two states or countries predicts a period of indecision. 237

BORE. Look out for articles falling from high places if you have a dream of having to talk with a bore or a tiresome person. 674

BORER. If you dream of seeing this boring insect boring into plant stems or the bark of trees, you are warned to pay more attention to business and less to frivolous occupations. You may have a rival in love. 754

BORROWING. To borrow denotes loss and a smaller income. If a banker dreams of borrowing from another bank, he may expect a run on his bank and possible failure. If someone borrows from you, you are assured of assistance being given you if you are ever in need. True friends will stand by you. 051

BOSOM. If a young woman dreams that her bosom is hurt, some calamity will overtake her. If she dreams of a flat or wrinkled bosom, she may expect to be heartbroken, although many rivals will contend for her. If the bosom is creamy and voluptuous, she will inherit a fortune. If her sweetheart peers at her bosom through her sheer gown, she will fall a victim to an ardent admirer. 056

BOSS. It is a good sign to dream of being on friendly terms with the boss, but it is also a warning against loafing on the job. 175

BOSTON TERRIER. A friendly but excitable Boston terrier seen in a dream predicts financial improvement but warns against "burning the candle at both ends." 693

BOTANY. The scientific study of flowers in a dream foretells calm after storm, but not much profit. 724

BOTCH. To dream of making a botch of anything you make with your hands is a forerunner of discovery if you have anything to hide. 702

BOTTLES. It is a good sign to dream of a bottle if it is full of a transparent liquid. You will be successful in love, and prosperous in business. If the bottle is empty, you will be faced with disaster, from which you must exert great pressure to escape. 769

BOTTOM. (See also Buttocks.) If in a dream you look at the bottom of a dish, you will quarrel with a relative. 307

BOUDOIR. (See also Bedchamber, Bedfellow.) For either a man or woman to dream of a scented, luxurious boudoir is a warning against indiscriminate alliances and careless behavior. If a man dreams of an amorous intrigue in a boudoir, it warns him to be exceedingly circumspect in all his relations with women. 291

BOUILLON. (See Soup.) 628

BOULDER. If one dreams of moving a large rock or boulder with ease, it portends better business conditions. It tells of bad luck when it cannot be moved at all. A falling boulder is a sign of change. 369

BOULEVARD. To dream of driving a car along a well-paved boulevard during the daytime portends favors from your creditors. At night if it is well lighted, the prediction is of a journey to a strange locality. A dark boulevard is a sign of disappointment. 964

BOUNTY. Hunters who dream of receiving a bounty from the statthe daytime portends favors from your creditors. At night if it is well lighted, the prediction is of a journey to a strange locality. A dark boulevard is a sign of disappointment. 964

BOUNTY. Hunters who dream of receiving a bounty from the state for the pelt of a wolf, coyote or other animal pest are warned against plots by designing men and women. 681

BOUQUET. A fragrant bouquet of bright-colored flowers signifies a bequest from some affluent and distant relative; also festivities among the young people. If you see a faded bouquet, it denotes illness and possible death. 982

BOURBON. To drink Bourbon whiskey in a dream is a prediction of a profitable real estate deal. 330

BOUT. (See Boxer.) 734

BOW AND ARROW. To dream of shooting at a target with a bow and arrow foretells that you will make a profit at someone else's expense. If you shoot at an animal, you will meet an old friend. 240

BOWER. Romantic dream meetings in a pleasant bower of vines, trees or flowers are a forerunner of happiness to young and old. 779

BOWL. An empty bowl signifies want. Filled with food, it is a generally good omen, but the nature of the contents will determine the omen. Look them up in other parts of this book, also the color of the bowl. 428

BOW LEGS. You should look to your own comfort if you dream of seeing a man, woman or child with bow legs. 507

BOWLING. You will be successful in your efforts to make a living if you dream of bowling, either in an alley or out of doors. 534

BOWSPRIT. A dream of climbing out on the bowsprit of a sailboat is a forerunner of exciting experiences. If the sea is rough, danger is ahead, but if you are shaken off, you will come through without harm. 355

BOW-STRING. To dream of stringing a bow in preparation for the shooting of arrows is a prediction of a great social achievement, whether you are a man or a woman. 667

BOX. To open a box of household goods foretells wealth and enjoyable travels in South American countries. If the box is empty you will be disappointed in your work. If you see boxes full of money you will have freedom from care and will enjoy your business.349

BOXER. A dream of men fighting in the prize ring is a sign of advancement through close attention to work. If you dream that you are a boxer, the augury is favorable if you hold your own against your opponent. Otherwise you will have a minor injury. 611

BOXWOOD. To jump over a boxwood hedge in a dream is an omen of a vexing problem that you will be able to solve without much difficulty. To dream of using a saw on boxwood predicts that you will help a good friend out of difficulties. 765

BOY. Boys at any kind of play are a good sign, especially if they are engaged in athletic events. Even a dream of fighting boys augurs well for the dreamer. A boy at play with a girl predicts happiness in marriage and love affairs. If one boy is at play with several girls, the prophecy is of an adventure that will turn out well. A boy at work to earn money is a fortunate omen for those who are contemplating marriage. 470

BOY SCOUT. Some wish that is close to your heart will be gratified if you dream of one or more Boy Scouts in the observance of their ritual. 329

BRACELET. If you wear a bracelet upon your arm or wrist, the dream augurs a present from your sweetheart or a friend and insures happiness in your marriage. Worn on your ankle, it predicts a scandal. If a young woman loses a bracelet she will have minor worries. If you find a bracelet you will inherit property. 108

BRACKEN. If you dream of lying among the bracken or other fern-like growth, there will be an exciting experience in store for you. Whether this will be agreeable or otherwise depends on the innocence surrounding your being there. 830

BRAGGART. A dream of hearing a person brag about his prowess in any line predicts a period of depression; but if you can put him to shame, the outcome will be hopeful. 867

BRAID. Uniforms or dresses trimmed with braid of gold or bright colors augur a promotion to a higher and better paying job. To see young girls with their hair done up in braids is a sign that you will be happy in your marriage. 276

BRAIN. To dream of your own brain foretells irritations. Your home and friends will displease you and you will become disgruntled and unhappy. If you see or eat the brains of animals you will hear profitable news from an unexpected source. 962

BRAKE. It is an omen of greater responsibilities ahead if you dream of applying the brake to an auto or other vehicle. If the brake does not slow down the vehicle, you must guard against making commitments that you cannot carry through. If the brake squeaks, you are in danger of being accused of a terrible crime. 506

BRAKEMAN. A woman who dreams of seeing a brakeman at work on a railroad train will live to see many changes for the better, both for herself and her friends. 351

BRAMBLES. If you are caught in brambles, beware of evil influences. Lawsuits will be settled unfavorably, and you or a member of your family may suffer from disease. 143

BRANCH. The branches of a tree waving in a gentle breeze predict new interests for those who have found life dull. If the tree is in bloom, there is an augury of increasing comfort. In a gale the omen is not so good, although there is nothing to disturb the dreamer. 274

BRANDY. Brandy signifies great wealth and affluence but you probably will lack consideration for others. The people whose friendship you would like to cultivate will avoid you. 210

BRASS. The dream of brass utensils of all kinds means that you will advance rapidly in your business, but while assured of success you inwardly anticipate misfortune. 014

BRASSIERE. If a man dreams of adjusting a brassiere, he is warned against making any false steps in his association with the gentler sex. For him to dream of acting the part of peeping Tom is to expect an occurrence that may exercise a profound influence on his life. If a woman dreams of forgetting to wear a brassiere she will be likely to have an altercation with someone she knows well. If she dreams that a strap breaks when she is in the company of a man, she will have an invitation to a party. 554

BRAT. Those who are employed in industrial jobs will be able to look forward to easier conditions if they dream of being annoyed by brats. For clerical workers, the dream predicts a happy home life. 524

BRAVADO. A show of fake bravery in a dream is a forerunner of quiet enjoyment from simple pleasures. 681

BRAVERY. One who dreams of being brave under unusually distressing conditions will have an opportunity to demonstrate that he can be brave. 799

BRAWL. To be a witness of or participate in a brawl is a good sign if no injury results for the dreamer. Otherwise it foretells misfortune. 434

BRAWN. A display of brawn by yourself or others in a dream foretells physical troubles. 820

BRAY. To hear an ass bray predicts bad news. 715

BRAZIL NUT. To dream of having difficulty opening these large nuts is an omen that you will have to contend with unreasonable people. 273

BREACH OF PROMISE. It is a warning against light love affairs if a man dreams of being sued for breach of promise. For a woman to dream of suing indicates that she should regulate her life so as to avoid criticism of her acts. 523

BREAD. If a woman dreams of eating bread, she will be the mother of obstinate children for whom she will work hard and worry. If any one eats bread with another, he will be certain of always being well cared for. If you see stale bread, unhappiness and illness will come to you. If the bread is fresh and you eat it, the omen is a good one. You will be prosperous. 783

BREAK. To break anything is a bad dream. If you break a leg or an arm, you are warned that you are mismanaging your affairs and are likely to be disappointed. To break a window foretells death. To break furniture means quarrels in the home and consequent worry. To dream of a broken finger ring warns that you will have heated arguments that will cause great unhappiness.274

BREAKDOWN. If you dream of a breakdown in health, you are warned against being too free with your money. 620

BREAKFAST. If your work is mental, to dream of breakfast is a good sign. To see fresh milk and eggs on the table and a well-filled bowl of fruit predicts hurried but propitious changes. To eat alone means that you will be overcome by your enemies. If you eat with others, the augury is good. 963

BREAST. (See Bosom.) 782

BREASTBONE. To eat the meat of the breastbone of a chicken, duck or other fowl indicates that you will be prosperous in your old age. 902

BREATH. If you dream of a person with a sweet breath, your conduct will be above criticism and a profitable business deal will be put through. If the breath is not sweet, sickness is foretold. To lose one's breath by over exertion denotes failure where success was expected. 089

BREEDING. You will have to struggle for an inheritance that is rightfully yours if you dream of breeding horses or cattle. 180

BREEZE. A strong and steady breeze felt in a dream predicts good business conditions. If it comes in gusts and then dies down, you will be worried. 589

BREVIARY. Reading this religious book in a dream is an augury of peace of mind. 254

BREWING. To dream of a brewery augurs injustice and ill treatment from public officials, but you will be exonerated and elevated to a high position. Brewing dreams point toward uneasiness at first, but they end in financial gain and contentment. 874

BRIBERY. To dream of offering a bribe is a warning against those who seek to exploit you for their own selfish ends. Accepting a bribe is a sign of serious illness. 153

BRIC-A-BRAC. It is a sign that your efforts will be wasted if you dream of collecting small ornaments and pieces of china to put around the house. You will have good fortune if you dream of breaking one or more of these. 255

BRICK. To dream of bricks foretells upset business conditions and upsets in your love life. If you manufacture bricks you will not make a great deal of money. 309

BRICKBAT. A dream in which you or others throw brickbats is the forerunner of success in the textile trades. If you are struck by a brickbat, you will meet a charming but unreliable person of the opposite sex. 828

BRICKLAYING. To dream of laying bricks foretells a slowly but surely increasing fortune. 043

BRICKYARD. Passing through a brickyard in a dream foretells years of travel before you finally settle down to a quiet life. It is a favorable sign for women who aspire to be in motion pictures. 104

BRIDAL WREATH. A woman who dreams of this lovely flower will have many proposals and will make a very advantageous marriage. 684

BRIDE. If a young woman dreams of being a bride she will inherit money, particularly if she appears in a happy frame of mind while dressing for the wedding. If she is displeased she will be disappointed in her husband. If in a dream you kiss a bride, you will be reconciled with former enemies. If a bride kisses others, it foretells many friends and much happiness. If the bride kisses you, your sweetheart will inherit some money. If you kiss a bride who looks tired and ill, it means you will not be successful and that you will be disapproved of by your friends. For a bride to dream of being indifferent to her husband predicts a short honeymoon. 009

BRIDEGROOM. A man who dreams of going through the marriage ceremony is likely to find a sum of money that will relieve him for the time being. If he cannot find the wedding ring in time for the ceremony, he will be criticized for his conduct by his superiors. If a man dreams of being nervous while being married, he will be confronted with the necessity of making a momentous decision. 781

BRIDESMAID. For a girl to dream of being a bridesmaid foretells a happy marriage within the year. If her dress is torn, she will find that her husband is secretive. 374

BRIDGE. To dream of a long wooden bridge with holes in it means that you will suffer distress over the loss of precious possessions. To single women and bachelors it predicts disappointments and broken engagements, as the beloved one will not live up to your ideals. To dream of crossing a bridge safely is an omen that you will eventually overcome obstacles. If a bridge falls while you are looking at it, be warned of seductive admirers. Clear water flowing under the bridge indicates wealth, but if the water is muddy, you may expect poor returns for your efforts in business. If you are seated at a table playing bridge and drop a card, you will lose money. If you win at bridge, you will receive a small legacy, but it will not last long. 632

BRIDGEWORK. Anyone who dreams of wearing dental bridgework will have to encounter several difficulties arising from failure to meet obligations. If the bridgework comes loose, the augury is of losing the friendship of an important person. 391

BRIDLE. To put a bridle on a horse in your dream means that you will undertake some unusual business that will cause you great distress, but will end profitably. If the bridle is old or broken you will encounter obstacles that are likely to defeat you. You will be deceived by some intriguing person or someone of the opposite sex will encourage you in a clandestine affair. 036

BRIDLE BITS. To dream of bridle bits is an omen that you will overcome an obstacle that has threatened your advancement. If the bits are broken, or appear to break in the dream, you will have to give in to your competitors. 696

BRIEFCASE. A business trip that will be both pleasant and successful is predicted by a dream of carrying a well-worn briefcase. If it is new and clean, it foretells disappointment resulting from lack of sufficient preparation. 622

BRIER. If you become entangled in a brier patch, it is a sign that unfriendly people are plotting to get ahead of you. Freeing yourself from the thorns predicts that friends will help you out of your difficulty. 345

BRIER PIPE. The ability to meet and solve your problems is promised if you dream of smoking a brier pipe. 461

BRIM. A hole in the brim of a hat portends physical pain. If one dreams of a chip out of the brim of a tea or coffee cup, there will be disagreeable people to contend with. To see a bowl brimful of food foretells joy. 288

BRIMSTONE. Brimstone suggests that you have been using dishonorable business tactics that will cause the loss of many friends, if you do not turn over a new leaf. To dream of seeing brimstone fires means that you will be alarmed and suffer loss through a contagious disease in your neighborhood. 421

BRISKET. Eating brisket is a good sign for those engaged in jobs where skill in the use of figures is required. To see it in a meat store augurs an increase in income. 796

BRISTLES. If you dream of brushing your hair or your teeth with a brush whose bristles are soft and flabby, you will be disappointed in the way your fortunes will turn. If the bristles are stiff and vigorous, good luck may be expected. 982

BROADCAST. Listening to a broadcast in a dream portends success for those who aspire to go into radio of any kind. To dream that you are broadcasting means that your ideas will be treated with respect. 159

BROADCLOTH. To dream of wearing broadcloth is a presage of prosperity through a wise choice of friends. 350

BROCADE. If you dream that your garments are of rich brocade, beware of hypocrisy on the part of those with whom you associate. 285

BROGUE. A dream of hearing someone speak with a brogue augurs a rise to affluence and power. 625

BROKER. No one who has a dream of a broker—whether in securities or commodities—ought to engage in speculation before a month has passed. 021

BROMIDE. It is distinctly unfortunate to dream of taking bromides to make you sleep. It foretells an accident. 932

BRONCHITIS. Bronchitis predicts that you will be prevented from carrying out your plans by illness in your immediate family. If one suffers with bronchitis in a dream, disappointment is in store and the possibility of attaining your objective will be doubtful. 916

BRONCO. No one can afford to disregard this warning against the underhanded activities of others if he dreams of being thrown by a bronco. 627

BRONZE. If a woman dreams of a bronze statue she will very likely fail to marry the man of her choice. If the statue moves or appears to be alive, she will fall in love but no marriage will take place. To see a bronze serpent or insect means that you will meet insecurity and jealousy. 830

BROOD. To dream of a hen with her brood of chickens foretells troubles to a woman. You will have several children under your care, and some of them will be stubborn and mischievous. If you see another kind of brood, it denotes the building up of a fortune. 472

BROOD MARE. It is an augury of definite improvement in home affairs to dream of seeing a brood mare with a young foal. A brood mare at the time of foaling predicts a happy event. 966

BROOM. To see a broom means that thrift and better luck will come to you in the near future, if the broom is new. If the broom is an old one, you will lose in the stockmarket. If a woman loses a broom she will be a cross wife and a poor housekeeper. 425

BROTH. To dream of broth predicts the loyalty of friends, who will always be true to you, and if you are in need of funds they will supply you with them. To lovers it denotes an enduring affection. If you make broth, you will govern your own and other destinies. 382

BROTHEL. It ought to be a forerunner of disgrace to dream of visiting a brothel, but instead it signifies honors and a dignified happy home life. For either a man or a woman the dream predicts an improvement in his or her condition. 153

BROTHER. A dream of loyalty and affection between brothers is a sign of increasing stability in financial and social position. 113

BROTHER-IN-LAW. If you dream of respecting your brother-in-law, you will discover that he lacks the very qualities that you had hoped to find in him. 483

BRUISE. Any accident in a dream that results in a bruise is a sign that you will be admired for your conduct in an emergency. A bruise on the leg, however, is a warning against carelessness at street crossings. 384

BRUSH. To use a hair or a toothbrush with flabby and ineffective bristles predicts disappointment, but if the bristles are stiff you will be pleased by developments in both home and business affairs. 920

BRUSHWOOD. Clearing away brushwood in a dream foretells a harrowing experience with one of the opposite sex. Burning brushwood warns against too great familiarity with chance acquaintances. 989

BRUSSELS CARPET. It is a forerunner of affluence and comfort if you dream of having this luxurious floor covering in your home. A dream of having it in the kitchen predicts an amusing experience with a new friend. 656

BRUSSELS SPROUTS. (See also Cabbage.) These little cabbages, as they are called by the French, are a sign of luxury ahead. To smell them cooking predicts a reward for work well done. To eat them signifies health and plenty. 273

BRUTALITY. A dream in which you are a witness to brutality predicts that you will revisit the scenes of your childhood. If you are the victim, you will see an improvement in income. 129

BUCKBOARD. Those who dream of riding in a buckboard may look forward with certainty to peace and comfort in their old age. With one horse it is a good dream, but if there is a team it is better. 172

BUCKET. To carry water or milk in a bucket is a sign that you will remember happier days. It foretells death if you stumble over a bucket. 629

BUCKLE. Numerous invitations will come to you to attend social functions if you dream of buckles, but you should be warned of neglecting your business or church duties. 148

BUCKSAW. A vacation is predicted by a dream of cutting wood with a bucksaw. If you dream of being very tired from this work, your vacation will be in the company of one of the opposite sex. 868

BUCKSHOT. Loading a gun with buckshot is a warning dream against giving way to bursts of ungovernable temper. 644

BUCK TOOTH. It is a premonition of sadness to dream of one or more prominently protruding teeth. On someone else it portends travel to faraway lands. 191

BUCKWHEAT. A thriving field of blossoming buckwheat is an omen of a calm but prosperous career. Buckwheat cakes signify that your ambitions will be realized, particularly in love. 525

BUDGET. A woman who dreams of budgeting her expenditures will not be popular with men. A man who has this dream will be likely to succeed in business. 742

BUGLE. To hear triumphant blasts of a bugle portends unexpected happiness through someone who is far away. It augurs good luck to dream of blowing a bugle. If you dream of a bugler sounding "Taps", you will have a sad experience. 270

BUGS. There is likely to be an event that will disgust you if you dream of bugs. If the house is overrun with bugs, the prediction is one of serious illness or worse. If in the dream you are successful in getting rid of them, the omen is better. 577

BUILDING. To dream of seeing magnificent and imposing buildings with flower gardens and lawns is a sign that you will be wealthy and that you will be able to indulge in the luxury of travel. If the buildings are of modest size and well kept in appearance, it predicts a happy home and good business. Old and unsightly buildings predict unhappiness. 383

BUILDING AND LOAN. It is lucky to dream of saving for a home. To open an account in a Building and Loan is a harbinger of contentment and a happy family life. 581

BULL. If in a dream you are chased by a bull, you should look out for grasping competitors for your business. If a woman encounters a bull, she will be likely to receive a proposal of marriage, but she should not accept it. You are warned against borrowing money if you dream of seeing a bull goring a person. It is a good omen to see a white bull in a dream, for it predicts promotion through understanding. 340

BULLDOG. If a bulldog attacks you while you are trespassing on another's property in a dream, you are warned against infractions of the law such as disobeying motor regulations, falsifying your income tax return, etc. 223

BULLET. The whine of a bullet, shot from a pistol or gun and heard in a dream, is an indication that you are in great danger and that you should use every precaution against exposing yourself to criticism. A lead bullet thrown at you by a strange person means that you will be slandered by someone you have trusted. To dream of finding a bullet is a sign that someone is plotting against you. To dream of being struck by a bullet is a prediction of illness or disgrace, or both. 569

BULLETIN. It is an augury of momentous happenings in your country if your dream of reading bulletins in front of a newspaper office. A bulletin of the death of a president of the country predicts a period of unrest. 866

BULLFIGHT. If you dream of being at a bullfight and appear to be interested and excited by it, you are warned of a none too pleasant experience inside your home circle. If you are disgusted by the exhibition, you will travel to foreign lands. 224

BULLFINCH. A dream of seeing this interesting bird predicts a short period of prosperity. 172

BULLFROG. To hear bullfrogs in a dream augurs peace of mind. To see them predicts meeting new and interesting people. To catch them indicates that you will be deceived by someone whom you have trusted. 496

BULLOCK. If you dream of a bullock, you may look forward to the pleasant companionship of friends who are tired and true, besides which you will enjoy good health. 851

BULLSEYE. A dream of engaging in target practice with any kind of weapon is a fortunate one if you are successful in hitting the bullseye once, but if you hit it every time you shoot, you should be on your guard against enemies who are trying to frame you. 824

BULL TERRIER. This dream predicts that you will win recognition from your employer through unremitting effort in his behalf. To be attacked by a bull terrier is not a bad sign, but carries a warning to give more attention to business and less to social diversions. 443

BULLY. If in a dream you take the part of someone against a bully, you will find that the people with whom you come in contact will show you great respect. You will have bad luck for a long time if you dream of bullying someone else. 947

BUM. To dream of giving money or food or encouragement to a bum is a sign that you will advance in your social relations. To refuse assistance or to criticize a bum harshly is a forerunner of disgrace. 326

BUMBLEBEE. If a bumblebee buzzes around your head in a dream, you will be able to carry out some great ambition that you have had. To dream of being stung by a bumblebee is a sign of coming prosperity. 686

BUMP. Those who have been contemplating some action that may not be lawful or ethical should be warned to go slowly if they dream of being in any vehicle that bumps another. It is a warning to be extremely careful in your actions. 422

BUMPER. If the bumper of your automobile comes loose in a dream and rattles as you drive, you must try to make amends for any wrong you have recently done to an acquaintance. If the bumper drops off the car, it is a sign of trouble for you. 712

BUNDLE. A mystery that will be difficult to solve is indicated by a dream of seeing someone carrying a bundle. If you dream of wrapping a bundle of any kind, you will be criticized by your friends for not being frank. 498

BUNGALOW. A bungalow in a dream predicts the friendly regard of people you meet. If you rent a bungalow you will be successful in business, but if you build one, you will also be advanced socially. 651

BUNGHOLE. To try to look into the bunghole of a beer or whiskey barrel is a sign that you will fail to achieve the purpose for which you have been working. If you dream of filling a barrel through the bunghole, you have a long period of distress before you. Driving a bung into a bunghole is a sign of successful achievement. 349

BUNION. Pain felt from a bunion in a dream is a sign of definite comfort in old age. To dream of having a chiropodist attend to a bunion is to look forward to improved financial circumstances. 443

BUNK. It is an unfortunate augury to dream of going to bed in a bunk, either on shipboard or in a backwoods cabin. You are likely to need money very soon, and it will be difficult to obtain. 947

BUNTING. A dream of seeing buildings or large rooms decorated with bunting presages a violent love affair for women and a hectic period of business for men. If you dream of using bunting for decorating, you will find yourself in an unusual dilemma. 326

BURDEN. Carrying a heavy burden, whether it is material or spiritual, is a dream that foretells grave responsibilities. Also someone will infringe on your rights in some kind of property, and you will have difficulty in straightening out your affairs. 968

BURDOCK. Too dream of getting a burr stuck in your clothes is a sign of family troubles. If the burr gets stuck in your hair, the prediction is one of disgrace that can be avoided only by the greatest circumspection in your actions. 067

BUREAU. You can be sure of a long period of freedom from care if you dream of laying away clothes in a bureau drawer. It is a sign of petty annoyances if you have to hunt for anything under a bureau. If you have to move a bureau in a dream, beware of those who flatter you. 892

BURGLARS. There is nothing to worry about after a dream about burglars, for they portend an increase in worldly goods. If a burglar points a pistol at you in a dream, the prediction is of an invitation to contribute to a charitable cause. If you are able to get rid of the burglars, you will receive money due you. 367

BURIAL. To dream of attending a relative's funeral is a sign of the marriage of another relative if the sun is shining. If it is raining, you will receive news by mail of the illness of a relative. Business reverses may also follow this dream. 859

BURIAL ALIVE. You are likely to make a grave mistake if you dream of being buried alive. If at the last moment you are saved from this fate, you are warned against practices that you know to be unethical. 925

BURLAP. The use of burlap in a dream, whether for making bags or covering walls, predicts that you will make a success of the work in which you are now engaged. 840

BURLESQUE. Attending a burlesque show in a dream predicts that you will have explanations to make for something that you are not responsible for. 212

BURNS. Burns in a dream are an omen of good luck. If you burn your hand, it predicts that you will have the approval of your friends, but if you burn your feet, it predicts that you will be successful in the accomplishment of some difficult task. 261

BURR. (See Burdock.) 678

BURRO. Riding one of these patient little animals is an omen of contentment in your daily life with your family. If the burro is balky, you will have minor irritations. 431

BUS. Riding in a bus foretells difficult times ahead, especially for those who are engaged in clerical or stenographic work. If the bus has an accident, there will be a long period in which the dreamer will be financially embarrassed. 452

BUSH. It is the forerunner of a shameful experience to dream of hiding under a bush if you are being pursued. To see a burning bush in a dream predicts the receipt of surprising but not gratifying news. 550

BUSINESS. Usually it is bad luck to dream about your business. It is likely to be the forerunner of embarrassment in a public place. 734

BUST. (See also Bosom.) It is a sign of a death among the circle of friends to see a sculptured bust of a well known person in a dream. 845

BUSTLE. If a woman dreams of wearing a bustle, she will have an adventure in which a handsome man can figure prominently. 176

BUTCHER. To dream of seeing a butcher kill cattle or sheep is a portent of a long and serious illness in your family. To see him slicing meat portends that your reputation will be besmirched, and it is therefore a warning against committing yourself to anything in writing. 076

BUTLER. One may expect a sudden reversal of fortune if he or she dreams of being waited on by a butler. To dream of being a butler is a sign that you will be able to pay your debts. 821

BUTTER. To eat fresh golden butter is a sign that you will enjoy excellent health and will have the financial means to enjoy it to the fullest. Even if the butter is rancid, you will be able to make a decent living by hard work. If the dream is of selling butter, you will have an opportunity to make a small amount of money. 844

BUTTERCUP. Wandering through a field of buttercups in a dream foretells a loving mate and happy children. To pick buttercups is an omen of relief from pressing obligations; to throw them away indicates dread of the future. 084

BUTTERMILK. To drink buttermilk in a dream means that you will worry about some indiscretion you have committed. It is bad luck to throw it away or to feed it to swine. To make an oyster stew with buttermilk is a sign that you will be in danger of making poor investments and that you will quarrel with a good friend. 128

BUTTERFLY. A butterfly fluttering its way through a flower garden and occasionally alighting on a blossom is an augury of good fortune. This dream foretells a handsome lover and an early marriage to a woman. 810

BUTTERNUT. If you try to crack a butternut in a dream, it is an indication that you will overcome your greatest difficulties. If you are successful in extracting the meat, you wll receive a legacy. 358

BUTTER SCOTCH. There will be a wedding among your circle of acquaintances if you dream of making or eating this kind of candy. If you dream of breaking a tooth while eating it, you will hear bad news. 640

BUTTOCKS. A dream of kicking a person in the buttocks augurs being promoted to a higher position but losing the respect of those under your authority. To have one's buttocks kicked is a sign of disaster. 275

BUTTON. If you dream of sewing colored or shiny metal buttons on any kind of uniform, you will win the love of a rich and handsome person. A young man having this dream has a good chance of receiving an appointment to a fine military school. Cloth buttons or those that have become tarnished are a portent of poor health and money losses. To lose a button from a garment is an indication that you will suffer embarrassment. 120

BUTTONHOLE. Worn buttonholes are an indication that you will have additional worries. New buttonholes predict new accomplishments. 569

BUTTONHOOK. Calm days ahead are predicted by a dream of using a buttonhook. 715

BUZZARD. This ungainly scavenger bird seen in a dream is a potent warning against repeating malicious gossip. If you dream of seeing it eat carrion, you are likely to regret some ill-advised action. 065

BUZZER. It is a sign that you will be appreciated at your proper worth socially and in business if you dream that you hear the sound of a buzzer calling you. 688

C

CAB. To ride in a cab foretells daily labor that you will enjoy. It will make for you a comfortable living. If you ride in the cab at night with one of the opposite sex, you will be in danger of telling your friends a secret that you should keep to yourself. If you dream of driving a public cab, you will work at manual labor with little promise of a salary, but you will enjoy yourself. 366

CABBAGE. It is good luck to dream of cooking a cabbage, but to eat green cabbage predicts a violation of the marriage contract. To cut a head of cabbage into shreds means that through extravagance you are in danger of want. 229

CABIN. To dream of being in the cabin of a ship points to misfortune. Trouble of a legal nature is ahead, and you are likely to lose the case through the perjury of your opponent. To dream of a cabin in the woods is a fortunate augury. 925

CABINET. To dream of putting away things in a cabinet portends that a secret of considerable importance will be revealed to you. It is a sign of improved financial conditions if you dream of locking a cabinet, but if you throw the key away, you will have to work hard for your money. It is not a good augury to dream of moving a cabinet. To take articles out of a cabinet signifies distressing news. 625

CABLE. Stretching a rope or wire cable foretells perilous work. If you accomplish it successfully, you will acquire much money and many honors. 477

CABLEGRAM. If you dream of receiving a cablegram, you will soon be the recipient of an important message that will be accompanied by unpleasant circumstances. 158

CACKLE. To hear hens cackle augurs news of the unexpected death of a neighbor amid circumstances that are not easily understandable. 382

CACTUS. If you dream of being thrown into a clump of cactus, it predicts a series of annoying occurrences. If you see a cactus plant in bloom, you may expect good luck in one form or another. To transplant cactus signifies going from bad to worse. To give a cactus plant in a pot to a friend portends a quarrel. 679

CADAVER. (See Corpse.) 871

CAFETERIA. Getting a trayful of food at a cafeteria is a dream that portends a small legacy from a deceased friend. If you dream of dropping the tray or otherwise spilling the food, you are in danger of illness. If you dream of going back to a counter for more food, you will receive good news. 192

CAGE. To dream of a cage in which many birds are flying about or roosting on perches foretells an inheritance of a large size and a sizable family. If there is only one bird in the cage, the dream is a good one for a woman, for she will marry to her great advantage. An empty cage predicts that you will see a serious accident while on your travels. 724

CAKES. To dream of pancakes shows that the future of the dreamer is secure and that a legacy and a home will be left him or her. Sweet cakes foretell advancement for the laborer and advancement for the industrious in every line. Those in love will be especially gratified. Layer cake denotes satisfaction in society or in business. If a young woman dreams of her wedding cake, it foretells bad luck. It is less fortunate to bake cakes in a dream than to eat them. Fluffy and rich icing on a cake predicts gay times. 941

CALENDAR. (See also Almanac.) To dream of marking off special dates on a calendar is a sign that you will have fewer things to worry about than formerly. 881

CALF. You may rest assured that your hopes will be realized if you dream of a calf receiving sustenance from its mother. To see a calf being butchered is an omen of disillusionment. For a man to dream of admiring the calf of a woman's leg is a sign that he will be hounded by his creditors. 540

CALICO. For a woman to dream of wearing a calico dress while at her housework is a sign of a delightful experience among men and women. If she wears calico at an evening party, she will receive a surprising message. 426

CALL. To dream of hearing your name called by a stranger you cannot see predicts that your financial affairs will be shaky and that you will be unable to meet your obligations promptly. If you hear the voice of a relative or friend, it augurs the sickness and possibly the death of one of them; in the latter case you may be importuned to act as guardian over a young person. For an engaged person to hear the voice of a fiance is a warning against negligence. Otherwise, the engagement is likely to be broken. Serious illness is predicted by hearing the voice of the dead. 726

CALLUS. To dream of having one or more calluses on your hands or feet predicts that you will shortly engage in a new and unusual kind of work. It will be interesting and remunerative. 615

CALM. One who dreams of a sudden calm in storms or periods of stress will have to take care of a noisy group of children. If you dream of calming an angry person, you will succeed in an important business deal. 411

CALOMEL. (See Laxative.) 642

CALUMNY. If in a dream you are the victim of calumny, your reputation will be attacked by evil-minded persons. If a woman has this dream, she should be careful to be guarded in all her acts. 634

CAMELS. To dream of camels portends that when you are beset with worries and irritations you will rise to the occasion and come through the ordeal with flying colors. You will inherit an important mining property if you dream of bringing a camel home. If you dream of seeing camels in a herd, you will be able to look forward to a bright future. 209

CAMEO. It is a sign or relief from storm and stress if you dream of seeing an old lady wearing a cameo ring or brooch. 184

CAMERA. If you dream of taking pictures with a camera, you are warned against gossiping tongues. If the pictures are still, you will be able to rise above scandal, but if they are in motion, it will be much more difficult. A dream of taking nude pictures, either still or in motion, portends disgrace. If you use a candid camera, you will be shunned by those who were formerly your friends. 049

CAMISOLE. (See also Slip.) A girl who dreams of wearing a soiled camisole will receive attention from a man of great learning. If the camisole is torn, she will be rebuked by an older person. 400

CAMP. An outdoor camp in a dream portends a change in your occupation, and that you will have a long trip to make. To come upon such a camp while in the woods is a prediction that one of your good friends will have to go away. A woman who dreams that she is camping will soon have to make up her mind which of two suitors she will marry. It is bad luck for a woman to dream that she is in a military camp. 630

CAMPAIGN. The dream of being concerned in a political campaign predicts family squabbles and added responsibilities. If you are engaged in a campaign to raise funds for a worthy cause, you will have a surprising letter from an old schoolmate. 948

CAMPFIRE. The cheerful blaze of a campfire is a forerunner of joy in married life. To dream of cooking over a campfire predicts great prosperity. Gay, though innocent times, are predicted by a dream of toasting marshmallows over a campfire. 934

CAMPHOR. If one dreams of smelling camphor, he or she will be annoyed by the attentions of one of the opposite sex. 654

CAMP STOOL. It is an augury of unexplainable conduct on the part of one of your friends if you dream of sitting on a camp stool inside a house or church. 194

CAMPUS. Walking across a college campus with one of the opposite sex predicts many petty disagreements after marriage. 640

CAN. To dream of opening a can of food is a sign that you will be shamed by someone of whom you are very fond. If you cut yourself on a can, you will lose money through a bad investment. 184

CANAL. A considerable loss of money is predicted by a dream of boating on a canal. To swim in a canal is an omen of disappointment in matters pertaining to love. To dream of seeing canal locks open and close is a sign of the unfaithfulness of a friend. 044

CANARY. If in a dream a canary bird shows signs of friendliness, you may be sure of good times ahead. If the bird is frightened, you will be beset by worries of various sorts. A dead canary is a prediction of illness. 774

CANCAN. This indelicate French dance performed by a woman in a dream is a forerunner of embarrassment in a public place. If a man dreams of being the dancer, he had better look well to his future conduct. 012

CANCER. Although it might seem to point otherwise, a dream of this disease portends an improvement in health. 146

CANDLE. To make candles in a dream promises hard work with little reward. To light them is a sign of improvement in your home affairs. To snuff them out portends unhappiness. 822

CANDLE-STICK. Candle-sticks in a dream predict joyous occasions if they are carried with lighted candles in them. To carry one in each hand portends a happy marriage in your family. If the candles are not lighted, there are troublous times ahead. Short, guttering candles are omens of new opportunities. 527

CANDOR. (See Honesty.) 153

CANDY. A woman who dreams of making candy will have many ardent suitors. If she dreams of eating it, she will have one suitor and an early marriage. If a man gives her a box of candy, she will receive many invitations to parties. For a man to dream of eating candy is a presage of worry. 152

CANE. To dream of seeing sugar cane growing is an augury of an increasing fortune. To see it cut predicts a lessening income. Affluence is predicted if you carry a cane in a dream. If you break the cane, your luck will come to an end. A white cane predicts disaster. 797

CANKER SORE. It is a sign of a major irritation ahead if you dream of having a canker sore in your mouth. 026

CANNED GOODS. You will not only have leisure time but the means to enjoy it if you dream of stocking your pantry with canned goods. To open canned goods predicts a series of enjoyable entertainments. 475

CANNERY. If the action of a dream occurs in a food cannery, the influence is a good one, no matter what the dream is about. 456

CANNIBAL. To be chased or captured by cannibals in a dream is a forerunner of dangerous events in your life. To see them cooking or eating human flesh predicts a dire happening close to home. 433

CANNON. The dream of a cannon being fired predicts an achievement of which you will be proud. If you dream of pointing and firing the cannon, you will be singled out for a high honor. If a young woman dreams of hearing cannon-fire, she will marry a soldier. 595

CANNON BALL. To see a cannon ball rolling downhill in a dream augurs an accident that you can avoid by paying more attention to those who are dependent on you. A pyramid of cannon balls in a public park is a sign of delightful experiences with persons of the opposite sex. 745

CANOE. Paddling upstream in a canoe or in rough waters is a sign of your being able to overcome serious difficulties. If you dream of being in a canoe on a calm lake or of going downstream with one of the opposite sex, you may look forward to many happy and carefree hours with your sweetheart. To dream of upsetting a canoe and being thrown into the water is a portent of quarrels with those you love best. 009

CANOPY. A canopy in a dream signifies protection, so that if you are under it, you may look forward to comfort and contentment. A young woman who dreams of leaving a church under a canopy stretched over the sidewalk will contract an early and favorable marriage. 677

CANTALOUPE. Illness of a minor nature is foretold by the dream of eating cantaloupe. To see these delicious melons ripening on the vine is a sign of prosperity. 691

CANTEEN. A narrow escape is predicted if you drink from a canteen in a dream. To find a canteen empty predicts failing crops. To lose a canteen means the loss of a friend. 114

CANVAS. If a woman dreams that she is wearing garments made of canvas, it is a sign that she will be loved for herself alone. To sleep under canvas predicts good health and a suitable income. To see the sun shining on the canvas sails of a ship is an augury of safe travel. 741

CANYON. To enter a wooden canyon on foot and follow a stream toward its course is, for single girls and youths, a presage of love and happy marriage. A trip through a canyon on horseback predicts a love life beset by many worries and misgivings. To be lost in a canyon indicates that you will hear bad news. 356

CAP. It is a good sign to dream of wearing a cap, whether you are a man or a woman. You will find that your worries will cease and that you will be fortunate in your investments. For a man who is wearing a cap to dream of meeting a lady friend and having to lift his hat, the omen is of minor difficulties that can easily be overcome. 711

CAPE. Worn in a dream by a person of either sex, a cape signifies that through the exercise of caution you will be able to avoid the consequences of your bad judgment. 996

CAPER SAUCE. You will meet new and interesting people if you dream of eating sauce flavored with pungent capers on roast lamb or other meats. 247

CAPITALIST. One who dreams of being a capitalist, with unlimited money to spend and invest, may look forward to easier circumstances but not to great affluence. 790

CAPITOL. It is a sign of unrest but minor achievement to dream of a capitol building with a dome. Better circumstances are predicted by a fire in a capitol, but is is also a warning against taking too great chances. 627

CAPON. To eat a capon predicts good health. To see it running in a barnyard is an omen of disappointment. To dress a capon indicates that one of your friends will be too curious about your comings and goings. 327

CAPSULE. Taking medicine in a capsule is a sign that your next business deal with one of the opposite sex will be successful. 069

CAPTAIN. To dream that you are a ship's captain or a captain in the army portends a rise in your fortunes. If someone gives you the courtesy title of Captain, you will have a period of depression. A woman who dreams that her lover is a captain must beware of being jealous of her friends. 130

CAPTIVE. A woman who dreams of being taken captive will be married before a twelve-month period has passed. If she dreams of taking a man captive, she will be disappointed in love. A man who dreams of capturing a woman and handling her roughly is warned against boasting. If he dreams of being captured by gangsters, he is likely to be double-crossed by business associates. 729

CAR. (See also Automobile.) Riding in a railroad car or electric car in a dream is a prediction of being able to make a decent living in spite of the obstacles you will meet. 709

CARAMEL. (See also Candy.) If in a dream a caramel gets stuck in your teeth and you are unable to open your mouth, the augury is of trouble with your relatives. If you offer a caramel to another person, you will regret some hasty act. A dream of exceptionally sticky caramels predicts a scandal. 184

CARAVAN. Travel in far lands with a loving mate is predicted by a dream of seeing a caravan winding its way across the desert. 554

CARAWAY SEED. To dream of being disgusted by the taste of caraway seeds is a sign that you will be received hospitably by those whom you have distrusted. If you dream of eating them with relish, you will receive honors from an unsuspected source. 170

CARBOLIC ACID. It is a distinct warning against a foolish display of pride if you dream of drinking this poison. To throw it in a person's face portends serious illness, but to have it thrown at you is a forerunner of happy days. 795

CARBON. If a young man dreams that his automobile engine is full of carbon, he is warned against associating with loose companions. To married people it portends family troubles. 791

CARBON MONOXIDE. Obviously this is a warning against letting an automobile engine run in an enclosed space. 402

CARBUNCLE. (See Boil.) 243

CARBURETOR. If a person dreams of a flooded carburetor in any kind of a gasoline engine, the portent is of accidents that may prove to be serious. 783

CARDIGAN. There will be explanations to make for your strange conduct in public places if you dream of wearing a cardigan. If it is old and worn, the consequences will not be unlucky. 613

CARDINAL. This dream is unlucky if you see the cardinal in his ecclesiastical robes. You will have to face a situation that may compel you to change your place of residence. 545

CARDS. (See also Playing Cards.) If you dream of writing greeting cards, you will buy new clothes for a gala occasion. If the dream is of looking at greeting cards, you will receive a small sum of money that you did not expect. To dream of working at a card index is a portent of suffering through the greediness of another. To buy buttons on a card is a sign that you will have to labor hard for a living. 693

CAREER. A woman who dreams of having a career will have many lovers but no husband. For a man to dream of making a success in a career is a sign that he will consummate an important business deal. 380

CARESS. The significance of a dream about caresses depends on whether they are given under appropriate circumstances. For a lover to caress his sweetheart augurs happiness in marriage. For a woman to caress her lover predicts early marriage and healthy children. It is a sign of unlucky investments if a married man dreams of caressing any woman other than his wife. 789

CARGO. To dream of loading cargo onto a ship foretells pleasant short trips and picnics. It is an augury of an accident to dream of throwing cargo overboard during a storm. 818

CARICATURE. If you dream of seeing a caricature of yourself, it predicts that you will be a target for abuse from others. A dream of drawing a caricature of someone you know is a warning not to speak ill of those whom you do not like. 167

CARILLON. (See also Chime.) Joy will be yours if you dream of hearing a carillon played from a church or other tower. Hearing it over the radio or on a phonograph record portends disappointment in love. You will inherit money if you dream of playing a carillon yourself. 669

CARNATION. You will rise to great heights in business if you dream of wearing a white carnation on your dress or in your buttonhole. A pink carnation augurs success in love affairs; a red one, an exciting adventure. To pluck carnations in a dream indicates trouble for those who drive automobiles. A dream of withered carnations foretells arguments with relatives. 295

CARNIVAL. Attending or participating in a carnival predicts that you will be invited to many parties; but if you wear a mask or appear in costume, be warned against drinking too much. 716

CAROL. Whoever dreams of hearing Christmas carols sung by fresh young voices will be happy during the forthcoming year. Singing carols yourself predicts success in love. 402

CAROUSAL. A dream of a carousal in which men and women are drinking, laughing and singing predicts that your actions are likely to be misunderstood by your associates. 170

CAROUSEL. (See Merry-go-Round.) 136

CARP. Try your utmost to avoid doing anything that may be criticized if you dream of catching, cooking or eating carp. 398

CARPENTER. One of the best auguries in all dreamland is that of being a carpenter. It predicts that you will be loved by your friends and respected by everyone. You will also have sufficient money to meet all your daily needs. 761

CARPET. To dream of walking on soft carpets denotes an easy and luxurious life in your own home. It is bad luck to dream of cleaning them with a carpet beater. 336

CARRIAGE. Drawn by a horse, a carriage in a dream predicts that you will have to answer embarrassing questions from one of your family. 104

CARRIER PIGEON. If you dream of catching one of these birds and finding a message on it, you are likely to receive astonishing news from an old and trusted friend. 037

CARROTS. A dream of raising carrots foretells a large income and good health. If a young woman dreams of eating them, she will marry early and have several healthy children. 314

CART. If you dream of riding in a cart, misfortune will follow and hard work will be necessary to care for your family. A cart foretells bad news from your relatives or friends. If you drive a cart you will be successful in your business and in your plans for the future. If lovers ride together they will be faithful to each other regardless of the interference of rivals. 975

CARTON. To dream of buying cigarettes or other packaged goods by the carton is a forerunner of prosperity. If you unload cartons of merchandise from a truck, you will be invited to a party at which you will meet influential people. If you receive a carton by mail and its contents are damaged, you will be disappointed in someone you considered your friend. 462

CARTOON. (See also Caricature, Comic Strip.) Cartoons that amuse you in a dream or that seem particularly appropriate augur success in business but bad luck in love. 563

CARTRIDGE. (See also Bullet.) To dream of slipping cartridges into a revolver or automatic pistol portends that you will be called upon to fill a much more important position than the one you now occupy. 048

CARVING. If you dream of carving a chicken, turkey, or any other kind of a fowl you will be unfortunate in your finances. Your ill-tempered friends will make trouble for you. If you carve meat, you will make unwise investments, but if you change your position, you will have greater success. 757

CASCADE. Water falling over rocks in a white cascade augurs a variety of experiences that will be not only interesting but profitable. If a woman dreams of a cascade, she will have difficulty in deciding which suitor to accept, but in the end she will make a wise decision. 657

CASEMENT. For a woman to dream of peering through a casement window is a portent of worry and possibility of disappointment. If she closes and locks the window, she will be lucky. 375

CASH. As might be expected, a dream of handling cash is an omen of prosperity. To dream of wrapping coins of any one denomination in paper indicates that you will be fortunate in business transactions. 801

CASHIER. If you dream of being a cashier, it is a sign that scheming people will lay claim to your property. If you owe money to a cashier, it denotes that some person of means will make things unpleasant for you. 514

CASH REGISTER. A dream of ringing up a sale and putting money in a cash register predicts an advancement in whatever work you are doing. 221

CASK. Rolling a cask aboard a ship is an omen of bad luck through association with loose-living companions. To dream of filling a cask with rum, fish or other foodstuffs predicts a period of plenty that will be followed by definitely hard times. 767

CASKET. Bad news and sadness may be expected by those who dream of a casket. If there is a body in it, the augury is of a public calamity. If the casket is empty, there will be a death among your circle of friends. 973

CASSEROLE. Food cooked and served in a casserole portends plenty of good times socially ahead. 249

CASSOCK. One will have every reason to expect a peaceful and quiet future if he or she dreams of seeing a priest or choir boy wearing a cassock. 071

CASTANETS. Physical disturbances are predicted by a dream of a Spanish dancer using castanets. The sound of these instruments in a dream foretells upset conditions also in family life. 729

CASTILE SOAP. It is an augury of an improvement in your general welfare if you dream of washing your body with castile soap. 506

CAST IRON. Dreaming of cast iron is a warning of accidents through bad judgment. To break anything made of cast iron predicts an occurrence that will cause you continuing trouble. 502

CASTLE. If you dream of living or visiting in a castle, you will be assured of having enough money to gratify your wishes. It predicts travel and meeting people from many different countries. If it is an ancient, moss-grown castle you must curb your romantic notions and exercise discretion in your love affairs. 410

CASTOR OIL. (See also Laxative.) If you dream of giving castor oil to another, the dream is a warning that you must not forsake the friend who is trying to help you. To dream of taking castor oil predicts that you must do a difficult and disagreeable task. 173

CAT. If you dream of seeing a cat asleep in a chair, either a rocker or a straight chair, you will be able to look forward to a gratifying love life. For a single woman it means marriage with a handsome and wealthy man, and for a married woman the adjustment of family difficulties. Usually a dream of a cat means bad luck unless you kill it or chase it away. If the cat should attack you, the dream signifies that you will have enemies who will besmirch your reputation for honesty. If you chase the cat away, you will have a stroke of fortune. If you hear the cat mewing or yowling, someone who dislikes you is talking slanderously and doing harm to your reputation. If a cat scratches you, an enemy will make an attempt to cheat you. For a young woman to dream that she is holding a cat or a kitten augurs committing an indiscretion that will mar her life. 677

CATACLYSM. (See Catastrophe.) 863

CATACOMBS. It is a sign of good health and fortune to dream of walking through a catacomb where skeletons are on view. 110

CATAFALQUE. The death of a person whom you greatly admire is predicted by a dream of seeing a catafalque. If there are many people to watch it, you will receive a legacy. 593

CATALOG. If you study a catalog in a dream, you are going to receive a letter that will contain good news. If you dream of ordering from a catalog you will receive money. 006

CATAMARAN. To dream of sailing in a catamaran denotes good luck in matters of business, unless you capsize, in which case you will have reverses. 532

CATARRH. This is a favorable dream for those who are in love. The more distressing the symptoms, the better is the augury. 522

CATASTROPHE. It is a sign of a radical change in your condition of life to dream that you are a witness to or a participant in a catastrophe. If you are not injured, or if you are able to help, the change will be for the better. Otherwise you are warned against taking chances. 290

CATCALL. To dream of being in an audience where there are catcalls for the performer is an augury of great embarrassment. If you dream of uttering catcalls at a public gathering, you will find yourself the object of shame. 138

CATECHISM. If you dream of the catechism it signifies that you will be offered a good paying job but that the conditions of the offer will cause you to think twice before accepting it. 058

CATERPILLAR. If you see a caterpillar, it foretells that deceitful people are about you and you must avoid false pretenses. Your business or love may be jeopardized. A caterpillar in your dream means you will be placed in a humiliating position and that there will be little respect or profit from it. 880

CATFISH. It is a portent of good luck to dream of catching or eating catfish. 329

CATGUT. This is a dream that predicts great annoyances. To dream of stringing an instrument with catgut foretells sleeplessness. 843

CATHEDRAL. A beautiful and inspiring cathedral seen in a dream is an omen that you will not be able to attain your desires but that you will be compensated for your struggle toward them. 365

CAT-O'-NINE-TAILS. It is a sign of sadness to come if you dream of seeing this instrument of punishment used in any way. If you are the one who uses it, you will have bad luck in your business for a long time and you will have family squabbles. 879

CATTLE. (See also Calf.) If you see fine-looking, well-fed cattle, contentedly chewing their cuds, your dream portends happiness and pleasant companions. If you see shaggy, underfed cattle, you will have to work hard all your life because of wasted time and inattention to details. Stampeding cattle foretell that you will attain wealth. A young woman who dreams of a herd of cattle will be happy in her love for her sweetheart. If you dream of milking cows that give their milk easily, you will make money; otherwise you will lose your sweetheart because of your coldness. 880

CAULIFLOWER. (See also Brussels Sprouts.) If you eat cauliflower, you are warned against taking your work too easily. To see cauliflowers growing means that your affairs will improve after a period of depression. 026

CAVALCADE. (See Parade.) 004

CAVALRY. A division of cavalry charging across a field predicts business promotion and personal honors. A party may be given in honor of your promotion. 739

CAVE. If you see the entrance to a deep cave in the moonlight, your business and health are in danger. If a woman dreams of going into a cave with a man, it foretells that she will fall in love with a gangster and lose many of her friends. 774

CAVE MAN. A woman who dreams of being captured and dragged away by a cave man may look forward to happiness in her married life. 716

CAYENNE PEPPER. There is travel to strange out-of-the-way places in store for a person who dreams of the burning taste of cayenne pepper. The hotter the sensation, the more interesting the places you will visit. 319

CAYUSE. (See Bronco.) 984

CEDAR. The smell of cedar is an augury of smooth sailing through life. If in a dream you smell it while sharpening a pencil, you will have success through something you write. This will not necessarily be literary work. It may be a letter or merely a signature to a document. If you dream of smelling a cigar box made of cedar, you will have many invitations to social events. 320

CELEBRATION. (See also Party.) A dream of celebrating an anniversary of any kind is a good portent for those who have been worried about the future. The larger the group present, the better is the augury. 264

CELEBRITY. If you dream of meeting a celebrity and he or she is stand-offish, you will suffer disillusionment of some kind. If the celebrity is gracious and agreeable, you have a pleasant surprise in store for you. This applies to such celebrities as movie actors and actresses, high government officials, novelists, painters and other artists; in fact, anyone who is in the public eye. 641

CELERY. To see white, crisp celery denotes wealth and prominence. To see the celery limp or spoiling is an augury of a dire happening in your family circle. To eat celery is an omen that you will be loved for your sterling qualities. For a single girl to dream of eating celery in the company of a young man is an omen of an inheritance. 908

CELIBACY. If you dream of living a life of celibacy, you will fail to accomplish something that is close to your heart. 138

CELL. Through something that you have failed to do you will lose a friend if you dream of being confined in a prison cell. 364

CELLAR. If you dream of a dank and musty cellar, you will become depressed with fear. You will not believe in your friends and will have evil presentiments from which it will be difficult to escape. If the cellar is dark and is stored with wines, liquors and canned goods, you are likely to get involved in a questionable deal. If a young woman has this dream, she will have an affair with a shady promoter. 327

CELLO. The heavy, satiny tones of a cello heard in a dream predict a strongly moving experience. If the cello is in tune, this will be something that will add depth and happiness to your life, but if it is played out of tune, there will be correspondingly discordant events. To see a beautiful woman playing a cello is a forerunner of a smooth and productive married life. A broken cello in a dream predicts severe illness. If you dream of putting new strings on a cello, you will receive good news either by mail, wire or radio. To break a string while playing the cello is an augury of a disturbing situation in a love affair. 449

CELLOPHANE. Good health is predicted if you dream of buying food, cigars, cigarettes, or other articles wrapped in cellophane. To wrap gifts in cellophane of any color is a sign that you will make new and interesting friends. 263

CEMENT. To use cement in fastening stones, bricks or porcelain together is a portent that you will keep your present position and advance to greater responsibilities and remuneration. To cement rubber or paper means that you will receive commendation for a noteworthy piece of work. 628

CEMETERY. To see an ill-kept and forsaken cemetery is a sign that you will outlive all your dear ones and will be left alone among strangers. A beautiful green burying ground is an augury of happiness. If young people dream of strolling through the quiet walks between graves, it denotes kind and loving friends but predicts that you will suffer many sorrows from which your friends cannot protect you. If a bride dreams of passing a cemetery on the way to her wedding, she will lose her husband while they are traveling. For a mother to put fresh flowers on a grave foretells good health and good fortune. For a young widow to dream of visiting a cemetery denotes that she will soon discard her widow's clothes for marriage clothes. If she is nervous and depressed, she will have other cares and rue the day she again became a bride. If you see small children gathering flowers and chasing butterflies in and out among the graves, it signifies a happy and healthy future. 286

CENSOR. If you dream of receiving a letter marked "Opened by Censor", you are likely to be criticized adversely by your associates. To dream of being a censor of books or public performances predicts that something you would prefer to have hidden will be revealed. 681

CENSURE. To dream of receiving censure by a lover is a forerunner of quarrels that will be serious unless you take it in your stride and admit that it was justified. If the censure is from a superior in business, it is a warning against taking things too easily, both inside and outside of business. 961

CENSUS. If a woman dreams that she is a census enumerator, she will be married to a hard-working and steady young man. To dream of answering census questions is a sign of moving to a new address. 915

CENT. A newly minted cent seen in a dream predicts that you will be deceived by someone in whom you put your trust. 313

CENTAUR. You will be shocked by news of one of your acquaintances if you dream of this creature that is half man and half horse. 304

CENTENARIAN. To dream of living to be one hundred years old and having your children and their progeny about you is an omen of happiness and the esteem of your friends. Two centenarians, man and wife, dancing with each other, predict a long life for you. 993

CENTERBOARD. It is a sign that you will escape the consequences of a foolish deed if you dream of letting down the centerboard of a sailboat. 394

CENTERPIECE. To spread a lace or embroidered centerpiece on a table predicts a slight increase in the amount of your income. 432

CENTIPEDE. This many-legged poisonous insect portends grief if you dream of seeing it. If it crawls upon you, the omen is sinister and warns against any kind of carelessness. 288

CENTURY PLANT. A dream of seeing one of these plants in bloom predicts that you will have a very unusual opportunity to make money. If it is not in bloom, the portent is of a slight accident. 741

CEREAL. Eating cold cereal for breakfast in a dream augurs success in a business deal, either through a rise in salary or by selling at a profit. Eating hot cereal is a sign of having to explain something you have failed to do. 239

CEREMONY. Religious, civil or fraternal ceremonies in a dream predict the sincerity of your friends. 317

CESSPOOL. Dreaming of a cesspool is a warning to avoid thoughts of evil and indiscriminate sex relationships. 391

CHAFF. To dream of seeing chaff predicts unsuccessful undertakings and that you will be the victim of ill health. For women to dream of piles of chaff warns against idle gossip and slander that will jeopardize their husbands' love. 052

CHAFING DISH. Good times are ahead for married persons who dream of cooking in a chafing dish. Those who are married are assured of one or more sturdy children. 076

CHAINS. If you dream of being bound by chains, heavy burdens will be put upon you, but if you can break the chains and set yourself at liberty, you will not be worried about your debts. 272

CHAIR. To dream of sitting in a comfortable chair is a good sign in connection with any dream in which chairs appear. If the chair causes you discomfort, the sign is not propitious. 953

CHAIRMAN. If you see the chairman of a civil organization, it signifies that a well-paid position will be offered you. If a chairman looks displeased, you will be dissatisfied with your job. If you dream that you are a chairman of a meeting or committee, it predicts that you will be well liked for your fairness. 608

CHAISE LOUNGE. A dream of reclining luxuriously on a chaise lounge is a fortunate dream for a woman in love, although she should give way slowly to her suitor's advances. 151

CHALET. One of these decorative Swiss houses lived in or seen in a dream predicts that you will be able to make someone happy and thereby gain happiness yourself. 012

CHALK. The use of chalk for marking or writing is an omen that you will not succeed in your next business project. If you write on a blackboard and the chalk squeaks, you are warned against vicious animals. 653

CHALICE. If you dream of a chalice or communion cup, it signifies that happiness will come to you through your manner of meeting your troubles. If you break a chalice, you will be unsuccessful in keeping your friends. 729

CHALLENGE. If someone challenges you to fight, either with fists or weapons, you will get into difficulties and have to apologize or be very unhappy. You will have a serious disagreement with someone of the opposite sex if you dream of challenging another. 567

CHAMBER. (See Bedchamber.) 086

CHAMBERMAID. For a man to dream of really falling in love with a chambermaid presages a rise in his fortunes, but if in his dream he trifles with her affections, he will suffer a serious illness. 723

CHAMELEON. This little animal that changes color according to the color it is on is a warning to beware of false friends and strangers. 948

CHAMOIS SKIN. Used for polishing furniture or automobiles, chamois skin is an augury of improved business conditions and an increased income. A soiled and wet, soggy chamois skin warns against having family arguments in public. 473

CHAMPAGNE. A dream of drinking champagne at a party at which both men and women are present and where hilarity prevails is a forerunner of going into debt. To toast a bride and groom with champagne is good luck, especially to those who are in love. 550

CHAMPION. To dream that you have become a champion in any sport is a sign that you will have a small business triumph. 943

CHANCEL. It augurs misfortune for a woman to dream that she enters the chancel of a church or chapel. A man who has the dream may look forward to promotion. 727

CHANDELIER. A dream of a brilliantly lighted chandelier is a forerunner of a rapid rise to business and social success. If a chandelier falls, it is a portent of a foolish act that you can avoid by using good judgment. To dream of anyone who hangs onto a chandelier either by the hands or feet is a portent of having a disquieting adventure outside of matrimony. 155

CHANT. To hear a choir chanting in a dream presages an achievement of which you may well be proud. 384

CHAPEL. You will repent of misdeeds if you dream of praying in a chapel. To dream of entering a chapel augurs peace of mind. 480

CHAPERON. A young woman who dreams of having an older one as a chaperon will find herself in a difficult situation. If a man dreams that the girl of his choice insists on a chaperon, he will be discomfited by someone he does not like. 711

CHARADES. It is a fortunate augury if you dream of playing charades, although it may not appear so for some time. Meanwhile you will enjoy simple pleasures. 202

CHARCOAL. A glowing fire of charcoal that is a feature of a dream exercises a beneficent influence, even if the rest of the dream points to misfortune. You will escape major difficulties. To dream of sketching with charcoal is an augury of easy living. 266

CHARIOT. Humorous developments in your love or family life are to be expected if you dream of driving a horse-drawn chariot such as the Romans used. A dream of a chariot race betokens an exciting episode in your social life, and is a warning against business upsets. 634

CHARITY. To give charity in a dream is a sign that if you refuse it to the needy, you will have bad luck for a year. If you dream of being the object of charity, your prospects are bound to improve. 493

CHARLOTTE RUSSE. It is exceedingly bad luck to dream of throwing one of these fluffy desserts at an enemy. You are likely to be very confused if you attempt even a good natured argument with your friends. To get cream on your face from eating one is a sign of being pressed by creditors. 041

CHARM. One may look for betterment in every way if one dreams of meeting and associating with charming people. To dream of wearing a watch charm is a sign of prosperity and good health. 371

CHARTREUSE. This agreeable cordial, if taken in a dream, portends a hearty greeting from old friends whom you will visit. 029

CHASE. If you dream of being a participant in a chase of any kind, it means that you will have to work hard for a living but that you will acquire enough money eventually to retire and live on the income. 886

CHASM. (See also Canyon.) If you dream that you are pursued and leap across a chasm, reaching the other side safely, you will be certain to solve any problems you may have that relate to finances. To fall into a chasm is a presage of woe. 614

CHASTISEMENT. A dream of being chastised is a forerunner of an upturn in your financial condition. If you dream of chastising another, you will suffer reverses. To chastise a child in a dream foretells illness. 512

CHEAT. Being called a cheat in a dream is a prediction of having a fortunate turn in your business affairs. If you call someone else a cheat, the augury is of being given a ticket by a traffic officer. 172

CHECK. It is good luck to dream of writing checks, and the larger the amount, the greater will be the fortune. You are likely both to inherit money and make large profits. 700

CHECKERS. Playing this ancient game in a dream augurs quiet pleasures and relaxation from worry. Win or lose, the augury is a good one unless you give way to an exhibition of temper, in which case the prediction is of harassing difficulties with your in-laws. If you dream of a sticky checker-board, you are likely to suffer from boils. 834

CHEESE. Eating cheese in a dream foretells that you will have a loving mate to help you weather the storms of life. As a rule, cheeses made of cows' milk are a better augury than those made of goats' milk. So-called "process" cheeses are omens of boredom, but any kind of strong-smelling cheese—such as

Roquefort, Limburger or Stilton—in a dream is a prediction of great embarrassment. To dream of making cheese augurs success in any job. Cheese that is dry and crumbly is a sign of finding money. 912

CHERRY TREE. Contrary to the moral of the George Washington story, it is very bad luck to dream of chopping down a cherry tree. You will lose money and reputation. To dream of picking ripe cherries from a tree is an augury of earning sufficiently for your immediate needs but not enough from which to build up a surplus. 796

CHERUB. You will have many pleasing and amusing experiences in the company of children if you dream of cherubs or baby angels. 109

CHESS. Unlucky is a dream game of chess if it is played by a man and a woman. To a man it portends that the woman he marries, or to whom he is married, will "wear the pants." To a woman the prediction is unfaithfulness on the part of her husband. If two men play chess, the augury is of a strenuous period in business. 684

CHEST. (See also Bosom.) If a woman dreams of seeing a man, with hair on his chest, she should regard it as a warning against unladylike behavior among the masculine sex. 974

CHESTNUT. Roasting chestnuts in a dream is an omen of good fortune to those who work with their hands. To eat raw chestnuts denotes alluring associations with persons of the opposite sex. If in a dream one is opening chestnut burrs, the augury is of a problem that you will solve with difficulty. 104

CHEWING GUM. This is a dream of lucky import when the chewing is done inside one's home. It predicts pleasant and wholesome social relationships among one's family and neighbors and a measure of content in one's sphere of life. If the flavor of the gum is apparent in the dream, it is an indication that an interesting and agreeable experience is in store for you. For a man or woman to dream of chewing gum in public—on the street, in a theater, church, railroad station, elevator, or elsewhere—is a forerunner of a humiliating experience. If in a dream, you step on a wad of gum that has been thrown away by a careless chewer, you should take warning against letting your judgment be warped by fits of temper. 270

CHIANTI. Serving chianti from the straw-covered bottle at a meal is a sign that you should be more reserved with people you do not know well. To spill chianti on a tablecloth is an omen of social misfortune. 582

CHICKEN. (See Hen.) 809

CHICKEN POX. Minor disappointments are indicated by a dream of having this disease. To dream that your child is ill with it is a sign that he or she will have a brilliant future. 191

CHILDBIRTH. (See also Labor.) For a man or woman to dream of being present at the birth of a child is a warning against putting things off that should be done immediately. Wills should be made, crops should be planted, bills paid, etc. It foretells ease of body and mind for a woman to dream of giving birth to a child, but a man who has this dream has a dark outlook in both business and social affairs. 567

CHILDREN. (See also Boy, Girl.) It is a fortunate augury to dream of having children. A single person may look forward to having a large and loving family. 719

CHILE CON CARNE. If this highly seasoned Mexican dish appears in a dream, it is a sign of upset love affairs. To eat it points toward trouble of one kind or another. 383

CHILL. You will have difficulty with your creditors if you dream of having a chill. 306

CHIME. (See also Carillon.) Chimes rung in tune are an augury of peace in the family circle and happy times for lovers. Out of tune, they predict the opposite. 480

CHIMNEY. If smoke is coming out of a factory or home chimney, the augury of your dream is of an increase in your earning capacity, but if sparks are rising, you will have family quarrels. A cold chimney predicts a change of occupation, perhaps for the better but not necessarily so. 743

CHIN. For a man to dream of kissing his sweetheart on the chin foretells that he will marry a nagging woman. To dream of striking a person on the chin is a portent of winning at cards; if you receive a blow on the chin, you will have surprising news. If you dream of being in a gymnasium and chinning yourself on a horizontal bar, it is a sign of being able to meet almost any situation with success. 769

CHINA. If you break china in a dream, it foretells good luck if you break it purposely, but bad luck if you break it by accident. 862

CHINESE. It is a fortunate augury if you dream of the Chinese people if they appear to be friendly. If they are hostile, you will have disquieting news from a source that will surprise you. 120

CHIROPODIST. The attentions of a chiropodist in a dream point to success in a new field of endeavor. Either you will get a better job at an increased salary or you will have an easier job in a different line at the same salary. If you dream that you are a chiropodist, you will receive news that will at the same time disgust and amuse you. 896

CHIVALRY. A dream in which a man shows evidence of chivalry to a woman—giving her his seat in a public conveyance, taking off his hat while talking with her, standing aside to allow her to precede him, assisting her to alight from a car—foretells success in the business world. 823

CHLOROFORM. Grief will come to those who dream of using chloroform to deaden pain. The dream also warns against association with people whom you distrust. 150

CHOCOLATE. To eat or drink chocolate in a dream is an augury of illness. Chocolate candies predict a large income, much of which will be spent on hospital bills. Chocolate ice-cream sodas foretell headaches, both physical and spiritual. 282

CHOIR. A dream of singing in a choir is a forerunner of being honored for some service to your community. If you dream of singing a solo part, you will be happy in your love life. To dream of listening to a boy choir means that you will have an opportunity to distinguish yourself in one of the artistic lines of endeavor. 380

CHOP. A thick juicy chop, broiled to perfection is a lucky augury for anyone in a dream, but if it is thin and either underdone or burned, the prediction is of illness or loss of money. 170

CHOPSTICKS. You are due to have a series of misunderstandings with people whom you like if you dream of trying to eat with chopsticks. To see Chinese people eating with them predicts a satisfactory unraveling of tangled affairs. 891

CHOP SUEY. You will solve a mystery if in a dream you eat chop suey in a Chinese restaurant. If you eat it at home, your chances for advancement are slight. 176

CHORUS. While it is a fortunate portent to dream of a chorus singing in tune, the augury is of death if you hear it singing off-key. A school or college chorus predicts that you will find something of value; a theatrical chorus, that you will lose it. 532

CHOW MEIN. (See also Chop Suey.) A dream of eating chow mein in a Chinese restaurant is a warning against a temptation by a glamorous person of the opposite sex. 116

CHRIST. Peace of mind through adjusting yourself to your condition in life and to the people with whom you have to live is predicted by a dream of our Lord. 951

CHRISTMAS. Most dreams of this holy season point toward advancement and prosperity. To dream of happiness among children at Christmas is a forerunner of satisfaction and repose. 323

CHRONOMETER. (See also Clock.) It is not a good augury to hold a person to strict time such as a chronometer tells. If you dream of this, you will be criticized by many people for your bigotry. To dream of consulting a chronometer on shipboard is to be warned that one of your friends or family is liable to be seduced. 709

CHRYSANTHEMUM. Dreaming of the scent of chrysanthemums is a forerunner of the fulfillment of a hope for the future. To pick these flowers in a garden or a greenhouse portends parties at which you will meet the right people. To give a bunch of them to a young lady foretells an understanding mate. 009

CHUCKLE. It is good luck to hear a chuckle in a dream if it is the result of pure amusement, but if it is cynical or gloating, it predicts a painful illness. 303

CHURCH. In general, a dream of going to church, of no matter what religion or denomination, augurs something better for you. If the dream is in the spirit of praise, the prediction is of improved circumstances surrounding love affairs. If it is merely fulfilling a duty, it predicts a humdrum existence with no change for the better. A dream of church social activities is a forerunner of depression in spirits. To see a church building in a dream foretells financial stability. If there is ivy growing on it, you may expect enduring love from your family. If you dream of seeing a church burning, you will lose a friend who has been tried and true. 961

CHURN. A woman who dreams of using a churn will shortly marry a man who is a good provider. If she upsets a churn, she will be disappointed in him. If the butter comes quickly, she will have many pleasant journeys. 440

CIDER. Drinking sweet cider in a dream predicts a slight illness; but if the cider is hard, the augury is of a boisterous party at the home of a friend. To dream of working in a cidermill is a sign that you will forget an important duty. To spill cider on your clothing predicts that you will win a prize in a lottery. Carbonated cider poured from a bottle into a champagne glass presages an invitation to a weekend party at which you will meet several worthwhile people. 584

CINDER. An old friend is in trouble of some sort if you dream of getting a cinder in your eye. To shovel or sprinkle cinders is a sign that you will receive an unexpected gift from an admirer. 158

CINNAMON. Used on food with which it is appropriate, cinnamon is a good augury, predicting enjoyable times. On such food as eggs, oysters or in soup it foretells heartaches. 813

CIPHER. A cipher may be a nought, o, or it may be a code. A dream in which the nought figures is a sign of failure to achieve something on which you have set your heart. If you dream of sending or receiving a message in cipher (code), the augury is of being deceived or double-crossed. 256

CIRCLE. To dream of drawing a perfect circle, either freehand or with the aid of a compass, is a prediction of the satisfactory working out of your plans and ambitions. 900

CIRCUMCISION. You will enjoy good health and success in business if you dream of being circumcised. If you dream of being present at the circumcision of an infant, it is a sign that you will make new friends who will help you toward advancement. 352

CIRCUS. If you dream of going to a circus, you are likely to receive good news from a person you see frequently. It is a warning against taking chances in automobiles if you dream of being a circus performer. If you dream of taking a child to a circus, you will be lucky with investments. 282

CISTERN. You will receive exciting news from someone you have not seen for years if you dream of getting water out of a cistern. If the cistern is empty, or foul, you will be likely to hear bad news. 321

CITY. A person who lives in the country and dreams of going to the city to live may look forward with certainty to many surprising adventures, especially with persons of the opposite sex. 954

CIVIL SERVICE. It is a sign that you will never be in want if you dream of getting a civil service job. To dream of working on a civil service job augurs good health and contentment. 061

CLAIRVOYANCE. You are likely to have a succession of difficulties in your love life if you dream of consulting a clairvoyant about your past or future. 957

CLAM. To open clams in a dream is an augury of a difficulty ahead that can be overcome by exercising great care and forethought. A dream of eating clams predicts relief from attacks by those who wish to do you harm. 579

CLAMBAKE. A dream of being present at a clambake predicts good times with your friends, but if you cannot eat a large quantity of food, you will be unhappy. 192

CLARET. Simple pleasures are foretold by a dream of drinking claret, but if you drink it from a bottle, you will be disappointed in love. 701

CLARINET. Those who dream of playing the clarinet have little more to look forward to than the applause they will receive for parlor tricks. It is an instrument that carries no particular rewards or penalties so far as dreams are concerned. 974

CLASSROOM. Women who dream of being in a classroom are likely to marry men whom they have known in childhood. A man who has this dream will meet and possibly marry an old school friend. 056

CLAY PIGEON. Shooting at clay pigeons augurs difficulties in your job. To fail to hit them is a sign that you will not succeed in your daily work. 170

CLEAVER. It is a fortunate sign if you dream of having some meat chopped with a cleaver at a butcher shop. If in a dream you attack someone with a cleaver, you will have bad luck in business for a long time. To dream of seeing a person's head cut off with a cleaver portends misfortune. 366

CLERGYMAN. A dream of a clergyman is a sign that you will need to explain your actions to a great many people. If you dream that you are a clergyman, the prognostication is one of family achievements. 348

CLIMBING. Anyone who dreams of climbing, either mountains or stairs, will have opportunities to better himself or herself financially. 569

CLINIC. You may look forward to excellent health if you dream of going to a clinic. 781

CLIPPER SHIP. If a young man dreams of being aboard a clipper ship, he will find that he is dissatisfied both with his job and his family. A woman who dreams of this vessel will have arguments with her sweetheart. For an elderly man it is an augury of comfort and many friends around him. 725

CLOCK. To hear the ticking of a clock in a dream denotes that you should not waste your time on unimportant matters. If you hear a clock strike, it is a sign that someone is waiting for you to make a decision. To wind a clock augurs happiness in love. 010

CLOISTER. To dream of walking through a cloister is a sign that you will have relief from your most pressing cares. A cloister in ruins augurs grief. 034

CLOTHES. A woman who dreams of buying new clothes will have a new admirer. If she dreams of putting on her clothes, she will be invited to many parties. If she dreams of taking off her clothes, she will have proposals that will offend her. If a man dreams of dressing or undressing, he should beware of those who seek to undermine his reputation for morality. 661

CLOUD. To dream of seeing a cloud obscure the sun is a sure sign that your fortunes will improve. If you dream of piloting an airplane through a bank of clouds, you will be likely to have interesting, although possibly innocent, experiences with the opposite sex. 134

CLOVE. A dream of eating cloves or using them as a spicy flavoring is a presage of relief from worry. To use oil of cloves for a toothache portends petty irritations. 912

CLOVER. A clover field in a dream is a fortunate augury, especially if the clover is in bloom. Bees in a clover field augur prosperity and contentment. 884

CLUB. For a married man to dream of going to a club for men only portends an argument with his wife. For women to dream of club activities is a forerunner of disquieting news. It is a sign of happy love affairs to dream of being hit by a club, but new responsibilities are augured by your hitting someone else with a club. 224

CLUTCH. A slipping or damaged clutch on an automobile portends that you will become estranged from an old friend. 822

COACH. To dream of riding in a coach drawn by two or more horses predicts the fulfillment of an ambition to be wealthy. If the dream is of driving the coach, the omen is of happiness in married life. If the coach overturns, you will make a change in your occupation and your place of residence. 119

COAL. To dream of buying coal means that your income will be doubled within the following few weeks. It is a sign of social advancement if you dream of delivering coal. Putting coal on a fire predicts business success. 467

COAL MINE. A dream of working in a coal mine is a forerunner of an increase in wages to those engaged in manual labor. 493

COAST GUARD. If you dream of seeing the coast guard in action, you will be likely to be involved in a dispute with your neighbors. A woman who dreams of a lover who is in the coast guard will receive news that will cause her grief. 696

COAT. If you dream of putting a coat on a hanger in a closet, you will receive the approval of someone whose opinion you value highly. To wear a ragged coat in a dream is a portent of riches and easy living. To help someone to put on a coat is a sign of lending money to a friend; but if another helps you to put on a coat, you will have to borrow. To lose a coat foretells that your feelings will be hurt by someone you admre. To throw away a coat is an omen of the loss of a friend; but to give one away predicts making new friends. 768

COAT OF ARMS. To dream of having a pretentious coat of arms framed on the wall, engraved on stationery, or embroidered on clothing predicts that you will incur jealousy through vanity. 434

COBBLESTONE. If you rumble in a horse-drawn cart or truck over a street paved with cobblestones, you will lose money through gambling. If you walk with difficulty over cobblestones, your dream portends that your work will bring you in contact with disagreeable people. To throw a cobblestone at someone or through a pane of glass means that you will suffer keen regret through forgetting to do something important. 207

COCA-COLA. Drinking Coca-Cola in a dream is a sign that you will succeed in the enterprise closest to your heart. 410

COBRA. Misfortune will follow a dream of this deadly snake, and unless you are constantly on guard, you will meet with accidents. To dream of a snake-charmer with a cobra denotes a painful illness. 258

COBWEB. (See also Spider.) It is bad luck to dream of seeing cobwebs on any article that should be kept bright with use, such as a Bible, toothbrush, etc. It is good luck to dream of cobwebs on bottles of wine. 075

COCAINE. Used in a dream as an antidote for pain, cocaine foretells an increase in income. If it is used because a habit has been formed, the augury is of depression and sorrow. 467

COCKADE. Wearing a cockade in a dream is a sign that you should be more self-assertive if you expect to succeed in business or social affairs. To tear a cockade off of another person's hat portends an encounter with someone who will be more than a match for you; it is a warning not to start anything you cannot finish. 340

COCK-CROW. The crow of a cock heard in a dream foretells that you will make a lucky discovery. It is a particularly fortunate dream for those concerned in mining enterprises. 406

COCKER SPANIEL. A dream of one of these gentle and lovable dogs foretells happiness with one's friends and an easy living. 204

COCKTAIL. The augury of drinking or mixing cocktails depends on the base with which they are made. If they are made of gin—martinis and the like— the portent is of unfortunate occurrences in your family. Made of whisky or rum, cocktails foretell pleasant diversions with your friends. 369

COCOA. To serve cocoa to friends in a dream is a sign that you will keep your friends through thick and thin. 788

COCONUT. Eating coconut in a dream foretells that when adversity comes to you, you will meet it with great fortitude. If you dream of opening a coconut, you will find a small sum of money. 421

CODE. To receive a message written in code betokens a long period of puzzlement over the behavior of a near friend. To send a message in code is a warning against trying to deceive people. 811

COD-LIVER OIL. It is a good augury to dream of taking cod-liver oil. It foretells an increased income, and to those who are in love, peace and fulfillment. 529

COFFEE. If you dream of drinking a good cup of coffee, you will receive encouraging news from a surprising source. If the coffee is weak or bitter, you will be disappointed by one of your friends. To dream of grinding coffee beans is a sign of happiness for those who are in love. To dream of spilling coffee means minor disappointments. 680

COFFEE-MILL. To dream of grinding coffee beans in a coffee-mill is an omen of success in any kind of mechanical work you may be doing. 221

COFFIN. It is good luck to dream of a coffin. If you see yourself in it, you may look forward to great peace and happiness. 120

COGNAC. This kind of brandy augurs success in social life that will lead to profitable business opportunities. To burn brandy on a plum pudding predicts a harmonious family life. 784

COGWHEEL. Those who are in love are likely to have slight disagreements if they dream of cogwheels in smooth motion. If a tooth on one of the wheels is broken it predicts disaster to a love affair. 270

COIN. To give one or more coins in payment for an article or service is a forerunner of a delightful experience with one of the opposite sex. To receive coins is a sign that your reputation is in jeopardy. To have a coin returned to you with the statement that it is a counterfeit is an augury of ill health. 287

COKE. A dream of shoveling coke presages that you will meet with great difficulties in your daily work, but these will not be insurmountable. 274

COLD. You are warned against having arguments with relatives if you dream of having a cold. If you dream of suffering with the cold or low temperatures, you may be certain of a change for the better in the position you occupy. 495

COLIC. It is a sign that you will shortly receive a legacy from someone for whom you have done a favor if you dream of having colic or cramps. 686

COLLAR. Having difficulty in putting on a collar is a dream that portends difficulties with your landlord. 599

COLLECTING. A dream of collecting stamps, bird's eggs, old furniture, etc. foretells meeting celebrities of the screen, stage and television. 993

COLLEGE. Lovers' quarrels are predicted by a dream of going to college. If you dream that you are a college professor, you will meet new friends who will contribute to your advancement. 534

COLLISION. (See Crash.) 805

COLOGNE. A married man who dreams of using cologne will have a serious falling out with his wife. Single women, wives or widows will meet interesting men, with whom they will have to exercise great discretion. 883

COLONEL. A woman who dreams of meeting a colonel socially will be much sought after by men. If a man dreams that he is a colonel, he will be successful in business. 128

COMB. Problems that have bothered you will be solved to your satisfaction if you dream of running a comb through your hair. For men to dream of combing a woman's hair is a warning against flirtations. 806

COMEDY. Dreams in which there is humor or fun are lucky, and so if you dream of seeing a comedy in a theater or movie house, you will be gratified by happenings that will eventually contribute to your advancement. 483

COMET. To see one of these tailed stars streak across the night sky is an augury of sudden and unexpected good fortune. To lovers it predicts early marriage and a congenial home life. 607

COMIC STRIP. Looking at a comic strip in a dream foretells more leisure and more money. 004

COMMAND. Giving commands in a dream portends a promotion if the commands are obeyed, but if no attention is paid to them, you will lose money. 444

COMMANDMENT. To dream of Moses holding the tablet of stone on which are the ten commandments is a warning to mend your ways. 558

COMMENCEMENT. The successful conclusion of a piece of work on which you are engaged is predicted by a dream of being present at a school or college commencement. 242

COMMITTEE. Being appointed to a committee in a dream is a presage of having to make a contribution to a public cause. If you are made the chairman, there will be an upheaval in your business affairs. 514

COMMUNION. It is a fortunate augury to dream of attending communion in any church, for it points toward a long period of peace and quietude. 431

COMMUNIST. You will be misunderstood and shunned by your friends if you dream of being a member of the Communist Party, or of attending their meetings. 672

COMPACT. If a girl dreams of using make-up from a compact in a public place, she will be disappointed in her lover. If a man should dream of carrying a compact, he will be shamed by his fellows. 269

COMPANION. The enjoyment of one or more pleasant companions of either sex in a dream predicts triumph over one's enemies. 183

COMPASS. Upset conditions, both in the home and in business, will follow a dream of using a compass whose needle will not point to the north. 539

COMPLAINT. To dream that you make a complaint against conditions that do not please you is a sign that you will make new and influential friends. If a complaint is lodged against you, the augury is of a quarrel with in-laws. 377

COMPLETION. It is a sign of easier living conditions to dream that you have completed a job on which you have been working. 226

COMPLEXION. A woman who dreams that she has a perfect complexion is likely to be courted by two men at the same time. If her complexion seems to be blemished, she will be in danger of malicious slander. 189

COMPLIMENT. To receive a compliment in a dream means that you will make a success of the work you are now doing. To give a compliment presages that you will be chosen to fill a position of trust. 250

COMPOSITION. Writing a composition in a dream as you did when you were a child at school foretells meeting an old friend whom you have not seen for years. 608

COMPRESSED AIR. The sound of escaping compressed air is a dream augury that you will be censured for something that was not your fault. It is a lucky sign if you dream of compressing air with a pump as, for instance, inflating an automobile tire. 233

COMRADE. (See Companion.) 100

CONCEPTION. For an unmarried woman to dream of having conceived a child foretells that she will have a proposal of marriage from a much older man. A married woman who has this dream will make new friends with whom she will be congenial. 315

CONCERT. If a young woman dreams of going to a concert with a man, she will be able to embrace an opportunity to go on the stage or into the movies. A dream of a tiresome concert, or one in which the music is off-key, predicts family quarrels. 295

CONCH SHELL. Strange but gratifying news from a far distant place is predicted by a dream of listening to the "roar of the sea" in a conch shell. 721

CONDEMNATION. If you dream of being a judge who is condemning a murderer to death, you will be slow to attain the goal that you have set for yourself. To dream of being condemned is an assurance that your friends will remain loyal to you. 778

CONDOLENCE. To offer condolences to a bereaved person foretells the unraveling of tangled threads. To dream of receiving them is a sign of happier days to come. 271

CONDUCTOR. Having an argument with the conductor of a train is a dream that portends an adventure in a foreign land. To dream that you are the conductor of a public carrier augurs a new responsibility. If you dream that you are the conductor of an orchestra, you will find a sum of money. 460

CONE. (See also Ice Cream.) A dream of anything shaped like a cone foretells pleasant experiences with a person of the opposite sex. 363

CONFECTIONERY. (See Candy.) 097

CONFERENCE. Sitting in a conference with a group of business or professional persons is an augury of news that you will be able to turn to advantage. A religious conference betokens social advancement. A political conference portends hard and unremunerative work. 761

CONFESSION. If in a dream you make full confession of one or more misdeeds, you are likely to buy a new and more comfortable home within a year. If you dream of hearing a confession, you are warned against gossiping. 580

CONFETTI. Throwing confetti at a carnival or other party is a dream that foretells a fantastic adventure with an actor or actress. 093

CONFIDENCE. If you dream of someone's showing confidence in you, you will be fortunate in your business relations, but in love you will be less lucky. To show confidence in another, especially a person who has not warranted your confidence, predicts the making of new and valued friends. 195

CONFINEMENT. It is good luck for a single woman to dream of her approaching confinement, but if such a dream follows an indiscretion, it foretells loss of reputation. For a married woman or a widow to have this dream foretells happiness. 069

CONFIRMATION. To attend a confirmation in a church is a dream that foretells understanding on the part of your friends. To be confirmed predicts calm days to come. To dream of confirming an order predicts business success. 115

CONFLAGRATION. (See Fire.) 240

CONFUSION. It is a sign that you will have a well-ordered life if you dream of being annoyed by confusion either at home or in public. 262

CONGESTION. (See also Constipation, Crowd.) Dreaming of a congested condition in any part of the body is a warning to take no chances with your health. 482

CONGRATULATIONS. To receive congratulations in a dream for any piece of work well done foretells a rise in the value of any property you may hold. If you give your congratulations to another, it is a sign that you will succeed handsomely. 772

CONGRESS. The temporary loss of an article that you value highly is predicted by a dream of being elected to congress. To sit in congress as a spectator foretells serenity in your life. 628

CONJURER. (See Magician.) 823

CONSCIENCE. If in a dream you feel that your conscience prevents you from doing an evil deed, or impels you to make restitution, you will retain the love of your friends and the respect of the community in which you live. 969

CONSERVATORY. Young women in love are assured of an early and desirable marriage if they dream of sitting amid plants and flowers in a conservatory. To dream of studying at a conservatory of music augurs success in any professional career. 907

CONSERVE. (See Jam, Jelly.) 516

CONSPIRACY. You will be successful in club work, church affairs and neighborhood activities if you dream that you are the victim of a conspiracy. If you dream of conspiring against anyone else, be warned against accidents. 529

CONSTIPATION. (See also Castor Oil, Colic, Congestion, Laxative.) If you dream of being a sufferer from constipation, you are warned against overindulgence in food and drink, especially beverages with an alcoholic content. It also predicts that you will regret your own selfishness. 993

CONSUL. Through no fault of your own you will get into trouble with the authorities if you dream of going to a consular office in country other than your own. To dream of being a consul in a foreign city is an augury of success in business undertakings. 637

CONSUMPTION. (See Tuberculosis.) 553

CONTAGIOUS DISEASE. It is a hopeful sign to dream of having a contagious disease, because it foretells that you will be able to distinguish between true friends and false. 815

CONTEMPT. If a person shows contempt for you or your judgment in a dream, you will make a success of your job. If you show contempt for another, you will fail. 449

CONTENTMENT. While it does not foretell unhappiness, a dream of contentment is a warning against smugness and a lack of interest in the trials of others. 468

CONTEST. (See Struggle.)812

CONTORTIONIST. Embarrassment in both social and business life is predicted by a dream of seeing a contortionist perform. It is bad luck for lovers. 064

CONTRACT. You are likely to get a good civil service position if you dream of signing a contract. If your dream is of tearing up a contract, you will be advanced at the expense of someone else. 048

CONTRADICTION. It is a sign of bad luck in any enterprise connected with the sale of goods to dream of contradicting a person. If someone contradicts you, the portent is of forgetting an important engagement. 661

CONTRIBUTION. If you dream of soliciting funds and someone makes a contribution, you are due to become a participant in a romantic episode. If you make a contribution to a worthy cause, you will be able to command the respect of others. 795

CONTROVERSY. (See Argument, Dispute.) 354

CONVALESCENCE. To dream of getting well after an illness is a sign that you will travel to countries that have a warm climate. 809

CONVENT. Dreaming of studying in a convent is a fortunate augury for women, for it portends freedom from worry and insures the friendship of many desirable people. 031

CONVENTION. There is a vigorous struggle in store for you if you dream of attending a convention. At the time it will seem vitally important for you to subdue your adversary, but even if you lose, you will eventually be reconciled to the outcome. 145

CONVERSATION. General conversation heard in a dream has no particular significance, but if it is conducted in loud, highpitched tones, it augurs aggravated discontent. A conversation in a language you cannot understand predicts that you will be snubbed by your relatives. 208

CONVERT. If you dream that you made a convert to your religion or politics, you will be worried for a long time about your own future. To dream of being converted augurs not only peace of mind but interesting business connections. 165

CONVICT. You will make a success as a musician or a singer, perhaps in opera, if you dream of being a convict. If you wear stripes, you are likely to become a composer of songs. 297

CONVULSION. Dire happenings may be expected if you dream of seeing anyone, baby or grown person, having a convulsion. It is a warning not to enter into any business or social agreements for at least a month. If you dream of having a convulsion yourself, you should check with your lawyer to see that your personal and business affairs are in order. 016

COOK. A dream of being a cook, either male or female, is one of the luckiest anyone can have. It foretells that you will soon be waited on by willing servants and loved by an adoring mate. 866

COPPER. (See also Cent.) One who dreams of mining copper will have a substantial income through his or her own efforts. To dream of receiving a large number of copper pennies in change is a sign of petty annoyances. To see bright copper dishes on serving tables or hung on a kitchen wall foretells a comfortable home life. To a woman it predicts marriage. 321

COPPERSMITH. A dream of seeing a coppersmith at work predicts that you will be invited to join a high-class social organization in your vicinity. 611

COPYING. It is good luck for a young man or woman to dream of making a typewritten copy of anything, but if the copy is made in handwriting, the augury is of censure from an older person. 617

COQUETTE. (See also Flirt.) A woman who dreams of coquetting with men will be invited out by a man she does not like. A man who dreams of a coquette who is unattractive will be offered a money-making proposition. 870

CORAL. Wearing red coral ornaments in a dream foretells happy days in the company of delightful people of the opposite sex. White coral is a prediction that you will have to take greater pains with the work you are doing. 029

CORD. (See also Rope, String.) Tying a package with a cord foretells accomplishment. Untying a knot in a cord predicts trouble through an incident with one of the opposite sex. To break a cord implies a serious accident. 876

CORDIAL. It is a happy augury, foretelling pleasant social relations, to dream of drinking a cordial, but if you spill it you will get into a jam with your associates. 806

CORDIALITY. A dream of being met cordially by a famous person is an omen of release from worry or pain. If you show cordiality to others in a dream, you will receive a message from a wealthy acquaintance that will give you much pleasure. 252

CORK. To pull a cork from a bottle of wine or other liquid signifies that a puzzling mystery will be solved. If there is a pop when the cork is removed, the solution of the mystery will be accompanied by sorrow. It is a prediction of a light amour to dream of inserting a cork into a bottle. 805

CORKSCREW. A warning not to trifle with another's affections is contained in a dream of using a corkscrew. If the dream is of hurting yourself with a corkscrew, you will have to defend your honor. 819

CORN. (See also Chiropodist.) Happiness in married life is foretold by a dream of a field of green corn. If there are many ears on the stalks, you will have attractive children. To eat corn from the cob is a forerunner of profitable business. If you pop corn in a dream, it presages good times if the kernels burst into fluffy white, but if they burn, look out for trouble. To dream of having corns on your feet is a sign that scandal-mongers are seeking to ruin your reputation. 754

CORNCOB. A pile of corncobs seen in a dream portends divorce in your close circle of acquaintances. To smoke a corncob pipe denotes that by meeting adversity with a stout heart you will accomplish your ambitions. 284

CORNED BEEF. Eaten with cabbage in a dream, corned beef is an augury of meeting new and pleasant people who will have interests similar to your own. In a sandwich it is an omen of discontent. 803

CORNER. To dream of waiting for someone on a corner means that you will make a date with a red-headed girl or man. 859

CORNET. To dream of playing the cornet in a band is a sign of having a proposition made to you that you should consider carefully. It is a sign of grief to dream of listening to someone practicing on a cornet. 431

CORNMEAL. Cooking or eating cornmeal in a dream is a sign that your health will improve and that you will have a corresponding increase in earning power. 954

CORONATION. Seen in a dream, the pomp and circumstance of a coronation are omens of a long pleasure trip in foreign lands. If you dream that you are being crowned, you are likely to make a great deal of money that will bring you added responsibilities and worry. A dream of a coronation scene in a play portends a succession of small successes. 822

CORPORAL. If a young woman dreams of going out with a corporal, she will be criticized for her boldness. A man who dreams of being a corporal is warned against being extravagant and wasteful. 215

CORPSE. (See also Dead Person.) A full life is predicted by a dream of seeing a corpse you cannot identify, for death precedes life as surely as life precedes death. Such a dream is nothing to alarm anyone. Frequently it is an augury of success and happiness. 508

CORPULENCE. A dream of many corpulent people, all of whom are fat to the point of grossness, means that you are in danger through intemperate habits. 266

CORRAL. A dream of horses or other animals in a corral portends exciting adventures in and out of doors, probably in mountainous regions. 408

CORRESPONDENCE. (See Letters.) 244

CORRESPONDENT. For a woman to dream of being named a correspondent in a divorce suit is a warning against even the appearance of being indiscreet with men. 328

CORSET. If a man dreams of seeing a woman with nothing on but a corset, he is likely to receive a letter containing shocking news. If he dreams of helping a woman to lace or otherwise adjust a corset, he will be able to solve his financial problems. 817

COSMETICS. It is a thoroughly good augury for a woman to dream of using cosmetics—rouge, lipstick, eyeshadow, etc.—if she does not dream of using them in public places. Otherwise it augurs discontent and an end to any love affairs. A man who dreams of the use of make-up is in danger of losing his reputation and his business. 870

COSSACK. To dream of a cavalry charge by a Cossack regiment forecasts danger from an unknown source and is a warning to be continually on your guard. 506

COSTUME. Wearing a fancy costume in a dream portends a happening that no one would have suspected. Whether it is fortuitous or not depends on the spirit of the occasion for which you wear the costume. 944

COT. It is a forerunner of good luck to dream of sleeping on a cot, unless the cot breaks down, in which case you are slated for trouble. 309

COTTAGE. For young people to dream of marrying and living in a cottage augurs a happy mating and a congenial wedded life. If there is a vine on the cottage, there will be healthy children to bless the union. 210

COTTON. It is a sign that you will never go hungry if you dream of picking cotton. To walk through a field of ripe cotton foretells ease unless you are accompanied by an undesirable companion, in which case the portent is of worry. To put medicated cotton in an aching tooth means that you will have a visitor. To see a cotton-gin at work is a sign that you will suffer a disability. 258

COTTON-GIN. If you dream of this machine separating seeds from cotton fiber, you are likely to be appointed to a position of trust and honor at a very satisfactory salary. 652

COTTONTAIL. To see a cottontail rabbit out of doors portends a vacation in pleasant surroundings, but to shoot one is an augury of disappointment. 014

COUCH. You will be unable to achieve success in a pet project if you dream of hiding under a couch. To dream of sleeping on a couch is a sign that you will be sucessful in buying and selling operations. If you dream of sleeping on a couch with a person of the opposite sex, you will be criticized by an employer for inattention to your work. 544

COUGH. It is a portent of impending disaster, such as flood, fire or physical disability, if you dream of having a cough. 872

COUNCIL. To sit in a council and discuss weighty matters is a dream that foretells a misunderstanding with one of your best friends. 404

COUNSEL. (See Lawyer.) 429

COUNTENANCE. (See Face.) 800

COUNTER. Working behind a counter in a dream foretells comfort in your old age and a family that will be a credit to you. 587

COUNTERFEIT. Deceit from a person whom you have trusted is predicted by a dream of trying to pass a counterfeit. It is good luck to dream that you destroy a counterfeit that you have received. If you dream of making or helping to make counterfeit money, you are in danger from an unknown enemy. 570

COUNTERPANE. A fresh, clean counterpane on a bed is an omen of harmonious life in the home. A soiled counterpane is an augury of discontent. 409

COUNTESS. If the countess you meet in a dream is young and beautiful, you will find it necessary to make excuses for something you have done. If she is elderly, you will receive an invitation that will help you in your social life. 610

COUNTING. Counting money in a dream predicts that you will have a larger income than formerly. Counting sheep portends family squabbles. Counting people is a good sign for those in show business. 306

COUNTRY. It is a pleasant omen to dream of being in the country in sunny weather. In the rain, or when the landscape is covered with snow, the forecast is of arguments with retail merchants. 675

COUPON. To dream of clipping coupons or of saving coupons given away with merchandise is a sign that you will be under close scrutiny and possible criticism from your superiors. 188

COURT. If you dream of being a defendant in a court of law, you are likely to be called upon to explain a statement or an act. If you are a plaintiff you will find yourself in an embarrassing position. 418

COURTESY. If in a dream someone is courteous to you in a manner that is unexpected, you will find an article that you had believed was lost. To dream of extending a courtesy to another is a sign that you will meet a new and charming person of the opposite sex. 668

COURTSHIP. It is a sign that you will have new and agreeable experiences if you dream of courtship. 704

COUSIN. A full life, a happy life and contentment are predicted by a dream of being in love with a cousin. To dream of being friends with cousins is an omen of freedom from worry. 386

COW. (See also Calf.) Chewing her cud, a cow is a portent of physical well-being. An ugly cow predicts dissension within the family circle. 952

COWARD. To dream of being a coward predicts that you will not be wanting when there is an occasion to prove your worth. 906

COWSLIP. To dream of picking a cowslip is a warning against association with people of doubtful reputation. You should watch your step. 241

COYOTE. The howls of this prairie wolf heard in a dream are an omen of criticism from your family. To dream of killing a coyote is a sign that you will achieve something very worthwhile. 360

CRAB. Be on the lookout for designing persons of the opposite sex after a dream of fishing for crabs or crawfish. To catch a crab and then lose it foretells that you will be criticized for failing in your duty to a friend. To cook crabs predicts a slight accident; to eat them, good luck at gambling. 179

CRABAPPLE. Eating crabapples off the tree signifies a disagreeable experience with a post-office employee. A dream of making or eating crabapple jelly is a forerunner of happiness in love and family life. 081

CRACKER. To dream of stepping on a cracker predicts a very annoying situation in connection with a fraternal organization. If the dream is of eating crackers in bed, the augury is of marital squabbles. To see a baker making crackers signifies good fortune and happy days. 746

CRADLE. Rocking a cradle in which there is a baby foretells a successful marriage and profitable business. If there are twins in the cradle, the augury is of a change of scene. An empty cradle presages illness. 226

CRAMP. (See Colic.) 894

CRANBERRY. Eaten raw, cranberries portend an encounter with a police officer. Sauce or jelly, they are a presage of your being involved in political disturbances. 020

CRANE. A lifting crane seen being used in a dream signifies that you will be relieved of worries and burdens. To see a broken crane augurs hazardous undertakings. To operate a crane means that you will be asked to fill an important job. The bird known as the crane is a good portent if in the dream you see it flying; if it is standing still, you are likely to have upsets in business or in love. 853

CRAPE. Hanging on a door to denote a death in the house, crape in a dream is a portent of a series of accidents. 456

CRASH. From whatever cause, a crash in a dream portends an achievement of some kind. If you are driving a car that crashes, the portent is not a happy one, but it does not necessarily point to tragedy. 604

CRAVING. A dream of an intense longing or craving for either pleasures or material things foretells that you will be offered a splendid position. 962

CRAWFISH. (See Crab.) 323

CRAYON. To dream of drawing with crayon is a sign that you will have to make excuses for overlooking something that was expected of you. 953

CREAM. A woman who dreams of skimming cream from the top of a pan of milk will have many admirers and one good husband. If anyone spills cream, the portent is not favorable to new enterprises. 298

CREDIT. If you dream of buying luxuries on credit, there will be dire happenings in your family circle. To dream of making a bank deposit to your own credit signifies increased earnings and added respect from your friends. To give a person credit for some worthy deed is to look forward to a season of prosperity. 139

CREEK. A dream of swimming in a creek is an augury of excellent luck in business and love. 521

CREMATION. Witnessing the cremation of a dead body in a dream portends a long journey with an interesting companion. 253

CREST. (See Coat of Arms.) 047

CREVASSE. You are warned against ill-advised behavior if you dream of falling into a crevasse in a glacier. To cross safely over a crevasse is a sign that you will overcome obstacles. 378

CRIB. (See also Cradle.) It is a pleasant augury of success in married life to dream of putting a sleepy child in a crib. 358

CRIBBAGE. Playing cribbage in a dream predicts many good friends throughout your life and an interesting job, although not very much money. 968

CRICKET. Indoors, a cricket seen in a dream is an omen of many family blessings. To hear crickets sing predicts long life. A game of cricket is an omen of health. But if you dream of simply watching it and not playing, it augurs boredom in social affairs. 498

CRIME. If you dream of committing any serious crime, you are warned to guard your actions and hold your temper in check. 281

CROCHETING. A woman who dreams of crocheting will have many admirers. To drop a stitch and have to undo one or more rows predicts an altercation with relatives. 298

CROCKERY. (See also Dish.) To dream of hearing the rattle of crockery in a kitchen is a forerunner of nervous exhaustion. The crash of breaking crockery predicts an international calamity with connections in the Orient. 794

CROCODILE. Good luck will follow a dream of being chased by a crocodile, but if he catches you, the augury is a very painful accident. If you kill him, you will be successful beyond your expectations. 909

CROCODILE BIRD. (See Birds.) 868

CROCUS. In a dream, a crocus is a harbinger of pleasant days to come, as it is a forerunner of springtime in reality. 739

CROIX DE GUERRE. To dream of seeing a soldier wearing this high military decoration foretells an encounter, either physical or otherwise, with someone whom you dislike. If you dream of wearing the croix de guerre, you will be lucky in your investments. 042

CROP. A small and disappointing crop in a dream augurs a setback in your business affairs, but a bumper crop is a sign that you will increase your holdings and build a competence. 619

CROQUET. Playing croquet is a dream that precedes wholesome and enjoyable pleasures among one's own circle of acquaintances. If it is played on a green lawn, the augury is better than if played on a dirt ground. 200

CROSS. (See also Crucifixion.) Any dream of a cross, of whatever description, portends a successful struggle, but one that will be accompanied by grief. 635

CROSS-EXAMINATION. If you dream of being cross-examined by a lawyer during a trial in court, you will be called upon to testify to the character of someone about whom you know damning things. 931

CROSSROADS. To dream of standing at the crossroads is a portent of a great change in your life that may bring you either happiness or sorrow. 706

CROUP. To see a baby with the croup in a dream is a sign that you will have to raise some money speedily. 048

CROW. The sight or sound of this black bird in a dream augurs a disappointment in love, but if you shoot it, the outcome will be satisfactory. 800

CROWD. (See also Mob.) It is a portent of profitable new associations to dream of being in an orderly or good-natured crowd. To be in a crowd that is reading bulletins of war outside a newspaper office predicts a business victory that will be unexpected. 509

CROWN. It is distinctly bad luck to dream of wearing a crown if you are in a palace, but if it is a paper crown in a masquerade or play, it simply means that you will be tempted. Be on your guard against yielding. 060

CRUCIFIX. You will have peace and comfort in your daily life, to say nothing of many true friends, if you dream of having a crucifix or of kneeling before one. 874

CRUCIFIXION. Hope for the future is promised by a dream of the crucifixion of Jesus Christ. 638

CRUELTY. (See also Brutality.) Either mental or physical cruelty in a dream is not propitious, whether you or another is the sufferer. 981

CRUISER. To dream of sailing in a cruiser for pleasure is an omen of having success in an important business deal. If the cruiser is a naval boat, you will be likely to have an enjoyable trip to a foreign land. 196

CRUST. If you dream of eating a crust with relish, you will have a pleasant vacation before long. 206

CRUTCH. It is an augury of ease and companionship among your circle of acquaintances if you dream of walking on crutches. If you dream of seeing a cripple hit a person with his crutch, you will have a prosperous month. 609

CRYING. To dream of crying betokens a heartache over someone else's misfortune. If you dream of hearing a baby crying, you will be surprised at news you receive through the mail. 667

CRYSTAL. A crystal with the sun shining through it and casting prismatic colors is, when seen in a dream, an augury of pleasing adventures in a brilliant and clever social group. 363

CUCKOO. The song of a cuckoo heard in a dream predicts meeting a genius who will be amusing but irritating. The sound of a cuckoo clock augurs contentment in home life. 293

CUCUMBER. Eating cucumbers in a dream is a sign of death in a family with which you are well acquainted. To dream of cooking cucumbers means that you are in great danger of making a serious business mistake. 344

CUDDLING. With a person of the opposite sex, cuddling is a dream that carries a warning against promiscuous relationships, but if it is between mother and child, it is an augury of contentment in the home. 075

CUFF. To write a memorandum on your cuff is a dream that should make you careful to avoid arguments with people who are in authority. To roll up the cuffs so that they will not become soiled predicts that your investments will require careful watching. 601

CULTIVATOR. Using a cultivator in a dream portends an improvement in your personal affairs. For a farmer it predicts good returns from his crops and livestock. 365

CULTURE. A dream of mingling with cultured people signifies that you will become esteemed for your bright conversation and your good manners. 011

CULVERT. If you dream of hiding from an enemy in a culvert, you will have trouble with your landlord and other creditors. 611

CUP. To drink out of a cup in a dream foretells pleasurable experiences with professional men and women. It also predicts success in the arts, such as painting, writing, and music. 536

CUPBOARD. A bare cupboard in a dream predicts a lean period in business, but if it is well stocked with food, you will have much success with your enterprise. 761

CURBSTONE. It is an augury of a hazardous occupation to come if you dream of sitting on a curbstone. 603

CURL. For a woman to admire her own curls in a dream means that she will be disappointed in her lover. For a man to dream of having his curls admired foretells disaster in his reputation. To dream of cutting off curls is a sign of better times. 907

CURRANT. Ripe, red currants are an augury of a splendid new opportunity, but if they are dry and dark, there will be a long period of unrest. 143

CURRY-COMB. Using a curry-comb on a horse in a dream is a sign of satisfaction because of a successful business deal. 026

CURSE. To utter a curse on anybody or anything in a dream is a prediction of destruction to your fondest hopes. To use curses indiscriminately foretells the loss of a friend's respect. 217

CURTAIN. Lowering a curtain means that you will not succeed in the enterprise that interests you most. Raising a curtain is an indication of the reverse. If a curtain snaps suddenly up to the top of a window, you will have a surprising message. 710

CUSHION. It is a sign of affluence to come if you dream of sitting or lying on a cushion. To throw cushions about is a portent of having to apologize for something. To tear a cushion indicates that you will be criticized for a misdeed. 405

CUSPIDOR. Spitting into a cuspidor in a dream is an augury of new friends if you do not miss the mark; otherwise it indicates the loss of friends. 351

CUSTARD. Eating custard in a dream is an omen of having to be in the company of uninteresting people whom you must not offend. To spill custard on your clothes is a sign of distress. 727

CUSTOM HOUSE. To dream of transacting business in a custom house presages good fortune in your dealings with high officials. 940

CUT. To dream of cutting yourself with a knife, razor, or other sharp edge is a sign of the loss of money or friends. 447

CUTAWAY COAT. It is a prediction of good fortune through close attention to business if you dream of wearing a cutaway coat at a social function. 863

CUTWORM. (See Borer.) 101

CYCLONE. A major catastrophe is predicted by a dream of being in a cyclone. You are warned to be careful at all times of your behavior, and to avoid taking any unnecessary risks to your person. 349

CYMBAL. An amusing experience is in store for you if you dream of playing cymbals in a band or orchestra. It is likely to be with someone of the opposite sex. 320

CYNIC. You will lose some money if you dream of hearing a cynic talk. If he is cynical about women, you will find it difficult to meet a note. 408

D

DACHSHUND If you dream of one of these quaint, lovable dogs, you will be successful in business, love and family life. 881

DADDY LONGLEGS. An amusing experience is predicted by a dream of anyone being frightened by one of these ungainly but harmless insects, but if you dream of trying to frighten a person by putting one on him or her, you will be unfortunate. 871

DAFFODIL. At any time of year, but especially in springtime, a dream of daffodils is an augury of hope, no matter what problems are besetting you. To dream of a field of daffodils in bloom is an especially good omen for those who are in love. 186

DAGGER. To dream of seeing a dagger is a warning to beware of your enemies. You will be embroiled in some heated argument and be mixed up in an unpleasant affair. To see a person stabbed with a dagger signifies a conquest over your enemies, but it warns you to watch your behavior carefully and keep it above reproach. 315

DAGUERREOTYPE. To see your own likeness in a daguerreotype is a prognostication that you are slipping into lazy habits that will mean your downfall if you persist in them. To look at daguerreotypes of your ancestors is a sign that you will make progress in the work you are doing. 503

DAHLIAS. To dream of seeing colorful dahlias in a vase foretells success in money matters, especially if they are in an old-fashioned farmhouse. 089

DAIRY. Peace and contentment in your home and with your friends are foretold if you dream of seeing a dairy. To see pats of golden butter and small cheeses in a dairy means that you will have fine, healthy children and a comfortable home. 114

DAIS. (See also Platform.) To dream of a dais denotes a secret ambition to go on the stage or into the movies. A successful screen career is predicted. 730

DAISY. The dream of walking through a field of daisies foretells a gift—something you have always wanted and never expected to have. A white daisy in a dream means that your love is true to you. If you dream of a yellow daisy (black-eyed Susan), beware of a rival. To pick apart a daisy in a dream, saying "He loves me, he loves me not," is a fortunate augury for young women in love no matter how it comes out. A parallel dream is lucky for young men. 697

DAM. To dream of seeing turbulent waters rushing over a dam is a bad omen. You will encounter losses suffered through lack of serious consideration before committing yourself to action. To see a dam across a calm water course foretells success if the sun is shining upon it; otherwise, failure. 707

DAMASK. Spotless white damask table coverings are a dream portent of a dignified, successful and worthy life. If the damask is soiled or spotted, or shows signs of having been used for a long time, it indicates that you will be severely criticized by your in-laws. 537

DAMNATION. (See Condemnation.) 465

DAMPNESS. A dream of dampness is either a lucky or an unfortunate dream according to circumstances. If it follows extreme thirst or drought, it is lucky, but if it is a mildewy, continuing dampness, it predicts disintegration. 767

DANCERS. To dream of seeing beautiful ballet dancers in a gorgeous setting foretells that you will make new friends and that you will enjoy many social activites. 567

DANCING. If young people dream of dancing with partners of the opposite sex, it denotes a happy conclusion to their love affairs. If married people dream of dancing, it signifies marital happiness and bright, healthy children. Ballroom dancing signifies the announcement of an engagement. 569

DANCING SCHOOL. To dream of going to dancing school portends several love affairs and an entanglement that you will later on regret. 207

DANCING TEACHER. If a girl dreams that her fiance is a dancing instructor, she may well suspect a rival for his affections. If a man dreams of a woman dancing teacher, he will find it hard to choose between two loves. 209

DANDELION. To dream of yellow dandelions dotting the lawn in the springtime is a good sign for those in love. If the blossoms have gone to seed and the fluff blows in the wind, beware of trouble in store for you. If you wear a dandelion in your buttonhole, you will be laughed eat and humiliated. 637

DANDRUFF. If you dream of seeing dandruff on someone's coat collar or on a dress, it augurs misunderstandings and a warning to walk the straight and narrow path. 513

DANGER. For one in love to dream of being in danger presages heartaches and jealousy, for it implies a broken engagement. If you dream of physical danger to yourself, the prediction is of the necessity to *go slow*, be moderate in everything, watch your accounts, your investments, your business and your heart interest. 149

DANGLING. If you dream of dangling from a high precipice or from a dangerous elevation, the dream foretells uncertainty in your business dealings. Be cautious, and look before you leap. 773

DAREDEVIL. To see someone taking undue chances with his life or happiness is a sign of hazardous undertakings. 229

DARKNESS. If in a dream the day grows suddenly dark or if there is an eclipse of the sun or the moon, it foretells what may appear to be supernatural happenings and telepathic messages. It may be the news of the passing of an old friend just as you are discussing him or her with another. 012

DARKROOM. Dreaming of working at photography in a darkroom predicts the unraveling of a mystery that has long given you trouble. 813

DARNING. If you dream of darning socks or a tear in a garment, it signifies new and pleasant companions. A woman who has this dream will marry shortly. 116

DARNING NEEDLE. A dream of seeing the beautiful insect known as a darning needle is an augury of travel to far-off lands. 527

DART. If you dream of taking part in an archery meet, or placing your darts in your bow, the dream foretells great ambitions happily realized. If you dream of the darts reaching their mark, you will know undreamed-of success. If the dart is broken or falls very short of the bull's-eye, failure is predicted. 322

DATE. To eat dates in your dream foretells a marriage among your friends. You may be the fortunate one. To make a date is a bad omen; your sweetheart will forsake you for another. If you see dates growing on a palm tree, you will become prosperous. 748

DAUGHTER. To dream of your daughter or daughter-in-law is a sign that some dependent will lean heavily upon your resources and may take advantage of you if you are not careful. 890

DAVENPORT. To dream of a new handsomely upholstered davenport foretells improvement in your business and social standing. If the davenport is shabby and old, disappointment and loneliness will be your lot. 496

DAVID. If you dream of David, the Biblical character, fighting with the giant Goliath, you will prevail over those who seek to do you harm. 487

DAVIT. (See Lifeboat.) 059

DAWN. To dream of the sun rising and the dawn of another day denotes the offering of a splendid opportunity to better your prospects. If it dawns gray and rain threatens, you will lose a large contract for which you have been working a long time. 956

DAYBREAK. A dream of seeing it grow light at the end of night is an augury of hope for those who are distressed. 453

DAZE. If you dream of walking about in a daze, you are warned against false rumors that people are saying things about you of a scurrilous nature. 900

DEACON. A dream of seeing a church deacon cutting capers is an indication that you will be severely criticized for your actions. If the deacon is walking toward the church and seems intent upon his thoughts, the dream augurs belated blessings. 115

DEAD FOLK. (See also Corpse.) If you dream of being dead, it signifies a release from your troubles and recovery from illness. To dream of conversing with dead people is a propitious omen, signifying strength, courage, and a clear conscience. 571

DEAD LETTER. It is a warning against carelessness to dream of receiving a letter from the Dead Letter Office. 393

DEAFNESS. To dream of being afflicted with deafness is to expect a happy solution of your troubles. To try to talk with a deaf mute is to experience disillusionment. 495

DEBATE. (See also Argument.) If a man dreams of engaging in a debate with a woman, the augury is of failure to achieve his purposes. If his opponent in the debate is a man, he will win promotion through close attention to the problems of his business. A woman who dreams of debating will find that she must exert herself more in order to keep her friends. 898

DEBAUCHERY. Any form of debauchery indulged in in a dream is an augury of family and social derangements. Such a dream is a warning against association with loose companions. 268

DEBTS. If you dream of paying your debts, it is a good omen. If you are in debt and dream of not being able to meet your obligations, business worries are bound to come. 732

DEBUTANTE. A charming and winsome debutante seen in a dream denotes the beginning of a new project, either business or social, that will reflect credit on you. For a woman to dream that she is a debutante predicts pleasant love affairs. 774

DECADENCE. It is a sign that you will have difficulty in explaining some of your actions if you dream of decadent art, poetry or music. 021

DECAY. No good may be expected from a dream of decay, whether it is of animal or vegetable matter. If one dreams of eating decayed food, the augury is of trouble that will be hard to bear. 615

DECEASE. (See Corpse, Dead Folk.) 720

DECEIT. It is fortunate to recognize deceit in a dream, for it predicts that you will be able to make a large sum of money through buying and selling. If you are caught in a deceitful action or statement, things will go hard with you. 700

DECENCY. Evidences of decency on the part of persons from whom you would not normally expect it presage a reconciliation with someone from whom you have been estranged. 337

DECIMALS. To dream of mathematical calculations in which you use decimals points toward the receipt of a message for which you had hoped but which you had not expected to receive. 087

DECK. For lovers to dream of being together on the deck of a large ocean liner is good luck. To stand, sit or walk on the deck of a ship, either under sail or power, is a good omen if the sea is calm. The prediction is that you will contribute some invaluable discovery to mankind. To dream of a deck of cards foretells deceit and loss of valuable property. 431

DECOMPOSITION. (See Decay.) 454

DECORATING. If you dream of decorating a house, room or clothing for some gala occasion, it foretells gay and festive times. 460

DECORATION. A dream of decorations that please you, whether they are inside a house, outside a building or elsewhere is a portent of success in artistic lines of all descriptions. 314

DECOY. Any kind of decoy seen in a dream, whether it is intended for animals or for people, denotes the deceit of someone for whom you have had affection. 808

DEDICATION. To be present in a dream at the dedication of a church, public institution, or other building or enterprise is a sign that you will rise to an influential position among your contemporaries. 336

DEDUCTION. It is a pleasant augury to dream of making a successful deduction in the manner of a detective. You will have increased confidence in yourself and will be able to make a satisfactory business deal. 121

DEED. To sign a deed in your dream presages legal action that will probably be unfavorable to you. To see someone perform a good deed, in the manner of a Boy Scout, for instance, or to give assistance to an elderly, infirm person, denotes that many unexpected personal kindnesses will be done for you. 574

DEER. For married people to dream of a deer foretells going to war or being called into court, or disagreeing with a best friend over a slight matter. For lovers to dream of deer or fawns denotes deep affection for one another and an early marriage. For a young man or woman to dream of killing deer indicates a broken engagement. 049

DELAY. Women who dream of anything or anybody who is delayed are not likely to enjoy peace of mind for some time. To dream of a train or bus that is delayed is an omen of trouble in connection with money. A delayed check portends family arguments. 060

DELIGHT. If you dream of the delight occasioned by the attentions of your sweetheart, it denotes unexpected pleasures. 091

DEMAND. (See also Command.) To dream of someone demanding that you do or give something is a sign that you will be in a position to refuse to comply with a demand from a person who believes that he or she is your superior. 959

DENTIST. To dream of having a dentist work on your teeth is a portent of receiving a letter that will give you much concern. If you have a tooth pulled, it means a loss of money. 498

DEPOT. To dream of seeing a depot means a change of residence or that you will live in some foreign country. A depot signifies change. 734

DERBY. If you dream of the Kentucky Derby and your horse wins, it foretells your ability to carry out successfully your business or social affairs. If your horse loses or there is an accident on the turf, it predicts failure in every direction. To wear a derby hat foretells advancement. 428

DERELICT. To see a derelict boat or person denotes discouragement in your business, but by using good judgment and common sense you will profit. 706

DERRICK. To dream of a derrick signifies hope and the achievement of your wishes. A derrick is an omen of optimism, realized ambitions and thanksgiving. 955.

DESERT. If you see the sands of the desert, bleak and baked by a burning sun, your dream denotes meditation and long hours spent alone with your books or your work. You will be very content if you have a resourceful nature. If there is a caravan on the desert, with camels and Arabs, the dream signifies long journeys by yourself into foreign lands. 547

DESERTER. For a man to dream of being a deserter from the army or navy is bad luck. He is likely to be severely criticized for some mistake he made a long time ago. If he dreams of standing before a firing squad, he is warned to be exceedingly careful of his conduct. 642

DESIGN. A dream of seeing designs, whether in color or black and white, and either simple or intricate, is a sign that one will be likely to have new responsibilities saddled on him or her. 021

DESIRE. (See Craving.) 906

DESK. To dream of working at a desk predicts irksome family affairs. To dream of cleaning out an old desk is a portent of new and interesting friends. 301

DESOLATION. To dream of being in a desolate house or neighborhood means that you will collect a group of articles that will increase in value as the years go by. 042

DESPAIR. If you dream of being in desperate circumstances either through danger or lack of money, it is a sign that your fortunes will improve before long. 189

DESPERADO. Meeting with a desperado in a dream portends that you will be dunned by your creditors. If you are able to capture or othewise humiliate the man, you will collect money that is due you. 214

DESPERATION. (See Despair.) 293

DESPOTISM. To dream of living in a country whose ruler is a despot, or of working for a despotic and tyrannical boss, is an augury that you will be able to solve your most pressing problems. 425

DESSERT. If you eat a rich dessert in a dream, you will be able to indulge in some luxury that you have not had for a long time. Simple desserts augur quiet contentment. 170

DESTITUTION. (See Poverty.) 399

DESTRUCTION. Dreaming of the destruction of a building or a country by natural causes, war or other vandalism warns you against being too quick to take offense. 189

DETAIL. A dream in which the small details stand out is a forerunner of many perplexities. These details may be those of a person's face, manners or clothing; or the intricate parts of a mechanism; or of any other variety. 964

DETECTIVE. (See also G-Man.) You may expect very irritating troubles if you dream of being a detective, but if you are successful at the job, you will be able to overcome your difficulties. 046

DETOUR. It is a sign of a new job in the offing, with new responsibilities and problems, if you dream of having to make a detour from the main road you are driving over. 542

DEUCE. (See Playing Cards.) 632

DEVIL. To dream of seeing a devil tormented and tortured signifies that the dreamer is in immediate danger of being punished by the law. If you dream of striking the devil and overpowering him, it is a sign that you will overcome your enemies to your satisfaction. To meet the devil on friendly terms augurs death, melancholia, anger, disagreements, or sudden illness. To dream that the devil speaks to you signifies that you will have a great temptation. 208

DEVILMENT. Innocent devilment indulged in, in a dream, augurs pleasant diversions in the company of well-bred people. 675

DEVOTION. To dream of devotional services or devotion in other ways foretells a faithful and loving mate. 706

DEW. To dream of seeing dew sparkling on the grass denotes marriage to a person of means. For a single woman or bachelor to walk barefooted in the dew presages a happy marriage in the near future. 475

DEXTERITY. (See Skill.) 352

DIAGRAM. (See also Map.) Drawing a diagram in a dream is a fortunate augury if the drawing is made with a pencil, but if pen and ink are used, it predicts complications in affairs of the heart. 746

DIAL. To break the dial of a watch or a clock indicates the necessity of inquiring into the stability of the bank where you keep your money. If you dream of calling a telephone number by using the dial, you will inherit a small sum of money from an old friend. 682

DIAMONDS. For a girl to dream of diamonds is a good omen; it indicates marriage to a man of distinction and great wealth. If a young man dreams of giving diamonds to his love, he must exercise great care in the choice of a wife. He must look for a girl who is a good home-maker rather than a social butterfly. To one who dreams of wearing diamonds there is an unpleasant experience in store with one whom they believed to be a friend. 492

DIAPER. If a man dreams of changing a baby's diapers, he will have a long and happy married life, but for him to refuse to do so predicts that he will have to spend many hours of overtime at his job. If a woman dreams of diapers it is an augury of marriage to a traveling salesman who will be away from home for long stretches. 048

DICE. If a woman dreams of her fiance throwing dice, it is a sign that he will be guilty of dishonorable actions. Anyone who dreams of throwing a lucky combination will have a fleeting financial success, but there will be unhappiness for someone in the family circle. 630

DICTAPHONE. To dream of using a dictaphone foretells wealth and an executive's position of trust and honor. To dream of seeing one in an office means that you may hope for a rise in salary or a betterment of your position. 064

DICTATION. To dream of giving dictation to a stenographer is a sign of complicated affairs in one's social life. If one dreams of taking dictation, the portent is of advancement in business. 259

DICTATOR. (See Despotism.) 063

DICTIONARY. To dream of seeing a dictionary denotes a wordy argument with an opinionated person. To dream of looking up a word in a dictionary means that you have a thirst for knowledge and that you may impress your superiors. 653

DICTOGRAPH. To dream of a dictograph denotes whisperings and gossip about you by your associates. 227

DIFFICULTY. If you dream of having difficulty with a simple task, you are likely to quarrel with a friend of long standing. 126

DIGESTION. If you dream that your stomach is upset and that your digestion is poor, the warning is to keep away from temptation or you will get into trouble. Don't turn the night into day. 827

DIGGING. To dream of digging signifies that hard work is in store for you, but it will bring its reward if you dig with a shovel. Digging signifies an inquiring mind, and if you follow the dream by applying yourself diligently to the study of your problem, you will succeed. 327

DIKE. To dream of a dike denotes repression. You fear that some catastrophe will befall you, and you might fight against it with all your might or it will ruin you. To dream of seeing the dikes and windmills of Holland is a good omen . You will know contentment and in a small way live in financial security. 232

DIME. To dream of seeing a shiny new dime means that you will be criticized for being mercenary. If you pick up a dime and give it away, you will receive an unexpected gift by air mail. 473

DIMPLES. To dream of seeing a pretty girl with dimples or a man with a dimple in his chin foretells summer flirtations and several affairs of the heart that will be soon forgotten. 077

DINNER. If you dream of eating your dinner in a hotel or cafe with friends, a quarrel is predicted. If you dine alone with your sweetheart, it foretells an early marriage. 338

DIPLOMA. To dream of students being given diplomas at graduation exercises is a good omen. You will become an honored person of wealth and distinction.

For a girl to dream of a diploma predicts that her pride will have a downfall. 607

DIPLOMAT. To dream of seeing a diplomat or someone in the diplomatic service foretells a delicate situation that will arise and will require in handling all the tact and skill of which you are capable. To say and do exactly what is expedient in the given circumstances is the warning of the dream. 691

DIPPER. There will be a family wrangle in which you will come off second best if you dream of drinking from a dipper. It is a warning to hold your tongue even when you have provocation otherwise. 961

DIRECTORY. To dream of seeing a telephone or business directory foretells paticipation in a game of chance, such as dice, numbers, and either horse or dog races. For a young woman to dream of looking in a directory also signifies an invitation to dinner with an admirer. 122

DIRGE. To hear a funeral dirge is, contrary to what one would expect, not always an unfavorable prediction. It foretells sympathetic understanding and helpful suggestions from a good friend. It may forewarn of a slight illness. 283

DIRIGIBLE BALLOON. (See also Airplane.) The significance of a dirigible in a dream is of achievements that will be accompanied by great hazards. 260

DIRT. (See also Earth.) The usual forms of dirt, such as dust and other accumulations of trash have an unfortunate augury if they are the results of carelessness or ill-breeding. They foretell disease and sorrow. 285

DISAPPEARANCE. To dream of seing someone walk off in the distance and disappear from sight foretells money losses and disaster. To see an object magically disappear means that although you will be bewildered by your problems, you must face them. 298

DISAPPOINTMENT. The contrary may be expected, as to dream of disappointment presages the fulfillment of your hopes. 681

DISARMAMENT. To dream that all nations are disarming is a prediction that you will be successful in love and in other high achievements. To dream that one nation alone is disarming is a forerunner of disaster and shame. 732

DISASTER. If you dream of being in a disaster, it foretells the loss of your sweetheart either by accident or through some lover's quarrel. 454

DISCHARGE. It is a favorable omen if you dream of being discharged from your position, but at the same time it is a warning against inattention to your work. To dream of discharging an employee is a sign that you will quarrel with a person whose friendship you need more than you think at the time. 922

DISCIPLINE. To dream of being disciplined by a superior for a misdeed or an infraction of rules is a portent of a fortunate business deal. If you dream of disciplining another, the prediction is of the loss of money through unwise investments. 297

DISCOLORATION. One may look for a setback in his or her relations with social groups after a dream of seeing an eye or other part of the body that is discolored. Any color off what may be normally expected is to be regarded as a discoloration. 705

DISCORD. If you dream of discord, either in music or in daily happenings, it denotes a heated dispute between you and your fellow employees. If a young woman dreams of discord, her engagement will be broken or her marriage postponed. 232

DISCOVERY. If you discover something unexpectedly, you will inherit some property. If someone discovers you, it indicates new friends and new places. 814

DISDAIN. (See also Contempt.) Something funny is likely to occur if you dream of being treated with disdain. This dream is also a warning not to take offense at fancied slights. 758

DISEASE. Dreaming of disease in most forms is not a pleasant augury, but if the dream is regarded as a warning, it may turn out to have a fortunate aspect. 284

DISGRACE. You will encounter some difficult situations with your circle of acquaintances if you dream of being in disgrace. They will have to do with someone of the opposite sex. 455

DISGUISE. If you dream of someone disguised, it denotes treachery and underhanded dealings by your enemies. It is a warning to be perfectly open and above-board in your affairs. 330

DISGUST. If in a dream your disgust for a foul odor, an ungentlemanly act, or cruelty of any sort, you will be likely to be brought into contact with successful people who will help you on toward your goal. If, however, your disgust is shown for someone who is doing his best, you will lose a good and influential friend. 538

DISH. A young woman will be lucky in love if she dreams of bright, new dishes. If the dishes are soiled and broken, she will be disappointed in love. 907

DISHONESTY. If you dream of someone being dishonest, it foretells a change in your plans. You will do something you thought unwise but which will prove to be of great benefit to you and your family. If you are dishonest, the dream predicts sudden disaster and serious illness. 609

DISINFECTANT. To sprinkle disinfectant in a dream is a sign that you will be exposed to a contagious disease but that you will escape infection through exercising great care. 389

DISINHERITANCE. If a young man dreams of being disinherited, it is a sign that his parents will in good time approve of his choice of a wife. If a young woman has this dream, it signifies a happy marriage after a long engagement. To dream of disinheritance means a righting of wrongs in general. 117

DISLOCATION. If anyone has a dream of dislocating an arm, leg, or other member, he or she should go slowly in making any new business arrangements involving a change of employer. 265

DISOBEDIENCE. To dream of being disobedient to an elder foretells unrest and a change of occupation. To dream of seeing a child disobey his parents denotes a long sea voyage to another country. 447

DISORDER. A woman who dreams that she meets a man when her hair or her dress is in disorder is warned against someone who is likely to try to take advantage of her innocence. For a housewife to dream that her house is in disorder is a sign that she will receive a letter from a former suitor. 056

DISPLEASURE. To dream of expressing displeasure to a young child is a portent of excitement over a small matter. 506

DISPUTES. To dream of having a dispute with your employer signifies a business depression and disastrous investments. If a woman gets into a dispute with a neighbor or friend she will be socially snubbed by a woman of prominence. 518

DISRESPECT. It is a fortunate augury if you dream of showing disrespect to those in authority, but if someone else shows disrespect to you, it portends a season of petty annoyances. 924

DISSIPATION. (See Debauchery.) 856

DISTAFF. If you dream of seeing a woman drawing flax from a distaff, it foretells a year of plenty and happy home surroundings. To dream of handling a distaff means that you will have to work hard for what you get, but that you will take pleasure in doing your work. 093

DISTANCE. A dream in which everything seems to be happening at a distance means that the portent will not materialize for a long time. 020

DISTILLERY. To dream of being in a distillery foretells a change in your business that will be more profitable than the one you now have. If a young woman has this dream, she will marry a man of means who is fond of the cultural things in life. 808

DISTORTION. If you dream of someone making a grimace or distorting any other part of his body, it foretells a rival, either in business or love. 723

DISTRESS. To dream of being in distress or of seeing others in distress denotes that you will have success when you feared failure. Distress is also a dream that forewarns of a slight illness. 382

DITCH. To dream of a ditch is a good sign, for it foretells that you will hurdle your obstacles with ease and will make your pastime into a business that will bring you surprising returns in a short time. A ditch signifies difficulties overcome and ultimate prosperity.116

DIVAN. If you dream of lying on a divan it denotes loss of personal property, perhaps the robbery or theft of your pocketbook. 233

DIVE. To dream of a dive frequented by dissolute persons augurs criticism of the company you keep and that you will suffer the loss of your good name unless you reform. For a woman to dream of being in a dive predicts illicit love affairs. 106

DIVIDEND. If you dream of receiving dividends on stock, you must beware of false friends. Do not confide in anyone except those who have proved their friendship. 405

DIVING-BELL. If you dream of seeing a diving-bell, it foretells a sharp loss in the stock market followed by small gains. Being in a diving-bell denotes unrequited love. 650

DIVORCE. To dream of divorce means that one should take warning. If you are married, it means that you must make every effort to establish better understanding with your mate and that you must look into your own misdeeds. If unmarried, the dream signifies an unhappy love affair. 511

DIZZINESS. You are likely to take a transcontinental trip by plane if you dream of being dizzy. 920

DOCK. A dream of being on a dock where they are loading ships foretells good health, wealth and great happiness. To see the dock from shipboard means that a pleasant surprise is in store for you. 324

DOCTOR. To dream of consulting a doctor foretells an accident. Seeing a doctor socially is a good sign, for it means better business and happy social contacts. 170

DOCUMENT. If you dream of receiving a legal document in the mail, it foretells bad news. To dream of seeing a document lying on a table means disaster. 944

DOG. To hear a dog bark means that you will make friends out of your enemies. If a dog bites you, you will disagree with your lover. If an unmarried woman dreams of petting a small dog, it is a sign that her sweetheart is unworthy. To be frightened by a large ferocious dog foretells a love affair with a person of great mental power. If you see a white dog and he is friendly, you will be successful in business and love. 789

DOGGEREL. To read doggerel foretells you will take part in a minstrel show or some comedy on the amateur stage. To write it forewarns of a visit from an unwelcome person. 029

DOLE. If you dream of receiving dole, it denotes a betterment in your finances. If you give dole you will be connected in some way with a grocery store. 634

DOLLAR. If you see a silver dollar it means good luck. If you see a dollar bill it means misfortune. The higher the denomination the better the luck. 675

DOLPHIN. Single women and bachelors should guard against the wiles of designing members of the opposite sex if they dream of seeing dolphins from the deck of a boat. 919

DOME. To dream of seeing a dome on a building such as the capitol or on a court-house signifies that great honors will come to you whether as a government official or as a professor or president of some university. 776

DOMINOES. To dream of playing dominoes predicts taking a chance on some stock that will prove to be of small value. To see dominoes in a box denotes an offer of a worthless article which you will refuse to buy. 315

DONATION. Giving a donation in your dream signifies a change of heart. Someone whom you have always disliked will prove to be a friend in need. 261

DONKEY. If in a dream you are thrown from a donkey's back, you will be likely to quarrel with your sweetheart. To be given a donkey as a present means good luck in business, but it is a warning against evil women. If you are kicked by a donkey, you may be discovered in a clandestine love affair. A white donkey signifies success in personal matters. 047

DOOMSDAY. A dream of doomsday is a sign that you will make a success of the job you are holding at present. 738

DOOR. To see a closed door foretells an opportunity missed. An open door through which one sees the open country denotes hopes realized; another chance will be given you to make good. 535

DOORBELL. To push the button of a doorbell in a dream augurs exciting adventures with a person of the opposite sex. 194

DOPE. Taking dope in a dream foretells a moral weakening. To see a dope addict denotes a leaning to take the easiest way instead of squaring your shoulders and making a success out of life. It is a warning to go straight. 479

DORMER-WINDOWS. Dreaming of dormer-windows is a good sign. It foretells brighter horizons. 984

DORMITORY. To see young people in a dormitory is a happy augury. To be in a dormitory means that through mental application you will arrive at your goal. 823

DOUGH. A woman kneading dough seen in your dream is a good omen. It means a season of plenty and good health. To ask for some "dough" meaning money is a sign that you will be publicly humiliated before some of your best friends. 485

DOUGHNUTS. To dream of eating doughnuts means that you will travel and circle the globe. To dream of frying doughnuts or seeing them fried by another foretells travel. If you are not careful you will become the proverbial "rolling stone." 673

DOVE. A dream of a white dove means contentment in the home and good business prospects. Seeing a flock of doves and hearing them coo foretells a trip in a plane, maybe an army plane in formation with others. 215

DOWNFALL. To dream of your own downfall foretells reverses from which you will quickly recover and profit by the lesson you have learned. Another's downfall signifies the news of friends being stricken with some muscular affliction. 458

DOWRY. For a young woman to dream of her dowry is an omen that she will marry a man of ample means. 015

DRAFT. If you dream of being drafted into the army, it predicts employment for you in work of a mechanical nature. If you dream of a draft of air, it means that you will be fooled into believing some hard luck story. Beware of panhandlers after this dream. A dream of a draft such as a money order, signifies that you will make a loan to one by whom you never expect to be repaid. 461

DRAGON. To dream of a dragon is a portent of riches and great treasures. You will have the pleasure of meeting some personage of note, possibly some member of a royal family. 637

DRAGON-FLY. A dream of seeing a dragon-fly in the garden denotes a voyage by sea to tropical lands. 305

DRAIN. A drain seen in a dream foretells sickness—such as anemia, poor blood. You must guard your strength and stay in the sunshine as much as possible. 074

DRAKE. To dream of seeing a sleek fat drake waddle across the yard denotes that festive times are in store for you. 851

DRAMA. To dream of a drama being enacted on the stage foretells a disagreeable encounter with an officer of the law. If in a dream you write a drama, you will be looked upon as a fool by your best friend. To play a part in a drama augurs success in family life. 975

DRAPERY. To dream of soft draperies signifies that you will enjoy a life of luxury. To see faded, torn draperies denotes the passing of prosperity. 030

DRAWING-ROOM. To be received in a formal drawing-room signifies high ambitions on your part that will not be realized. To lie down in a lovely drawing-room foretells jealous enemies who are plotting against you. 042

DRAW-KNIFE. Using a draw-knife in a dream presages a thrifty helpmate. If you appear to be doing a good job with it, the omen is of heartening news from a wealthy friend. If you cut yourself, you will be dunned by your creditor. 024

DREADNOUGHT. Dreaming of a dreadnought in battle presages disaster and quarrels with your relatives and in-laws. 051

DREAMS. To dream that you dreamed is a sign that your dream will come true sometime in the future. 759

DRESS. For a woman to dream of seeing a pretty dress on another woman means that she will become socially prominent. To dream of a dress in a shop window signifies a social ambition or a political ambition that will benefit both you and your family. 790

DRIFT. A snowdrfit seen in a dream foretells a difficult problem that you must solve or lose all that you have gained so far. Seeing the leaves drift down from the trees in the fall of the year denotes a disinclination to meet your difficulties and overcome them, but soon you will face a situation that must be solved successfully or you will regret it as long as you live. 554

DRILL. If you dream of seeing cadets drilling on the parade ground, you will be in line for a splendid position that will pay you well. If you dream of drilling, it foretells some time spent in preparing yourself for a fine opportunity either in your home town or in some large city nearby. To see a hand drill in your dreams is a sign that you will be surfeited with frivolous pleasures that will get you nowhere. 410

DRINK. To see someone drinking (anything) in your dream foretells years spent in academic learning. You will add many degrees after your name. To dream of yourself drinking to excess denotes many acquaintances who will take advantage of your easy going, indolent nature and rob you of your money. 446

DRIVING. Fast driving in a car, that is, exceeding the speed limit, foretells a hasty marriage and an unfortunate one. To dream of driving at a moderate speed through the open country implies success in a small way and much happiness. To drive a car into some object denotes frustration. You will break your engagement, or lose out in some business deal. Driving a nail bespeaks unfailing energy. You will realize your ambitions and become a prominent citizen. 853

DROMEDARY. A woman who dreams of riding a dromedary will be wise if she does not believe all that men, including her husband, tell her. If she rubs the animal's hump, she should beware of flirting with men she does not know. 208

DROOL. To dream of drooling like a baby means that you will enjoy good times with a group of young people. 050

DROPSY. A journey across the ocean is predicted by a dream of this disease. Something is likely to occur on the trip that will cause you concern. 586

DROWNING. To dream of drowning forebodes bitter sorrows. 122

DRUG. A dream of being drugged and unable to move about denotes that an enemy is watching his chance to harm you. 845

DRUGGIST. If you dream that you are a druggist, you will have to spend longer hours at your job to make the same amount of money. 127

DRUGSTORE. To dream of being in a drugstore is a sign that your investments will turn out favorably. 596

DRUM. To hear a drum in your dream is a forerunner of the long awaited success from your discovery, invention, or ideas. The muffled beat of a drum heard in the distance is a portent of dire calamities, a series of misfortunes that will overtake one of whom you are very fond. 228

DRUMMER. To see a drummer in your dream in some gala parade or orchestra signifies gay times and over-indulgence. 150

DRUMSTICK. Eating a turkey drumstick in your dream means good luck. Handling wooden drumsticks is a warning against making boastful statements. 823

DRUNKARD. To dream that one is drunk is unfortunate for it signifies indiscretions and disorderly living that will cause your ruin. To dream of seeing a drunkard means loss of money through the mail. 865

DUCHESS. To dream of seeing a duchess beautifully gowned, and wearing a tiara foretells many social engagements, perhaps a house party where there will be distinguished guests. 635

DUCK. If you see many ducks in your dream and hear them quacking, it foretells good luck. You will have a great deal to be thankful for. 294

DUDE. To see a dude or fop in your dreams points to a disappointment in love. For a man to dream of being one augurs loss of standing. 251

DUET. To dream of hearing a duet sung predicts a happy marriage among your friends in the near future. It also foretells harmonious surroundings and freedom to work upon your hobbies. 362

DUGOUT. If you dream of being in a dugout, it foretells the need of keeping a friend's secret to your own detriment. Paddling in a dugout canoe signifies that through your own resourcefulness you will come out of an emergency unscathed. 272

DUKE. To dream of seeing or talking to a duke denotes a betterment of your circumstances. You will be looked up to by your acquaintances. 456

DULCIMER. To dream of playing the dulcimer promiss sweet moments with your best beloved, but if the music sounds sour, you are warned against associating with loose characters. 438

DUMMY. A dummy seen in your dreams foretells the failure of your plans that might have meant success if you had used better judgment. 806

DUMP. A dream of a trash dump forewarns of a trying circumstance where you will be forced to bear the brunt of another's burdens. 203

DUN. It is a sign of approaching prosperity if you are dunned for money by creditors, either in person or by mail. 974

DUNGEON. To be confined in a dungeon in a dream predicts a visit from wealthy relatives whom you do not admire. 909

DUNGHILL. Scandalous things are likely to be said about you if you dream of shoveling manure on a dunghill. 480

DUSK. If you dream of the dusk gathering at the close of the day, the prediction is unfavorable. It foretells discouragement and misfortune, especially for merchants. 483

DUST. Seeing a cloud of dust denotes a new and irritating problem. Evil influences are about you. Watch your new acquaintances and your health. Seeing dust upon the furniture means that you will have an embarrassing moment. To be covered with dust signifies that you will be jilted by your sweetheart. To married people it means trouble with in-laws. 433

DWARF. To dream of a dwarf is a prediction of health and wealth. Your complex problems will be solved as if by magic. 294

DWARF. (See also Midget.) Little people with oversized heads and hands are a sign, when seen in a dream, that your future is menaced by someone who wishes you ill. 315

DYEING. If you dream of dyeing your hair, it foretells business success. If you dream of dyeing a garment, it means social honors. 039

DWELLING. Seeing an old dwelling in a dream is a sign that you will take a trip and on the way visit school friends. If you see a new dwelling in the process of construction, the dream foretells an unexpected legacy. 637

DYNAMITE. If you dream of seeing an explosion of dynamite, your new made plans will go awry. If you see dynamite being loaded onto a ship, it means that the danger to which you have been exposed is over. 594

DYNAMO. To dream of a dynamo foretells that you will be put on night work, or that you will suffer from insomnia and will write or read a great deal during the night. 742

EAGLE. To see an eagle in a high place is a good sign. If the eagle lands upon your head, it is a sign of death; if the dreamer is carried up into the air by the eagle, a serious accident. If one dreams of seeing a dead eagle, it means a fatality to the rich, and to the poor some profit. To see an eagle flying foretells good business prospects. An eagle flying also portends the return of a good friend from a distant country. To see eaglets in the nest means that you will accept a position of trust and will be successful in your work. 899

EAR. To dream of people's ears implies startling news in the mail. To dream of pulling someone's ear signifies an altercation with your employer. 030

EARRINGS. If you dream of seeing an attractive woman wearing earrings, it foretells an affair with an adventuress. She will lead you a merry dance and leave you regretting your folly. If you wear earrings, you will win some money in a lottery. 198

EARTH. To dream of seeing the earth through a telescope means that you will inherit a large sum of money, but it will be held in litigation for some time before you will receive your share from the estate. 379

EARTHQUAKE. To see the horrors of an earthquake portends the dissolution of your affairs, but you will manage to go on, and out of your difficulties you will reap a well-deserved reward. If you are unfortunate enough to be in an earthquake, you will have troubles aplenty but will overcome them. 944

EASEL. To dream of seeing an artist painting at an easel foretells a life of ease. You will have many hobbies and live in a southern country. 075

EASTER. A dream of the lovely Eastertime portends a change of business that will be to your benefit. It means for a woman new furnishings in the home and pleasant social gatherings. If you dream of rolling Easter eggs on a green lawn, it foretells freedom from worries and the celebration of some joyous event. 793

EATING. Eating with guests in a dream portends good luck and happy times. If you eat alone, it is an unfortunate augury. 400

EAVESDROPPING. If you dream of seeing someone eavesdrop, it signifies a dilemma from which you will have difficulty in finding a way out. If you eavesdrop in your dream, you will be put on the spot and if you are not tarred and feathered, it won't be the fault of your enemies. 836

EBONY. To handle an object made of ebony, means that you will write a letter that will cause you no end of trouble and bring you unwelcome notoriety. Ebony foretells personal entanglements. 648

ECHO. To dream of hearing the echo of your voice portends a strange experience with one of the opposite sex. 015

ECLAIR. If you dream of seeing eclairs on a tray with French pastries in a restaurant or hotel dining room, it is an omen that an old sweetheart is in town and that you will meet her or him and recall the old days. 469

ECLIPSE. To see an eclipse, either of the sun or the moon, denotes dread and forebodings of impending harm to yourself or to a member of your immediate family. 738

ECSTASY. To dream of being in a state of ecstasy signifies a proposal of marriage or the acceptance of your hand in marriage. To dream of ecstasy while dancing denotes amorous affairs and a case of "off with the old love and on with the new." 446

EDEN. If you dream of being in the garden of Eden, beware of rivals. You will be flattered but not loved. 473

EDITOR. To dream of seeing an editor at his desk is a warning to go over your accounts and balance your budget. To dream of being an editor shows dissatisfaction with your lot in life. 151

EDUCATION. To dream of working hard at your studies, trying to get an education, signifies that you will receive honors and know success but not in a cultural way. 493

EEL. To catch an eel is a good sign if it doesn't wiggle out of your hands. To dream of seeing a school of eels in the water warns you to look out for your pocketbook. 471

EFFIGY. To dream of seeing an effigy foretells the discovery of fraud in the accounts of one whom you believed the soul of honor. To see a straw effigy hanging from a tree means deceit and treachery among your acquaintances. 367

EGG. Eggs in a dream are a good omen. They portend success in any new venture. To dream of finding fresh eggs in a nest means financial profit. To eat eggs foretells good health. 391

EGGNOG. Drinking an egggnog denotes household activities, such as cleaning the house or the garage or the cellar. 065

EGGPLANT. To dream of preparing an eggplant for the table predicts social festivities and simple home entertaining. To see an eggplant growing foretells moderate success and the gift of several new books to read. 126

EGOTIST. Talking to an egotist in a dream signifies an inferiority complex that will cause you to boast of your knowledge. 919

EIGHT. To dream of seeing the number eight on an object portends disaster and disillusionment. To dream of an eight coupled with other numbers is a good augury. 283

EIGHTEEN. To see the number eighteen in a dream foretells a calamity, but you will escape unharmed. 361

EINSTEIN. To dream of the Einstein theory foretells many complex problems in your life that will require your close attention. 723

ELASTIC. If you dream of snapping elastic, you will encounter hazards that will try your courage but whet your appetite for more. To dream of elastic bands means that you will stretch a point to do a favor for a friend. 024

ELBOW. Elbowing your way through a crowd in a dream foretells a career in movies or on the lecture platform or in some profession where you will be before the public. To be elbowed by another who arouses your temper foretells mismanagement of your affairs and possibly a lawsuit. 277

ELDERBERRIES. Picking elderberries in a dream is a portent of making a friend of an old and delightful person. Making or drinking elderberry wine forecasts having to clean up the litter left by a wedding party. 976

ELDERS. To dream of your elders, that is, of being among a group of older people, signifies the coming of a momentous occasion in your life when you will be called uponto prove beyond a doubt your knowledge of a certain subject. 041

ELECTION. If you dream of celebrating an election, it foretells the offer of a small position in some department of the Government, from which you can rise to great heights if you put your shoulder to the wheel. If you dream of being elected to some office, it prophesies failure in business. 304

ELECTRICITY. To dream of seeing an electrical storm in the sky or the cross-circuiting of electric wires means the loss of property. To dream of turning electricity on and off is a sign of public acclaim; through your winning personality you will be accorded great honors. 587

ELEPHANT. To dream of seeing an elephant is an omen of good luck. To see elephants performing signifies a happy family life. Elephants at work denote a prosperous business outlook. 693

ELEVATOR. Being in an elevator with many people and going to the top of a high building augurs good luck and a bright future. To dream of descending forecasts poor investments and unsettled business conditions. Love affairs will be uncertain and unsatisfactory. 729

ELEVEN. The number eleven is auspicious. To dream of the number eleven means that good things are in store for you. Eleven is a good luck number. 512

ELK. If a man dreams of seeing or hunting elk, he will have a strong influence over women. 796

ELM. Dreaming of a beautiful elm tree predicts a carefree life, but if it is eaten with worms, you will have many annoyances. 961

ELOPEMENT. To dream of eloping with your sweetheart is a warning to take your head out of the clouds and look at realities. To dream of seeing others elope signifies that you will take a sentimental journey that will plunge you into serious difficulties. 650

ELOQUENCE. To be conscious in a dream of the eloquence of a preacher or orator is a warning not to yield to the flattery of persons who have an axe to grind. 558

EMBALMING. To dream of being engaged in embalming a body, or of looking on when an undertaker is doing this work, is a sign that a perfectly innocent action of yours will be misunderstood by your friends. 683

EMBANKMENT. To see a high embankment in your dream is a sign that you should put your pet project into cold storage for a while and await developments. 280

EMBARRASSMENT. To dream of being in an embarrassing situation means just to sit tight and avoid letting people persuade you against your better judgment. 833

EMBASSY. Being received at an embassy in a dream foretells a gay social season ahead of you. You must spring into action and not sit around waiting for things to happen. To see gentlemen at the embassy in the uniforms of their respective countries predicts social responsibilities of great importance to you and your family. 906

EMBER. To see embers, fires of live coals, on the hearth is a good omen if the dreamer does not get burned. It signifies harmonious surroundings and a peaceful if not eventful existence. 891

EMBEZZLER. To dream of being an embezzler portends a disturbed state of mind that will respond only to an immediate discussion of your problems with those who understand them best. To dream of another person embezzling implies a secret fear that clouds your happiness and makes your progress doubtful. 479

EMBLEM. An emblem of any description in your dream foretells a journey, either to foreign countries or on a long transcontinental trip. 122

EMBRACE. To be embraced by one of the opposite sex is a sign that you will be accused of an indiscretion that will blight your good name, though there may be no truth to the rumor. To see others embrace foretells that you will be criticized to balance the praise you have received. 303

EMBROIDERY. To see a woman embroideirng in your dream denotes innocent peccadilloes and good fun. To work upon fine embroidery with many bright colored silks is a sign that someone is plotting against you. 822

EMERALD. Wearing a beautiful emerald in a dream predicts a life of affluence. You will marry into a wealthy and respected old family. To dream of seeing an emerald among other jewels implies riches and social prestige. To dream of an old emerald foretells the inheritance of money and real estate coming from an unexpected source. 909

EMIGRANT. To dream of seeing emigrants from another land coming to this country aboard a ship foretells bright prospects and a change of address. To dream of being an emigrant is a sign you will be in need before the year is out. 421

EMISSARY. Seeing an emissary holding a message in his hand is a foreboding that a great calamity of national import will occur within the week. 872

EMPEROR. (See King, Queen.) 901

EMPLOYMENT. To dream of being in an employment agency predicts a happy solution to all your troubles. You will make use of something close at hand that will prove a bonanza. Offering employment to others is a sign of the opening of some project, like a mine, or oil field or something that will come out of the ground to bring you riches and great joy. 237

EMPTINESS. Opening a box, basket or bag and finding it empty when you expected to find it full, denotes futility. Do not undertake anything out of the ordinary for a while; it would prove a waste of time and a keen disappointment. 604

EMU. To dream of seeing an emu in strange surroundings is a sign you will meet a fool. 750

ENAMEL. To dream of handling enamelware foretells mistaken friendship with one whom you believed to be worthy but who will prove a thorn in the flesh. 081

ENCAMPMENT. An encampment of either soldiers or people intent on a good time is an omen of the necessity for preparedness. You must prepare for a concerted attack from the outside. Line up your assets and liabilities and balance your books. You have nothing to fear. Stand at attention. 996

ENCHANTMENT. If you dream of being enchanted by a sorceress, the prediction is that you will fall into idle ways and the society of undesirable peoples. 261

ENCORE. To dream of being in an audience that encores a famous artist, and of his gracious response, signifies that you will reap the reward you have worked for. If the artist fails to respond you will be disappointed. 276

ENCOUNTER. To encounter a person whom you have not seen for years is a good sign. To encounter a person or any object suddenly and unexpectedly denotes news from afar. 0.24

ENCYCLOPEDIA. It is a fortunate omen for all those who wish to become successful writers to dream of looking up a subject in an encyclopedia. 443

ENDIVE. Eating endives in a dream is a sign that you will become engaged to a foreigner, one who does not speak your language nor think your thoughts but who will give you much love. 743

ENEMY. To dream that you overcome an enemy is a good sign for anyone, but to dream that he or she overcomes you is a prediction of danger and warning against taking chances. 285

ENDOWMENT. To dream of endowing a college or some other large institution denotes an undertaking that will prove to be definitely unwise. You will bite off more than you can chew and cry for help. To dream of being entrusted with an endowment foretells trouble ahead, complications that are so involved that it will seem a physical impossibility to overcome them. 962

ENERGY. Being full of pep and energy in a dream, as though you would like to tear the world up is a sign that "pride goeth before a fall." You will be guilty of a tactical error that will make your ears red. 328

ENGAGEMENT. If you dream of being engaged, you will be disappointed. Celibacy will be your lot. If you dream of breaking your engagement, you will be allergic to marriage for some time and will make of yourself a nuisance to your friends. 226

ENGINE. To dream of an engine doing at top speed portends the accomplishment of an arduous task that has taken you a long time to complete but for which you will receive many honors and material awards. To dream of an engine is a good sign. You will go far in your chosen profession or job. 822

ENGINEER. Happy and successful will be the man who dreams of doing engineering work of any kind—civil, electrical, mechanical, chemical, or otherwise. 640

ENGLISH. To see and hear an Englishman speak foretells a situation that will require great diplomacy and tact. You will have to be broadminded and look at it from all sides. 972

ENLISTMENT. If you dream of enlisting in the army or in any project of public concern, you will suffer the loss of a good friend and a home. You will become a cog in the wheel and it will be many years before you settle down. 130

ENTERTAINMENT. Dreaming of a sumptuous entertainment portends curtailment of income and pecuniary troubles. If you dream of entertaining simply in your home, it warns against extravagance; you must curb your desires, for you cannot eat your cake and have it too. 735

ENTOMBMENT. If you dream of the entombment of someone you loved, you will awake to hear of the loss of some personage famed the world over for his contribution to the arts. To dream of being entombed is a warning to relax and to stop fretting over the impression you make. Forget yourself and others will remember you. 295

ENTRAILS. (See Intestines.) 372

ENTRANCE. To dream of an ornate entrance to some public building signifies the desire for higher learning. You may be an adult, but you will continue your studies to your great profit. If you are young, you will receive scholastic honors. An entrance denotes higher learning and greater knowledge. 115

ENVELOPE. Sealing an envelope in a dream foretells a happy marriage. To dream of addressing an envelope is a sign that you will meet the one to whom you address it very soon. 319

ENVY. To dream of envying someone his possessions foretells good fortune. To envy his or her good looks is prophetic of a marriage in which ill temper will mar the happiness of both parties. 444

EPAULET. If you dream of seeing epaulets on a uniform, it signifies the crushing of one's foes. To dream of wearing epaulets foretells a love afair with a girl who is famous on the stage. 869

EPICURE. To dream of being an epicure is fair warning to restrain your desires and be more discreet with acquaintances of the opposite sex. 073

EPIDEMIC. If you dream of being in an epidemic, it denotes mental disturbances. It would be well to consult a doctor and to observe the rules of health, regarding diet and exercise. 480

EPISTLE. If the epistle is delivered by hand, it indicates a troubled conscience. If it is written in colored ink, it is a portent that you will separate from your mate or break your engagement to your sweetheart. To dream of hiding an epistle is a warning to beware of a fair-haired rival. 829

EPITAPH. To see epitaphs on tombstones in a cemetery is a sign that you will become interested in work concerned with a library, either as librarian, recorder, or researcher. If the epitaphs are plainly discernible, you will overcome all the obstacles that confront you. 008

EQUATOR. If you dream of crossing the Equator it denotes a certain indecision about you. You are unsettled in your mind as to the best course to pursue. If it touches interests of the heart, consider well your choice. If it relates to living with your in-laws, ponder well. Your finances require close attention. If you approach the Equator in your dream and do not cross, you will rue the day you let a good opportunity slip through your fingers. 354

EQUESTRIAN. To dream of seeing equestrians in riding togs surrounded by hounds and going to the hunt, you will in the near future receive an unexpected dividend from stock that you feared was worthless. To dream of being an equestrian is a good sign, for you will meet your Prince Charming or the Beautiful Lady within the year. 495

ERASER. An eraser foretells that a close friend will suffer from loss of memory and will disappear from his usual haunts. To use an eraser on paper or on the blackboard foretells a broken heart. You will be jilted by your sweetheart and made to face your rival socially. 802

ERIN. To dream of Erin, the land of the shamrock is a happy omen. Like a prince or princess in a fairy tale, you will ride through life on the wings of success and be well loved for your priceless gift of humor, always seeing the silver lining in every cloud. 060

ERMINE. Ermine in your dream bespeaks quite the reserve from what one would expect. It implies a life of sackcloth and ashes unless one gives it to another, in which case you will werar diamonds. To wear an ermine wrap augurs cold and famine. 833

ERRANDS. To be sent on an errand in your dream means that you will lose your loved one through your selfishness. If someone comes to you on an errand it is prophetic of a future interest in politics. 203

ERROR. If you dream of committing a slight error, it betokens a happy adjustment of your difficulties. If you see someone in error, the dream denotes an unfortunate affair in which you will be mixed up with a lot of silly busybodies. 724

ERUPTION. To dream of an eruption on your face or body foretells the breaking away from old beliefs and joining a new cult or group of agitators. To dream of the eruption of a volcano is a forerunner of disaster and calamity. 590

ESCALATOR. An ascending escalator signifies new hopes and ambitions, new friends and new places. A descending escalator means probable defeat that you must fight against and turn into success. 629

ESCAPE. To escape from some danger implies a speedy recovery from what will threaten to be a serious illness. To see someone escaping from a fire or an explosion, or some dire disaster foretells a check in the mail. 227

ESCORT. To escort a fair lady to the opera or theater or some other place of amusement is a good omen. You will be taken into the partnership of your concern. To be escorted denotes material help in a time of need to promote your business interests. 383

ESKIMO. Eskimos dressed in their native costumes, riding on dog sleds or standing in the snow, foretells a rebuff to your request for a loan of money. To be with Eskimos is a sign that you will meet a cool reception at the home of your best girl. 449

ESSAY. To write an essay denotes an ambition to be acclaimed by the public as a conquering hero. To read an essay foretells success as an executive or leader of men. 448

ESTATE. Grand estates, large green lawns, gabled castles, swimming pools and tennis courts, point to the necessity of your facing the realities of life. To become the owner of a small estate is a forerunner of unpleasant circumstances that could be avoided if you forgot yourself and thought of others for a while. 718

ETCHINGS. Etchings, either in a shop window or in a museum or on the walls of your home denote a refinement of taste that will serve you well in your profession or job. Etchings when admired by the dreamer foretell cultural connections. 510

ETHER. To smell ether in your dream and see an operating room in a hospital implies a great change in your life for the better. 913

ETIQUETTE. To dream of not observing the rules of etiquette among a group of strangers is a warning to overcome your inferiority complex or it will get you down and you will miss out in a great many ways. Being over punctilious in your behavior foretells a public snubbing from one of social prominence whom you hoped to number among your friends. 386

EULOGY. To dream of being eulogized signifies the receipt of an expensive gift from some temple in a foreign land. To dream of eulogizing another points to hypocrisy on your part that will ultimately carry you to defeat. 443

EUROPE. If you dream of being in Europe when it is at peace, it is a happy augury; but if the continent is at war, it is the opposite. 419

EUNUCHS. To see eunuchs in a harem denotes a separation. It implies pain and sorrow and misunderstanding. 379

EVANGELIST. To dream of an evangelist is a foreboding of illness either in mind or body. 742

EVE. To dream of an eve, as the night before a great occasion, such as Christmas Eve or New Year's Eve, is a sign of discontent and the desire to outshine your friends. To dream of Eve in the Garden of Eden is a sign of fecundity and plenty. 822

EVENING. If your dream is concerned with a summer's night luminous with moonlight, it signifies a case of love at first sight. If you see the evening star in the sky and make a wish, happiness will be yours and the future will be very rosy. 734

EVERGLADE. To dream of walking in the everglades denotes an entanglement with one of the opposite sex that will cause you grave concern. 358

EVERGREEN. An evergreen shrub or tree seen in a dream is a sign of lasting friendship. 345

EVICTION. An eviction is not a pleasant dream. It foretells financial troubles and wraps your problems in a blanket of fog compelling you to wait for the sun. But it will shine, as it always has. 065

EVIL SPIRITS. To dream of evil spirits around you shows that you will be prevented from realizing your ambitions but will find happiness and contentment in another channel. If you dream of seeing evil spirits about you, grotesque faces that appear and disappear, unaccountable situations will develop that will confuse and mystify you. 560

EWER. If you dream of seeing an old-fashioned ewer, it is a good sign. You will be talked about, but pleasantly, and compliments will be tossed your way like nosegays to a star performer. 007

EXCHANGE. To dream of exchanging goods at the store signifies a change of heart. To make an exchange denotes a rearrangement of your plans. 412

EXECUTION. A prolonged illness is predicted if one dreams of an execution by either hanging or electrocution. 530

EXILE. To dream of being an exile in a foreign land predicts difficult times ahead. Your most honorable intentions will be misunderstood, and you will be subject to calumny. 264

EXPEDITION. To go on an expedition to a strange and fearsome land foretells marriage to one you have known only a short while. You will marry and travel by boat a great distance and make your home among strangers. Whoever dreams of going on an expedition will handle strange merchandise to his great profit. 749

EXPLOSION. The terrific report of a high explosive heard in a dream is an augury of permanent improvement in your finances and health—unless it is from a death-dealing gun, which is a forerunner of the opposite. Explosions for useful purposes are of lucky import. 662

EXTRAVAGANCE. To dream of being extravagant when those about you are in want foretells a scandal in which you will be the center of interest. 639

EYE. To see eyes dancing around in space and not related to any particular face signifies an improvement in your financial condition and a hankering to play the stock market. 734

EYEBROWS. To see a face with heavy eyebrows is a sign the dreamer will be honored and esteemed by all. The dark, heavy, well-arched eyebrow is called the mandarin eyebrow and denotes aristocracy and cultural background. If the eyebrows are thin and colorless, the dreamer may expect little success either in his business or in his love affairs. 482

EYEGLASSES. If you dream of seeing your sweetheart wearing eyeglasses, you may be sure it means an end to your love affairs. 622

EYELASHES. Long, silken eyelashes predict the sharing of a secret that disconcerts you and makes you appear at a disadvantage. 261

F

FABLE. To dream of reading a fable predicts that someone will give you a sharp lecture regarding your shortcomings. 541.

FABRICS. To dream of handling beautiful fabrics, noting and feeling their color and texture, draping the material into graceful folds, foretells a bright career in one of the arts. 397

FACE. A sweet, happy, smiling face signifies new friends and pleasures to which you are unaccustomed. Faces distorted or seemingly grotesque denotes disaster, privations and possible death. To wash your face and dry it on a clean towel is a sign you will repent of your sins. To see a black face means a long life. Faces that grimace at you denote a quarrel with your sweetheart. If you dream of seeing your own face, the prediction is of great unhappiness. 392

FACIAL. To dream of having a facial at a beauty parlor implies the need to scurry about and cover up some indiscretion of which you are ashamed. Don't be so selfish. Think of the other fellow for a change and see what happiness it will bring you. 232

FACT. To dream of recording facts or searching for facts denotes a law-suit and unpleasant notoriety. 622

FACTORY. A factory, full of busy, contented employees portends splendid business prospects. To dream of working in a factory signifies that you will be rewarded for your service and share in the proceeds. 982

FAD. A new and interesting fad in your dream portends a series of adventures that will take you far afield. 093

FAILURE. If you are in love and dream that your sweetheart refuses to marry you, it is a reminder to pursue your suit with great diligence, for if you do, you will succeed and live happily ever afterward. To dream of a failure assures success in your affairs. 564

FAINTING. To dream of fainting is a warning to stop and consider your frivolous ways and renounce the questionable associates you now call your friends. If you see a beautiful girl faint and you rush to her assistance, beware of designing women. Don't let a pair of blue eyes cause your downfall. 985

FAIR. For a young woman to dream of being at a fair means that she will marry a good-natured man of fine principles who will provide well for her. To dream of attending a country fair augurs well for you. You will enjoy life to the fullest. 317

FAIRY. You will have an opportunity of making children happy if you dream of the elves, pixies and gnomes of forest and field that you have read about in fairy-tales. If your dream is of imagining yourself a fairy or being recognized as such, you are warned to guard your conduct against possible misunderstanding. 654

FAIRYLAND. To dream of being in the land of the fairies peopled with elfin sprites signifies unexpected riches that will come to you through some simple invention of yours that is needed in the commercial field. To dream of fairies coming into this workaday world and of your talking to them denotes an artistic talent that you will make use of to your great profit and gratification. 528

FAITH. A dream of an abiding faith in someone or of faith in yourself means that you will finally make some decision that you have put off making and that has prevented you from going ahead with your plans. The decision will be to your advantage and you will be free to carry on. A dream of faith always predicts a happy ending. 722

FAITHFULNESS. If a married person dreams of the faithfulness of his or her mate, the augury is one of peace and prosperity. 915

FAKE. To dream of a fake, something that isn't what it seems, or of some person who pretends to be other than what he is, predicts a situation that will occur in which you must be on your guard and not jump to conclusions. Don't gamble. Stop, look, and listen, and then, don't do it, whether it concerns love or business. 751

FAKIR. These East Indian holy men met with in a dream are a forecast of being disgusted by the behavior of one of your close relatives. 126

FALCON. The dream of seeing a falcon poised for flight is a good omen; it signifies honor. If you hunt with a falcon on your wrist, beware of thieves and robbers. If a young woman dreams of catching a falcon, it indicates that her desires will be fulfilled but that she will have a rival. 714

FALLING. To dream of falling is not propitious, for sickness, failure, and disappointments in love are foretold. If one dreams of falling and actually crashes to earth, the ominous prediction is death or a prolonged illness. 884

FALSEHOOD. It is good luck to dream that someone tells you a lie. If you dream of telling a lie to someone, you will suffer some physical injury. 532

FALSETTO. To hear someone singing in a falsetto voice is auspicious. To those in love it means an early marriage and happy dreams coming true. 509

FAME. If you dream of becoming famous and accepting the adulation of the people, it signifies a turn for the worse in your affairs. Keep plodding along. Don't reach for the fruit on your neighbor's tree. If you dream of seeing a famous person, it means that help will come to you from some unexpected source. 977

FAMILY. To see a large and happy family in your dream predicts a holiday spent alone in some strange city far from home. To see a family of animals nuzzling at their mothers breast signifies a pickup in business. To see a destitute family augurs an upheaval in national affairs. 201

FAMINE. To see a country in the throes of a famine predicts unsettled conditions from which you will suffer but eventually struggle through to enjoy days of peace and contentment. To be encircled and made to endure the privations of a famine augurs troublesome times and searching for the leadership of the right man. 366

FAN. To dream of seeing a pretty girl fanning herself foretells a broken engagement and jealous heartaches. To dream of receiving a lot of fan mail is a sure sign that you are regarded as fickle. To fan yourself predicts a love entanglement. To lose a fan means that your lover is becoming cold. 433

FANATIC. Meeting a fanatic in a dream predicts a long period of illness whether the fanaticism is about religion, politics or any other subject about which there maybe conflicting opinions. 257

FANCY WORK. For a woman to dream of doing fancy work such as embroidery, knitting, crocheting, or drawn work is an augury of the renewal of an old romance. 697

FANFARE. To dream of being greeted by a fanfare of trumpets is a sign that jealous parties are seeking to do you harm by ridiculing you. 456

FANG. Seeing the fangs of an animal in a dream is a warning to pack your bags and leave before you are kicked out. Fangs foretell trouble with your in-laws. 377

FANTASY. It is a forerunner of a fortunate business adventure if you dream of a fantastic occurrence in your love life. 925

FARCE. To sit in a theatre and watch a farce on the stage presages an uncomfortable visit with people whom you dislike, where you will be ridiculed and belittled to the point where you will protest and cause a scene. 061

FAREWELL. If you bid farewell to your lover in a dream, very shortly he will become indifferent to your love. If someone bids you farewell, you will be looking for a new job. 490

FARM. To see a carefully tended farm in your dreams means a life of plenty, simple joys and good health. To own an unprofitable farm and see poor crops and lean cattle augurs a run on the bank and a small loss of money. 645

FASCIST. A dream of living under a Fascist regime foretells having to admit being in the wrong regarding something that happened many years ago. 690

FASHION. To dream of being dressed in the height of fashion foretells a season of social activities and of your taking a prominent part in them. To dream of being out of fashion predicts all work and no play, if you do not exert yourself and meet your friends at least halfway. 465

FASTDAY. To dream of observing a fastday means that you will right a wrong and be much happier for it. 466

FATNESS. If you dream of being exceedingly fat and very uncomfortable, you will have few worries and many friends. 346

FATALIST. To dream of being a fatalist shows a troubled conscience. Brush out the cobwebs and begin a new day. You will be given an opportunity to do this very soon; take advantage of it. 334

FATE. If you dream that fate has been unfair to you, you may rest assured that good luck is coming your way. If you dream that fate has played into your hands, you will marry the one you love and build the home you want. 972

FATHER. To dream of one's father presages a change of environment. If you are a city resident, you will move to the country; if you live in a rural community, you will move to the city or to another state. If you dream of being a father with your children about you, it foretells a rise in your fortune and a change in business that will be to your advantage. If a wife dreams of the father of her children she will get a new dress. 544

FATHER TIME. To dream of Father Time augurs a national crisis in which you will play a prominent part. You will be chosen to carry burdens of state and because of your aptitude for supervision you will direct the work of others and be honored and revered. The dream of Father Time predicts anticipation in public affairs. 454

FATIGUE. It is a fortunate augury to dream of being tired. You will enjoy good health and an income that will be sufficient for your needs. 493

FAUCET. To dream of a dripping faucet means that you will be guilty of divulging a secret of great importance so that it will change your entire future and not to your liking. To dream of a new, shiny faucet signifies a great happiness that will come to you unsolicited. 225

FAULT. You will be delighted by news that you will hear if you dream of admitting a fault. Finding fault with another person in a dream prophesies that you will win a promotion. 851

FAVOR. To dream of asking a favor of someone predicts loss of face or social standing. To dream of conferring a favor means that you will receive a compliment from someone you esteem. 052

FAWN. To see a fawn in your dream portends a serious disagreement with one you love; it may result in a broken engagement or the divorce court. 113

FEAR. To experience the sensation of fear in your dream foretells a decision that you alone must make, and upon it hinges your future happiness. To dream of allaying the fears of another presages a righting of wrongs and a clearing of the atmosphere from petty annoyances that threaten your peace of mind. 976

FEAST. To dream of feasting is propitious. It indicates a period of plenty, during which you will enjoy the good things in life. 076

FEATHER. Dreaming of eagle feathers denotes success, the realization of your ambitions. To dream of ostrich feathers predicts a fortunate business transaction. To dream of a cloud of feathers as though they were coming from a pillow means unprecedented good fortune that will please your pride as well as your purse. 620

FEEBLENESS. If you dream of being feeble and infirm, you are likely to be approached by a solicitor of funds for a charitable cause. 352

FEEDING. A dream of feeding animals foretells a journey. Feeding a baby denotes a happy family reunion. Feeding a family predicts the undertaking of some civic project that will bring you great personal satisfaction. 597

FEET. To dream of bathing the feet foretells a pleasant relief from anxiety. If you dream of seeing your own feet, it means that your position is insecure. To dream of seeing many feet walking along a pavement portends material loss. 437

FELICITATIONS. To dream of being felicitated denotes a marriage in the near future. Offering felicitations to another augurs the celebration of some big event. 007

FELON. To dream of a felon or crook indicates that your secret fears will interfere with your plans unless you bring them into the open and crush them. 795

FEMALE. A sex disturbance of some kind is foretold by a dream of using the word "female" as a substitute for *woman, lady* or *girl.* 321

FENCE. If you dream of building a fence, you will be lucky in love. If the fence falls, you will lose your sweetheart. If you dream of climbing a fence, you will reach the height of your ambitions. To have dealings with a fence, or buyer and seller of stolen goods, is a dream that portends failure in business. 952

FENDER. To dream of a broken fender on an automobile signifies that your pride will take a fall. A fender in front of a fireplace denotes family unity. 667

FERMENTATION. A dream of the fermentation of wines predicts a temporary mental disturbance. If you dream of fermented canned goods or preserves, you will receive gratifying news. 086

FERN. A bank of fresh ferns seen in a dream predicts a threat of coolness between you and one of your friends. To gather ferns foretells an adventure of a startling nature that will be both enjoyable and thrilling. 257

FERRET. To dream of one of these little animals is a prognostication of disease either in your immediate family or among your circle of acquaintances. 628

FERRY. Being ferried across a river in a dream means that you will accomplish what you have set out to do, and your rewards wil be commensurate with the labor you have expended. 259

FERTILITY. A new and unexpected source of income is predicted by a dream that indicates either fertility of the soil or of the body. 307

FERTILIZER. It is auspicious to dream of putting fertilizer on any field or garden. It predicts an increase in income and good fortune in love. 622

FESTIVAL. If you dream of participating in a festival where there is much gayety, you will rejoice at the good fortune of a friend. To dream of attending a musical festival predicts the introduction of a new interest into your life, either a rare friendship or a fascinating hobby that will make you famous. 231

FESTOON. To dream of seeing ribbons or greens festooned about a room foretells a happy occasion among friends and relatives. 554

FETLOCK. If you dream of grasping a horse's fetlock, it forecasts new business hazards. 958

FETTER. To dream of being fettered with chains, ropes or conditions predicts a new and successful love affair. 466

FEUD. A person who dreams of taking part in a feud can look forward to a long period of contentment. 791

FEVER. If you dream that you have a fever, you are likely to have upsets in your love life. Your love affairs will take a sudden turn for the worse. 683

FIASCO. A dream of a ridiculous failure or any sudden reversal of your fortunes denotes the ability to pay your debts and hold up your head. 320

FICTION. (See Novel, Story.) 012

FIDDLE. (See Violin.) 741

FIDELITY. (see Faithfulness.) 940

FIELD. It is a sign of great perturbation just around the corner if you see one person running across a field. If there are several, you will find yourself in legal difficulties. To see animals pastured in a field predicts easier work. 616

FIEND. If you have the misfortune to dream of a fiend from hell, you will be liable to punishment for some misdeed that you would prefer to forget. 567

FIESTA. (See Festival.) 340

FIFE. To play or hear a fife in a dream is a portent of an upset in love affairs. If accompanied by drums, however, it foretells an easy conscience. 263

FIG. Shame will come to you if you dream of eating figs. If you pick figs from a tree, your difficulty will be with a member of the opposite sex. 886

FIGHT. If you dream of being in a fist fight, you are likely to find that people will regard you highly. If you see others fighting, you will find happiness in your own sphere. 105

FIGHTING COCK. If you dream of attending a show of fighting cocks, some covetous person will try to get hold of your possessions. A dream of putting a fighting cock into a ring signifies a gain of minor proportions. 208

FIGURE. (See also Accounting.) To dream of a hodge-podge of unrelated figures is a sign that you will meet a combative person and come off second best. For a man to notice a woman's figure in a dream forecasts pleasant and innocent diversions out of doors. 053

FILBERT. Trouble and anger are the portents of a dream about eating filberts. To buy a bag of them indicates that you will take a short trip. 714

FILE. Using a file on wood in a dream is an augury of criticism from a person older than yourself; on iron or steel it portends a reconciliation with an enemy. Used on one's fingernails, it predicts the fulfillment of expectations. 330

FILET OF SOLE. You will be disturbed by the actions of someone you know who will avoid you if you dream of eating filet of sole. To cook it augurs worries of a personal nature. 703

FILIGREE. It is an augury of receiving a package in damaged condition if you dream of handling silver or gold filigree work. 449

FILING CABINET. Unless one is searching for a lost letter, it is good luck to dream of working at a filing cabinet. Where a letter is lost it portends a lowering of moral standards. 801

FILLING STATION. Buying gas at a filling station predicts an increase in your income, but to dream of buying anything else is a portent of illness. To visit the washroom of a filling station is a sign of less worry than you have been undergoing. 330

FILLY. You will have more leisure time for your avocations if you dream of seeing a filly in a pasture. If she is inclined to be friendly, you will make money in your spare time. 983

FILM. To dream of threading film into a motion picture projector is a sign of being able to buy new clothes. To load a camera with a roll of film signifies gratification of a love for jewelry. To make prints from photographic film is an augury of disappointment. 709

FILTH. If you are not constantly on your guard, circumstances will work toward your degradation after a dream of filth, either actual or mental. 996

FIN. A dream of seeing a fish wave its fins is an augury of freedom from detestable work. If, in preparing a fish for cooking, you cut off the fins, you will lose a valuable trinket and have great difficulty in finding it. 633

FINANCIER. It is a sign that you will have bad luck with your money affairs if you dream of being a financier. To dream of meeting on equal terms with financiers is a sign of good luck in buying and selling. 198

FINE. No good will come of a dream of having to pay a fine, no matter what the offense, even if it is for failure to return a public library book on time. You will have an altercation with one of your neighbors and you are likely to have to apologize. 873

FINERY. Girls who dream of wearing finery will be certain to have plenty of attention from men, probably men twice their age. 500

FINGER. (See also Thumb.) Scornfully to point your finger at another person in a dream is to look forward to being neglected by those whom you had considered your friends. To blow a kiss from your fingers to a person of the opposite sex is an augury of finding a new and exciting friend. To cut your finger predicts a long season of discontent. To dip your finger into food for the purpose of tasting it foretells jealous relatives. 196

FINGER BOWL. Someone will criticize you for snobbishness if you dream of using a finger bowl after a meal. To drink out of a finger bowl predicts money from a surprising source. 915

FINGERNAIL. To dream of trimming your fingernails is an augury of greater usefulness to the community in which you live. If you trim them too close, you will have troubles that will take some time to overcome. To bend back a fingernail predicts a period of unrest caused by critical relatives. For a woman to polish her fingernails is a sign that she will be criticized for her conduct. 657

FINGER PRINT. A friend will come to your aid if you dream of being fingerprinted by the authorities. To dream of finger prints on light-colored woodwork signifies financial distress. 604

FINGER WAVE. Young women who dream of getting a finger wave at a beauty parlor will meet new and intriguing men of whom they should be extremely careful. 435

FINISH. It is a prediction of a new association, either in business or social life, if you dream of finishing a job. 798

FINN. To dream of one of the natives of Finland is an augury of good health, honor and a large income. 718

FIORD. You may look forward to calm, peaceful days in a happy home if you dream of sailing on a fiord of Norway or on any other narrow bay with mountains on either side. 219

FIR. It is a sign of disaster if you dream of cutting down a fir tree, but to walk through a forest of fir trees is a forecast of good fortune, especially when you can smell the piney odor. 567

FIRE. This is a bad sign when it burns you, but an auspicious one when it provides comfort. To build a fire portends an adventure with a person of the opposite sex. To dream of setting fire to a building is a sign of impending harm. If you dream of putting out a fire, you will overcome your enemies. Looking at a building that is on fire means that you will have a call on your sympathy. 081

FIREARMS. (See Gun.) 683

FIREBOAT. In action, with jets of water spraying from its nozzles, a fireboat is a presage of nervous disorders that should receive medical care. 152

FIREBRAND. To dream of snatching a brand from a fire is a prediction of being able to save somebody from death. If the dream is of throwing a firebrand into a house or any other inflammable material, you will have to make amends for a misdeed. 575

FIRECRACKER. The sight and sound of the explosion of firecrackers in a dream portends irritations of a serious nature. If you dream of setting off firecrackers, you will have an interesting experience that will not be wholly to your liking. 781

FIRE ENGINE. Good luck in money matters will be yours if you dream of seeing any kind of fire apparatus on its way to a fire. To be at a fire-house when the engine is leaving is especially good luck, but to see it returning forebodes evil days. 640

FIRE ESCAPE. It presages pressure on you from your creditors if you dream of being on a fire escape either through necessity or for relaxation. 637

FIREFLY. Young men and women who dream of seeing fireflies in a summer garden should take warning that their conduct will be severely criticized by their elders. 227

FIREMAN. A man who dreams of being a fireman will be invited to an exclusive stag party composed of influential citizens. If you dream of driving a fire-engine, you will have a narrow escape from an accident. To dream of saving the life of a woman at a fire presages amorous adventures under very peculiar circumstances. 082

FIREPLACE. (See also Fire.) It is an augury of home comforts to dream of sitting in front of a fireplace in which a fire is burning, but if there is no fire, it predicts an upset in love affairs. 714

FIREWOOD. To gather firewood predicts a happy family life with the girl or man of your choice. To split firewood augurs success in the affairs of your community. 634

FIREWORKS. Skyrockets, Roman candles, pinwheels and other such displays forecast lack of success in the accomplishment of the work you have planned. 070

FIRST AID. To dream of administering first aid to a disabled or wounded person predicts that you will be called upon to fill a high position. 386

FISH. A dream of fish predicts a death in your family or among your circle of friends. To catch fish with a hook and line is a forerunner of illness; if with a net, it foretells an accident. 042

FISH-HOOK. Baiting a fish-hook in a dream is a fortunate prediction for men and women in love, no matter what their age. To get a fish-hook into any part of the body foretells a long period of distress through family troubles and lack of money. 399

FISH-MARKET. Dreaming of a fish-market in which the fish are attractively displayed foretells a pleasant vacation. If the fish appear to be spoiling, you are likely to have to pay a large income tax. 992

FISHNET. The use of a fishnet in a dream is a lucky omen only when he net is empty; if it has fish in it, there will be a mortal illness in your family or in your immediate circle of acquaintances. 597

FISH STORY. If in a dream someone tells you a "fish story"—one that you cannot believe—and you say that you do not believe it, you will find yourself in a difficult love entanglement. 418

FIST. (See also Fight.) Success in love and business will come to those who dream of making up a fist. 163

FIT. If a person dreams of seeing another in a fit, he or she will be in a quandary over family problems. To see a dog, cat, or other animal in a fit is a sign of vexation on account of one's work. 763

FIZZ. Young women who dream of taking any kind of drink that fizzes are likely to be held to account for unseem behavior. 604

FLAG. You may be sure of pleasant association with friends if you dream of seeing the flag of your country floating in the breeze. To dream of hoisting one on a flagpole is a forerunner of an increase in your worldly estate. If you dream of saluting your country's flag, you will win acclaim for an outstanding achievement. To lower a flag at sunset predicts finding a large sum of money. 111

FLAKE. A dream of any kind of flakes—corn, snow or what not—presages a difficult situation in which you will have to use more than ordinary discretion in order to keep from making a serious mistake. 218

FLAME. (See Fire.) 395

FLAMINGO. This long-legged, web-footed red bird is an augury of are exciting adventure far from home when seen flying in a dream. If it is standing or walking, it predicts worry. 281

FLASH. A flash of light that occurs in a dream portends that you will cash in on an idea and be able to live in comfort. 920

FLASHLIGHT. To use an electric flashlight indoors foretells that you will have a strong temptation to do wrong. It is therefore a warning to be on your good behavior. To use a flashlight out of doors is a sign that you will make a new and valuable friend. 183

FLATTERY. You are warned against repeating reports that are damaging to another if you dream of being flattered. If you dream of flattering someone else, you will have an illness. 543

FLATULENCE. A dream of being flatulent in the company of others is a presage of a violent quarrel with one of your best-liked associates. If the flatulence is that of someone else, you will go on an extended journey. 534

FLAVOR. To taste any definite or pronounced flavor in a dream portends good luck if it is to your liking. Otherwise it is a sign of petty annoyances. 267

FLAW. If you dream of finding a flaw in an otherwise perfect thing, you are likely to be blamed for something for which you are not responsible. If someone else points out the flaw, it predicts an altercation with a traffic officer. 969

FLAX. Growing in a field, flax is an augury of being admired for your sterling qualities. 073

FLEA. To dream that you are a flea, with the flea's great power as a jumper, is a warning against going into business deals without very careful consideration. If you dream of being bitten by fleas, it is a sign that you will be harassed by your creditors. Better luck will follow a dream of killing a flea. 359

FLEECE. You will have to go through a period of depression if you dream of wearing garments or gloves lined with fleece. 800

FLEET. A fleet of battleships at anchor in a river or bay betokens freedom from the worries that beset you. Streaming out to sea, they predict travel. A fleet of fishing boats seen in a dream augurs worry if they are going out to sea— contentment if they are returning to a harbor. 802

FLESH. (See also Meat.) A dream of human flesh, if it is regarded from the personal standpoint, is an omen of distress through ill-advised behavior with one of the opposite sex. 349

FLEUR-DE-LIS. (See Iris.) 160

FLIGHT. (See also Airplane.) For a person to dream of flying like a bird is a sign that he or she is in some way attempting the impossible; but if the dream is of flight in an airplane, the augury is a good one. 194

FLINT. Young people who dream of striking fire with flint and steel will have love affairs that will probably lead to an early marriage. 758

FLIRT. (See also Coquette.) For a man or woman to dream of meeting a flirt and encouraging him or her predicts a short and unsuccessful love affair. 439

FLOAT. A dream of lying on a float in a bathing suit is a portent of a heavy disappointment. To step out of a boat onto a float is a sign of making up after a quarrel. 376

FLOCK. Birds seen in a flock are usually a propitious augury in connection with other items in a dream. 499

FLOGGING. After a dream of seeing a person flogged you will have an opportunity to seek revenge on someone who has done you wrong. Be warned against all ill-advised acts. 119

FLOOD. This is a dream that should put you on your guard against crooks, gangsters and other evil persons. If you are swept away by a flood, you are in danger of losing your head over some unscrupulous person of the opposite sex. 726

FLOOR. To dream of laying a new floor in a house is a sign of activity and profit in business. To lie on a floor predicts an alliance that will cause you misery. To sweep a floor foretells a journey that will bring you much pleasure. 277

FLOORWALKER. A woman who dreams of a floorwalker in a store will receive flowers and other simple gifts from an admirer. 858

FLOP-HOUSE. You are on the point of having to decide whether to go to a distant city if you dream of sleeping in a flop-house. 726

FLORIST. To dream of being in a florist's shop forecasts a romance for the unmarried, but for those who have wives or husbands it foretells a scandal. 304

FLOSS. Any flossy material seen or handled in a dream is a forerunner of slander and ugly gossip. 798

FLOUNDER. It is a sign that a pet project will fail to materialize if you dream of catching or eating flounder. 641

FLOUR. Any dream in which flour is used for baking is a forerunner of contentment in the home. 104

FLOW. Any kind of gentle flow is an augury of peace of mind to those who dream of it. 133

FLOWER. Luck will follow dreams of most of the garden flowers. Wild flowers predict adventure. 388

FLU. (See Grippe.) 733

FLUKE. To dream of an achievement made through a lucky fluke is an omen of a rise in salary or a small legacy. The flukes of an anchor betoken misery, but the flukes of a whale's tail are a sign of freedom from worry. 288

FLUME. A dream of a flume down a slope through a forest is a portent of increasing good fortune through the years. 088

FLUNKEY. You will be likely to have a humorous experience with one of the opposite sex if you dream of being a flunkey in uniform. To dream of having flunkeys in your employ portends embarrassment. 217

FLURRY. A flurry of snow or dust in a dream is an omen of temporary prosperity. 089

FLUTE. The sound of a flute in a dream augurs peace and contentment in family life. To dream of playing a flute predicts being caught in an embarrassing situation. 698

FLY. A dream of being annoyed by common house-flies portends a variety of difficulties with which you will have to contend. You are warned against losing your temper. If you dream of killing flies with a swatter, you will have good fortune of a minor sort. If you see flies that have been caught on flypaper, your future will be beset with many annoyances. 062

FLYING. (See Flight.) 229

FLYING FISH. Travel to the Eastern Hemisphere and a variety of odd experiences are predicted if you dream of seeing flying fish from the deck of a boat. 440

FLYPAPER. To see or use flypaper in a dream augurs getting into a jam through repeating gossip. You should regard it as a warning. To dream of seeing a cat walk across a sheet of flypaper predicts that someone will laugh at you for attempting the impossible. If you dream of sitting on flypaper or of getting your hands in it, you will be accused of taking advantage of someone. Getting it in the hair is a sign of having to defend yourself in a court of law. 576

FLYSPECK. A disgusting episode is likely to occur if you dream of seeing flyspecks on anyplace that is connected with the preparation or the serving of food. 192

FOAL. (See also Filly.) It is a sign that you wil hear interesting news, some of which will prove advantageous, if you dream of seeing a foal. If it is accompanied by a mare, the augury is especially lucky. 479

FOAM. (See also Soapsuds.) On a glass of beer or other beverage, foam seen in a dream indicates that you will have pleasure with light-hearted (and perhaps light-headed) companions. The foam generated by the propeller of a ship or motor-boat is an omen that you will travel both for business and pleasure. 743

FOG. If you dream of being in a fog at sea, there will be disturbing occurrences that will require your utmost patience and skill to overcome. If the fog lifts, the outcome will be entirely favorable. A dream of being in a fog on land is an indication of a coming dilemma that will cause you and your family much concern. 626

FOGHORN. To those who are harassed by worry and poverty a dream of hearing a foghorn offers hope of speedy relief. 188

FOLIAGE. If the foliage of trees, flowers or vegetables is fresh and green, seeing it in a dream is a pleasant augury for those who are in love. If it is brown or eaten by worms, there will be quarrels and perhaps broken engagements. 138

FOLK-SONG. As a rule, a dream of hearing people sing folk-songs forecasts much pleasure in the company of your family and friends. 265

FOLLY. A dream of folly that is not vicious indicates a calm period during which you will have an opportunity to readjust your finances so as to better your condition. 490

FOOD. (See also separate items of food.) In general a dream of seeing or eating food is auspicious; a dream of wanting it, the reverse. 280

FOOL. If you dream of playing the fool, the augury is directly along the line that the foolishness takes. You will reap according to the manner in which you sow. 804

FOOT. Looking at your own bare foot in a dream is a sign that you will laugh before you will cry and suggests that you should cultivate the habit of looking on the bright side of life. Seeing the bare foot of another signifies a new acquaintance who will prove to be an excellent friend. If the foot is deformed, you will hear disturbing news. Stocking feet betoken a mystery; with shoes on them, they point to new experiences in the company of one of the opposite sex. If someone steps on your foot, you are warned to guard your tongue lest you get into trouble. 885

FOOTBALL. You are headed toward a large sum of money if you dream of playing football before spectators. If you dream of witnessing a football game, you are warned against making friends too easily. 546

FOOTLIGHTS. Beware of entanglements with those in public life after a dream of seeing a row of footlights either from backstage or from the audience. To dream of seeing them go out predicts disaster. 166

FOOTMAN. (See Flunkey.) 536

FOP. (See Dude.) 245

FORCEPS. (See also Dentist.) To have forceps used on your teeth during a dream is a forerunner of a difficult period from which you will emerge triumphant. 881

FORECAST. To dream of hearing or reading a forecast of events is a warning to exercise great care in your behavior and your investments. 025

FOREHEAD. (See also Headache.) You may expect difficulties of a serious nature if you dream of looking at your own forehead. If the dream is of smoothing the forehead of another, you will be happy with your mate. A wrinkled forehead seen in a dream is an augury of security and peace. 519

FOREIGNER. If he or she is inclined to be friendly, a foreigner in a dream, whatever the nationality or race, is an auspicious augury. 174

FOREMAN. It betokens good tidings about money if you dream of being a foreman in a shop or of a jury. 547

FOREST. If in a dream of being in a forest you are alone and frightened, it foretells that someone will break a solemn promise made to you. 128

FOREST. If you dream of being lost in a forest, you are likely to receive a puzzling and disturbing message about an old wrong. 555

FORFEIT. To have to forfeit anything in a dream—money, honor, even a kiss— is a sign of having to make amends for a wrong you have done. 813

FORGE. It is a sign that you will make definite progress if you dream of seeing a blacksmith working at a forge. 276

FORGERY. Dire misfortune is likely to follow a dream of committing a forgery. If you dream of having your name forged to a check or document, you are warned against trusting strangers. 292

FORGETFULNESS. A dream of forgetting things is an admonition to younger persons to be kind and considerate to their elders. 672

FORGIVENESS. One may look forward to a long period of relaxation and comfort if he or she dreams of forgiving a wrong. To dream of being forgiven has much the same augury. 501

FORK. It is a sign of relief from pain if one dreams of eating with a fork. To dream of stabbing a person with a fork is a prediction of the loss of one's position. 719

FORM. A dream about the beautiful form of one of the opposite sex indicates that you will find it possible to invent a gadget that will bring you much fame and a little money. 534

FORMALITY. Any occasion in a dream that is accompanied by great formality is likely to be followed by an increase in your worldly estate. 159

FORMULA. It is a good sign for lovers if they dream of making up solutions and preparations from formulas. 164

FORNICATION. (See Adultery.) 433

FORSYTHIA. Joy of living is predicted by a dream of seeing a yellow forsythia bush in bloom. To make a bouquet of it foretells a happy love affair. 528

FORTIFICATION. A dream of fortifications is an excellent augury because these indicate defense against an enemy. To dream of being in command of a fortification is a sign of increasing responsibility and commensurate reward. 100

FORTITUDE. If in a dream you show bravery and strength of character, you are warned that these qualities will be required of you in the near future. 315

FORTUNE. A dream of a large legacy or a fortunate turn in your business affairs is a forerunner of conditions in which it will be necessary for you to exercise the best judgment at your command. 117

FORTUNE-TELLING. Having your fortune told in a dream points to a successful love life, whether or not the fortune is a favorable one. 047

FOSSIL. To find a fossil in a dream is a warning against taking things too easily in your job. If someone calls you a fossil, it is a warning against carelessness. 220

FOUNDATION. Working on the foundation for a building or a bridge is a dream that presages good over a long period. 476

FOUNDLING. To dream of finding a baby that has been abandoned by its parents and seeing that it is taken care of is an augury of peace of mind over a long period. If a woman has this dream, she may look forward to a happy wedded life. 305

FOUNDRY. Achievement is the forecast of a dream of working in any kind of a metal foundry. 515

FOUNTAIN. Frustration is predicted by a dream of a dry fountain, but if it is working and the water spurts, it augurs a contented and fruitful married life. 882

FOUNTAIN PEN. If you have any literary aspirations, a dream of using a fountain pen assures you of success. 021

FOWL. (See also Hen.) Any kind of fowl—hens, geese or ducks—seen in a dream are a sign of being able to hold up your head among the best people. 197

FOX. Beware of those who are seeking to do you harm if you dream of seeing a fox. If you dream of a fox hunt on horseback, you will be likely to receive an invitation for a week-end party. 182

FOX TERRIER. Nervous disorders are indicated by a dream of a fox terrier, but you will have good luck in your financial affairs. 468

FRACTION. It is a prediction of vexatious circumstances if you dream of figuring in fractions. 457

FRAGRANCE. Any pleasing odor in a dream is a harbinger of delight to those who are in love. 516

FRAME. The successful completion of a job or project is foretold by dreaming of putting a picture into a frame. 815

FRAME-UP. If you dream of being a party to any kind of a frame-up, you are likely to be asked for money by your creditors. If you dream of being "framed", you will find that your friends will rally round you in time of need. 046

FRANKFURTER. Eaten at a roadside stand, frankfurters predict grievous misunderstandings, but a dream of eating them at a picnic is a sign that you will work out your problems satisfactorily. 612

FRATERNITY. If a man dreams of being in a fraternity or brotherhood of any kind, he will be likely to meet influential people. 669

FRAUD. A dream of fraud perpetrated on yourself, is a warning against having a too trusting nature. If you dream of being the perpetrator, you will lose a valued friend. 221

FRECKLE. Young men or women who dream of having freckles are sure to find successful and steady-going mates. 074

FREEDOM. The sensation of freedom, felt in a dream, is a presage of contentment with the man or woman of your choice. 899

FREE LANCE. There is inspiration and an augury of happiness in a dream of being a free lance and earning your living by writing books and magazine articles, or by painting and drawing pictures. 196

FREE LOVE. (See also Adultery.) Everyone who has a dream of indulging in free love must make up his or her mind whether it is love or lust. If it is free *love*, the augury is of better days through closer attention to personal and business duties. This dream does not condone marital relations outside of marriage, but it does point toward better contacts with life. 520

FREE MASONRY. You will have many loyal friends if you dream of taking part in any of the rites of free masonry. 724

FREIGHT TRAIN. Improved business conditions may be confidently expected if you dream of riding on or seeing a freight train. 530

FRIAR. In person or in a picture, a friar seen in a dream is an augury of a pleasant, comfortable existence. 198

FRICASSEE. Whether of chicken or of veal, a fricassee in a dream is a sign that you will find it hard going for the next few weeks. 511

FRICTION. In general, a friction element in a dream predicts a heartache. 878

FRIEND. Anything in a dream that goes to prove that a person is a real friend is a wholesome and heartening prediction. 498

FRIGATE. Love affairs will come to a happy ending if you dream of seeing a frigate under full sail. At anchor, it predicts adventure of a dangerous sort. 061

FREIGHT. Things will turn out for you better than you had feared they would if you dream of being frightened; but if you dream of purposely frightening another person, you will suffer reverses. 195

FRITTER. Eating fritters—corn, clam or other varieties—is a dream that forecasts amazing adventures both with men and women. To dream of making them portends new work without additional compensation. 550

FRIVOLITY. (See Folly.) 805

FROCK COAT. A man will be criticized for loose behavior if he dreams of wearing a frock coat. You are warned against indiscretions. 615

FROG. Frogs in a dream are an omen of restfulness in your life. To hear them is an augury of steady and quiet progress in your business and community life. To eat their legs predicts that your friends will understand and love you. 266

FROLIC. It is an auspicious augury if you dream of frolicking either with children or grown-ups. You will have good luck at home and abroad. 080

FRONTIER. (See Borderland.) 844

FROST. It is an augury of an exciting experience to dream of seeing frost in patterns on a window. 991.

FROST BITE. If you dream of being frostbitten, you are warned against doing things that will endanger your health or your reputation. 925

FROSTING. There is a sermon on frivolity in a dream about the frosting on a cake—a simple warning against taking things the easiest way—going for the sweet things of life first without thinking of those which are more lasting. 825

FROST. (See Foam.) 514

FROWN. You will be pretty certain to have a humorous experience if you dream of seeing a person frown. If you dream of frowning yourself, you are likely to have an encounter with a law officer. 021

FROZEN FOODS. You will take a pleasure trip to a warm climate if you dream of eating or preparing frozen foods. 927

FRUGALITY. (See also Stinginess.) It is a sign that you will not want for creature comforts if you dream of practicing frugality in your home. 773

FRUIT. Generally speaking, fruit in a dream augurs good health if it is ripe; if it is green, the reverse. 612

FUCHSIA. This old-fashioned flower is not a good sign for those who are afflicted with skin diseases. 411

FUDGE. A warning to save money for a bad day is contained in a dream of making or eating fudge. One who dreams of buying it will have upsets in his or her love life. 473

FUGITIVE. Dreaming of being a fugitive from justice foretells a violent alter- cation with a member of your immediate family. To dream of helping a fugitive escape augurs money troubles. 450

FULLBACK. A woman who dreams of the fullback on a football team had better be on her guard against unscrupulous men. 473

FUN. Good clean fun in a dream foretells general good luck; but fun at the expense of others' feelings predicts loss of money and health. 166

FUNERAL. The death of either a relative or a friend is foretold by a dream of going to a funeral. To dream of being at your own funeral portends a national calamity. 982

FUNGUS. You are pretty certain to have tooth trouble if you dream of seeing fungus growths on trees. It is a sign that you should guard against conspir- acies of your competitors if you dream of fungus on any part of your body. 974

FUNNEL. Using a funnel in your dream to pour liquid from a container into a bottle is a sign that you will receive a message that will be difficult to understand. 946

FUNNY-BONE. It is not a funny dream where hitting the funny-bone is con- cerned, for it portends dismay at a sudden downward turn in your fortunes. 005

FUR. A woman who dreams of wearing luxurious furs is warned against the appearance of evil in her relations with men. If the furs are worn and ratty, she will be singled out for honors. A man who dreams of wearing a fur overcoat may look forward to a long season of prosperity. 830

FURLOUGH. A dream of being on a furlough from military or naval duty is a forecast of relief from pressing financial obligations. For a woman to dream of meeting a soldier on furlough presages a happy love affair. 917

FURNACE. (See also Coal.) A cold furnace seen in a dream is an omen that you will be able to add to your savings account. With a fire in it, the augury is that you will be invited to social functions. 115

FURNITURE. (See Bed, Chair, etc.) 572

FURROW. (See also Plow.) A straight furrow in a dream portends hard but productive work. If the furrow is crooked, it is a sign of new problems. 641

FURY. A dream of being in a fury foretells that you are in danger of doing something that will make you appear ridiculous. If someone else is in a fury, you are warned against loose companions. 637

FUSE. It is a sign that you are wasting your time on a useless project if you dream of having to replace an electric fuse that has blown out. 863

FUSELAGE. (See also Airplane.) You will be likely to find a sum of money if you dream of climbing in or out of the fuselage of an airplane. 804

FUTURE. Good tidings from a person you have not seen in many years may be expected from any dream that looks ahead into the future. 986

GABLE. To dream of a house with many gables is a sign that you will go adventuring. You will visit strange places, both in your own land and in foreign countries.

GALE. If you dream of going through a devastating gale, it indicates that you will have a series of misfortunes that may be partially averted if you take care in every step you take. If, aware of your own security, you dream of watching a gale, you may expect financial difficulties, but you will emerge from these battered but undefeated. 748

GALLEON. An old-time Spanish galleon, well manned and riding the waves, signifies a blessed escape from your troubles if it is seen in a dream. You will enjoy a period of peace and plenty. 545

GALLERY. Visiting an art gallery in a dream denotes a happy climax to the project on which you have set your heart. If the paintings are by the fine old masters, you will renew an old and pleasing acquaintance, but if they are of the modern school, the friends you will make will lead you on a merry chase. 218

GALLOWS. To dream of seeing a gallows is an omen of a broken engagement or a divorce. If there is a victim hanging on the gallows, you will have to overcome a great obstacle before you will be happy. 790

GALLSTONES. A dream of having gallstones foretells a bright future in spite of obstacles. 192

GALOSHES. Wearing galoshes in a dream is a forerunner of being able to save a considerable sum of money. If they are too large for you, the augury is even better, but if they leak and allow your feet to get wet, you are in danger of being called to account for some sin of omission. 042

GAMBLING. To dream of sitting in at a game of chance surrounded by gamblers of a vicious nature foretells that opportunity is on the point of knocking at your door and that you must prepare yourself to embrace it. If you dream of having losses at gambling, it portends a healthy readjustment of your mode of living; if you dream of winning, it is simply a warning against gambling. 576

GAME. Playing any game in a dream is an omen of a proposal of marriage or of a love affair that will bring you the greatest possible joy. 902

GAMEKEEPER. It is a thoroughly heartening dream to see a gamekeeper because it means that you will check up on all your affairs and adjust yourself to the manner of living that will be most advantageous to you, both spiritually and financially. 943

GAMIN. To dream of a poor little gamin, an Arab of the streets, foretells an election to public office in which you will be able to help others to help themselves. 374

GANDER. (See also Goose.) A gander in a dream warns you to watch your weight lest you become too heavy for your height. To catch and hold a gander means that you have a happy surprise in store for you. 035

GANG. If you dream of being one of a gang, it portends a weak submission to your lot and a warning against having too little initiative. To be the head of a gang foretells a curtailment of your income. To see a threatening gang of ruffians signifies a period of unrest ahead of you. You must exercise great will power to rid yourself of despondency and to force yourself to do the things that make a successful career. 905

GANGRENE. It is a sign that you will have a nagging wife or husband if you dream of a gangrenous wound. 023

GANGSTER. A dream of gangsters is an augury of easy money but a terrible catastrophe resulting therefrom. If you are captured and tortured by gangsters, you are likely to go through a long period of distress. To dream of being a gangster yourself predicts many difficulties of a financial nature. 510

GANGWAY. To dream of a gangway from a boat filled with gay, chattering, happy tourists denotes a stage of transition in your life—a change of occupation, a new home and pleasant associates. You will slip from a difficult past into an easy future. If the gangway is crowded with harassed, jostling refugees, or of people worried and fearsome of their destiny, the dream foretells a change for the worse, but it does not mean there will be a tragedy. 826

GARBAGE. Strange as it may seem, a dream of garbage is a good omen. From a small beginning you may reasonably expect to develop a big future. 758

GARDEN. Lucky is he or she who dreams of a garden in bloom, for it is a portent of happiness, not only in love and married life, but in the things of the spirit. The opposite may be expected from dreams of a garden neglected and gone to seed, for it foretells adversity and misfortune. 294

GARDENIA. To dream of the heavy-scented gardenia is a forerunner of passionate embraces from the one you love best. 363

GARGLE. Some distasteful task is predicted by a dream of gargling. You are warned that you must make the best of it and exercise sportsmanship. 505

GARGOYLE. To see a gargoyle in your dream signifies a humorous experience that will temporarily get you into hot water. 992

GARLAND. A garland of flowers is a good sign. It signifies unity of purpose. By putting your thinking cap on you will meet and jump a hurdle with ease and come out of a difficulty with flying colors. 075

GARLIC. To dream of smelling garlic foretells some achievement that will bring you recognition in the field of sports. If in your dream you use garlic as a seasoning, you will receive a letter that for a time will give you much concern. 017

GARMENT. If you wear a new garment in your dream and receive many compliments about it, you will have an invitation to spend the week-end with some new and wealthy friends. If you dream of wearing an unbecoming or torn garment, it foretells a disappointment or a pleasure that you must forego. 982

GARNET. To wear jewelry with garnets in it is not a propitious dream. Garnets are harbingers of hard work and little to show for it. To see garnets worn by others denotes a futile longing for old times. You must forget the past, and live for today. 327

GARRET. An orderly garret seen in a dream is a good sign, and it foretells family gatherings, pleasant home interests and contentment. If the garret is used as a catch-all for trunks and boxes, and is covered with dirt and cobwebs, the dream is a warning to renew your home ties before it is too late. 690

GARRISON. A garrison of troops in a dream is a sign that you should put your affairs in order. Don't be caught napping, but prepare for the future. A deserted garrison foretells disaster. 945

GARTER. To dream of your garters being unfastened indicates that you will come to grief unless you signify your disapproval of loose morals. To dream of finding a pretty feminine garter is a sign that you are at the present time skating on thin ice and you are likely to go through. For a man to dream of putting a garter on a young woman is a warning against taking chances. 190

GARTER SNAKE. It is a sure sign that someone is talking behind your back if you dream of seeing a garter snake in the out of doors. To dream of handling a garter snake is a warning against repeating ugly rumors. 497

GAS. The smell of escaping gas in a dream is a warning not to interfere in the business of other people. Seeing a victim overcome by gas predicts a scandal. Lighting a gas stove or other kind of outlets foretells the necessity to go slow in making commitments. 770

GASH. To dream of seeing a person with a deep gash in his or her body is a sign that your feelings will be hurt. It is a warning not to harbor grudges over personal slights, but to speak kindly of others even if you do not like them. 972

GAS LOG. If in a dream you see a gas log burning cheerily on the hearth, it forecasts a party at which there will be conviviality and simple good times. 146

GAS MASK. Calamity is foreboded by a dream of a person wearing a gas mask. If you dream of wearing one yourself, you will find that your creditors will be on your trail. 346

GAS METER. Seeing a man read your gas meter in a dream portends the receipt of a bill that does not concern you but which will cause you considerable inconvenience. 192

GATE. To dream of coming to an open gate predicts that there are opportunities for you ahead. A closed gate indicates that you will be thwarted in your plans for the immediate future. 095

GAUZE. Applying a gauze bandage to a cut or other wound in a dream foretells relief from harassing mental upsets. To dream of seeing a willowy young woman in a gauze dress predicts that you will be invited to an exhibition of famous paintings and sculpture. 195

GAVEL. A gavel, seen or used in a dream, portends the righting of a wrong. You will doubtless have a great deal of trouble, but if you remain firm and stick to your plan, you will come through with flying colors. 204

GELATINE. Gelatine used in a salad or dessert foretells a long walk through open country with a congenial companion of the opposite sex. If you dream of seeing powdered gelatine in a package, you will be likely to meet a famous dancer with whom you will have much in common. 993

GEM. (See also separate items.) Seeing many beautiful gems in a dream predicts fantastic happenings and a possible psychological upset. On the other hand, something unusual and unexplainable will possibly happen that will cause you much delight. 550

GENEALOGY. If you dream of studying your genealogy, you are likely to marry beneath you and rue the day. 768

GENEROSITY. A dream of being generous to your family and others predicts many honors to be showered on you. You are assured of an exalted position and more than the usual share of worldly goods. 500

GENII. Genii of the fairy tale variety in a dream are a sign of difficult but successful struggles with the world. 323

GENIUS. To dream of genius with extraordinary talents foretells an unpleasant episode caused by your jealousy. Be warned against losing a friend. 255

GENTIAN. The lovely blue gentian in its native setting is a dream promise that you will return to live in the country and enjoy again the pleasures of life close to nature. For a woman to wear a blossom is a sign that she will marry her true love. 519

GENTLEMAN. To dream of a gentleman, a man with courtly manners and kindly spirit, a man set apart and above the rest, means an invitation to the opera, a concert or some classical entertainment by someone you have not known for long but for whom you have the greatest admiration. 757

GEOGRAPHY. If you dream of studying geography, you will soon have an opportunity to visit foreign lands. 135

GERANIUMS. Geraniums in bloom in a dream foretell a journey in a trailer or a large bus. 211

GERMS. To see germs through a microscope denotes pleasure through the study of the things closest to you. To dream of being afraid that germs will attack you is an augury of a visit from distant relatives. 815

GERMANY. Dreaming of Germany and of the German people at peace denotes a full pantry in your home and peace of mind through the use of the mind. 359

GESTURE. If you see a group of people making strange gestures, the dream foretells a successful career on the stage or in the movies. 606

GIDDINESS. If you dream of feeling giddy, you will soon be called upon to make a momentous decision concerning your future and that of two near relatives. 545

GIFT. To offer a gift in a dream foretells happy responsibilities. To receive a gift denotes unexpected pleasures of a social nature. 921

GIGGLE. A dream of giggling in the midst of a solemn gathering foretells that you must pay your debts to save your honor. To see a group of giggling schoolgirls is a sign that you will be invited to see one of the current plays by an admirer. 808

GIN. Drinking gin in a dream foretells that a surprise is in store for you. To see others drinking gin denotes an unsettled state of affairs that will cause you much worriment. 341

GINGER. Tasting or smelling ginger in a dream signifies a passionate romance that may or may not turn out to your liking. 790

GINGERBREAD. To eat gingerbread in a dream portends a wedding. To bake it foretells a happy family life. 142

GINGHAM. To dream of bright-colored gingham, either in a dress or upon the counter, is a sign you have come to a crossroads. You must make a decision between two loves. 670

GIRAFFE. To see a giraffe in your dream is a warning to keep out of other people's affairs. 793

GIRDER. Trouble ahead and danger to your reputation are indicated by a dream of seeing a girder swung into place on a new building under construction. 302

GIRDLE. To dream of a girdle is a good sign. It means that you will accomplish the job that you have set out to do. 752

GIRL. To dream of a pretty girl means love, of course, but following the old adage that the course of true love never dud run smooth, you will have your ups and downs. If you dream of a homely girl, proffered love will be refused. The standard of beauty in a dream is your own taste. 188

GLACIER. If you dream of seeing a glacier on a slope or mountainside, you will go on an extended tour of northern countries. 724

GLADIOLUS. In a dream, this beautiful flower signifies that someone will make you a straightforwaard proposition to take on new responsibilities with added compensation. 989

GLAMOUR. Since this means so many things to different people, it can only be said that in general a glamorous person in a dream is a warning against indiscretion. 767

GLAND. The dream of a swollen and painful gland foretells worries over nothing in particular—worries that are perhaps foolish and unnecessary. 965

GLASS. Glassware for the table or bar, used or seen in a dream, foretells a short, sharp and unfortunate argument with a person of the opposite sex. To dream of breaking glass indicates a change in your condition of life. To dream of putting a glass pane in a window is an augury of contentment. 968

GLASS-BLOWER. Seeing a glass-blower at work in a dream presages promotion in your job, and additional compensation. 482

GLASSES. You will be fortunate n your family life if you dream of wearing glasses and you will find a way to clear up all of your obligations. 389

GLEN. To dream of being in a mountain glen portends the recurrence of an old ailment if you are alone. If you are accompanied by one of the opposite sex, you will be able to look forward to better relations with your family. 053

GLIDER. In a glider, or airplane without an engine, riding the winds is a portent of regaining the respect and cooperation of a business friend who will wish you to help revive a dormant business. 586

GLOBE. Dreaming of a globe of any material—metal, glass, wood, etc.— foretells a great many new diversions and the wherewithal to enjoy them. A globe map is an omen of wide travel and adventure. 490

GLOOM. If in any dream there appears to be an atmosphere of gloom, you are likely to be afflicted with severe headaches. 675

GLOVE. Gloves worn in a dream portend security, marital happiness and pleasant surroundings. New gloves, never worn, assure one of promotion to a higher-salaried position. 467

GLUE. To dream of spilling glue on your clothing is a sign that you are likely to be held up by a robber. If you dream of using glue to mend anything, you will lose money through unwise investments. 673

GLUTTON. Seeing a glutton eat in a dream signifies that you will be snowed under with invitations to social functions. You should try to accept as many of these as possible, for they will help you in your business career. If you dream of acting the part of glutton, you will be successful but not popular. 236

GNASHING. If you dream of gnashing your teeth in rage, it is a sign that you will become embroiled in some low affair, and that you will suffer humiliation. 168

GNAT. To dream of gnats is to be warned against investing in any proposition that you have not thoroughly investigated. 194

GNAWING. Much trouble that will be your own fault is predicted by a dream of gnawing a bone. 699

GNOME. The augury of a dream in which gnomes and other unreal people are figures is that you will have to face a certain problem and that the sooner you do so, the better off you will be. 598

GNU. To see one of these animals in your dream is a warning to spend more time out of doors. 237

GOAL. Reaching the goal you have set for yourself is a dream that augurs success. If you dream of playing a game in which there is a goal, and you are successful in reaching it, you will find that new friends and new opportunities will come to you. 492

GOAT. Grazing goats seen in a dream are a warning against associating your self with any enterprise in which there is the slightest suspicion of graft. General irritations will follow a dream of milking a female goat. 923

GOATEE. To dream of a man wearing a goatee is a warning against taking chances with your health. If you wear one yourself, the omen is of scandal. 971

GOBLET. To dream of drinking water out of a goblet portends a quarrel with someone you know slightly. If the goblet holds beer, you will be welcomed into the homes of wealthy people. To break a goblet is an omen of losing a small amount of money. 238

GOD. Any dream in which you seen to be standing in the presence of God is an augury of new opportunities to be of service to the world. It is also a promise of peace through adjustment to circumstances. 057

GODPARENT. If you dream of being a godfather or a godmother, you will be enabled to engage in a new business under propious circumstances. 758

GOGGLES. Wearing goggles or sun-glasses in a dream signifies that you will be called a flirt and taunted for your boldness. 841

GOITER. To dream of having goiter indicates that you will have petty anxieties that will be depressing to you but that can easily be overcome. 353

GOLD. To dream of gold is an indication that you are avericious, and that because of your miserly inclinations you will suffer the loss of many good friends. To dream of mining for gold signifies dissatisfaction with your home surroundings. 883

GOLD BRICK. If you foolishly buy a gold brick in your dream and are chagrined, it denotes a secret shame that you are trying to hide from the world. 016

GOLDENROD. To dream of seeing goldenrod growing by the roadside is a warning to stop meddling in your friends' affairs. To gather goldenrod denotes a new friend who will teach you many things that are worthwhile. 920

GOLDEN RULE. If you dream of following the golden rule, you will be able to learn to play some stringed instrument. 691

GOLDFISH. A woman who dreams of seeing goldfish in a bowl or aquarium is warned to make sure that her shades are drawn when she retires to her room. Peeping Toms will be seeking to look in on her. 799

GOLF. To play golf in your dreams means that you will turn over a new leaf and be able to right a wrong. 137

GONDOLA. To dream of a gondola on one of the canals of Venice signifies a honeymoon on foreign shores. 066

GONG. To hear a gong clanging in your dreams is A warning to go back to your former occupation. If you do this, you will make a success of it. 779

GOOD FRIDAY. If you dream of going to church on Good Friday, you will be rewarded for the patience and care you have given to one of your family. 294

GOOSE. To dream of seeing a goose in a barnyard is a sign that you should watch the scales. Correct your diet, either to reduce or put on weight, according to the doctor's orders. It is a sign that you will enjoy good health if your diet includes plenty of goose-grease. 314

GOOSEBERRY. Eating gooseberries from the bush in a dream is a forecast of being derided in public for some folly for which you are not directly responsible. To make or eat gooseberry jam is a sign that you will get a ticket from a traffic officer on a highway. 685

GOOSEFLESH. If gooseflesh breaks out all over your body in a dream, you will fall in love with a good-natured fat person who is not particularly moral. 655

GOPHER. If you should see one of these little rodents in a dream, the augury is of poor business and troubles within the family circle. 282

GORE. (See Blood.) 555

GORILLA. A dream of a terrifying gorilla that haunts you even after you are awake is a portent of an embarrassing moment in which you will be misunderstood and unjustly criticized. 380

GOSPEL. If you dream of reading the gospel, you will soon be able to confer a favor on someone who is in a position to do you a great deal of good. 259

GOSSIP. To dream of being the object of malicious gossip, you will quarrel in some public place with strangers who are likely to have the better end of the argument. If you dream of idly gossiping about another, you will be involved in the love affair of another person. 786

GOSSIP. If you dream of being with people who are gossiping, you are bound to have disagreements over one or more wills in which you are mentioned. If you dream of being accused of malicious gossip by a person of either sex, you are warned against repeating confidences. 807

GOSSIP. If you dream of being with people who are gossiping, you are bound to have disagreements over one or more wills in which you are mentioned. If you dream of being accused of malicious gossip by a person of either sex, you are warned against repeating confidences. 807

GOULASH. A merry weekend party is foretold by a dream of eating Hungarian goulash. 197

GOURD. A gourd used or seen in a dream, is a sign of friendship, amiable companions and comfort. 403

GOUT. To dream of having gout foretells postponement of a long anticipated visit to old friends. It is also a warning to cut down on your consumption of alcoholic beverages. 906

GOVERNOR. If you dream of seeing or meeting the governor of your State, you will soon be able to buy a new automobile. 707

GOWN. A new gown in a dream denotes to a woman a desire to be the center of interest. You will bbe, but it will not be entirely satisfactory to you. A dream of wearing an old and ragged gown is a sign that a skeleton will be dragged out of the closet. 486

GRACE. To say grace in a dream before partaking of food is an omen of receiving a handsome gift that you will always treasure. 675

GRADUATION. To dream of being present at a graduation, whether as a participant or a spectator, denotes a rise in fortune and a much better position in business and social life. 963

GRAFTER. To dream of being approached by a grafter is a sign that you contemplate some questionable undertaking. You are warned against trying to make easy money. 007

GRAIL. A dream of the Holy Grail foretells that you will be called upon to share your estate with others. This omen is one that should be taken very seriously. 333

GRAIN. Feeding grain to horses or cattle n a dream is a sign of prosperity for you and your family. Handling bags of grain portends a visit from relatives. 544

GRAMMAR. It is bad luck to dream of correcting another person's grammar, but good luck if someone else corrects yours. 816

GRANARY. To dream of a full granary is a sign that your wishes will be fulfilled. To see an empty granary foretells a lonely heart. 847

GRAND JURY. A lawyer who dreams of seeing a grand jury in session is likely to be accused of malpractice. Anyone who dreams of sitting on a grand jury is in danger of being accused of double dealing. 201

GRANDPARENT. If you dream of your grandfather, you will receive high honors from the community in which you live. A dream of your grandmother is an omen of plenty. 485

GRANGE. If you dream of being a member of a grange, you will be called to officiate at a meeting of a community group. 725

GRANITE. To dream of blocks of granite portends sickness and a slow recovery. 192

GRAPES. A dream of picking grapes and eating the luscious fruit augurs well for you. You will be appointed to a high position and will be able to set aside enough money for a rainy day. 349

GRAPEFRUIT. Golden grapefruit eaten in a dream foretells a division of interest. Your love affairs, business and sports will draw you in varying directions. 334

GRASS. If you dream of green grass bordering a flower garden, you will make money at the same time that you are making love. Brown, sunburned grass, neglected and gone to seed, predicts that you will have to work very hard for what you get. 068

GRASSHOPPER. To dream of grasshoppers foretells unsettled times ahead. You will be bewildered by the complexities of life. You are advised too take advice from your elders. 840

GRATE. If you dream of sitting before an open grate with a brisk fire burning, you will have many convivial companions and not a few good friends. 540

GRAVE. A grave freshly banked with flowers is an omen of a broken vow. A forsaken grave means that unkept promises will cause you many a heartache. 901

GRAVEL. If you dream of driving a car over coarse gravel, you will court a girl who is on the stage, and you should beware of skidding. 411

GRAVESTONE. (See also Grave.) To dream of seeing a new gravestone in a lot where the other stones are moss covered is an omen of having a new chance to make good. Old gravestones in a rural cemetery are a sign that you will meet a long lost friend at an opportune time. 639

GRAVY. If you dream of passing a bowl of gravy at a dinner party, you are likely to overlookan opportunity that might have brought you fame and fortune. If you dream of making gravy, you are sure to select the lucky number in a lottery. 787

GREASE. Getting grease on your clothes in a dream portends a stupid blunder that will make you simply sit down and think things over. You are warned to use the judgment with which you were endowed. To dream of greasy pots and pans or dishes predicts that you are likely to rush in where angels fear to tread. Be advised especially against giving advice where it is not asked—and then be careful. 943

GREAT LAKES. To dream of flying over the Great Lakes or driving around them or sailing on them is an augury that you are likely to be stuck in one position all your life. It is a warning to get out of the rut you are in. 924

GREEK. To dream of either modern or ancient Greeks is a sign that you will be very successful in your business ventures. 261

GREEK CROSS. Good luck may be confidently expected after a dream in which the Greek cross figures. 612

GREENBACK. If you dream of finding a greenback of whatever denomination, you will be likely to ask a friend for a loan. If you dream of having a pocketful of greenbacks, it is a sign that you will soon be in need of financial assistance. 912

GREENHOUSE. To dream of being in a greenhouse, smelling the damp earth and vegetation therein, is a sign of a bright future. Love, laughter and adventure will be yours. 760

GREEN ROOM. If you dream of an actors' green room, you will soon be able to rest on your laurels and enjoy the satisfaction of your art. 133

GRENADE. (See Hand Grenade.) 507

GREYHOUND. To dream of seeing a greyhound running foretells a sudden collapse of your plans for the future. 369

GRIDDLE CAKES. If you dream of making griddle cakes, the portent is that your love will be sought by at least two ardent suitors. To eat griddle cakes in a dream means that you will have a love affair with the next dark-eyed person you meet. 528

GRIDIRON. A football gridiron in a dream, if a game is being played, is a sign that you will have an interesting time with one of the opposite sex. 952

GRIEF. To dream of being grief-stricken portends a slight digestive disturbance that may lead to amore serious ailment if not given proper attention. 378

GRILL. Being in a grill and surrounded by many people of both sexes points toward an affair of the heart with a married person. 974

GRIN. It is a sign, if in your dream you see a person grin, that you will be sent tickets for a high class concert or stage performance. If you grin at someone else, you are likely to achieve some success as an amateur actor or actress. 180

GRINDSTONE. To dream of turning a grindstone is a sign that you will encounter hazards in your business but that through attention to the ins and outs you will overcome them. 989

GRIT. If you dream of eating grit in your food—spinach, asparagus or what not—you will be compelled to retract some statement that you have made about another person. 588

GROAN. To groan in your dream signifies that your last year's income tax is likely to be investigated. If in your dream you hear another person groan, the augury is of an unfulfilled wish. 601

GROCERY. To dream of a grocery store well stocked with goods is a sign that you will meet with success and be able to take time out for a pleasant vacation. 338

GROOM. Seeing a groom in a dream currying a horse means that you will make an overland trip within a fortnight. A man or woman who dreams of a bridegroom will not be married within the year. 392

GROTTO. A grotto deep in the earth, or a religious retreat in a mountainside, foretells an illness of a muscular nature that will be cured through faith and taking good care of your health. 641

GROUND HOG. If you dream of seeing a ground hog, you are apt to fall in love with a genius. This may or may not be a fortunate dream. 830

GROVE. To dream of a grove of trees is a sign that you will preside over a meeting where there will be many people who will hold different opinions. 374

GROWL. Hearing a dog growl in a dream means that you are likely to have an encounter with a person whom you have never liked but who never gave you any real cause for actual criticism. 751

GRUNT. Hearing an animal grunt in a dream means that you will have to consider changing the kind of work that you are doing. If you dream of grunting yourself, you will be likely to have a troublous experience. 883

GUARD. If you dream of seeing a police guard for any kind of valuables, it foretells the loss of some sort of valuables. If the dream is of your being on guard, the prediction is of an increase in salary. 119

GUARDIAN. To dream of being made guardian of a young person forecasts many worries arising from both financial affairs and the criticism of your friends. 770

GUERNSEY. To dream of Guernsey cattle signifies that someone will ask you for a small loan. 678

GUEST. Entertaining guests in a dream is an augury of great satisfaction through an achievement. To dream of being a guest in another's home is a sign that you will shortly take a trip to a city you have never visited before. 439

GUIDE. If you dream of being a guide to someone from out of town, you will have an opportunity to make money through a new invention. If you are the one to be guided, the augury is of a discovery that is likely to make a great deal of money for you. 948

GUIDE BOOK. Referring to a guidebook in a dream signifies that you will attend a cocktail party at which there will be many famous people present. 786

GUILLOTINE. You will have a serious misunderstanding with a friend if you dream of seeing a person brought to the guillotine. If you dream of being the victim, you are in great danger of an illness that may prove fatal. 037

GUITAR. To dream of playing a guitar is a sign that you are apt to have your pocket picked. Listening to a guitar in a dream is a portent of pleasant love affairs. 803

GULL. If you dream of seeing ulls flying, you are very likel to have adventure of an exciting but innocent nature. 236

GUM. Chewing gum in a dream is a sign that your best girl will break a date with you; or, if you are a woman, it warns against too much familiarity with men you have but recently met. 235

GUM DROPS. To dream of gum drops means that you will see a friend or a relative whom you have not seen for many months or years. 897

GUN. Injustice either to you or to one of your family or friends is foretold by a dream of firing a gun—a pistol, rifle, shot-gun, or large-calibered cannon. To hear the sound of guns in a dream is a sign of unrest. 928

GUTTER. A dream of lying in a gutter predicts a period through which you will pass in which you will have many things to explain. Trying to clean out a gutter in a dream is a sign that you will be successful in the next job you undertake. 930

GYMNASIUM. Gymnasium exercises in a dream augur invitations to functions on the same date, and consequent embarrassment. 007

GYPSY. Amorous adventures are predicted by a dream about gypsies. If a gypsy tells your fortune, you are likely to find a mate. 408

H

HABERDASHERY. Clean haberdashery—shirts, collars, neckties, scarves—is a fortunate augury when seen in a dream. If these articles are soiled, the omen is of business failure. 267

HABIT. To dream of having formed a habit—drink, tobacco, drug, etc.—is a portent of difficulty in social relationships. 477

HABITATION. (See Home.) 884

HADDOCK. Lovers may look forward to unhappiness but eventual marriage if they dream of eating this kind of fish. 152

HADES. (See Hell.) 494

HAG. No good comes of a dream of a hag. Men will find themselves snubbed by their sweethearts, and women will have disillusioning experiences. 962

HAIL. A hailstorm in a dream is a forerunner of a succession of grievous occurrences. 264

HAIR. Combing onne's hair in a dream signifies a solution of annoying problems. To comb another's hair indicates that you will be called upon to help a friend, and if you are wise, you will help him or her. If you comb the hair of a person of the opposite sex, you will be able to solve any sex problems that you may have. To have your hair cut is a sign of success in a new sphere of life. To cut another's hair is a warning against those who are unfriendly to you. To braid your own hair signifies that someone will make an explanation to you; to braid another's is a sign that you will have to explain something. For a woman to wave her hair portends new men friends, but if a man dreams of waving his hair, it is an omen of shame. 884

HAIRDRESSER. A woman who dreams of going to a hairdresser should guard against repeating any scandalous gossip she may hear. 647

HAIRPIN. Happy is the man who dreams of seeing a woman arranging her hair wit hairpins. If there are hairpins in her mouth, so much the better. He can look forward to a calm and fruitful married life. It is also a good sign to dream of making minor repairs to machinery with hairpins. 175

HALF-BREED. If you dream of a half-breed Indian, you are likely to have an exciting adventure, but you should be on guard against treachery. 128

HALF COCK. To dream of carrying a gun or pistol at half cock is a warning against losing your temper. If you dream of such a weapon going off half-cocked, you are bound to regret a hasty action. 880

HALF DOLLAR. If you dream of receiving a bright new silver half dollar in change or for payment, you are likely to have a disappointing experience. 590

HALF-MAST. A flag at half-mast seen in a dream is a sign of calamity, although it does not necessarily portend death. 920

HALF MOON. In a clear sky a half-moon is an omen of travel to foreign lands. If the sky is partially obscured by clouds, the portent is one of dissatisfaction with your position. Guard against complaining to your boss. 303

HALITOSIS. To dream of seeing a person turn away from you in disgust because you have halitosis is a warning against too great self-assertiveness. If you dream of another person's having it, the omen is of either a business or social obstacle that will have to be overcome. 879

HALL. You may as well make up your mind to be ready for a long period of fear and worry if you dream of being alone in a long hall. 962

HALLELUJAH. This exclamation of joy, heard or spoken in a dream, is a portent of the succesful culmination of an ardent love affair. 308

HALLOWE'EN. To dream of high jinks on Hallowe'en presages increased influence in club, church, lodge or community liife. 143

HALLUCINATION. If you dream of having hallucinations, you will be called upon to testify in behalf of a friend. Be on your guard against perjuring yourself. 891

HALO. To see a person wearing a halo in a dream predicts a death among your circle of close friends. If the halo is on someone you know, it foretells a death in your family. If it is on yourself, it predicts travel to a far-off land. If you dream of taking off a halo, you will have business advancements. 754

HALTER. Putting a halter on a horse in a dream is a sign that you will be able to control your own destiny in spite of the forces that seem to be working against you. 299

HAM. Smoking hams in a dream is a sign of a year of plenty. To dream of baking a ham augurs a difficult time that will work out to your ultimate good. If you dream of eating ham in any forms—smoked or fresh—you will be lucky in business affairs. 456

HAMLET. A dream of a hamlet, or small village, is an augury of defeat in a project that is close to your heart. To dream of Shakespeare's play "Hamlet" predicts that you will have much comfort in the bosom of your family. 806

HAMMER. Using a hammer in a dream, whether for driving a nail or for other purposes, predicts an achievement for women and an accident for men. 294

HAMMOCK. Sitting in a hammock alone in a dream foretells a succession of irritations arising from a selfish attitude. If you are with a person of the opposite sex, it predicts wholesome recreations. 778

HAMPER. It is a sign that you will make progress if you dream of putting soiled clothing into a hamper. 989

HAND. A dream of any beautiful hands is an augury of satisfaction in life. A dream of busy, skillful hands predicts recreation aftter toil. If you dream of bent and gnarled hands, you will find relief from your financial worries.

Waving hands predict separations. Caressing hands foretell romance and marriage. 444

HANDBAG. A mystery is predicted if you dream of a lady's handbag. To dream of a woman or girl opening and looking through a handbag foretells an episode in which all your sympathies will be brought into play. 039

HANDBALL. It is a sign that you have varying fortunes for a period but final success if you dream of playing handball. 669

HANDBILL. A dream of distributing handbills is an augury of great content in your everyday life. To dream of seeing handbills strewn around the street is a prophecy of an upset condition. 926

HANDCUFF. If you dream of having handcuffs snapped on your wrists, there is no need to worry about an encounter with the law, but a man who has this dream will have mother-in-law complications if he is married, and if he is single, he will be likely to be criticized by his boss. A woman having the dream should guard her good name. If you dream of putting handcuffs on another, the augury is of an unexpected promotion. 993

HAND GRENADE. The deepest shame may be expected after a dream of throwing a hand grenade. It is also a warning not to do anything against your better judgment. 222

HANDICAP. To succeed in a dream in spite of a handicap is a sign that you will have a better position offered to you. If you dream of receiving a handicap in any kind of contest, you will be very likely to make a success in business. 995

HANDICRAFT. It is a fortunate augury of better times if you dream of being skilled in handicrafts such as weaving, wood-working, book-binding, printing and the like. You will always be able to make a living. 917

HADKERCHIEF. To dream of using the handkerchief for blowing the nose is a prophecy of an increase in your income; for wiping perspiration from your forehead, release from worry. If you wave your handkerchief to someone, you will have an interesting though not passionate love affair. To wash a handkerchief is a sign of losing money. 911

HANDSPRING. Women who dream of doing handsprings had better keep a watchful eye on their behavior while in the company of young men. A man having this dream should be careful to keep his mind on his work. 518

HANDWRITING. It is a sign that you will succeed in business undertakings if you dream of trying to decipher illegible handwriting in a letter or document. To dream of reading handwriting of the "copperplate" variety means that you must be on your guard against deception. means that you must be on your guard against deception. 374

HANDY MAN. Enlisting the services of a handy man in a dream for any sort of cleaning or repairs portends a series of difficulties with your landlord. 520

HANGAR. You are certain to have a rise in your fortunes if you dream of being locked in a hangar where airplanes are kept, but if the hangar is empty, you will suffer disappointment and chagrin. 649

HANGER. It is a sign of freedom from care if you dream of putting away a suit of clothes or a dress on a hanger in a closet. 875

HANGING. To be present at the hanging of a condemned person in a dream is a prophecy of having to give an alibi of some sort. 563

HANGMAN. You will have worries aplenty if you dream of fulfilling the duties of a hangman. It is a distinct warning against being too critical of your friends. 432

HANGNAIL. An ailment that, unless it is given prompt and careful attention, may lead to serious consequences is predicted by a dream of having a hangnail. If you dream of pulling it off, the dream signifies an even worse state of affairs. 637

HANGOVER. This is a serious dream for a single woman to have. She must be very careful not to make any false moves where young men are concerned. For men or married people the dream portends relaxation from worries regarding their financial affairs. 699

HAPPINESS. After a dream in which you get the impression of happiness, you are advised to take particular care not to do anything that may impair your health. A dream of happy children is a pleasant augury. 051

HARA-KIRI. This Japanese method of suicide by disembowelment is a sign of distressing circumstances both in your personal and business life. 374

HARANGUE. You will have difficulties with your relatives if you dream of delivering a harangue to several persons. If you dream of listening to a harangue, you will be likely to be given a civil service job. 247

HARBOR. To dream of coming into a harbor in a sailboat or steamship denotes that you will be successful in meeting your obligations. If the ship is leaving a harbor, you will doubtless take a trip abroad. 817

HARDWARE. Many items of hardware seen in a dream is an omen of general good fortune in business. 940

HARE. To kill a hare in a dream predicts a change of occupation. To eat a hare is an omen of good times. To prepare a hare for the table forecasts pleasant family surroundings. 770

HAREM. A woman who dreams of being a member of a harem is apt to have upsets in her love life. A man who dreams of keeping a harem had better watch his step, or he will be criticized. 387

HARLEQUIN. Dancing in a pantomime with the fair Columbine, Harlequin in a dream is an augury of happy hours in the company of your best-beloved. 386

HARLOT. Dreaming or harlots is a sign of impending illness for a man, but if a woman dreams of being a harlot, she will be likely to have good news from an unexpected source. 576

HARMONICA. Played in tune and with a vivacious lilt, a harmonica in a dream portends pleasant hours spent in the company of one's best beloved. 588

HARMONY. There can be no other interpretation of a harmony dream than that harmony in your life is predicted. 064

HARNESS. (See also Halter.) It is an augury of an interesting achievement of a minor nature if you dream of putting a harness on a horse or other animal. 642

HARP. Playing a harp in a dream portends a reawakening of your spiritual life. If you see a beautiful woman playing a harp, you will find that someone will do you a favor of considerable importance. 334

HARPOON. To dream of having a harpoon buried in your body is an omen of great distress over the loss of money. Using it on a large fish or a whale portends increased earning capacity and a better place in which to live. 264

HARPSICHORD. A tuneful harpsichord on which is played refined music is a favorable augury to those in love. Jazz or swing music played on a harpsichord portends a puzzling experience. 159

HARVEST. It is a sign of good circumstances if you dream of gathering a satisfactory harvest, but if it is disappointing, you are likely to have difficult ties in business. 888

HARVEST MOON. Lovers will come into their own if they dream of a large harvest moon. If it becomes obscured by mist, the augury is of quarrels that should not be allowed to become serious. 254

HASH. A dream of hash predicts that something will happen that for a time wiill be unexplainable. To make hash in a dream is a sign of having trouble with machinery; to eat it portends a mystery. 467

HASHISH. (See Marihuana.) 072

HASSOCK. To dream that you are a child sitting on a hassock at the feet of someone you love is an augury of peace after a period of distress. 052

HASTE. To do anything in a great hurry in a dream augurs difficulties that you could have avoided by exercising a little forethought and care. You are warned against doing your work in a hurried and sloppy manner. 153

HAT. For a gentleman to dream of lifting his hat to a lady is a sign of promotion in business. If he dreams of keeping his hat on under such circumstances, he will meet with a puzzling problem that will require skillful handling. To dream that your hat is blown off by the wind portends irritations in business. It is a sign of good fortune that will arrive soon if you dream of buying a new hat. To wear a hat that is much too small for you predicts a heartache; if it is too large, you will be called to account for an indiscretion. 060

HATCHET. It is an augury of disturbances both at home and in the business world to dream of cutting down a tree with a hatchet. To split kindling wood with a hatchet predicts that you will make up any differences you may have with your family. It is a sign of an increased income if you dream of sharpening a hatchet. 124

HATE. Sad happenings are forecast if you dream of hating anyone, but if you dream that someone hates you, the augury is of an improvement in your affairs. 481

HAUGHTINESS. Watch out if you dream of acting in a haughty manner to another person, but if someone similarly tries to snub you, there will be a mildly amusing experience in the near future. 967

HAVOC. For whtever cause—wind, rain, fire or other disaster—a dream of the havoc that has been wrought bespeaks a new opportunity for you before long. 516

HAWAIIAN. (See also Hula Hula.) If they are in their native costumes, Hawaiians seen in a dream foretell stirring adventures in love. Dressed in European clothes, they are an augury of boredom. 196

HAWK. A hawk flying augurs new business opportunities. Otherwise it foretells a period of depression. 038

HAWSER. Reaching from a large boat and made fast to a dock, a hawser is an augury of a secure future for yourself and family. To dream of seeing a hawser break foretells dire happenings from the effect of which you will find it difficult to escape. 252

HAY. Contrary to what might be expected, to dream of making hay under sunny skies is a sign that you will lose money and get into debt. If it is cloudy, the dream is of beetter import, for you will receive money that you never expected to get. It is a good sign to dream of playing in a haystack; it is a presage of happy love affairs to young men and women. 664

HAY FEVER. No good will come of a dream of suffering from hay fever unless you take it as a warning to guard your health. 238

HEAD. A disembodied head seen in a dream is a sign of a new situation in your life that must be met with fortitude and good sense. 600

HEADACHE. To dream of suffering from a headache indicates that if you will keep your own counsel regarding your job and your investments, you will make a success of a pet project. 751

HEADDRESS. (See also Hat.) An opportunity will be offered for you to make progress in your community if you dream of seeing a striking headdress on a woman of the Old World. 795

HEAD HUNTER. A dream of being captured by head-hunting savages is a prediction that you will have a chance to retaliate for a wrong that has been done you. It is also a warning against associating with wild company. 322

HEADLIGHT. One or more glaring headlights coming toward you in a dream, either on an automobile or a railroad locomotive, are a portent of a disaster that you can avert only by quick and decisive action. 953

HEADLINE. To dream of seeing your name in a newspaper headline is an augury of an unpleasant occurrence in your neighborhood. 741

HEADSTONE. If you dream of erecting a headstone on a grave, you will have to call upon a friend to help you out of trouble. A headstone that has fallen over portends a narrow escape. To dream of reading your own name on a headstone is an omen of exciting news from afar—perhaps to your great advantage. 766

HEALTH. Accent on health in a dream ortends joy to the dreamer. 639

HEARSE. It is a sign of increasing responsibilities if you dream of being asked to ride with the driver of a hearse. To dream of occupying the interior of a hearse predicts a sudden business trip. 414

HEART. The augury of a dream of losing one's heart to a person of the opposite sex is of meeting a new and eligible person. To dream of having a heart attack augurs many years of happy and productive living. 513

HEARTACHE. For whatever reason, a heartache in a dream predicts better times through a release from worrisome responsibilities. 667

HEARTBURN. An attack of heartburn felt in a dream presages a return to simpler pleasures than those to which you have become accustomed. 594

HEARTH. (See Fireplace.) 432

HEAT. To dream of suffering from heat is a portent of having to apologiize to someone for an ill-advised action or remark. 759

HEATER. (See Furnace.) 653

HEATHEN. Unfortunate is he or she who dreams of referring to a person of another faith as a heathen. 468

HEATHER. Lying in the heather under a sunny sky is a dream that portends simple but lasting pleasures. If the sky is cloudy, the portent is of hard work and little reward. Heather at night predicts sorrow. 069

HEAT STROKE. To dream of passing out because of extreme heat is a presage of difficulties of a physiological nature. 696

HEAVEN. Dying and going to heaven in a dream portends a new and more difficult job; and it may be a better one for you. 715

HEBREW. (See Jew.) 238

HEDGE. It portends good luck to dream of clipping a hedge; bad luck to dream of jumping over one. If you dream of crawling hrough an opening in a hedge, you will be snubbed by a society matron. 871

HEDGEHOG. (See Porcupine.) 180

HEEL. If you dream of losing a heel from one of your shoes, you will find yourself at odds with long-established friends. To dream of nailing a heel on one of your shoes is a portent that you will make a social error. A dream of rubber heels is an omen that you will be deceived. 573

HEIFER. (See Calf, Cow.) 625

HEIR. A small sum of money will be yours if you dream of falling heir to a large fortune. 721

HEIRLOOM. The significance of an heirloom in a dream is one of dignity in your association with the people you meet. 332

HELIOTROPE. This old-fashioned purple flower predicts a quiet and sensible love affair to the unmarried and a secure future to all who dream of it. 626

HELIUM. Safe and profitable investments are forecast by a dream of this gas used for inflating dirigible balloons. 546

HELL. A dream of the orthodox hell described by Dante and the great religionists of old and illustrated by Dore and such artists is a sign that you will have an easier time financially but that you will have disagreements with your neighbors. If you dream of going through "hell on earth", you are warned that you should try harder to understand people you do not like. 145.

HELMET. If you dream of seeing soldiers wearing steel helmets, you will have an internal disturbance that may prove serious. To wear a helmet yourself portends better health. 289

HELP. A dream of calling for help is a sign that you will shortly need help, and get it. If you dream of hearing a call for help and answer it, you will find that you are in a good position to make money. 897

HEM. To stitch or sew a hem on a garment or other piece of cloth denotes the completion of a creditable job. 556

HEMORRHAGE. Any kind of a hemorrhage seen in a dream—whether it is yours or another's—is a warning against over-exertion in both manual and mental work. 859

HEMORRHOIDS. A dream of this affliction, commonly known as piles, is a warning against foolishly exposing yourself to physical danger or contagious diseases. 747

HEMP ROPE. (See also Rope.) The successful termination of a long and arduous job is portended by seeing a coil of new hemp rope. To uncoil it presages the beginning of an important piece of work. To make a noose with a hemp rope is a prediction of misfortune. A mystery will be unraveled for you if you dream of seeing the manufacture of hemp rope. 867

HEN. General comforts in life varied by ups and downs and family worries are predicted by a dream of feeding hens. To dream of seeing a hen sitting on eggs is a sign of plenty. Killing a hen in a dream signifies a visitor. Plucking a hen means that you will have to spend more money than you had planned to. 765

HENNA. New scenes and new friends are promised the woman who dreams of putting henna on her hair. 415

HEN-PECKING. A man who dreams of being hen-pecked is warned thereby against losing his temper. 655

HERALD. To dream of seeing a young man in the costume of a herald delivering a message of importance is a forecast of an advance in your fortunes. 909

HERALDRY. (See Coat of Arms.) 378

HERB. Contentment in your daily life, in love and in marriage is predicted by a dream of growing herbs in a garden. The pungent, unusual aroma of herbs in a dream is a sign of new and pleasing adventures. 393

HERESY. A dream of being accused of heresy foretells that you will assert yourself in your community and thereby make greater progress than formerly. 976

HERITAGE. (See Legacy.) 676

HERMAPHRODITE. You will have many disquieting experiences if you dream of being a hermaphrodite. If you dream of seeing one, you must behave with more circumspection in the company of the opposite sex. 886

HERMIT. To dream of visiting a hermit in his retreat portends the early solution of a vexing problem. If he or she shows anger, this solution will cause you no end of trouble. 850

HERNIA. (See Rupture.) 086

HERO. If in a dream you appear to play a hero's part by doing brave acts in the face of death, you are likely to be criticized by someone younger than yourself or called to account by your employer for unseemly actions. To dream of seeing a heroic act performed by another is a sign that you will engage in a new business deal and make a handsome profit. 521

HEROIN. (See also Marihuana.) You will be despised by someone whose good opinion you value highly if you dream of experimenting with this drug. 797

HERON. Things will move faster in your business career if you dream of herons, and the gains will be greater than the losses. 104

HERRING. Smoked herring eaten in a dream is a portent that warns against over-indulgence in wines and hard liquors. To buy herring foretells that people will be suspicious of your actions. 820

HICCOUGH. A dream of hiccoughing seldom comes except in connection with liquor, and therefore it is to be regarded as a warning against drinking too much. 952

HICKORY. Using the wood of the hickory tree in a dream foretells hard going in your business. Eating hickory nuts predicts that you will succeed in the job you are doing. 500

HIDE. A dream of the hides of animals is a sign that you will be invited to take a vacation with a wealthy friend. 164

HIEROGLYPHICS. Dreaming of making an attempt to read the hieroglyphics or inscriptions on ancient Egyptian monuments is an augury of making a discovery that will bring you renown. 930

HIGHBALL. To drink one highball in a dream—either Scotch or rye—is a good augury. To drink two or more forecasts an argument with an associate. 101

HIIGHBROW. If someone calls you a highbrow in a dream you will be shamed by a person for whom you have little regard. To dream of a person who shows evidences of being a highbrow portends that you will distinguish yourself by an intellectual achievement. 876

HIGH JINKS. If the high jinks in your dream are conducted among low company, you are likely to be successful in business dealings with people of inferior intelligence, but you will get no personal satisfaction therefrom. 084

HIGH SCHOOL. To dream of being back in your high school days is a sign of a love affair that will be both exciting and disturbing. 642

HIGH TIDE. There is great promise in a dream of high tide. You should take the greatest possible advantage of any opportunities you may have offered after such a dream. 121

HILARITY. If you dream of being hilarious at a gathering of men and women, the augury is of time-wasting festivities. 460

HILL. To dream of climbing a hill augurs some small success. Standing or sitting on the top is a sign of an established income and contentment. 140

HINDU. A mysterious but enjoyable person will come into your life if you dream of associating with one or more Hindu men or women. 409

HINGE. A rusty hinge in a dream foretells difficult times in connection with personal affairs. One that squeaks is a prediction that someone will be cruel to you, either physically or mentally. 867

HIP. For a man to dream of a woman who is carrying a burden of any kind on her hip is a portent of a love affair in a foreign land. To dream of the naked hips of a person of the opposite sex betokens a succession of small troubles. 750

HIPPOPOTAMUS. You will soon have to run to escape danger if you dream of a hippoptamus in its native lair. If it is seen in a zoological park, you will run the risk of being very much bored by people from whom you cannot escape. 171

HISS. To hear a snake hiss in a dream portends that you wil make a grave mistake through not controlling your temper. It is an augury that you will be held in contempt if you dream of hissing at an actor or a speaker. To dream of being hissed at predicts slow but sure progress in your work. 837

HISTORY. If in your dream your mind goes back over historic episodes, you will be likely to have an opportunity to better yourself financially by showing good judgment. This dream is a warning to be ready. 029

HITCH-HIKING. You will be criticized for your dependence on others if have a dream of hitch-hiking. If you dream of taking on a hitch-hiker while driving a car, it is a sign that you will have to have a show-down with your creditors. 988

HIVE. A beehive in a dream is a sign of freedom from worry, but if you overturn it or otherwise damage it and set the bees loose, your dream will have exactly the opposite import. 421

HIVES. This skin eruption in a dream portends unexplainable occurrences that will cause you no end of concern but that will not be serious if you do not allow them to become so. 556

HOARSENESS. If you dream of being hoarse and unable to speak above a whisper, you are likely to have an affair that will put you in an embarrassing situation. 803

HOAX. To perpetrate a hoax in a dream, even if it is an innocent one, presages that you will have explanations to make for apparently strange actions. 694

HOBBY HORSE. It is a fortunate augury if you dream of riding a hobby horse. This may be the kind of hobby horse you had when a child or it may simply mean following a hobby such as collecting things, photography, or other recreations. 542

HOBGOBLIN. Hobgoblins in a dream are not to be taken seriously by themselves. They seldom mean anything more than indulgence in too rich food before going to bed. 498

HOBO. Easy times are ahead if you dream of being a hobo, but if you are concerned in nefarious actions, the augury is anything but auspicious. You are likely to be shamed in public. 194

HOCKEY. A rough game of hockey in a dream is a portent of success through close attention to business. This is true whether the game is played on the ice or elsewhere. 412

HOCKSHOP. (See Pawnbroker.) 869

HOE. The use of a hoe in a dream portends good fortune in the sale of farm and dairy products. 093

HOG. A dream of a clean, well-groomed hog forecasts an unusual experience in connection ith a factory of some sort. If a hog is wallowing in mud, the portent is success in a new business enterprise. 303

HOLE. A hole in a garment predicts better luck in financial affairs. If you dream of seeing a bullet hole in a body, you are warned against believing what strangers tell you. 944

HOLIDAY. A dream of having a holiday and being able to rest from your labors is a sign that you will have to work even harder but that your efforts will be effective in procuring for you greater rewards. 585

HOLINESS. It is an augury of peace and understanding with family and friends if you dream of the holiness of any particular person. 968

HOLLAND. The countryside of Holland, with its windmills and its people in wooden shoes, is the setting for a dream that will bring you content in your family circle and in your community. 041

HOLLY. If in a dream you hang wreaths of holly in windows or on a door, you will have good luck in both material ways and in your friendships. 279

HOLLYHOCK. This old-fashioned flower seen in a dream is a portent that you will be happy in spite of present poverty. 209

HOLY COMMUNION. To partake of Holy Communion in a dream points toward making a friend who will stand by you through life. 430

HOME. If the dream is of a happy home life, it portends success of small dimensions and great contentment. 262

HOME RUN. You may be sure that your next business venture will be successful if you dream of making a home run in a baseball game. 215

HOMESICKNESS. This dream is a sign that you will receive good news from an old and valued friend and that you wil use this news to good advantage. 076

HOMICIDE. (See Murder.) 401

HOMINY. Dull days are predicted by a dream of eating hominy. Eaten cold, it also predicts illness. 309

HONESTY. It is a particularly fortunate augury in a dream if someone whom you believed to be dishonest turns out to be honest. To dream that you yourself are honest means nothing, for that should be the normal expectation. 749

HONEY. Going will be slow and difficult if you dream of eating honey. Hard times are predicted if you dream of getting your fingers sticky with it. If you call someone "Honey", you will be placed in an embarrassing position. 461

HONEYMOON. To dream of being on your honeymoon is a sign of wedded bliss. 544

HONEYSUCKLE. The sweet scent of honeysuckle in a dream is an augury of love to the unmarried. To pick sprays of it indicates real contentment in home life and among your neighbors. To others it is a sign that you will be able to make the most of your opportunities. 984

HOOD. It is not a good sign to wear a hood in a dream. You will be deceived by those whom you have trusted. 099

HOODLUM. Unfortunate is he or she who dreams of hoodlums. It signifies that you will be shamed and held up to public scorn. 195

HOOF. The hoof of a horse, cow or other animal, seen in a dream, indicates that you are in danger of being swindled. If the hoof is cloven, the augury is of complications in love affairs. 694

HOOK. To be caught on a hook of any kind in a dream presages difficulties that will give you much concern. If you are able to wriggle free, it will be at the expense of much sorrow and grief. 139

HOOP. If you dream of rolling a hoop as you did when you were a child, you are likely to hold your present job as long as you wish to. 881

HOPE. Any dream that seems to hold out hope in the face of difficulties is to be regarded as a good dream in the long run. 505

HOPS. Picking hops in a dream prophesies love affairs that will carry you away for the time being and then suddenly cease. 761

HOPSCOTCH. If the game of hopscotch you play in a dream gives you pleasure, the augury is of an entertainment in store for you; otherwise it means a defeat of some kind. 202

HORIZON. To see a far horizon in a dream is a sign of success in your business life and your love affairs. If the horizon seems close at hand, the augury is of incidents that are likely to give you much concern for a long time. 968

HORIZONTAL BARS. Exercising on horizontal bars in a dream is a sign that you wil be called upon to exhibit courage in the face of danger. 584

HORN. The sound of a horn heard in a dream haas different meanings according to circumstances. An automobile horn is, of course, a warning against danger. A horn in an orchestra or band predicts family difficulties. 525

HORNET. To dream of being stung by a hornet is, strangely enough, a forerunner of good luck in your next business undertaking. 497

HOROSCOPE. The best of luck may be expected from a dream of having your horoscope read by an expert. 769

HORROR. This note in a dream should be interpreted in connection with the other elements that figure in it. It is not necessarily unfortunate. 303

HORS D'OEUVRES. Your expectations are good after a dream of being served with hors d'oeuvres at a restaurant or a bar. They predict that you will make progress with your business associates. 502

HORSE. In general, dreams about horses portend acts of faithfulness on the part of your frieds. If you dream of riding horseback, the omen is of achievement in affairs relating to your community. To dream of training a horse is an augury of resistance from someone you want to be friendly with. If you dream of being kicked by a horse, it is a warning against over-confidence in strangers. Seeing two horses fighting in a dream portends ill luck. 030

HORSE CHESTNUT. You are likely to have a short illness if you dream of eating horse chestnuts. To dream of throwing them at an enemy is a sign of failure in business. 641

HORSEFLY. Minor annoyances are portended by a dream of being bitten by a horsefly. 593

HORSESHOE. (See also Quoits.) To dream of nailing a horseshoe over a door augurs a series of happenings that appear to be unlucky but that will add up to something extremely good for you. 657

HORSERADISH. If you dream of eating horseradish, you will be beseet by doubts of the fidelity of your friends. 402

HORSE-TRADING. To dream of trading horses is a sign of having to contend with a trying business situation that will require careful handling. 044

HORSEWHIP. (See Flogging.) 229

HOSE. (See also Stockings.) Squirting a hose in a dream portends new adventures, perhaps of a dangerous nature. If it is directed on a fire, the adventures will be in a foreign land. Playing with a hose on a lawn predicts new friends. 735

HOSIERY. (See Stockings.) 885

HOSPITAL. Dreaming of being taken to a hospital means that although you will get into difficulties, you will overcome them and be ahead of where you were before. 210

HOSPITALITY. If you are shown hospitality in a dream, the augury is of a comfortable home life. To show it to others is a sign of increased income. 869

HOST. To dream of being the host or hostess to visitors or guests at a dinner party points toward successful handling of your financial affairs. 680

HOSTILITY. If it is directed at you, hostility in a dream betokens keen regret for some unworthy action. If you show it to others, you are likely to find yourself in a compromising situation. 484

HOTBED. Working with plants in a hotbed is a dream that foretells delightful experiences with new friends. 543

HOT DOG. (See Frankfurter.) 218

HOTEL. A dream of registering at a hotel is a sign of increasing responsibilities in your job if you are alone in the dream. If you are accompanied by one of the opposite sex, it is a portent of having to meet an emergency. 249

HOTHOUSE. (See Conservatory.) 539

HOUND. Riding to hounds in a dream is an omen that you will have much leisure time but by the same token it is a warning that you should make good use of it and not waste it at gay parties. To dream of being pursued by bloodhounds is a sign that unless you slacken the pace at which you are going, you will suffer a breakdown. 748

HOUR-GLASS. It is a portent of woe resulting from wasted opportunities if you dream of looking at an hour-glass with the sand running through. 933

HOUSE. Dreaming of building a house portends good fortune in business; of buying a house, a short and mad love affair. 809

HOUSEBOAT. A dismal outlook for those in love is predicted by a dream of living on a houseboat. If the houseboat slips its moorings, the augury is one of disquieting adventure with loose companions. 734

HOUSEKEEPER. For a woman to dream of being a housekeeper for a wealthy man is a prophecy of an increasing incom but much criticism from the world at large. 212

HOUSEMAID. If a man dreams of companionship with a pretty housemaid, he is likely to be invited to a school reunion. If he dreams of kissing her, he will be dunned by those to whom he owes money. 037

HOUSEWIFE. A woman who dreams of being a housewife will be likely to marry an actor or some other professional man who must be more or less constantly on the move. 381

HOVEL. You will not want in your old age if you dream of living in a hovel. If the hovel burns down, however, you will hear good news. 601

HOWLING. The sound of howling in a dream—either from an animal or a human—portends misery and pain. 359

HUBBUB. A dream of being in the center of a hubbub foretells a great many vexatious occurrences inside your family group. 480

HUCKLEBERRY. A warning to investigate all unsanitary conditions around you is contained in a dream that in any way concerns huckleberries. To dream of picking them augurs a slight illness. 688

HUG. A warm hug, if unaccompanied by passion, is a fortunate portent in a dream by young persons. It points toward a happy marriage and healthy children. If the hug is lacking in innocence, the augury is of a trip around the world. 397

HULA HULA. This highly insinuating dance, performed by grass-skirted Hawaiian girls in a dream foretells stirring adventures with persons of the opposite sex. 573

HUM. The sound of humming in a dream is a forerunner of disaster. If it seems to stop for no particular reason, the augury is one of shame. 802

HUMIDITY. Great embarrassment is foretold by a dream of suffering from the humidity. 531

HUMILITY. To display humility in a dream is a warrning against being bigoted and arrogant when in the company of others. 577

HUMOR. (See Fun.) 575

HUNCHBACK. It is a sign that you will be financially fortunate if you dream of seeing a hunchback. 405

HUNGER. Better times are sure to come if you dream that you are hungry. To dream that you satisfy the hunger of another predicts that you will receive a legacy and be able to take a long vacation. 541

HUNTING. If you dream of hunting for something you have lost, you will be talked about scandalously by your enemies. To dream of hunting for game is a sign of impending physical danger. 724

HURDY-GURDY. The sound of a hurdy-gurdy heard in a dream portends a new opportunity to make good. If you dream of turning the handle of one, you will have interesting adventures with strange but likeable people. 252

HURRICANE. (See Cyclone.) 961

HURRY. The cause for hurrying in a dream has a bearing on its significance. If it is selfish, it predicts worries; if it is to help others, the portent is auspicious. 727

HURT. To dream of being hurt is a warning against carelessness in crossing streets or roads. 750

HUSBAND. If a woman dreams that she has a husband and yields to his embraces joyously, she will be married within a year. 440

HUSTLE. (See Hurry.) 533

HUT. (See Hovel.) 563

HYACINTH. Growing out of doors in a garden, hyacinths portend visitors whom you have not expected and who are not entirely welcome. In pots, hyacinths are a sign of improvement in finances. 042

HYDRANT. To dream of a hydrant that is flowing is a sign of good luck to those who are oppressed. Seeing one burst denotes a large fortune in the distant future. If you dream of a fireman attaching a hose to a hydrant, you are likely to have a disquieting experience. 967

HYDROPHOBIA. Sad happenings are predicted by a dream of seeing a dog with hydrophobia. 287

HYDROPLANE. Whether landing on or taking off from the water, a hydroplane in a dream foretells a successful outcome to a perplexing situation. 952

HYENA. To be attacked by a hyena in a dream augurs ill unless you kill the animal or get it to go away. To see hyenas pacing back and forth in a cage is a sign that you will be afflicted with boils. 435

HYMN. To hear a hymn being sung in a dream portends new and constructive occupations in connection with your life in the community where you live. 670

HYPNOTISM. Being hypnotized in a dream and doing what someone wills you to do is a portent of having to account for something you would rather keep hidden. If you dream of hypnotizing someone else, you will have difficulty in meeting your debts. 710

HYPOCRITE. If in a dream you seem to discover that one of your friends is guilty of hyprocrisy, you are warned against jumping too quickly at conclusions. If it is you who acts the part of a hypocrite, the augury is of illness. 942

HYSTERIA. Sorry consequences may be expected by the man who dreams of a woman having a fit of hysteria. He will suffer business losses and have family troubles. Mob hysteria in a dream forecasts national calamities. 418

ICE. This is a contrast dream in most of its phases. To sit on a cake of ice foretells comfort in daily living, while to slip on the ice is a sign that you will have a vacation in a warm climate. If you dream of ice skating, you will merit applause for some worthy action, but a dream of skating with a person of the opposite sex is a warning against unseemly behavior. To put ice into drinks foretells discomfort during warm weather. 427

ICE-CREAM. Eating ice-cream in a dream foretells a happy experience in which children will figure prominently. 487

ICICLE. A dripping icicle seen in a dream portends trouble unless you arrange to save a certain sum each week. To eat an icicle foretells sickness. 665

IDEA. Getting what appears to be a brilliant idea in a dream foretells great irritation of mind unless you can remember the idea when you awaken. Then it is excellent luck. 951

IDEAL. If a man dreams of a girl as his ideal, he is warned against making a fool of himself in the company of women. 280

IDIOT. Grave trouble is foretold by dreaming of trying to talk with an idiot. 431

IDLENESS. If you dream of doing nothing while others about you are busily working at their jobs, you will find that you will have to make explanations to your associates. 434

IDOL. To dream of seeing a person worshipping an idol is a sign that you are due for an increase in income. If in the dream you are the worshiper, you are likely to have differences with your employer. 290

IGNORANCE. If you are disgusted in a dream at a person's ignorance of any well known fact, you are in danger of being exposed for doing something that you would prefer to keep hidden. If your ignorance is shown, you will have a rise in salary. 142

ILLEGIBILITY. Trying to decipher illegible handwriting in a dream is a sign of having to prove your identity in a court of law. 910

ILLNESS. Arguments with those you love are predicted by any dream of being ill; if it is others who are ill, the augury is of distress through worry. 563

ILLITERACY. To meet in your dreams a grown person who is unable to read or write is a sign that you will take on added responsibilities in connection with your job. 204

ILLUMINATION. Any brilliant illumination in a dream—by whatever means—presages the solution of a perplexing problem. 374

ILLUSION. If in a dream you are aware that what you are seeing is an illusion, you will be able to discover secrets of considerable value. 020

ILLUSTRATION. To be interested in an illustration for a story in a dream is a sign that your love will be requited. 622

IMAGE. (See Idol, Picture, Statue.) 825

IMAGINATION. In a dream if you come in contact with a display of imagination, such as that of a writer, poet, artist or inventor, the portent is likely to be of an inspiration that will make money for you. 564

IMBECILE. (See Idiot.) 658

IMITATION. A dream of finding out that something you treasure is only an imitation of what you thought it was prophesies being disillusioned by someone in whom you believed. 524

IMMODESTY. A dream by men of women being immodest in behavior, speech or dress is a portent of making errors that will cause shame and heartaches. 424

IMMORALITY. A warning is contained in a dream of immorality to be on guard against judging others until you are sure that your own conduct is above reproach. 651

IMMORTALITY. Dreaming of immortality, either of the body or soul, is a portent that you will have to put additional energy into the work you are doing. 380

IMP. (See Devil.) 535

IMPACT. (See Crash.) 845

IMPATIENCE. A dream in which you show impatience with someone who is doing his or her apparent best foretells a grievous condition within your immediate circle of friends. 900

IMPERFECTION. (See Flaw.) 618.

IMPERSONATION. For whatever purpose the impersonation is made—disguise, masquerade, or theatrical performance—if you dream of impersonating another, you will have to make excuses for being remiss in your duty. If you dream of being fooled by an impersonation, you are likely to make new friends unexpectedly. 703

IMPLEMENT. (See Tool.) 373

IMPOSTOR. To dream of being swindled by an impostor is a portent of hard times in your business. 405

IMPRISONMENT. (See Prison.) 976

IMPUDENCE. If you have a dream in which you are impudent to someone who normally would have a much higher business or social rank, or whose authority is undeniable, you will find yourself in line for advancement in business. 438

IMPURITY. Discovering impurities in food, drink, or anywhere else where they are a menace is a sign of happiness in love affairs and married life. 988

INAUGURATION. It is a lucky portent to dream that you are present at the inauguration of the president of a republic. 809

INCANTATION. Humorous experiences may be expected if you dream of hearing a person uttering incantations at a weird ceremony. 135

INCENSE. You may be certain of pleasing adventures with persons of the opposite sex if you dream of burning incense or seeing it burned. To smell the odor in a dream foretells travel. 198

INCEST. A dream of incest is a warning against lowering the standards of your life for any reason whatever. 348

INCISION. To dream of showing another person where the incision was made for an appendicitis operation is a sign that you will show increasing efficiency in your job. If you dream that you are a surgeon and make an incision in a patient, you are likely to have trouble with the authorities. 242

INCOHERENCE. If you dream of hearing a person talk without being able to understand what he is driving at, you will be in danger of having to explain something that will embarrass you. 549

INCOME. To dream of an increase in your income is a sign that you will have additional worries. If the dream is of smaller income than that to which you have been accustomed, you are likely to have a rise in salary. 824

INCOMPATIBILITY. For a married person to dream of incompatibility with his or her mate is a warning against loss of temper that may lead to serious consequences. 784

INCUBATOR. Baby incubators seen in a dream are portents of better health for you and your family. Chicken incubators are an omen of being able to meet your obligations. 604

INDELIBLE INK. Marking clothes with indelible ink in a dream is a sign of a new accumulation of money, but if you dream of trying to erase indelible ink, you will have trouble with your landlord. 735

INDEMNITY. There will be little peace during the following month for the person who dreams of levying an indemnity on another. 523

INDEPENDENCE. To feel or show your independence in a dream is a warning against being too sure of yourself in the next business deal on which you are working. 538

INDEX. To search for an item in the index of a book is a sign that a man will have a better understanding of women and vice-versa. If you dream of indexing a book, you will advance to a higher and more lucrative position. 626

INDIAN. Either North or South American Indians seen or met within a dream are a good sign if they are friendly, but if they appear to be hostile, the dream is a warning against placing too great a trust in your business associates. 098

INDIFFERENCE. If you dream that someone you love is indifferent to you, it is a sign that you should exert yourself to make yourself more agreeable to others. if you dream of showing indifference to others, you will find yourself in want. 001

INDIGESTION. A dream of indigestion is usually the effect of either over-eating or over-drinking, so it seldom has any meaning other than that you should be more discreet. 636

INDIGO. Dreaming of this shade of blue is a presage of a cruise in southern waters. 368

INDUSTRY. A dream in which you are conscious of the industry of others foretells new responsibilities both in your business and your home. If you dream of being industrious, you may look forward to a period of rest and relaxation. 870

INFANT. (See Baby.) 056

INFANTRY. On the march, infantry in a dream foretells adventure and, for the unmarried, love affairs that are short-lived. 019

INFECTION. It is a warning against taking chances if you dream of having even a small wound infected. 662

INFERIORITY COMPLEX. Friends will stand by you if you dream of strutting by reason of an inferiority complex. 428

INFERNO. (See Hell.) 984

INFIDELITY. A man or woman who dreams of being unfaithful to his or her mate is warned to be extremely careful in their dealings with the opposite sex. 083

INFIRMARY. If you dream of going to an infirmary to be treated for some sickness or disability, the chances are that one of your friends will do something nice for you. 543

INFIRMITY. If in a dream you notice and comment on someone else's infirmity, you will have to explain a misdeed to someone outside of your family. 211

INFLUENCE. To dream that a person of either sex has an influence over your actions portends that mischief makers will plot against you. 971

INFLUENZA. To dream of being ill with influenza is a forerunner of a vacation during which you will have an opportunity to travel. 328

INFORMALITY. This dream depends for its import on whether there is occasion for formality or not. If one dreams of being informal at a very impressive occasion, the augury is of disgrace through unworthy actions. If, however, a great dignitary meets you with informal charm, the augury is of advancement in social life. 986

INHERITANCE. Receiving an inheritance in a dream usually foretells receiving one in real life. 981

INITIATION. Being roughly handled by your fellows in an initiation ceremony is a forerunner of sound friendship and good times. 191

INJURY. No dream of receiving a physical injury has a good portent, but if the injury is to your reputation, it is a sign that you will be well thought of. 887

INK. Spilling ink in a dream is nothing to cry about, but to write with ink is a warning to go slowly in giving confidences even to your best friends. 163

INN. (See Hotel.) 455

INNOCENCE. A dream of taking advantage of another's innocence is an augury of defeat in all your undertakings. 714

INOCULATION. You may rest easy regarding your most insistent creditors if you dream of being inoculated against any disease. 061

INQUEST. To be present in a dream at an inquest over a dead body foretells that very soon you will have to assume a new responsibility. 270

INQUIRY. If in a dream an inquiry is made that you are unable to answer, the portent is of sorrow through someone's leaving you. If you are able to answer the inquiry, you will receive an important letter. 129

INQUISITION. You will be subjected to the closest supervision of your employer if you dream of having to submit to an inquisition. It is a warning against loafing on the job. 655

INSANITY. A dream of an insane person forecasts an uncomfortable session with hostile relatives. If you dream that you are insane, the omen is of good news. 943

INSCRIPTION. Reading the inscription on a gravestone or monument is a sign that you will be promoted to a higher and more difficult position. 265

INSECT. Indoors, insects portend annoyances through minor afflictions and skin irritations. 867

INSOLENCE. If you dream of being insolent to an inferior, you will have to answer for a misdeed to a superior. If a young person is insolent to you, it is a warning not to lose your temper. 729

INSOLVENCY. If you dream that you are insolvent, either personally or in business, you will be much better satisfied with the job you now hold. 219

INSURANCE. A dream of taking out life or accident insurance portends a difficult time with your financial affairs. If an insurance salesman approaches you in a dream, you are likely to be offered a new job. 334

INTEMPERANCE. Dreaming of being intemperate in the use of liquor, in eating, or in other ways augurs that you are likely to lose one or more staunch friends. 291

INTERPRETER. If in a dream you have to speak with a foreigner through an interpreter, you are likely to have difficulties with your investments. 133

INTERRUPTION. To dream of being interrupted either in your work or while speaking, is an augury of discontent in your marital relations or the upsetting of a love affair. 548

INTESTINES. A definite warning against overexertion is contained in a dream of your own intestines. If there is excruciating pain, it is a sign that you will be ill unless you are checked by your physician. 921

INTOLERANCE. If you dream of being intolerant of anyone else's views on religion, politics or other controversial subject, you will be disappointed in the attitude adopted by your warmest friends. If others are intolerant of your viewpoint, you will have a small legacy. 020

INTRIGUE. To dream of being a party to a love intrigue means that people will discuss your personal affairs to your detriment. 183

INUNDATION. (See Floods.) 795

INVALID. If you dream of taking care of an invalid, you are certain to receive good news through the mail. 873

INVENTION. Good news is in store for you if you dream of working on an invention. It portends that you are likely to receive the thing for which you have hoped the most. 592

INVENTOR. To dream of being an inventor foretells good fortune. If in the dream you invent something that seems to be successful, it is a portent of success in whatever business you are engaged in. 178

INVITATION. A dream of receiving an invitation of any description forecasts additional expense that you probably do not wish to incur. 274

IODINE. Swallowing iodine in a dream is a warning to snap out of your depression and a forerunner of better times. 857

IPECAC. If you dream of taking ipecac as an emetic, you will receive news that will at first disgust you and then amuse you. 443

IRIS. This beautiful purple or yellow flower is a harbinger of peace and plenty when seen in a dream. if it is bordering a pool, you will realize your fondest wish for a faithful mate. 767

IRON. From a dream of iron in any form one may expect a slow but steady progress to prosperity. 475

IRONING. For a woman to dream of ironing clothes is an omen that she will be relieved of burdens she has borne for a long time. If a man has this dream, it portends an increase in salary. 153

ISLAND. If you dream of living on an island, you are liable to find that for a time things will not go well with you but if you keep your chin up, things will get better. For a man to dream of being alone with a girl on an island is an omen of exciting and dangerous adventures. 901

ITCH. Unimportant but irritating troubles are predicted by a dream in which any part of the body itches. 997

IVORY. To dream of hunting in African jungles foretells that a wealthy relative will make you an offer which you should accept. If you dream of carving ornaments and objects of art out of ivory, you will make a reputation for your honesty and ability. 974

IVY. The constancy of those you love is insured by a dream of a fine, healthy growth of ivy on a wall or building. Tearing it off in a dream portends woe and disappointment. Planting it is a presage of good times to come. 730

JAB. If you dream of being given a jab, you will soon suffer an imagined wrong due to your super-sensitiveness. It will make you and others miserable unless you can rise above it. 349

JACKASS. A jackass in a dream portends that you will be made a fool of in the company of someone whose esteem you crave. 586

JACKET. Wearing a fine jacket in a dream foretells that you will be invited to a select dancing party where attractive favors will be handed to the guests. A worn jacket is a sign that you will not have a good time at the next party you attend. 755

JACK-KNIFE. To dream of a jack-knife is a sign that you will be accused of being two-faced. 773

JACK-POT. Winning the jack-pot in a poker game is a portent of going to the races and placing a bet on a dark horse. If you lose the jack-pot and see another take it, you will not get married this year. 200

JADE. Dreaming of beautiful jade set in gold foretells that you will be asked to contribute to some relief fund. Buying a rare piece of jade in a dream means that you will have visitors from another city. 213

JAG. If you dream of going on a jag, you will have to answer to your employer's criticism that you are paying too much attention to the opposite sex. 937

JAGUAR. To dream of one of these tiger-like South American animals is a warning to beware of some catty woman's slanderous tongue. 960

JAIL. To go to jail in a dream is a sign that you will be caught in a white lie to your great embarrassment. To see prisoners being committed to jail foretells that you are in danger of infection by a contagious disease. 562

JAILER. If you are a jailer in a dream, you will be called to account for some infraction of the motor laws. For a woman to dream that she marries a jailer is a sign that she is in danger from an unknown source. 483

JAM. To get in a jam—traffic or personal—in a dream where there seems to be no possible way out augurs a quarrel with someone whose friendship you should cultivate. To put up jam and put it in jars signifies that you will be invited to a neighborhood party. 521

JANITOR. A disagreeable task is sure to be assigned to you if you dream of being a janitor of an apartment house or public building. 138

JAPAN. If you dream of being in Japan and seeing the Japanese people, you will have an unusual experience, doing something quite apart from your everyday pattern of living. 820

JAR. A row of jars on a shelf, seen in a dream, means that you will find pleasure in social activities. A family "jar" or quarrel is a sign of illness. 146

JARDINIERE. To dream of a colorful jardiniere with a plant in it signifies a new romance to those who are unmarried, but it is a warning to others to watch their step. An empty jardiniere is an indication of adventure. 728

JASMINE. Young men and women who dream of jasmine will win their hearts' desire. 269

JAUNDICE. Your efforts at making money will come to naught if you have a dream that you are afflicted with jaundice. 669

JAUNT. A dream of taking a jaunt or short trip is a favorable sign for those who are in love. 163

JAVELIN. Broken friendships are foretold by a dream of throwing a javelin at a human being, but if it is thrown as a pastime in athletics, the augury is favorable to business men. 087

JAW. Dreaming of one's jaw portends a humiliating experience, but another's jaw is a sign of a rise in salary. 992

JAYWALKER. Seeing a jaywalker in a dream means that you will be called to account for a slight infraction of the law. If you are the jaywalker, you will have a serious altercation with an officer. 680

JAZZ. A dream of hearing jazz music is a forerunner of gayety that will cost you more money than you can afford. Dancing to jazz music with a good-looking partner foretells that you will have to borrow carfare shortly. 689

JEALOUSY. To dream of being jealous of a person of the opposite sex means that you will have a burst of despondency or at least a fit of the blues. If you can snap out of it, it will be much better for your future. 682

JEER. Being jeered at in a dream portends that someone will cancel an engagement with you. If you jeer at another, your sweetheart will quarrel with you. 438

JELLY. (See Jam.) 773

JERUSALEM. If you dream of the city of Jerusalem, you will suffer an injustice and know the misery of loneliness. Visiting Jerusalem in a dream means that a relative will come to stay with you. 531

JESSAMINE. Happy will be the person who dreams of this fragrant flower. It portends health, wealth, and peace of mind. 509

JEST. (See Joke.) 855

JESTER. To dream of a jester at the court of an ancient king portends adventures among strange and amusing people. 662

JESUS. To dream of Jesus augurs peace of mind and contentment. 645

JET. (See also Fountain.) Pieces of polished black jet on a woman's dress portend the enjoyment of luxury that will not be good for you. A burning gas jet, seen in a dream, signifies a love affair with a person of wealth. 124

JEW. The presence of Jewish people in dreams pesages a career that will be varied both in occupation and place of abode. 075

JEWELRY. A display of jewelry seen in a dream signifies social activity among community-minded persons. To dream of buying jewelry is a sign that you will have to answer for peccadillos that you believed you could keep hidden. 634

JEW'S-HARP. If you play a jew's-harp in a dream, you are likely to visit some eastern country within a year. Hearing a jew's harp played is an augury of having to choose between two loves. 375

JIG. To dance a jig in your dream is a good sign. You will win the favor of an elderly person who will leave you his money. 466

JIGSAW. Dreaming of using a jigsaw portends a broken engagement. 588

JILT. If you jilt your sweetheart in a dream, you are in danger from failing to keep an important appointment. If you are the jilted one, your investments will yield a larger return. 229

JINGLE. To dream of hearing someone repeat a silly jingle is a sign that you will receive a wedding announcement from a long forgotten acquaintance. The jingling of bells heard in a dream foretells a pleasant outing with a person of the opposite sex. If you hear money jingle, you will lose an opportunity of a semi-business nature. 380

JINRICKISHA. Riding in a jinrickisha is a portent of travel to a country you have never visited. If you dream of pulling a jinrickisha, you will have to meet an emergency that no one could have predicted. 843

JITNEY. If you dream of riding in a jitney bus, you will be likely to have a visitor whom you will have to take on a sightseeing trip. 865

JITTERS. Having the jitters in a dream signifies that you will have an important part in amateur theatricals. 931

JIU-JITSU. Your carefully conceived plans for the future are in danger of collapsing if you see someone in a dream practicing jiu-jitsu. To take an active part in this form of self-defense foretells a successful business trip. 812

JOB. To dream of finally getting a job after many discouragements is a sign that you will find a purse with a large sum of money in it, personal belongings, and the name and address of the owner. If you dream of losing a job, you must be on your guard against losing your temper with those to whom you are responsible. 167

JOCKEY. Young people who dream of seeing a jockey ride a horse in a race will shortly take a civil service examination in which they will make a satisfactory showing. 648

JOHN DOE. If you dream of hearing a person describe himself as John Doe when booked in a police court, racket. 002

JOKE. Hearing a joke in a dream and laughing heartily at it means that you will have an unwelcome visitor, perhaps your mother-in-law. If you dream of telling a joke that makes a hit with your audience, the omen is of successful business; if no one laughs, you will be disappointed in someone you have trusted. 268

JOKER. To dream of holding the joker in a card game presages loss of business due to the efforts of a competitor who is more energetic than you. 111

JONAH. If Jonah and the whale get all mixed up in your dream, it means that you will have a family dispute over money matters. If you dream of being a "Jonah", you will be made to apologize for a remark you have made about a friend's wife. 286

JONQUIL. Yellow jonquils in a dream foretell the receipt of a passionate love letter. 009

JOURNAL. If you dream of reading a journal, you will receive a telegram. If you buy a journal, you will receive word that a dividend has been declared on a stock you believed worthless. 937

JOURNEY. To dream of going on a journey foretells a nervous affliction that will require medical attention. 416

JOWLS. If you dream of a person whose cheeks, or jowls, are heavy and pendulous and thickly bearded, you will meet with a narrow escape on the road. 024

JOY. A dream of joy, whether yours or another's, is a prophecy of happiness in the home circle. When it is the joy of children, the prophecy is much better. To dream of being joyous on an occasion that is not creditable is a sign that you will have to answer for something that you would prefer to forget. 714

JOY RIDE. Going on a joy ride in a dream presages that you will abandon yourself to circumstances. You may, however, turn defeat into an amazing success if you give your problems proper attention. 719

JUBILEE. To celebrate with a jubilee portends recognition of long and faithful service. You will receive either a sum of money or a vacation with all expenses paid. 408

JUDAS. If you dream of a false friend (a Judas), you will turn your hand to a new trade. Go slowly. 811

JUDGE. To dream of appearing before a judge in a courtroom is unlucky for married men. It forecasts having to explain satisfactorily an absence from home. If you dream of passing judgment upon another, you will be assigned a thankless task that entails much work. 563

JUDGMENT DAY. Dreaming about appearing on Judgment Day foretells a robbery. 135

JUG. Days in the country are predicted by a dream of drinking out of a jug. 702

JUGGLER. To dream of a juggler practicing his art is a sign that you will compete in some popular contest where the prize is of considerable value. 200

JUGULAR VEIN. You will have an illness and require a change of climate if you dream of having your jugular vein cut. 912

JUICE. Financial help will be forthcoming if you dream of drinking vegetable or fruit juices. To serve these to your guests is a sign that you will come to the aid of another. 883

JULEP. To dream of drinking a mint julep is a portent that you will be host to a group of old friends. 264

JULY. It is a sign that you will meet your fate at a post-office if you dream of going on a vacation in July. 878

JUMPER. If you dream of a horse in the jumping class going over high hurdles, you are likely to find leisure to go on a hunting trip. 416

JUMPING. If you dream of jumping over obstacles, you will be able to meet your difficulties with assurance and overcome them. 566

JUMPING-JACK. A dream of a jumping-jack being played with by either a child or a grown-up person augurs new agreeable companions. 091

JUNE. A thrilling success will be yours if you dream of being married in June. If you dream of a girl with this lovely name, you will be married within a year. To dream of attending a June wedding is an augury of advancement in your job. 237

JUNIOR. Naming a child junior in a dream is an omen that you will forget to mail an important letter and thereby bring trouble upon yourself. 816

JUNIPER. To cut down a juniper tree in a dream is a portent of good luck. To pick the berries warns against associating with loose characters. 264

JUNK. A pile of junk in a dream predicts that you will be confused regarding a decision you will have to make shortly. 931

JURY. To dream of sitting on a jury foretells a serious difference of opinion with your sweetheart. It is possible to arbitrate the matter, but unless you use considerable tact and discretion, you will be unhappy. 473

JUSTICE. In a dream if you are of the opinion that justice is being done, the augury is of a successful future. If you are the person who metes out the justice, you will be subject to criticism by your neighbors. 396

JUVENILE COURT. Being present in a dream at a session of a juvenile court means that you will fail to keep a promise and thereby be in danger of losing a good friend. 119

K

KALEIDOSCOPE. To dream of looking into a kaleidoscope and watching with interest the ever-varying pattern before you signifies that you will take a new interest in your dress and in the creation or designing of new costumes. 335

KEG. To see a new keg in your dreams means that you will attend a masquerade party where there will be much hilarity and a great deal too much to drink. 624

KELP. Gathering kelp on the seashore in a dream is a sign that you will visit a naval academy and see the cadets on parade. 436

KENO. To be in a game of keno in your dream is an excellent portent. You will meet Lady Luck in the person of a blue-eyed blond and embrace her heartily. 632

KANGAROO. Dreaming of a kangaroo jumping nimbly about foretells a journey by airplane. If the kangaroo is a female and has one of its young in heer pouch, the journey will be full of adventure. 262

KATYDID. To hear the summer song of a katydid denotes a visit to a Spanish or Mexican night club where you will dance to music punctuated by castanets. 814

KEEPSAKE. If you are given a keepsake in your dream by one of the opposite sex, it augurs a serious illness in your immediate family. 146

KERNEL. To dream of feeding kernels of corn to a flock of birds is a sign that you will be ecstatically thanked. 315

KEROSENE. To fill lamps or stoves with kerosene in your dream portends a walking tour through a country with an understanding companion. 424

KETCHUP. To season your food with tomato ketchup is a sign that you will be kept guessing by a handsome and intriguing person of the opposite sex. 001

KETTLE. Dreaming of a kettle boiling on the stove points towad a pleasant and enjoyable family life. A kettle that boils dry is a sign of woe. 790

KETTLEDRUM. If you play the kettledrum in an orchestra, you are in danger of overindulgence in both food and drink. 024

KEY. Dreaming of having a key in your hand foretells a mild flirtation. If you dream of putting a key in a lock, you are very likely to be rebuked by someone you like very much. 206

KEYHOLE. Peeping through a keyhole in a dream is a prophecy of shame. To put a key in a keyhole predicts an amorous adventure. 758

KHAKI. Domestic troubles are foretold by a dream of seeing anyone wearing clothes made of khaki. 524

KICK. You will be reprimanded by a superior if you dream of being kicked either by man or beast. This is a warning against loafing on the job, for you are in danger of having your salary docked on account of infractions of office discipline. 697

KID. To see a young goat or kid in your dreams presages the meeting of a bearded man of great learning and influence. 364

KIDNAPING. If you are kidnapped in your dream, you should watch your step. You are likely to marry great wealth, but it will bring you no happiness and much shame. To dream of kidnaping someone means that thieves will steal your most treasured possession. 574

KIDNEY. To dream of your own kidney indicates that you are in danger of investing in worthless stock. It is a sign of physical deterioration if you dream of eating kidney stew. 537

KILLING. If someone is killed in your dream and you are a terrified witness to the crime, you will change your place of abode and be sorry for it. To dream of killing a person, whether purposely or by accident, is an omen that you will be criticized for bad manners. 409

KILT. To see a Scotchman wearing kilts in a dream is an indication that you will have to buy new luggage in preparation for a long trip. 967

KIMONO. Pretty Japanese girls wearing kimonos in your dream are a sign of attending a festival at which you will meet your fate. To dream of a woman wearing a faded and soiled kimono is a portent of a love affair that you will some day wish to forget. 806

KINDERGARTEN. To dream of seeing little children in a kindergarten is a sign that young men and women will marry early and have healthy progeny. 350

KING. (See also Queen.) If a man dreams that he is a king, the interpretation is similar to that for a woman who dreams of being a queen. 280

KISS. The portent of a kiss in a dream depends on the circumstances surrounding it. Kisses between married people are an omen of content; between unmarried people they predict happiness. A woman who dreams of kissing an old man will suffer disappointment. To dream of kissing a baby indicates success in a difficult undertaking. Kisses given in hypocrisy or contrary to the moral code are a sign of illness or disgrace. 077

KITCHEN. If one dreams of being the happy possessor of an attractive modern kitchen, it is an omen of being the host or hostess to a group of congenial dinner guests. A dream of a dirty, cluttered-up kitchen is a portent of having to make a visit to the doctor. 970

KITE. To fly a kite in your dream is an augury of trying a job that will be too much for your capabilities. If the kite-string breaks, the omen is of bad luck in business. 064

KITTEN. For a woman, playful kittens in a dream portend a suitor who will be more interested in dalliance than in the serious side of love-making. A man who dreams of kittens is in danger of being played with b the object of his affections. 786

KLEPTOMANIAC. If in a dream you have the urge to steal things that you do not need, it is a sign that there are people who seek to work your undoing. It is a warning against the appearance of evil. 972

KNAPSACK. A full knapsack denotes a pleasant journey. An empty knapsack denotes hard going financially. 782

KNAVE. To dream of holding the knave of any one of the four suits indicates that you will be tricked into doing something against your better judgment. 948

KNEADING. Kneading dough for bread is a sign that you will be visited by your female relatives. 923

KNEE. If you dream that your knees are quaking, it is a sign that you should kneel on them for the sins that you have committed. For a man to dream of dimpled knees is a portent of a liaison with a foreigner. 956

KNEELING. To see a person kneeling in prayer in an incongruous setting, such as a bus or in a cafe, is a sign that you are in danger of breaking at least two of the ten commandments. 995

KNELL. To hear a funeral knell in a dream is an ill omen. You will miss an opportunity to better yourself. 976

KNIFE. An open knife in a dream is a sign of strife to come. A closed knife indicates that someone is trying to swindle you. A very dull knife portends difficult times in making a living. 237

KNIGHT. Knights of old dressed in full armor presage the discovery of valuable family papers that will be turned to advantage. 230

KNITTING. Plying the knitting needles in a dream is a good sign. You will be blessed with children and grandchildren who will love you. 472

KNOB. To dream of a door-knob indicates that you are likely to enter a new business. The augury is of success if you go slowly. 424

KNOCK. If you hear a knock in your dream and then hear it repeated several times, it denotes that you will come in contact with a mysterious stranger whom you will never get to know. 437

KNOT. Dreaming of tying knots in a string or rope without any particular purpose is a warning against riding horseback, for you are likely to fall. To knot a necktie in a dream forecasts a meeting with a charming person of the opposite sex. 259

KU KLUX KLAN. Dreaming of hooded figures in white gathered about a fire at night is a warning against sacrificing the good name of a friend for the purpose of furthering your own interests. 909

L

LABEL. To dream of paying special attention to the label on a bottle, can, jar or garment is a forerunner of success in a business enterprise. 708

LABOR. Solid achievement is predicted by a dream of laboring on construction work. To dream of being affiliated with a labor party is an omen of better living and working conditions. To be ashamed of honest and productive labor is a sign of the deterioration of the mental faculties. If a single woman dreams of having labor pains, she may expect an early marriage and a large family. If a married woman dreams of having labor pains, she may expect to become pregnant in the near future. 869

LABORATORY. You will unravel a mystery of long standing if you dream of working in any kind of laboratory. 165

LABYRINTH. To lose your way in the tangled paths of a labyrinth is a portent of having to untangle a problem of your own making. If there appear to be wild beasts in the labyrinth, you will be beset by difficulties purposely thrown in your way by enemies. 697

LACE. Women who dream of lace will be loved for their feminine traits. Lace on women's undergarments dreamed of by a man foretells an episode that has possibilities for either good or ill. It warns against using bad judgment in casual social relations with women. A dream of lace on a man's underwear is a sign that you will make money in a questionable manner. Lace curtains in a dream are a portent of easy living. Lace made of paper portends accidents. 838

LACERATION. Painful lacerations of your flesh suffered in a dream portend a combination of circumstances that will cause you both discomfort and embarrassment. 475

LACKEY. (See Flunkey.) 739

LACQUER. Using lacquer in a dream to cover furniture or a floor predicts a whirlwind love affair with a foreigner. 009

LACROSSE. To dream of seeing a game of lacrosse played is a warning against giving credence to superstition. If you play the game yourself, you should guard against accidents. 465

LADDER. If in a dream you are climbing a ladder and a rung breaks, you will not need to worry about your financial future. If a ladder falls on you, the augury is of malicious gossip about you. To dream of entering a house by way of a ladder predicts a message that will cause you some concern. 147

LADLE. Using a ladle in a dream—serving soup or other food—portends visitors who will impose on your hospitality. 259

LADY. If you dream of meeting a woman with the title of Lady—Lady, the augury is good or bad according to whether or not she acts like a lady. 372

LAGER BEER. (See Beer.) 669

LAGOON. Boating alone on a quiet lagoon in your dream predicts danger from traffic accidents. If you are accompanied in the boat by one or more people, you will meet an old friend under surprising circumstances. 816

LAIR. Discovering the lair of a wild animal in a dream portends a struggle. If the animal is present, you will overcome the difficulty; if not, you will not be successful. 541

LAKE. Dreaming of a stormy lake predicts a disaster that, if you do not let it overwhelm you, will lead to eventual triumph. If you are sailing on it and are overturned, you will have family troubles as well. To sail on the calm waters of a lake in fine weather is an augury of peace and interest in life. Sailing on a lake by moonlight portends happy love affairs. 548

LAMB. (See also Sheep.) New lambs in a dream predict an experience that will soften you and make you a better man or woman. To dream of lambs playing together is an omen of happy family affairs. If you dream of eating lamb chops or roast spring lamb, you will be able to turn a fortunate business deal. 278

LAMENESS. If in a dream you feel sympathy for a lame person, or if you give assistance to a lame person, the prediction is one of good health. If you dream of being lame yourself, you will have to go slow in any enterprise that you are considering. Bad times are ahead for one who dreams of pushing or crowding a lame person. 892

LAMENTATION. Hearing the lamentations of one or more persons in a dream foretells a season of unhappiness. 080

LAMP. The interpretations of these dreams relate to oil, gas or electric lamps, but not to neon signs. To light a lamp signifies that someone to whom you have done a kindness will reciprocate. To put out a lamp is a sign that you will be able to take a long needed vacation. To hang a lamp so that it will guide people predicts that you will have of good luck. To break a lamp is an omen that someone will distrust you. 682

LAMP-POST. To dream of leaning against a lamp-post in a state of inebriation is an omen of trouble in the family circle. If you dream of a lamp-post that has been broken, you are likely to have a serious quarrel with a neighbor. 395

LANCE. If you dream of bbeing a doctor and using a lance on a patient, you will find that friends will avoid you for some unexplainable reason. To dream of having a boil lanced is a sign that you will have trouble with your in-laws. 925

LANDING. A landing of any kind in a dream, whether in connection with an airplane or a boat, denotes the successful completion of a hard job. 491

LANDLADY or LANDLORD. To dream of being asked for the rent by your landlady or landlord is a sign that you will have lucky in business and buy your own home. 951

LANE. Young men and women who dream of meeting each other in a shady lane will be fortunate in love if they are discreet in their actions. 894

LANGUOR. Active participation in games is predicted by a dream of relaxation and languor. 876

LANTERN. (See also Lamp.) A dream of trying to signal a railroad train by swinging a lantern is a presage of grave danger through designing women. If your lantern is blown out by the wind, you are likely to have trouble with a law officer. 832

LAP. Sitting on the lap of a person of the opposite sex predicts love affairs of a passionate nature. To dream of falling off a person's lap signifies the loss of a good position. 161

LAPDOG. If you dream of being bitten by a lapdog, you are likely to have difficulties with jealous women. A dream of a dead lapdog foretells prosperity within a short time. 152

LAPIS LAZULI. This beautiful blue gem is an augury of blessed contentment when seen in a dream. If you receive it as a gift, you will be able to take a long and enjoyable trip to the Orient. 038

LARCENY. (See Stealing.) 097

LARD. Dealings with people of doubtful morals are predicted if you dream of using lard in your cooking. 274

LARIAT. (See Lasso.) 907

LARK. The song of a lark heard in a dream presages joyous experiences of an innocent nature. If you kill a lark in a dream, it is a forerunner of an agonizing experience. 422

LARYNGITIS. A dream of having laryngitis is a sign of having to endorse a note for a friend. If it results in making you lose your voice, you will be unlucky in gambling. 541

LASHING. (See Flogging.) 836

LASSO. To throw a lasso in a dream is a good augury for married people if it is a successful throw. To have the rope looped about you presages embarrassment among your friends. 783

LATIN. To dream of anyone speaking in the Latin tongue augurs a long period during which you will be forced to give way to others. 656

LAST SUPPER. To dream of being a witness to the Last Supper portends the making of a new friend who will prove to be invaluable. 046

LATCH. If in a dream you leave the latch off, you will have delightful experiences in the company of the opposite sex. 961

LATHE. Working at a lathe in a dream portends working out an idea that will be of immense value to you. 972

LATHER. If you dream of lathering your face or underarms for shaving, you are likely to solve a pressing problem. Lathering the body in a bath forecasts getting good news by mail. 360

LATRINE. Business affairs will come to a satisfactory conclusion if you dream of visiting a latrine. 217

LATTICE. Opening a lattice window onto a summer garden is a portent of ease and contentment. 839

LAUDANUM. (See Opium.) 031

LAUGHTER. (See also Comedy, Fun.) If you dream of laughing, the augury can be nothing but good. To hear a good joke that provokes your laughter means that you will have good luck over a long period. To make another person laugh indicates profitable investments. 384

LAUNCH. To see a boat launched in a dream foretells exciting and profitable adventures. If you dream of sailing in smooth waters in a launch, you will have a satisfactory love affair. 289

LAUNDRY. To dream of being in a laundry is a sign of meeting a person on a train, bus or airplane and finding that you have friends in common. To dream of sending soiled linen to a laundry sounds a sharp warning against gossiping. 840

LAUREL. This lovely flower seen on bushes in a dream portends success in an important enterprise. 604

LAVA. Issuing from a volcano in eruption, lava seen in a dream warns you that unless you pay stricter attention to your work, you will be discharged. If it is sweeping over the countryside, destroying houses and trees, it is a sign of illness. 987

LAVATORY. Visiting a lavatory or washroom in a dream foretells a sharp altercation with a tradesman. To slip on the floor of a lavatory is a sign that you are in danger of forgetting to execute an important commission. 206

LAVENDER. The scent of lavender in a dream foretells pleasant companions in whose company you will improve your mental status. Lavender-colored dresses portend exciting adventures with members of the opposite sex. 773

LAW. To dream of being in the legal profession presages many harassing experiences in your business. If you retain a lawyer to bring suit against a person or company, you are warned against carelessness. To dream of winning a lawsuit foretells that you will lose money. To dream of laying down the law to another person is a portent of success in business. 781

LAWN. A fine green lawn seen in a dream foretells contentment in your home life. If you dream of mowing a lawn, you will be invited out by one of your neighbors. A lawn that is brown and gone to seed portends illness. 946

LAWYER. A woman who dreams of marrying a lawyer is likely to be caught in an embarrassing predicament. Here is a warning against loose morals. 790

LAXATIVE. Taking a laxative in a dream is an omen that someone whom you believed to be stingy will treat you with great generosity. 400

LAZINESS. (See also Leisure.) Being lazy in a dream is a good augury, but if someone chastises you for it, you will have family difficulties. 743

LEAD. Grievous troubles will beset your path if you dream of carrying a load of lead. If you dream of moulding bullets out of lead, you will have a serious accident. To hit a person with a length of lead pipe portends business upsets. 046

LEAF. (See also Foliage.) One leaf remaining on a tree is a sign of pleasure in the company of people older than yourself. To press a leaf between the pages of a book foretells having to answer embarrassing questions. To tear a leaf out of a book is a warning against repeating rumors. 616

LEAK. A leaky faucet in a dream is a forerunner of having to account for something you have said about another. Leaky galoshes portend illness. A boat that is leaking is a forecast of accidents. 203

LEAP. To dream of leaping over a fence is a sign that you will overcome an obstacle that has been in your way for some time. If you dream of leaping over a house or some other impossible object, you will attain social prestige. 854

LEARNING. People in dreams who display their learning in an obnoxious manner are an augury of a prolonged illness. If you dream of seriously trying to learn a new trade, language or some difficult subject, you will discover a new friend in whom you may place your trust. 863

LEASE. To lease a dwelling-house, building, or plot of ground in a dream is a sign that you will increase your income. 232

LEATHER. Leather in a dream augurs advancement by hard unremitting toil. To dream of working with leather is a sign of having to meet some overdue bills. 156

LEAVE. (See also Furlough.) If you dream of being on leave from a job without pay, you have a good chance of having your salary raised. 649

LECTURE. Anyone who dreams of going to a lecture by an important figure in politics, literature or art will be fortunate in love affairs. If you dream of being a lecturer, you will take an extended trip. 931

LEDGER. (See Accounting.) 625

LEECH. To dream that a leech is sucking your blood predicts that demands will be made upon you by relatives. 759

LEG. Dreaming of a single leg is a portent of failure to accomplish your ambition. Crooked legs in a dream foretell that you will suffer from a lack of capital with which to further an enterprise. Beautiful, shapely legs are a sign of success in social enterprises. To break a leg signifies discontent. 059

LEGACY. A dream of receiving a legacy foretells pleasant days if it does not come as the result of death in your immediate family. Otherwise, it portends woe. 587

LEGERDEMAIN. (See Magic.) 946

LEI. This garland of flowers that the Hawaiians hang on the necks of their friends is a fortunate augury in a dream. It foretells happiness to lovers. 951

LEISURE. To dream of spending your leisure in quiet and dignified pursuits is a sign of an increase in your fortune and respect in your community. 279

LEMON. Sucking a lemon in a dream predicts that you will be unpopular among professional people. To squeeze a lemon for use in making mixed drinks portends difficult times ahead. 992

LEMONADE. Making lemonade in a dream is a portent of making new friends who will stand by you in time of need. Drinking lemonade is a forerunner of being looked up to by your friends. 581

LENTIL. A woman who dreams of cooking lentils will thereby be assured of winning a handsome husband and a happy home. To eat lentils portends several healthy children. 920

LEOPARD. To be attacked by a leopard in a dream predicts trying experiences, but if you succeed in killing it or getting it to go away, you will achieve your ends. 266

LEPER. Difficult times are ahead for the person who dreams of associating with lepers. 371

LETHAL CHAMBER. If you dream of being led into a lethal chamber for execution, you are warned against investing your money without making a thorough investigation of its honesty. To see another person go into a lethal chamber means that you will make money by buying and selling. 719

LETTER. In any dream regarding letters the portent varies acccording to whether they contain good or bad news or simply routine information. To dream of receiving good news by mail—and that of course includes money—is an augury of good business prospects. Letters in which the news is either distressing or disappointing portend a battle to protect your good name. To receive a batch of unimportant letters is a sign that you will be harried by your creditors. To dream of writing an impassioned love letter is an augury of regret for a wrong you have done someone long ago. To dream of tearing up or burning a letter before you have read it predicts a money loss. Shame is the portent of reading a letter intended for another. It is a sign that your fondest wish will come true if you dream of dropping a letter into a mail-box or mailing it at the post-office. 015

LEWDNESS. A dream of being present when people are behaving in a lewd manner augurs new opportunities to make money, but in a questionable mannr. 602

LIAR. If you dream of calling a person a liar, you will have to defend yourself against a vicious attack on your character. To be called a liar by someone else in a dream is a portent of quarrels. To dream of calling yourself a liar presages illness of a serious nature. 971

LIBEL. To dream of being libeled is a warning against any actions that you are well aware may cause criticism. To libel another is a portent of continuing hard luck. 855

LIBRARY. You will be applauded for your cleverness if you dream of going to a library. It is a particularly fortunate dream for those who are engaged in creative work. 146

LICENSE. Being asked by a traffic officer in a dream to show your license is an omen of good fortune in love unless you are unable to produce the license, in which case the omen is of family squabbles. To dream of buying a license for a dog presages a long period of home comfort. 618

LICKING. (See Flogging.) 389

LICORICE. It is a sign that you will begin to go places in your business life if you dream of eating licorice. 500

LIE. It ought not to be so, but a dream of telling a lie is a forerunner of good luck in financial affairs. If a married man dreams of telling his wife a lie, he will have to buy her an expensive present, but he will be able to. If you dream of having someone tell you a lie, you will fail in an important enterprise. If you tell a lie to save someone shame or embarrassment, you will have good luck socially. 424

LIFEBOAT. Launching a lifeboat in a dream means that you will embark on a new venture that may be either business or love. As long as the lifeboat is steady, the venture will be successful, but if it overturns, the opposite may be expected 472

LIFEBUOY. If you dream of being taken off a wreck by means of a lifebuoy, you are in danger of being put to great inconvenience by a member of the opposite sex. 140

LIFEGUARD. A woman who dreams of being rescued by a lifeguard at a beach or pool will meet a likeable sort of fellow with whom she will have many good times. 316

LIFE INSURANCE. To dream of being turned down for life insurance after you have been examined by the physician predicts a long and happy life. Paying a premium on your life insurance in a dream is an augury of new opportunities to make money. 527

LIGHT. Light in a dream is always a more favorable augury than darkness. To turn on an electric light indicates a pleasant party. Lighting a candle augurs a happy meeting. 658

LIGHTHOUSE. Seen from a deck of a ship at night, a lighthouse in a dream signifies good going in love and in business. A lighthouse in the sunshine with waves breaking about its base is a portent of travels abroad. 652

LIGHTNING. Accompanied by rain and thunder, streaks of lightning seen in a dream are a forerunner of disaster. Heat lightning foretells pleasant days with one's friends. 950

LIGHTNING-ROD. It is a sign that you are in danger from a mysterious source if you dream of seeing a lightning-rod on a house or other building. 266

LILAC. A lilac bush in bloom, either lavender or white, predicts illness of a young friend, but it will turn out for the best. 601

LILY OF THE VALLEY. A dream of picking this sweet-scented spring flower augurs happiness for lovers. 927

LIMA BEAN. Canned lima beans predict business disappointments, but if they are fresh, they foretell solid achievement. 629

LIMBURGER CHEESE. There is a forecast of embarrassment in any dream in which this foul-smelling cheese figures. 769

LIME. If you dream of squeezing limes for limeade or cocktails, you are likely to meet a person who is in some way peculiar or outlandish. To dream of mixing mortar with lime is an augury of a promotion in business. 989

LINEN. Clean linen in a dream predicts easy living. Bed linen is an augury of romance. Table linen is a sign of social distinction. 841

LINER. An ocean liner lying at a dock foretells adventure. For a woman to dream of seeing people off on a trip and being carried away on the liner portends a new lover. To dream of being on a liner in mid-ocean is an omen that someone will distrust you. 161

LINGERIE. (See also Lace.) Men who dream of lingerie—of silk, fine linen or rayon—are warned to guard against loose talk while in the company of the opposite sex. For a woman to dream of lingerie foretells social advancement. Black lingerie predicts adventurous companions in night clubs. 326

LINIMENT. Rubbing lame parts of the body with liniment foretells a legacy consisting of valuable personal effects. 298

LINSEED OIL. A dream of mixing paint with linseed oil predicts success in a difficult undertaking. 431

LION. You will be looked up to by your associates if you dream of being on friendly terms with a lion. If a lion attacks you and you overcome him, you will develop greater leadership socially and in business. 272

LIP. (See also Kiss, Mustache.) To dream of the lips of an old person is a sign that you will have a problem to solve. Deeply reddened lips portend illness and loss of business. Thick, sensual lips foretell disappointment in love. 153

LIPSTICK. To dream that you see a woman using a lipstick in a public place is a portent of defeat in a struggle. You will be the butt of a practical joke if you dream of seeing a man use lipstick. 138

LIQUOR. Drinking hard liquors in a dream is a warning against over-indulgence in alcohol. 240

LITERATURE. (See Reading.) 698

LITIGATION. (See Law.) 290

LIVE-OAK. Peaceful days are assured if you dream of live-oak trees, but if they are hung with moss you will have to stay pretty close to home for one reason or another. 595

LIVER. If you appear to be having trouble with your liver in a dream, you are likely to find a purse full of money. To eat liver in a dream is a sign of good health. Taking cod liver oil predicts a love episode that will make you happy. 082

LIZARD. This reptilian creature seen in a dream is an augury of being caught in some unimportant misdemeanor. It is chiefly a warning to watch your step. 174

LLAMA. A dream of a llama carrying its burden in the Andes of South America is a forerunner of success in business where merchandise is dealt in. If you dream that a llama spits at you, the augury is one of great perturbation. 337

LOAD. Carrying a load of any kind in a dream is an omen of having to begin work early and continue until late. 136

LOAN. Dreaming of getting a loan from a bank or other moneylending institution is a portent of hard going in business that will eventually work out to your financial benefit. Making a loan to another presages a new and lasting friendship. 790

LOBSTER. A live lobster in a dream portends petty difficulties. To eat lobster in any form is a sign that you will receive some money that has been long overdue. 208

LOCK. To lock a door or a box, trunk or other container in a dream indicates that someone will be suspicious of you. To pick a lock with a skeleton key or piece of wire presages great embarrassment. If you dream of finding a padlock on the door of your home, you are likely to run afoul of the law. To be locked in a room or prison cell predicts being called upon for a speech at a public gathering. 011

LOCKET. For a woman to dream of wearing a locket in which there is a man's picture predicts a love affair of a warm and passionate nature. 152

LOCKJAW. You will have little peace for a long time if you dream of having lockjaw. 597

LOCOMOTIVE. Driving a locomotive in a dream is a portent of realizing an ambition. To ride in the cab of a locomotive is an augury of promotion in business. 028

LOCUST. The whirring sound of locusts heard in a dream predicts grief through the loss of a friend. To dream of a plague of locusts is a forerunner of business losses. 293

LODGER. If you dream that you are a lodger in a rooming or boarding house, you will see an improvement in your affairs before the week is out. 983

LOG. To dream of sitting on a log is a signal of contentment on a small but steady income. You will have leisure to follow your favorite hobby. Sawing logs for use in a fireplace predicts new home comforts. 827

LOLLYPOP. If in a dream someone hands you a lollypop as a pacifier, you will be elected to office in some social group such as a club, church organization, lodge or community association. To dream of sucking a lollypop in church, school or other public place portends embarrassment. 123

LONELINESS. A dream of being lonely is a sure indication that you will have company. 072

LONGSHOREMEN. Seeing longshoremen in a dream loading or unloading a ship is a prophecy that you will have a job offered you within a month—a job that you should accept. 238

LOOM. To dream of weaving cloth on a loom foretells pleasant days doing constructive work. If the loom breaks or the threads get twisted, there is trouble in store for you, but with patience it can be straightened out. 480

LOON. A dream of seeing a loon diving under water is a sign that you will travel to faraway lands. 728

LOOT. If you dream of coming upon a quantity of loot left by burglars, you are warned against being too grasping in your dealings with business men and women. 835

LORD'S PRAYER. You will meet a most interesting person of means and refinement if you dream of reciting the Lord's Prayer. 172

LOSS. Losing anything in a dream is an unfortunate augury unless you find it again. The loss of reputation portends sickness and death. 788

LOTTERY. To dream of buying a lottery ticket is a sign that you will be held up to ridicule by someone you have always liked. If you dream of winning in a lottery you will get into a jam with your relatives. 480

LOTUS. Lotus blossoms seen in a dream predict romance to the unmarried. To inhale their fragrance at dusk is a sign that you will have ecstatic happiness. 045

LOUD SPEAKER. A blaring loud speaker on a radio is a portent of woe, but if you dream of turning down the volume, you will have good luck in community affairs. 738

LOUNGE. In a cafe or theatre, a lounge is a prophecy of luxury. To meet your friends there portends difficulties in business that can be overcome by hard work. 691

LOUSE. Being afflicted with lice in a dream is a sign that you are going to be approached by an unscrupulous person who will propose an alliance for dishonest purposes. To see lice on another foretells a keen disappointment. 918

LOVE. Dreams of honest love foretell happiness and contentment. Illicit love affairs foretell disappointment. The greater the passion in a love dream, the greater the possibilities for reaching the heights or the depths. To dream of witnessing the love-making of others is a sign that you will succeed in the project on which you are at present engaged. 829

LOZENGE. Taking a throat lozenge in a dream means that you will be chastisedfor talking too much. If you swallow a lozenge whole, you will have to do a disagreeable job that you have been putting off for some time. 609

LUBRICANT. (See Oil.) 990

LUCK. To dream of having luck is a sign that you will be lucky, but it is also a warning against taking things too easily. 577

LUGGAGE. (See Baggage.) 023

LUMBER. Piles of lumber seen in a dream augur prosperity through increasingly good business. To see lumber carelessly strewn about a yard betokens harassing family squabbles. 894

LUNACY. (See Insanity.) 047

LUNCH. If you dream of eating lunch from a box or basket in the out of doors, you will find that your health will improve and you will gain weight. To eat lunch in a restaurant at a table is an indication that you will have difficulty with your employer. Eating at a lunch counter is a sign of a raise in salary. 764

LUNG. To dream of having your lungs congested or otherwise affected is a warning to guard both your conduct and your health. 083

LUST. If you are not additionally careful of your conduct, you are in great danger if you dream of giving way to lustful impulses. 888

LUTE. Playing this old-fashioned stringed instrument in a dream portends happy love affairs. 429

LUXURY. Any dream of luxury is a warning against indolence. Keep your mind on your job during working hours and let nothing interfere with your advancement. 407

LYE. To dream of using lye in cleaning or making soap is a forerunner of being investigated for your integrity. 929

LYING. (See Liar.) 397

LYNCHING. Death is predicted by a dream of taking part in a lynching; disgrace if you are simply a witness. 191

LYNX. A young woman who dreams of having a fur piece made of lynx will marry a handsome editor or author. 285

LYRE. To dream of playing this ancient stringed musical instrument presages an adventure in a garden of love, but if you break a string, it is probable that evil days will befall you. A lyre that is out of tune predicts a menace in your life. 190

M

MACAW. A macaw of bright plumage hopping about a cage, denotes an escape from an unpleasant and boring conference. 035

MACHINERY. (See also Cogs, Wheels.) If in a dream you see machinery in motion and it is clean and well cared-for, you will make good with your employer. If the machinery is idle or rusty, you will have difficulties with your car, your employer or your family. 451

MADNESS. (See Insanity.) 573

MADONNA. A picture or a statue of the Madonna is a propitious omen. You will win the love of a gifted and beautiful child. 934

MAGAZINE. To see many magazines on a newsstand portends a budding romance with a foreigner who does not speak your language. To write for a magazine in a dream is an augury of success in literary work. 697

MAGIC. Magic in any form in a dream foretells a strange coincidence. To see a magician at work and to be mystified by his tricks foretells meeting someone whom you never expected to see again. 481

MAGNET. To dream of the attractive power of a magnet portends many palpitating love affairs and much admiration from the opposite sex. 030

MAGNIFYING GLASS. You will have more money to spend if you dream of examining articles with a magnifying glass. 387

MAGNOLIA. To dream of a beautiful magnolia tree in bloom foretells to unmarried people a happy spring wedding. To wear a magnolia blossom indicates that you will lose your heart to a Southerner. 610

MAIL. If you dream of calling for mail at the post-office, it is a sign that you will buy a new piece of furniture. If you receive mail, it predicts a good buy; if not, you will not get a bargain. To dream of mailing a letter predicts a better than ordinary chance of making money. 004

MAILMAN. (See Postman.) 685

MAILBOX. To drop a letter into a mailbox and have difficulty in getting it in is a sign that the answer will be No to anything you propose. 757

MAJOR. If in your dream you meet a major in uniform and recognize him as such, it means that you will have an invitation to join a civic association. 223

MAKEUP. (See also Cosmetic, Lipstick, Rouge.) If you dream of making up for the stage, you will be asked to solicit funds for a community chest. If in making up for some social engagement you get powder on your dress, you are likely to make a faux pas at a party. If you dream of making up someone else, you are in danger of burning a hole in your clothes with a cigarette. 139

MALARIA. To dream of having malaria means that you will fail to get a hoped-for position. 160

MALLET. Handling a mallet in your dream portends a labor disturbance in which you will have a part. It may be in the office or factory where you work or it may be in your own kitchen. 600

MALTESE CAT. To fondle a maltese cat in your dream and hear him purr with delight at your attentions is a sign that a woman whose reputation is not of the best will make advances to you. 890

MAN. To dream of man in the abstract is a warning against too much brain work. For a woman to dream of a man foretells a meeting with an interesting person who will be a platonic friend. 751

MANE. A horse's mane seen in a dream, whether it is black, white or roan, foretells a telephone call and an invitation. 528

MANGER. To dream of the Christ child in a manger is a happy omen. You will inherit property and be happy in your married life. 714

MANIAC. One is likely to have a nightmare if one dreams of seeing a maniac. One is likely to be falsely accused of appropriating another's belongings. 873

MANNERS. Being conscious in a dream of the good manners of someone present portends better circumstances surrounding the main interpretation; bad manners suggest the reverse. 576

MANNIKIN. If in a dream one sees a fashionably dressed mannikin parading before a group of women, it signifies that you will have a dispute with one of the opposite sex. 068

MANSION. To dream of living in a mansion and enjoying all the luxuries that go with it is a sign that you will travel with the mate you have selected. 548

MANUFACTURING. A dream of being engaged in manufacturing of any kind augurs respect from the community in which you live. 092

MANUSCRIPT. Typing and editing a manuscript for publication in a dream means that you will be likely to be called for jury duty. To dream of submitting a manuscript to an editor augurs probable disappointment. 424

MANX CATS. Tailless, green-eyed Manx cats in your dream foretell trouble with a neighbor over the behavior of one of your family, probably a child. 443

MAP. To consult road maps and colored plates in a world atlas portends a marriage alliance with a person of another race and creed. 010

MAPLE. Maple furniture in a dream is a good sign. It indicates that you will have happy family connections and home life. 364

MARATHON. Watching a marathon race or dance in a dream is a portent of nervous strain. If you dream of being a contestant you are in danger of having to answer for a misdeed that you did not intend. 980

MARBLES. Playing a game of marbles in a dream signifies that if you meet a former suitor, you will find his sentiments unchanged. 475

MARDI GRAS. You will sign an important document if you dream of celebrating Mardi Gras, and the chances are that this will make you independent for life. 684

MARE. (See Horse.) 049

MARIHUANA. A dream of smoking this drug foretells a serious illness coupled with disgrace. 451

MARIONETTES. To stage a marionette show for the entertainment of children foretells much joy in family life. 136

MARKET. Dreaming of an outdoor market in which all sorts of foodstuffs are temptingly displayed is an omen of prosperity, but if the food is wilted or otherwise spoiled, it predicts hard times. 185

MARRIAGE. A dream of being happily married and proud of your mate portends a quarrel with a lover. If a woman dreams of being a bridesmaid at the wedding of a friend, it is a sign that she will have a whirlwind courtship and marriage within a year. A divorce is indicated if a marriage ceremony is accompanied by many tears from those assembled. 647

MARSH. To walk through marshy ground in a dream is a sign that you will go through a period of bad health. 655

MARSHMALLOWS. Toasted or served from the box, marshmallows portend the introduction of a tall, handsome man into your circle. He will be popular among the feminine members of your group. 154

MASCOT. To see a mascot paraded before a crowd of people at any kind of game is simply a portent that you will have a serious argument with a taxi driver. 375

MASK. The interpretation of a dream in which one wears a mask is that you will be deceived by someone you trusted. 052

MASQUERADE. To dream of attending a gay masquerade party with sprightly music and amusing companions predicts that there is a surprise in store for you—probably concerning a fascinating person of the opposite sex. 416

MASS. For a person to attend mass in a dream is a good augury. He or she will be blessed with fine, healthy children. 493

MASSAGE. A facial or body massage in a dream is a portent of going to a party where you will have a good time but where you will lose some important belonging. It is a lucky augury if you dream of massaging a sick friend. 299

MAT. Going to the mat with anyone in your dream and fighting it out denotes overconfidence in your abilities. To lay a mat in front of a door foretells visitors. 417

MATCH. If you strike a match in your dream, the portent is one of good luck. You will fall in love, and what is more, your love will have what it takes to create a happy home. 725

MATE. If a woman dreams of matching things up—such as a pair of stockings, gloves or shoes—she will be married shortly and have identical twins. If you dream of your mate, fearful that he or she is lost or hurt, it is a reminder that there is an anniversary of some kind that you should remember. 460

MATERNITY. A dream concerning maternity is a forerunner of increasing responsibility. 502

MATHEMATICS. To work on a mathematical problem in your dream and despair of its solution is an indication that you have no hope of fulfilling your plans. 081

MATTING. A dream of laying matting on a floor portends that some people you do not know are conspiring to do you harm. 478

MATTRESS. To be lying on a soft mattress in your dream, luxuriating in its comfort and ease, is a sign that you are in danger of losing your initiative. If you have a companion of the opposite sex, you will have to look to your conduct. 473

MAUSOLEUM. To walk in a cemetery and see magnificent mausoleums in memory of the dead warns against unworthy attentions to a wealthy relative in the hope of inheriting his money. 326

MAYOR. If you dream of becoming the mayor of your city and being acclaimed by the citizens, you are likely to be called for jury duty. 412

MAYPOLE. Dancing about a maypole in a dream is a good omen for lovers. It predicts an early marriage and healthy progeny. 405

MAZE. (See Labyrinth.) 498

MEADOW. Meadows and rich pasture lands in a dream foretell a season of plenty during which you should provide for the future. If there is a stream flowing through the meadow, your fortune will be that much better. 203

MEALS. (See Dinner, Eating, Lunch.) 383

MEAT. To dream of buying meat foretells that you will be very busy in your work for a long time, with little opportunity for recreation. 247

MECHANIC. A woman who dreams that her lover is a mechanic will have a struggle to hold him, but she should consider it worthwhile. 237

MEDICINE. Taking medicine in a dream augurs good health, but to give it to another is a sign of disappointment. 528

MEDIUM. To dream of visiting a spiritualist medium foretells learning something about your forebears that you never knew before. It may or may not be to your advantage. 256

MEDUSA. You are warned against illicit love if you dream of this mythical woman whose hair changed into snakes. Be very circumspect in the company of the opposite sex. 057

MEGAPHONE. A night-club singer crooning through a megaphone is a sign of disturbances that will annoy you for some time. Dreaming of a megaphone used out of doors is a good portent for young people in love. 660

MELODY. Hearing a melody in a dream is a good portent. If it seems new, you are likely to meet influential and agreeable people. If it is a melody that you recognize, there will be a meeting with a well-loved friend of long standing. 144

MEMORIAL. Pausing in a dream to do homage to a great man or woman in front of a memorial is a forerunner of deceit on the part of one of your acquaintances. 294

MEMORIAL DAY. You will be loved by your friends and respected by your neighbors if you dream of taking part in Memorial Day services or of putting flowers on the graves of those who have gone before. 015

MENAGERIE. (See Zoo.) 982

MENDICANT. (See Beggar.) 325

MENDING. To dream of mending socks or other clothing forecasts a new means of making money that will add a considerable amount to your income. 575

MENU. To dream of studying the menu or bill of fare in a restaurant is an omen that you need not worry about having plenty for comfortable living. 716

MEPHISTOPHELES. (See Devil.) 331

MERCHANT. If you dream that you are a merchant and are prospering through the buying and selling of necessary and staple goods, you are assured of hard work but a reasonably good income. 173

MERCY. Showing mercy to a person who has wronged you in a dream predicts a long and happy life with the object of your affections. If you dream of being at the mercy of a cruel and savage person you will have to answer publicly for a misdeed. 591

MERINGUE. Eating this frothy mixture of eggs and sugar in a dream predicts an adventure with some person of a lighthearted disposition. 475

MERMAID. A dream of discussing matters of general interest with a mermaid indicates that you will suffer a keen disappointment. 286

MERRIMENT. (See Frolic, Fun.) 784

MERRY-GO-ROUND. If you dream of riding with happy children on a merry-go-round or carousel, you will have an experience that will change your life for the better. 834

MESH. (See Net.) 363

MESSAGE. (See Letter.) 411

MESSENGER. Acting as a messenger in a dream is a sign of making money in real estate. To send a package or letter by a messenger augurs the success of a pet project. 675

METAL. (See Gold, Iron, Platinum, Silver, Steel.) 191

METEOR. To dream of a streaming meteor flashing across the sky denotes sudden success that will be of short duration. 641

METER. Reading a gas or electric meter in a dream is a portent of having to listen to good advice that you ought to follow. 156

METRONOME. To dream of playing the piano or other musical instrument to the clicking of a metronome is a forecast of having to do a disagreeable task. 665

MEW. The sound of a cat or kitten mewing in a dream is an augury of accidents in which you will receive several superficial wounds. 944

MICROSCOPE. Looking at objects under a microscope in a dream is an omen of being surprised at the behavior of someone you thought you knew well. If you dream of breaking a microscope and being greatly worried thereby, you will fail to persuade someone of your good intentions. 720

MIDDLEWEIGHT. If a girl dreams of being in love with a pugilist in the middleweight class, she is likely to marry a man of literary or artistic tastes. 997

MIDGET. To dream of one or more midgets foretells making the acquaintance of a man connected with books and pictures who will prove to be a good friend. 515

MIDWIFE. (See also Childbirth.) A man who dreams of calling a midwife to deliver a child is likely to suffer for his extravagant habits. If a woman dreams of officating as a midwife, she will have a quarrel with her husband about money. 481

MIGRATION. Dreaming of the migration of birds predicts freedom from worry; of the migration of animals, a new opportunity in business. 493

MIKADO. Japanese rulers in a dream are a portent of lighthearted diversions in unusual surroundings. 625

MILDEW. Disappointment in love or the loss of a friend is forecast by a dream of finding mildew on clothing. You are also warned against placing too much confidence in strangers. 064

MILE-POST. A succession of mile-posts seen in a dream portends a long and enjoyable cross-country motor journey. 647

MILK. A dream of milk is one of the luckiest dreams you can have, for it foretells lasting happiness that is the result of the right kind of a marriage and calm, peaceful home life. To drink cows' milk in a dream predicts good health; to drink goats' milk, business progress. If one dreams of milking a cow or a goat, the augury is comfort and prosperity through hard work. 294

MILKY WAY. You will be successful in acquiring further education if you dream of gazing at the Milky Way. 788

MILL. If it is driven by water-power, a mill in a dream portends happy hours with the person you love. If the mill is large like a factory, the augury is of money acquired through the toil of others. 252

MILLER. A miller at work is a sign of greater industry on your part and corresponding higher wages. 222

MILLIONAIRE. To dream of being a millionaire and spending money lavishly on the things you have always wanted to have is a portent of receiving money in a roundabout way for a service you had rendered and forgotten. To dream of helping out your less fortunate friends with your money is a sign of good fortune just around the corner. 717

MIMIC. To see a mimic imitating the peculiarities of a worthy person is a warning not to place too great confidence in casual acquaintances. If you dream of mimicking another, you are likely to have great difficulty with your work. 570

MINARET. If you dream of seeing the minarets of a Mohammedan mosque, you will have many opportunities to travel and meet interesting people. If there is someone on the minaret calling to prayer, you will be financially fortunate. 248

MIND READER. Nothing but bad luck can come from a dream of visiting and paying money to a mind reader. 203

MINE. (See also Bomb.) To dream of working in a mine—coal, gold, silver or other metal—predicts that you will make a great deal of money through your own efforts. To feel suspense and fear from mines while on shipboard in the area of warring countries augurs worry from some indiscreet remark or action. If the ship is blown up, it is a sign that you should be constantly on your guard in all your dealings with strangers. 290

MINISTER. If in your dream you talk over your troubles with a minister of the gospel, you will be able to clear up all your outstanding obligations, both financial and social. To dream of social contacts with a minister from a foreign government is a sign of increasing prosperity. 384

MINSTREL. A dream of attending an old-fashioned minstrel show predicts that you will meet a valued friend whom you have not seen for years. Minstrels of the Middle Ages in a dream foretell meeting fascinating companions of the opposite sex. 686

MINT. The flavor of mint in a dream predicts that your next trip will be in a northerly direction. 567

MINT JULEP. To mix or drink a mint julep in a dream foretells enjoyment through making an effort to understand the viewpoint of others. 791

MIRACLE. If in a dream you witness a miracle, or something that could not happen without Divine intervention, you have every reason for looking toward the future with confidence. 055

MIRAGE. A mirage or scene that fades away as you watch it is an augury that you will be confronted with an apparently hopeless task. Do not, however, fail to try it; for you are likely to succeed. 237

MIRE. Being stuck in the mire—on foot, horseback or in a car—is a dream that foretells a difficult situation arising from failure to meet obligations. 559

MIRROR. You will be unfortunate in your love affairs if you dream of breaking a mirror. To dream of seeing yourself in a mirror is a sign that you will be admired by one of the opposite sex. 953

MIRTH. (See Fun.) 251

MISCONDUCT. (See Adultery.) 180

MISER. A dream of a miser counting his money and gloating over it is a portent of getting riches in a manner of which you would be ashamed if you did not heed the warning. 434

MISSIONARY. You will fail in an important enterprise if you dream of being a missionary. If you dream of being converted by a missionary, you will be successful in business. 110

MIST. (See Fog.) 508

MISTLETOE. (See also Kiss.) Young people who dream of kissing under the mistletoe have much to look forward to. A woman who dreams of hanging mistletoe will win a charming and ardent lover. 089

MISTRESS. A married man who dreams of keeping a mistress is warned against yielding to the lures of designing women. A woman who dreams of being mistress to a man, whether married or single, will have difficulty in meeting her debts. 763

MOB. If in a dream you are pursued by a mob, you are in danger from one of the social group with which you associate. Do not be suspicious, but be careful. 320

MOCCASIN. On an Indian in a dream, moccasins portend disappointment in a friend whom you trusted. If you are wearing moccasins, you will be given a job supervising others. 453

MODEL. Dreaming of mechanical or shop models portends commendation for a job well done. Artists' models in a dream are an omen that you will be distrusted by the people who know you best. 991

MODESTY. Any exhibition of modesty in a dream, whether it is by a woman or a reprobate, is a sign that has a good influence on other factors in the dream. 074

MOHAMMEDAN. To dream of a person of this faith in the performance of his or her religious duties is a sign that you will have an opportunity to travel in foreign lands. 780

MOLASSES. Eating molasses in a dream foretells that you will be censured for some ill-advised statement you have made concerning another person. 065

MOLE. Burrowing into the ground, a mole in a dream is an augury of success in work that is in any way connected with engineering. To wear a mole-skin coat predicts unwelcome attention from the opposite sex. 303

MONARCH. (See King.) 789

MONASTERY. (See also Monk.) It is a sign of bad luck generally if a woman dreams of being in a monastery. She will be accused of deception by persons of rank. For a man to have this dream is a portent of smooth sailing in his affairs. 193

MONEY. If it is come by honestly, money in a dream is a sign that you will develop your resources to the point where you will have ample for your needs. To give money away is a forecast of having an interesting job but a small income. 838

MONK. (See also Monastery.) It is an augury of good fortune to dream of talking things over with a monk. You will have easier work and an easier mind. 537

MONKEY. To dream of keeping a monkey as a pet indictes that you are going to meet with treachery. A chattering monkey denotes that people will gossip about you and your personal habits. Monkeys in a cage at the zoo are a portent of coming trouble with hostile competitors. 034

MONOPLANE. (See Airplane.) 550

MONUMENT. (See Memorial.) 976

MOON. To dream of looking at the new moon over your left shoulder augurs a month of good luck. A clear, silvery moon in a cloudless sky foretells that you will devote your energy to a new and worthwhile project, but if it becomes clouded over, you will have many discouragements. A full moon denotes success in love affairs, particularly if you see it reflected in water. To dream of the harvest moon is an omen of excellent returns on your investments. 293

MOONSTONE. If someone hands you a moonstone in a dream, either in a setting or not, you will be mystified by the behavior of one of your friends. 047

MOP. Using a clean new mop in a dream foretells favorable comment on some of your work. Seeing an old and dirty mop in a pail of filthy water is a warning not to repeat evil rumors that you hear. 331

MORGUE. To dream of looking through a morgue and finding the dead body of someone you are acquainted with is a forerunner of disaster and a warning to guard your health in every possible manner. If you dream of being a corpse and lying in a morgue, you will soon be called upon to perform a disagreeable duty. 654

MORNING AFTER. If you have the experience of dreaming of having what is inelegantly called a "hangover" or "katzenjammer," due to overindulgence in alcohol the night before, you are likely to be reprimanded by someone who has authority over you. This may be your employer or your wife. 754

MORNING GLORY. This bright-colored climbing vine in bloom seen in a dream foretells carefree lazy days. 459

MORPHINE. If you dream of taking morphine in any shape, form or manner, you are warned that you must not shrink from facing a disagreeable duty. You will save yourself and others a heartache if you seize the bull by the horns. 413

MORTAR. Mixing mortar in a dream for use in bricklaying portends the successful accomplishment of a difficult job. Carrying mortar in a hod or other receptacle foretells a better position. 590

MORTGAGE. Great hardship is predicted by a dream of paying off a mortgage, but if you dream of foreclosing one, you will be fortunate in business. To put a mortgage on a house or other piece of property foretells a lucky business turn. 057

MOSLEM. (See Mohammedan.) 236

MOSQUE. (See also Minaret.) To dream of a mosque with its domes and minarets in the bright sunshine or moonlight is an omen that you will take renewed interest in the affairs of your own particular religion. 328

MOSS. Soft green moss in a dream is an omen of happy, fruitful romance and married bliss, but dry gray moss predicts disillusionment. 885

MOTH. Slanderous statements will be made about you and your family if you dream of trying to catch a moth. If you succeed in getting it and killing it, you will overcome your enemies. If you find clothing full of moths, there will be sadness in your family. 706

MOTHER. If you dream of a mother who has gone to her reward, you will have many happy hours in the company of dear friends. If you dream of being a child and being hugged to your mother's bosom, the omen is a fortunate one, for your family and friends will rally to your aid in time of trouble. To see a new mother with her baby at her breast betokens peace and security for the future. 982

MOTHER-IN-LAW. For a man or woman to dream of having an altercation with a mother-in-law is a portent of a situation that will require skill and patience to adjust. For a woman to dream of being a mother-in-law is a sign that she will have to apologize for angry words. 860

MOTION PICTURE. If in a dream of being at the movies, the picture gives you great pleasure, you will overcome an obstacle that is in your way. If the pictures are depressing or disgusting, you will lose a piece of jewelry. 501

MOTOR. Any motor seen in a dream, be it electric or gasoline, is a sign of progress. If you cannot make it function as it should, the portent is of trouble ahead. 918

MOTOR BOAT. Freedom from business and family cares is predicted by a dream of operating your own motorboat. If you race with another power boat and win, you will have business worries that will cause you concern for only a short time. If you lose the race, you will make new friends. 131

MOTOR CYCLE. For a woman to dream of riding on a motor-cycle behind a young man predicts that she will have an adventure that may lead to serious consequences. It is a warning not to be careless of appearances. 094

MOUNTAIN. Climbing a mountain in a dream foretells a promotion in business, but it also warns you not to say you can handle a job unless you are sure that you can do so. If the mountain is very steep or if it is covered with ice and snow, you will be likely to succeed in spite of great difficulties that will be put in your way. 669

MOURNING. It may seem strange, but a dream of being in mourning is a portent of better times to come. If one dreams of seeing a city or community in mourning, the omen is of happenings that will be hard to bear but that will work out to a good end. 619

MOUSE. For a woman to dream of being frightened by a mouse is an augury of being put to shame by a younger person. If she kills the mouse, she will be able to buy new clothes and millinery. To catch a mouse in a trap is a sign that you will receive a letter from someone you do not like. 465

MOUTH. (See also Lip.) Cruel mouths seen in a dream are a warning against being too quick to criticize the actions of others. If the teeth show, you are likely to be hurt by base insinuations from those whom you had trusted. A beautiful mouth is a portent of great happiness for lovers. The mouth of a baby is a sign that the person you had trusted least will turn out to be a firm and lasting friend. 829

MOVIES. (See Motion Picture.) 816

MUCK. Dire consequences are predicted by a dream of falling down in the muck of a barnyard. You are warned against evil companions. 935

MUD. To get mud on your clothes in a dream is a sign that someone who wishes you ill is trying to influence people against you. To drive in a car down a muddy road presages trouble with people to whom you owe money. 043

MUFFIN. Eating tasty hot muffins in a dream foretells pleasant family relations. To dream of baking muffins is a sign that you will receive a small legacy. 291

MULE. Driving one or more mules in a dream is a portent of loss of reputation through talking out of turn at a social gathering. If a mule kicks you in a dream, you are likely to get into business difficulties. To see a mule kick another of his kind is a sign of a pick-up in business. 601

MUMMY. To dream of discovering a mummy in an underground tomb predicts new and unusually prosperous undertakings. If you unwrap the mummy, you are liable to be talked about by people who do not like you. 800

MURDER. It is distinctly bad luck to dream of committing murder, the more so if the victim is a baby or young person. This is a dream that warns you against loss of temper, association with people of little or no moral scruples, and extravagance. 090

MUSCLE. If you dream of displaying your muscles to an admiring audience, you are likely to be snubbed by someone you would like to have for a friend. 433

MUSEUM. Good luck in your social contacts will follow a dream of going through a museum of art or science and studying the exhibits. 095

MUSHROOM. To pick mushrooms in a dream is an indication that through taking intelligent chances you will make considerable money. To eat them signifies achievement in social life that will help you financially. 343

MUSIC. Hearing music in a dream portends good luck so long as it is played or sung in tune; otherwise it means that you will have reason to be discouraged. 590

MUSK. Dreaming of the odor of musk is a forerunner of exciting love affairs. 755

MUSKRAT. To trap or kill muskrats in a dream is a prophecy of want. To wear a coat made of the skins of muskrats is a sign of irritations from a relative who wishes to regulate your life. 383

MUSTACHE. For a woman to dream of kissing a man who wears a mustache is a forerunner of discontent with her surroundings. If a man dreams of shaving off his mustache he will lose a valuable feminine friend. 502

MUSTANG. (See Bronco.) 958

MUSTARD. Putting mustard on a sandwich or frankfurter in a dream portends a new interest in which will figure a person of the opposite sex. To see mustard growing predicts happiness in love. 858

MUTINY. If you dream that you are an officer on a ship and the crew mutinies, you are in danger of being accused of double-dealing. Be on guard against those who seek to do you harm. 017

MUTTON. Eating mutton in a dream foretells comfort with one's family. If it is served with caper sauce, the augury is of a celebration. 394

MYRTLE. Young men and women who dream of myrtle trees will have many lovers. 116

MYSTERY. Any dream in which you are introduced to a mystery is a portent of worry over an unimportant matter that will eventually be straightened out. 242

MYTH. You will be fortunate in love if you dream of being a character in one of the great myths of the ages. 133

N

NAGGING. If you have a dream in which someone nags you for something you have done or left undone, the augury is of having to visit either a doctor or a dentist. 735

NAIL. To drive nails in a dream means that you will accomplish a task that you had believed was beyond your powers. 610

NAKEDNESS. To dream of finding yourself naked in a mixed group of dignified people is a portent of being found out in some minor deception of which you have been found guilty. 053

NAME. If in a dream you meet someone whom you know perfectly well and cannot remember his or her name, you will have trouble in explaining your conduct to your family. 612

NAP. To dream of lying down to take a nap during the daytime is an augury of having plenty of money to spend. 087

NAPKIN. Using a napkin in a dream, whether to wipe off your mouth or your hands, indicates that you will complete in a satisfactory manner a job that has been assigned to you. If you fold a napkin, you will receive an invitation to a house to which you have long wished to go. 553

NAPOLEON. If you dream of seeing Napoleon, you are likely to be restless for a long time. If you dream of being Napoleon, you will suffer from the criticism of your fellow men. 912

NARCISSUS. Your friends are likely to make fun of you if you dream of this lovely flower. It is a warning against self esteem. 417

NASTURTIUM. A dream of picking nasturtiums is an augury of meeting with interesting people through whom you will achieve advancement. Eating the stems of nasturtiums in a dream is a sign of pleasant adventure. 459

NAUSEA. Being sick to one's stomach in a dream portends a situation in which you will be suspected of stealing a sum of money. Be on your guard against a frame-up. 874

NAVEL. To dream of having a sore navel indicates that you will visit the scenes of your childhood. To look at your own navel is an omen that you will win the respect of your associates. To look at another's is a sign of a coming adventure. A dream of Buddha contemplating his navel portends a season of excellent luck. 334.

NAVIGATION. There will be problems in your life that will be difficult but not impossible to solve if you dream of being the navigation officer of either a ship or an airplane. To dream of studying navigation portends traveling through many parts of the world. 239

NAVY. If you dream of being in the navy, you will have many admirers of the opposite sex. 748

NECK. Dreaming of a pain in the neck is a sign that someone who does not like you will try to make you uncomfortable. Seeing a woman's beautiful neck predicts social advancement; if her neck is thin and scrawny, you will lose money in business. 174

NECKING. It depends on what is in your mind in your dream of necking whether this is a good or a bad portent. Innocent love-making portends happiness in married life, but if the necking is done with little feeling or concern, there will be grief in your family. 877

NECKLACE. A woman who dreams of wearing a necklace will meet a distinguished gentleman and spend many happy hours with him. If a man dreams of giving his sweetheart a necklace, he will find that he will be fortunate. 303

NEIGHBOR. You are warned against losing your temper too quickly if you quarrel with your neighbors in a dream. If you dream of helping a neighbor who is in any kind of trouble, you will receive a legacy that you never expected. 045

NECROMANCY. (See Magic.) 695

NEON LIGHT. A dream of neon lights of any color predicts that you will be prodigiously bored by the conversation of a new acquaintance. To dream of smashing a neon light is an augury of a raise in salary. 590

NEPHEW. To dream of being asked for money by a nephew forecasts many calm and happy hours among genial companions. 329

NERVE. It is a sign of coming good fortune to dream of having a nerve removed from a tooth by a dentist. To dream of tortured nerves predicts that you will find contentment in your family circle. 748

NEST. Birds building a nest are an augury of marriage to the young and of happiness in home and children to their elders. It is a portent of woe if you dream of stealing a bird's nest, especially if there are eggs in it. 173

NET. Women who dream of wearing net dresses must be on their guard when they are being courted by suitors. To use a fishnet in a dream augurs an experience with the opposite sex that you would rather forget. For a man to buy a hairnet for his wife predicts that his family life will be smooth and happy. 877

NETTLE. To dream of being irritated by a nettle is a sign that there will soon be an occasion on which you should assert yourself in no uncertain terms. Stand up for your rights and you will get them. 303

NEURALGIA. Family upsets are predicted if you dream of having an attack of neuralgia. 043

NEWS. (See also Letter.) To dream of receiving news is a sign of good fortune if the news is in any way encouraging; otherwise it portends distress. 845

NEWSPAPER. To buy a newspaper in a dream augurs a surprise, although it may be an unhappy one. To dream of using newspapers as a means of procuring warmth is a sign of good health. 695

NEWSPAPER REPORTER. You will have many petty annoyances if you dream of being interviewed by a newspaper reporter. If the dream is of being a reporter, you will make a success in your business and love life. 590

NEW YEAR. If you dream of seeing the New Year come in, you may look forward to hopeful developments in your career. Gay New Year's eve parties in dreams portend happiness. 056

NICKEL. To hand a nickel to a beggar in a dream is a prophecy of making a lucky turn in business. To drop a nickel into a slot machine portends a disappointment with regard to financial affairs.261

NICKNAME. For a man to dream of calling his wife by a nickname—or vice versa—predicts happy days in the out of doors. To dream of familiarly addressing a dignified person by a nickname is a sign of great prosperity. 962

NIGHT-CAP. To dream of wearing a night-cap augurs an altercation with a husband, wife or sweetheart. If you dream of taking an alcoholic drink as a "night-cap" you are sure to be able to relax for a period. 356

NIGHTINGALE. The song of a nightingale heard in a dream is a happy portent for lovers. For married people it prophesies social advancement. 187

NIGHTMARE. It is unusual to dream of having a nightmare, but it is not unheard-of. It portends serious trouble of a kind that you have never experienced before. 357

NIPPLE. If a grown person dreams of taking sustenance through a nipple, the augury is of worry about personal debts. 461

NOBEL PRIZE. To dream of winning the Nobel Prize is a warning against too great satisfaction with your own achievements. 701

NOISE. If in a dream one hears noises that do not readily lend themselves to any particular happening, the portent is of having to meet bills of long standing. 696

NOMINATION. If you dream of being nominated for any sort of office, you will be likely to have a season of difficulties in business and family life. 240

NOODLES. Dreaming of eating crisp noodles such as those served with chow mein portends a change of address to a quieter location. If the noodles are of the soft variety, you will be enabled to carry out a plan on which you have set your heart. 374

NORTHERN LIGHTS. If you see this brilliant electrical display in a dream, and the sky shows many bright colors, you are assured of great success in your work. 988

NOSE. For a man to dream of tweaking a girl's nose is a sign that he will be married within twelve months. If a girl dreams of kissing a young man on the nose, the augury is of trouble with her relatives. Blowing one's nose in a dream predicts relief from the pressure of creditors. 103

NOSEDIVE. For a person to dream of piloting an airplane and going into a nosedive is a portent of an exceedingly interesting experience with a member of the opposite sex. 348

NOTARY. It is a sign that you will be asked for a contribution to a worthy charity if you dream of taking a document to be attested by a notary. 462

NOUGAT. Eating the candy known as nougat in a dream portends coming in contact with a group of exotic persons whom you will not understand at first and whom you will never quite like. 812

NOVEL. It is bad luck to dream of writing a novel, but to read one is a prophecy of happy hours in congenial company. 870

NOVOCAINE. Having novocaine administered in a dream foretells that you will be given a vacation, but it will be at your own expense. 552

NUDITY. If in a dream of nudity you are aware of the beauty of the human body, it is a sign of happiness for lovers. If it is accompanied by libidinous thoughts, the augury is one of discontent. 693

NUGGET. To find a nugget of gold in a dream augurs a new set of friends and new occupation. 710

NUN. To dream of seeing and talking with nuns is a sign that you will be able to square yourself with the world and your problems. 382

NUPTIAL. (See Marriage.) 479

NURSE. A uniformed and trim looking nurse seen in a dream is a portent of a new source of income. For a man to dream of falling in love with a nurse predicts a lucky break in his business. 003

NURSING. It is good luck in family life to dream of seeing a mother nursing her child. If a young woman dreams of being a trained nurse, she will marry a rich and handsome man. 533

NUT. To crack a nut in a dream augurs success in whatever project you are working on. Eating nuts is a sign that you will be tempted and that you will yield unless you are exceptionally strong willed. 604

NUTMEG. Grinding nutmeg in a dream portends a party at which you will enjoy great popularity because of your joviality. The taste of nutmeg is an omen of missing a date that will cause you great embarrassment. 060

NYMPH. To dream of a nymph wearing a flowing diaphanous robe is a sign of a strange but enjoyable experience in the out-of-doors. 559

O

OAK. Lovers who dream of oak trees may be certain of a long, happily wedded life and a suitable number of healthy children. If oak is used in the construction of a building or furniture, the prediction is sound health, a comfortable income, and more than usual harmony in the family group. 415

OAR. To dream of breaking an oar while rowing is an omen that you will get into trouble that, by using your brains, you can get out of. 879

OASIS. To arrive at an oasis after a hot, tiresome trip across the desert is an augury of great importance to the dreamer, for he may expect forthwith phenomenal success in a new venture quite outside of his usual line of endeavor. 173

OATH. It is a good sign to take an oath in a dream if it is to help an innocent person to escape suffering. 801

OATS. Whether growing in the field or prepared for the breakfast table, oats in one's dream are a prelude to a fortunate and prosperous business season. 711

OBEDIENCE. A dream in which there is a display of obedience to a higher power portends a better understanding with a former enemy. 691

OBELISK. An obelisk in a dream foretells that you will plan a tour of foreign countries, gathering pamphlets and information, and getting advice from those who have traveled, but it is probable that your trip will have to be deferred for some time. 900

OBESITY. If you dream of being too fat, it is a warning against over-indulgence in food and drink. 238

OBLIGATION. To dream of being under an obligation to someone is a sign of distress, but if you are able to meet your obligations, you will be given a long vacation with pay. 989

OBITUARY. To read an obituary in a dream and to be startled by it is a sign that an old friend will have decided to move to a distant city. 666

OBOE. Playing an oboe in your dream, or hearing one played, is a definite warning to be cautious of your eyes and ears. 992

OBSERVATORY. To look out from an observatory and see a beautiful panorama of the countryside is a good omen. You will not only enlarge your business but you will find great content in the friendships you have made. 199

OBSTETRICS. Any dream of the delivery of a child is an augury of good fortune. To dream of assisting a doctor in an obstetrical operation predicts that you will have good luck in whatever projects you engage in that relate to family matters. 635

OCCULT. If you dream of attending a spiritualist meeting or any other gathering of investigators of the occult, you will find that your friends will be likely to criticize you for being over-sensitive. 231

OCEAN. An ocean voyage in your dream denotes an escape from a troublesome person. To swim in the ocean is a portent of an opportunity to relax from your cares and worries. To look on the ocean when it is calm is an augury of prosperity, but if the sea is angry, it foretells business depression. 706

OCULIST. To visit an oculist in your dream is an augury of having to meet a serious situation in your family life. 554

ODOR. A pleasant odor permeating your dream is auspicious, and you will meet no opposition from your lover. A stench is the reverse. You will run into difficulties wherever you go and you will, moreover, be suspected by members of the opposite sex. 257

OFFENSE. To be offended in a dream and show every evidence of resenting the behavior of another means that you are likely to speak in haste and repent at leisure. If you give offense in your dream and are punished for it, the portent is that you will lose a friend and make an enemy. 489

OFFERTORY. To dream of being in church as the offertory is being played on the organ is an omen of embarrassment. To dream of forgetting to bring any money with you is a sign that you will be called on to pay the check the next time you are dining at a restaurant.

OFFICER. To be bawled out by a traffic officer for some infraction of rules for driving foretells the receipt of a check that will bounce. 472

OGLER. A girl who dreams of being ogled will be likely to have a flirtation with a sailor who is just off a ship. 621

OGRE. If you dream of a terrifying ogre, you are in danger of doing something that will prey on your conscience so that you cannot sleep. 511

OIL. Money in your pocket is foretold by a dream of a rich oil field. To oil machinery is a sign that you will receive commendation for your work. To purchase oil from a roadside service station foretells a telephone call from a sweetheart who is worried about you. To sell or try to dispose of oil is an omen of being approached by someone who will try to get you to cooperate in a crooked deal. 297

OILCLOTH. Bright, new shiny oilcloth laid upon a table in your dream denotes that you will have a rendezvous with a member of the opposite sex. Guard against any illicit love affairs and you will be happy. 003

OIL PAINTING. A fine oil painting in a heavy gold frame, if it is hung on the wall of your home, is a dream that warns against false pride. Accept the invitation that you will receive, for it may mean that you will meet people who will be able to do you much good. 806

OILSKINS. If you dream of wearing oilskins in a dream, be sure to wait a full week before drawing any money out of your savings account. 173

OINTMENT. The use of ointment in a dream, whether it is rubbed on your own or another's body, is a sign that you are in danger of flattering the wrong person. Be discreet in your dealings with anyone of the opposite sex. 717

OLD-FASHIONED. Dreaming of drinking an old-fashioned cocktail foretells that you will live in a small town and be a member of a select group of people. 650

OLD GLORY. If you dream of seeing Old Glory, the American flag, waving from a flagpole, you will acquit yourself with honor in a difficult task. 966

OLD MAID. To dream of being an old maid is a sign that you will marry a fiery black-eyed musician. 261

OLD TESTAMENT. To read the Old Testament in a dream or hear someone quote passages from it portends a welcome visit from an elderly and well-loved relative. 526

OLIVES. Juicy ripe olives eaten in a dream portend an unexpected experience in kissing. Green olives are a sign of meeting someone of an unusual type. Stuffed olives are a warning against talking with people you do not know. 837

OLIVE OIL. To dream of using olive oil in salad dressing is an omen of falling in love at first sight. Using it for deep frying predicts pleasure at a house party. 942

OMELET. Young people who dream of eating light, fluffy omelets portend a swift courtship that will make the head spin but which will result in a happy marriage. A flat, heavy omelet predicts that you will have to kiss someone as a matter of duty. 309

ONION. (See also Halitosis.) If you dream of peeling this vegetable and shedding oniony tears, you are likely to go to a circus or some other kind of joyous entertainment. To eat boiled onions signifies good health; fried onions indicate the making of an enemy. 028

ONYX. To be given an onyx ring or brooch in your dream foretells that you will change your mind on some important question. To break an onyx table signifies good fortune. 252

OPAL. Contrary to the popular belief that opals portend bad luck, to dream of them is a sign of both prosperity and popularity. 660

OPERA. To dream of going to the opera and enjoying it is a portent of being tempted to deceive a friend. 393

OPERA GLASSES. To gaze through opera glasses at a well-known person in a dream presages meeting a theatrical manager who will prove to be a good friend. Using opera glasses as a peeping Tom is a sign that you will be accused of deception. 981

OPERA HOUSE. If you dream of going into a darkened opera house, wandering about through the aisles and backstage, you will suffer a keen disillusionment through the perfidy of an old acquaintance. 120

OPERATION. You will have an ordeal of some kind to meet if you dream of being operated on by a surgeon. This may be either physical or mental. You should have an understanding with a friend and agree on some sort of procedure. To dream of being a witness to an operation is a portent of the satisfactory completion of an important and difficult job. 547

OPIUM. Opium administered to another or to yourself in a dream warns you against associating with people of loose morals and convivial habits. 071

OPOSSUM. An early celebration of some accomplishment is predicted by a dream of eating this animal roasted. 655

OPTICIAN. To dream of going to an optician for eyeglasses is a portent of worry about the possible loss of your position. It is a good dream, however, for the extra effort you will put forth will insure your keeping it. 119

OPULENCE. (See Money.) 742

ORACLE. To consult an oracle in your dream is a sign that you should not allow yourself to be tied to a woman's apron strings. If the oracle predicts dire happenings, you will find that your fortunes will pick up. 230

ORANGE. Eating an orange in your dream foretells happy days ahead. To pick oranges from the tree is a sign of a love affair that you will never forget or regret. Squeezing an orange and drinking the juice means that you will lead a happy-go-lucky existence. To see oranges graded, sorted and boxed in a packing house is a portent of a slowly increasing income. 059

ORANGOUTAN. The best advice on a dream about this great ape is: don't dream about him. A ruthlessly cruel person will seek to destroy your credit, your home and your happiness. 589

ORATION. To be bored in a dream by a long and stupid oration is a sign that you will submit to an injustice to save the honor of another person. To deliver a lengthy oration in your dream is an augury of having to make good on an old promise. 460

ORCHARD. Lucky is he who dreams of an orchard in bloom. He will be blessed with a happy home and a full pantry. 055

ORCHESTRA. To hear a jazz orchestra in a dream predicts gay times, especially if there is swing music played. A symphony orchestra is a portent of being entertained at a fine home in the suburbs. 449

ORCHIDS. Dreaming of orchids worn as a corsage denotes that you will be accused of extravagance by someone who has no business to do so. To present your lady love with orchids is a sign that you will borrow money to pay the rent. 194

ORGAN. Listening to the strains of organ music in a dream foretells being loved by someone of the opposite sex. If you play the organ, you will be a bridesmaid or best man at a wedding. 322

ORGY. If you dream of being in a drunken orgy, it is a sign that you should be more careful of the company you keep. You are likely to run afoul of the law unless you take great care after this dream. 752

ORIENT. To dream of being in an Oriental country and mingling with the common people is a prophecy that you will try to deceive an associate to further your own interests. You are warned not to yield to the temptation. 382

ORIOLE. These black and gold songbirds foretell a change of abode to a higher altitude. You will live up in the hills or perhaps in a higher apartment than the one you now occupy. 469

ORNAMENT. (See also Decoration.) You will be successful in a selling proposition if you dream of applying ornaments to anything. 490

ORPHAN. To dream that you are a child in an orphanage is a warning against self-pity that will make you tiresome to your friends. If you dream of adopting an orphan, you will be the victim of jealousy from your neighbors. 261

OSTEOPATH. If you are treated by an osteopath in a dream and feel as if your bones are being cracked, you should take special care in crossing streets because an accident is indicated. 414

OSTRICH. An ostrich dream is a good sign, particularly if the great bird kicks you. You will carry a bankroll and have many friends. 604

OTTER. In the water or out, an otter in a dream signifies a period of financial stress. Save now for the future. 014

OTTOMAN. To dream of putting your feet on an ottoman foretells that young people of different foreign origins will visit you and fall in love. 075

OUIJA BOARD. Someone of the opposite sex will divulge a secret that you have shared if you dream of getting messages by means of a ouija board. 021

OUTBOARD MOTOR. If you dream of sailing in a boat with an outboard motor, you will be the victor in a dispute with a disagreeable person. If your outboard motor stalls, it is a sign that you will lose a sum of money. 574

OUTLAW. If you dream of harboring an outlaw, you are likely to be made a fool out of by an unscrupulous group of persons. To bring an outlaw to justice means that you will have an opportunity to make money. Do not fail to grasp it. 905

OVEN. To use a hot oven for cooking in your dream predicts that you will be made an officer in a church or community organization. A cold oven is a sign of yearning for days and people who can never return. 917

OWL. An owl in a dream portends evil, but if the dreamer is able to scare it away, the prophecy is of improved circumstances. To dream of an owl coming into your room predicts a visit to quarreling relatives. 269

OXEN. The simple life is predicted by dreaming of a yoke of oxen, but though you will be poor in worldly goods, you will have many friends. 062

P

PACIFIC OCEAN. To dream of cruising on the Pacific Ocean or of crossing it for the first time is a sign that you will invest in oil stocks. 300

PACKAGE. If you carry a package in your dream, it indicates that you will shoulder a heavy responsibility that should be shared by another member of your family. To wrap up a package carefully denotes the finishing of a job with which you have taken infinite care to bring to a satisfactory conclusion. 235

PADDLE. If you dream of being dextrous with a canoe paddle, you will be able to handle your own affairs with great success. You may be placed in the position of mentor or guardian over young people. 432

PADDLE-WHEEL. To dream of seeing an old boat with a paddle-wheel is a sign that you will venture forth from your home in quest of fortune. You are warned not to take too many chances. 339

PADDOCK. Horses in a paddock attended by their grooms are a dream portent of being able to provide handsomely for your family. 806

PADLOCK. If you dream of trying to open a padlock on a door or chest, your ambitions will be thwarted and you will have a long season of discontent. 497

PAGE. Turning the pages of a book or magazine in your dream indicates that you will make a sound investment and reap a rich reward. To dream of handsome young pages in uniform is a forerunner of better business. 593

PAGODA. If you see a Chinese pagoda in your dream, it is a sign that you will plant a lovely garden. 459

PAIL. To carry a pail in your dream implies that you will move to a better neighborhood. Shiny milk pails in a row are a portent that you will take a trip and have to make an early start. 509

PAIN. To feel pain in any part of the body in a dream means that someone will try to defame you. Watch your step. 840

PAINT. To see a house being painted in a dream is an augury that someone is keeping news from you that you ought to hear. If you dream of painting anything, you will have to hide something from your best friend. 210

PAINTINGS. To dream of having paintings of your ancestors hung in your home, framed in heavy gilt, is a sign that you will receive a small inheritance from a relative you believed to be hostile to you. 933

PAJAMAS. Luxurious pajamas worn in a dream for the purpose of impressing others foretell a sordid affair with a very common person. Taking your ease in lounging pajamas in the comfort and privacy of your home is a forerunner of a mild flirtation. 981

PAL. Dreaming of having a real pal, one who goes everywhere with you, shares your secrets, and enjoys the things that you like, is a sign that you will have general good luck for a long time to come. 079

PALACE. Living in a dream palace, surrounded by much pomp and ceremony, augurs marriage with a wealthy old person with one foot in the grave. 444

PALETTE. Seeing an artist's palette smeared with colors is a portent that you will be a guest at a tea or cocktail party where there are people who represent all the arts. 137

PALISADES. To dream of seeing beautiful and imposing palisades against a sky brilliant with the colors of sunset is an omen that you will go on a western trip for a visit. 123

PALLBEARER. If you dream of being a pallbearer at a funeral, you will be promoted to a higher position. 468

PALMIST. Having your palm read in a dream presages a period during which you will do considerable worrying about your home life and finances. 344

PALM SUNDAY. To dream of attending church on Palm Sunday dressed in new spring finery is a sign that you will have a religious argument with a well-loved friend. 502

PALM TREE. If in a dream you try to climb a palm tree, you are likely to fail in an enterprise that you have in mind. To cut down a palm tree augurs deceit on the part of one whom you believed to be your friend. 808

PALSY. If you see someone suffering from palsy in your dream, you are likely to outlive your children. 909

PAN. A dream concerning the god Pan is a good omen for young and old of either sex. It foretells that you will bring a sense of humor to bear on your troubles and thereby minimize them. To use a frying pan or other kind of pan used in the kitchen is a sign of coming prosperity. 508

PANAMA HAT. Wearing a Panama hat in a dream indicates that you will be invited to engage in recreations that you cannot afford. 844

PANCAKES. Making pancakes in a dream foretells an invitation to a sumptuous banquet where you will meet worthwhile people. Eating them portends being called upon to make a speech. 155

PANHANDLER. (See Beggar.) 925

PANIC. If you dream of being caught in a panic-stricken crowd, you are warned against losing your temper when your work is criticized by your employer. 231

PANSY. To wear pansies in a corsage or in your buttonhole foretells a dinner date with people who are not quite normal. To pick pansies in a garden is a forerunner of a misunderstanding with a person of the same sex. 497

PANTHER. A panther seen in a dream portends misfortune through a neighbor who is a busybody and a gossip. If you kill the panther or get it to go away, you will make a large sum of money. 039

PANTOMIME. If you dream of watching a pantomime, either on the stage or between two people who cannot talk, you are likely to meet some very interesting people of the stage or screen. 866

PANTRY. Dreaming of a well-stocked pantry means that you will be well loved. You will have a schoolteacher for a visitor if you dream of someone robbing your pantry. 108

PAPER. The broad significance of paper in dreams is of exertion. White paper portends the possibility of success, while colored papers are an omen of wasted effort. Paper that is ready to be thrown out or burned is a sign of new opportunity. 124

PAPOOSE. To see an Indian papoose in your dream is a prophecy of a broken engagement. 079

PAPRIKA. Using paprika to season your food predicts a heated argument with someone of the Latin race. 617

PARABLE. (See Fable.) 434

PARACHUTE. To dream of bailing out from an airplane in a parachute, having difficulty in making it open, means that you will be criticized severely by someone you love. If the parachute opens easily and you float down to a safe landing, you will have a smooth and happy love life. 521

PARADE. You are likely to be elected to public office if you dream of leading a parade. If you are simply one of the rank and file, you will find that relatives will visit you and overstay their welcome. To watch a parade and be thrilled by the music and pageantry is a sign of an increase in income. 022

PARADISE. To dream of being in Paradise, a place more beautiful than you believed possible, in the companionship of charming people, portends a state of both spiritual and material happiness. 715

PARAFFIN. Using paraffin for covering jars of jelly or preserves is a dream that signifies making a call on a new neighbor. To use a paraffin candle indicates that you will receive money. 487

PARALYSIS. Temporary disability is predicted by a dream of being paralyzed. It is a warning to avoid danger so far as possible. 657

PARASOL. For a woman to dream of carrying a pretty parasol in the bright sunshine is a portent of a love affair at a summer resort. To open a parasol in the house predicts a visit to a savings bank for the purpose of depositing money. 037

PARCEL. To carry parcels in a dream prophesies discontent but eventual success in your work. To receive a parcel by mail or express is a prophecy of profitable ventures. 028

PARCEL POST. To send a package by parcel post in your dream and have to wait in line to have it weighed and stamped is a sign that you will receive a gift from across the water. To receive a parcel post package by insured mail denotes a surprising experience with a person of the opposite sex. 761

PARCHMENT. Dreaming of an ancient and yellowed parchment manuscript presages that you will make a discovery of great value in a bookshop that specializes in first editions. Parchment lampshades portend a release from pain and sorrow. 534

PARENTAGE. A dream concerning doubt as to the parentage of a child augurs quarrels among your family circle. 801

PARIS. If you dream of visiting or living in Paris, you will be likely to find happiness and success in the study of art. To imagine that you are a French resident of Paris, dressed in the latest style, is a sign that you are in danger of making a purchase that will be very extravagant and disappointing as well. 867

PARK. Someone will give you a young puppy if you dream of walking alone in a public park. To dream of a sentimental meeting with a person of the opposite sex in a park is a sign of love affairs that will prove exciting. If flowering trees are in bloom, it foretells marriage. 892

PAROLE. Dreaming of talking with a person of either sex who has been released from prison on parole, and being interested in helping that person, is an indication that you will have an opportunity to do newspaper work. 003

PARROT. To dream of having a caged parrot using profane, abusive or disgusting language is a sign that you will have to defend your name against calumny. A group of noisy, squawking parrots foretells having to attend a gathering composed chiefly of women. 601

PARSLEY. Pleasant social relations in your neighborhood are predicted by eating parsley that is used as a garnish. 839

PARSNIPS. Parsnips in a dream portend a broken friendship. If they are the only available food, you are warned against being too easily satisfied. 673

PARSON. If you dream of talking with a parson in his church, you will come under the spell of a foreign missionary. A parson in his shirtsleeves is a sign of being disappointed in a friend. 363

PARTNER. You will be financially successful if you dream of having an agreeable partner, and this relates to marriage as well as business. It portends bad luck if you are suspicious of him or he of you. 720

PARTNERSHIP. To dream of going into a business partnership predicts buying a home and being a power in the community; but to dream of dissolving a partnership augurs misfortune. 272

PARTRIDGE. (See Quail.) 701

PARTY. A dream of going to a party connotes either pleasure or distress, according to the character of the party and its guests. 879

PASSENGER. Being a dream passenger in any wheeled vehicle is a sign of slow but steady improvement in your work. 475

PASSPORT. To dream of going through all the formalities of obtaining a passport predicts travel in foreign lands and a chance to make money as well. Losing a passport is a sign that someone will belittle your best efforts. 152

PASSWORD. Going into some forbidden place by giving a password is a dream that prophesies many new friends. 918

PASTRY. (See also Cake, Pie.) Rich pastries eaten in a dream are a portent of having to miss an important engagement. 221

PASTURE. (See Meadow.) 002

PATCH. To dream of having a patch on the seat of your pants or on some other conspicuous part of your clothing is an omen of luck in games of chance. A patch worn over an eye predicts adventure in foreign lands. Seeing a patch on a beautiful woman's face is a forerunner of an adventure that you will not tell your grandchildren. 597

PATCHWORK. (See Quilt.) 907

PATENT. To dream of receiving a patent for something you have designed or invented is a sign that you will win at card-playing and the races. 752

PATENT LEATHER. Wearing shoes of patent leather and suffering because they are too tight is a prediction that you will have to make excuses to a wife, husband or sweetheart. 989

PATENT MEDICINE. Any dream of buying or taking patent medicine is a forecast of getting into a situation that will make you appear ridiculous. 498

PATH. (See also Trail.) To walk down a shady path in your dream is a prediction that you will keep a love tryst. To shovel a path through the snow portends that you will meet people of extraordinary charm. 223

PATIO. To be welcomed onto the patio of a Mexican or other Latin-American home and entertained as a guest is a sign that you will be invited to a party where you will meet celebrities of the motion-picture world, artists, writers and dancers. 880

PATTERN. If you dream of seeing fantastic patterns formed with kaleidoscopic colors that change as you watch them, you will have a succession of surprising adventures with a radical person of the opposite sex. They will be diverting, but they are likely to be as dangerous as they are alluring. 547

PAUPER. If you have a dream in which you are a pauper and resort to begging, you are in danger of becoming a very selfish miser. 875

PAVEMENT. Driving a car over a pavement full of depressions and bumps is a sign that you will feel badly because your best friend is more fortunate than you. Resist feelings of envy if you value your peace of mind. 326

PAW. If a dog or cat gives you a paw in a dream, it is a prophecy that someone you do not like will make friendly advances. If a young woman dreams of being "pawed" by a man, she is thereby warned not to engage in conversation with strangers. 893

PAWNBROKER. To go to a pawnbroker in a dream and get a loan on one of your treasured possessions is a sign that you will have an upturn in fortune within a short time. 809

PEA. For a man to dream of shelling peas means that he will meet a dark-haired, blue-eyed woman who will be the means of his climbing high on the ladder of success. A woman who shells peas will have a talkative visitor. To work in a garden of peas signifies that you must apologize to someone for your thoughtlessness. To open a can of peas augurs a family disagreement that will soon be straightened out. 927

PEACE. To dream of a world at peace is a presage of having a spiritual uplift that will help you and others in your daily life. 482

PEACH. Eating ripe peaches in a dream is a portent of a leisurely trip by automobile to the places you have long wished to visit. Green peaches are a sign that unless you right an injustice, you will suffer great regret. 935

PEACOCK. A dream of peacocks strutting about a large estate spreading their beautiful tail feathers fanwise indicates that you will be criticized for your manner toward someone less fortunate than yourself. 557

PEANUT. Eaten from the shell or salted, peanuts in a dream indicate that you will be invited to a party by people whom you have known only a short time. Eating peanut butter is a sign of regret for a white lie you have told. 107

PEAR. Seen in a dream in connection with other fruits, pears foretell a pleasant picnic in the country or in the woods. To eat fresh pears foretells hearing a scandal; canned pears, a church supper. 470

PEARL. New friends of wealth and social position are foretold by a dream of wearing pearls. You may meet one of the nobility or a distant relative of the royal family. 621

PEBBLE. A pebble tossed into water in a dream is a warning against being careless with jewelry when you bathe either at home or at the beach. If you dream of walking barefoot on pebbles, you will have an opportunity for revenge on someone who has misused you. You should weigh the consequences. 572

PECANS. Eating pecan nuts in a dream is an augury of an invitation to a delightful dinner party. 438

PEKINESE DOG. To own or care for a Pekinese dog in your dream is a portent of being complained of by your neighbors for having your radio turned on too loud. 587

PELICAN. To dream of pelicans means that you will be invited to dinner by a friend who has returned from a fishing trip with a full creel. 467

PEN. (See also Fountain Pen.) Dreaming of using a pen that spatters ink on the page is a sign you are in danger of hurting your reputation by associating with a person of doubtful character. 301

PENCIL. Trying to write in a dream with a very blunt, badly sharpened pencil portends being criticized for slovenly dress. To dream of breaking a pencil point while you are writing is a warning to look out for accidents to your person. 946

PENITENTIARY. (See Jail.) 383

PENNY. To give a child a penny in a dream foretells pleasant experiences in the woods and fields. 537

PENSION. If you dream of receiving a pension from a corporation or the government, you will be likely to receive a position doing some kind of manual work that will be both agreeable and profitable. 969

PENTHOUSE. To dream of living in a penthouse from which you have a view over a large area and in which you entertain your friends lavishly is an indication that the next place you live in will be a basement. If you dream of being a house-guest in a penthouse, you are warned against living beyond your means. 011

PEPPER. (See also Cayenne.) To dream of shaking pepper on your food and sneezing because of its pungency is a sign that you are likely to lose your temper in a manner that will bring you regret. 013

PEPPERMINTS. Eating peppermints from a paper bag in a dream is a prophecy that a distant relative will leave you all his money and heirlooms. 545

PERCOLATOR. Dreaming of making coffee with a new percolator signifies that you will move into another house; but if the percolator is old and battered, it means that your present quarters will be re-decorated. 248

PERFUME. For a woman to dream of spraying or dabbing perfume on herself predicts that she will meet a man who will fall in love with her. If a man has this dream, he will be misunderstood by both men and women. To smell a heady perfume is a prophecy of an exciting taxi ride with a person of the opposite sex. Delicate perfume that stirs pleasant emotions foretells meeting a young and beautiful woman. 562

PERISCOPE. To dream of looking through a submarine periscope is a portent of receiving a letter containing news that will cause you great concern. 282

PERMANENT WAVE. Admiring one's own permanent foretells approaching marriage to a single waman and social success to a married woman. To dream of having one's hair waved is a prediction of the receipt of money. 573

PEROXIDE BLOND. A dream of a blond whose hair has obviously been chemically treated is an omen that you will be invited to a dinner party and draw a partner who will bore you stiff. 956

PERSIAN LAMB. To dream of wearing Persian lamb predicts trouble with people in the educational field, either professors, teachers, principals or members of the board of education. 783

PERSIMMON. Eating a persimmon in a dream is an augury of an unexpected holiday. If the persimmon is unripe, you will not have a good time. 334

PERSPIRATION. (See Sweat.) 478

PESSIMIST. It is a sign that your fortunes will improve if you dream of being with a person who looks on the dark side of life. To dream that you are a pessimist is a warning against taking the burdens of the world on your shoulders. 558

PET. (See Cat, Dog, Etc.) 302

PETAL. To pull the petals from a rose or other flower in your dream is a portent of a broken engagement or friendship. 204

PETROLEUM. (See Oil.) 670

PETTING. (See also Necking.) Petting an animal in a dream foretells pleasant home affairs. For young people to dream of "petting" is a sign that they must learn to be discreet in their social contacts. 073

PETUNIA. A man who dreams of wearing a petunia in his buttonhole is likely to be disappointed in love. To set out petunias in a flower bed portends an enjoyable party in the near future. 091

PEWTER. You will enjoy the friendship of an older person if you dream of having pewter dishes and utensils in your home. 871

PHANTOM. (See Ghost.) 519

PHARMACIST. (See Druggist.) 231

PHEASANT. To hunt pheasants in a dream foretells that for a short time you will have easy going, but it is also a warning to save your money for a rainy day. Eating roast pheasant portends a new source of income. 305

PHONE. (See Telephone.) 294

PHONOGRAPH. (See also Record.) Hearing your own voice from a phonograph in a dream is a portent of being disillusioned about your ability to impress others. To listen to phonograph music predicts a new kind of adventure that may or may not be agreeable. 353

PHOSPHORESCENCE. It is an augury of a strange and exciting experience to dream of seeing the glow of phosphorous at night upon the sea or in the woods on decaying tree stumps. 418

PHOTOGRAPH. (See also Camera.) To dream of looking over old photographs and renewing your youth thereby predicts that you will meet an old school friend who has made a great success. To see a photograph of a former sweetheart whom you had almost forgotten is a sign of content in your present life. 866

PHYSIC. (See Laxative.) 569

PHYSICIAN. (See Doctor.) 854

PIANO. To dream of being able to play the piano with ease and enjoyment, even if you have never taken lessons, is a forerunner of success in drawing, painting or writing. You will stand a good chance of making your mark as a movie actor or actress if you dream of being a piano tuner. To dream of lifting a piano presages a long period of achievement and good health. To hear an artist play the piano beautifully is a promise of more money in your pay envelope; but if it is played out of tune, you are likely to be discharged. 957

PIAZZA. (See Porch.) 424

PICK. (See also Toothpick.) You are likely to have hard going in your work if you dream of using a pick, but in this dream there is a promise of better times if you will persist in trying to better yourself in education. 877

PICKEREL. Catching this kind of fish in a dream augurs an exciting experience with a member of the opposite sex. If a pickerel bites you with his saw teeth, you will have trouble with an acquaintance you had trusted. 651

PICKET. In climbing a fence in a dream, if you get caught on a picket you will have to answer for a minor misdeed. If you dream of picketing a factory or a shop for being unfair to union labor, you will win admiration for the completion of a difficult job. 219

PICKLE. Eating pickles in a dream denotes being satisfied with the state of your health and your bank account. 935

PICKPOCKET. If you dream of catching someone who is picking your pocket, you are likely to have an altercation with a person to whom you owe a sum of money. 657

PICK-UP. A man who dreams of picking up a girl on the street is in danger of severe criticism from his employer. If a girl dreams of being picked up, she will marry in haste and repent all her life. 509

PICNIC. (See also Camp, Frolic.) Dreaming of going on a picnic portends joyous association with friends. 234

PICTURE. (See Motion Picture, Painting, Photograph.) 415

PIE. (See Cake, Pastry.) 491

PIER. (See Quay.) 583

PIG. A dream of pigs in a sty predicts a comfortable home, children, and plenty to eat and drink. 339

PIGEON. To dream of pigeons flying through the air in circles is a prophecy of family trouble. Feeding pigeons in a dream portends distractions on account of business conditions. 795

PILE. (See also Hemorrhoids.) To put articles into a pile in a dream is a sign of having to account for an omission of duty. 157

PILGRIMAGE. Dreaming of a pilgrimage to a shrine of some kind portends good luck both in business and social life. 975

PILGRIM FATHERS. You will find that you can enjoy life better after a dream of the austere and unbending Pilgrim Fathers of New England. 881

PILL. To take a pill in a dream is a sign that you will move to a new address. 805

PILLORY. This old-fashioned means of punishment seen in a dream is a forerunner of great embarrassment. If you dream of being pilloried, you will have to pay a debt that you had believed was outlawed. 726

PILLOW. To dream of laying your head in comfort upon a soft pillow is a prophecy that you will not have to worry about your ability to make a living. If the pillow seems hard and uncomfortable you will have difficulty in meeting your just obligations. 550

PILOT. If you dream of being a pilot of either a ship or an airplane, you will be asked for advice by a person who is much older than you are. 720

PIMPLE. Being annoyed by a pimple in a dream augurs difficulties with people to whom you owe money. If you pick a pimple in a dream, you are apt to be ill for some time. 546

PIN. To dream of hearing a pin drop is an augury of contentment. Sitting on a pin prophesies a pleasant surprise. If you dream of pinning up a dress, the augury is of embarrassment at an evening party. 313

PINAFORE. It is a wholly pleasant augury if you dream of seeing little girls who are wearing pinafores. 992

PINCHERS. To dream of trying to make repairs on machinery with a pair of pinchers is a prediction of success in your business. 210

PINCUSHION. A woman who dreams of making a pincushion will have many invitations to parties from interested men. 177

PINE. A pine tree in a dream is a sign of health and well-being whether it is a large or small one. 644

PINEAPPLE. Love adventures in tropical lands are predicted by a dream of working in a field of pineapples. Drinking the juice portends a successful business career. Eating the fruit is a forerunner of social success. 723

PINE CONE. Long life is presaged by a dream of picking up pine cones in a forest. To burn them portends the birth of a son to one of your friends. 148

PINFEATHERS. To dream of picking pinfeathers off a chicken or other fowl foretells ease and plenty for a housewife and good business for a man. 434

PING-PONG. If you dream of playing a fast game of ping-pong with the odds about even, you will have new responsibilities given you and a corresponding increase in your weekly remuneration. 947

PIN MONEY. A woman who dreams of being given pin money by a husband or lover will be likely to inspire jealousy in one of her acquaintances. 687

PINOCHLE. Good friendship and conviviality in your social circle is predicted by a dream of playing this card game whether you win or lose. 247

PIONEER. To dream of pioneering in an uncultivated country points to success in your chosen work. 228

PIPE. For a man to dream of smoking a pipe augurs eventual success and an adequate income. For a woman to have this dream is an augury of being publicly rebuked for an indiscretion. 864

PIRATE. Armed and dressed in eighteenth-century clothes, pirates in a dream portend a car accident. You are warned to exercise great caution. 749

PISTACHIO NUT. To eat this green-colored nut in a dream augurs a loving friend of the opposite sex. A dream of its use as flavoring and coloring for food is a prophecy of social entertaining. 213

PISTOL. (See also Gun, Revolver.) It is bad luck to dream of pointing a pistol at anyone, even if it is only a toy pistol. It prophesies that you will suffer from some physical ailment. To shoot at a target with a pistol foretells success if you score a hit; otherwise failure. 714

PITCH. To dream of getting pitch on your hands or your clothing is a sign that unless you select your friends with greater care, you will be involved in a scandal. 922

PITCHER. Pouring from a pitcher in a dream is a sign of plenty. To break a pitcher augurs foot trouble. To piece together a broken pitcher foretells a party where there will be considerable drinking. 579

PITCHFORK. Handling a pitchfork for hay or barnyard uses is a forerunner of good health. To dream of being chased by a devil or a human being holding a pitchfork augurs worry over money affairs. 302

PITH HELMET. You will visit a tropical country if you dream of wearing a pith helmet. 584

PITY. If you pity another in a dream, you will have to share your home with an in-law. If someone pities you, the omen is good for business. 353

PLAGUE. To dream of a terrible plague visiting the city or community in which you live is a sign that you should have a physician check up on your health. 218

PLAID. Wearing plaid materials in a dream means that an old and trusted friend will visit you and make you much happier than you have recently been. To see a Scotch highlander in a plaid kilt is a sign of a whirlwind love affair. 324

PLAN. To dream of going over the plan of your house with an architect or contractor is a forerunner of getting some new and becoming clothes. If you dream of drawing your own plans, you are likely to be cheated in a land deal. 156

PLANE. (See Airplane.) 483

PLANK. To dream of walking on a plank predicts that you will be in danger of being robbed. If the dream is of being made to "walk the plank" by pirates, you must also guard against personal injury. 749

PLASTER. Mixing plaster in a dream foretells a lucky break with a lottery ticket. Applying it to a wall is an omen of continued prosperity. 832

PLATE. (See Dishes.) 173

PLATE GLASS. If you dream of passing a plate glass window and seeing your reflection in it, you should be warned against flirtations. To break a plate glass window is a sign of your having to relieve somebody's distress. 803

PLATFORM. You will be called upon to make a public address if you dream of standing on a platform. You may have an offer from not too far away. 688

PLATINUM. For a woman to dream of platinum foretells that she will meet the man of her choice and that he will lead her shortly to the alter. To lose a platinum ring is an omen of having to apologize for forgetting an important duty. 270

PLAY. Seeing a play in your dream is a good portent if it gives you enjoyment but if it is sad or disagreeable, you will be dunned by your creditors. 810

PLAYER. (See Actor.) 798

PLAYGROUND. To dream of happy, noisy children at a playground forecasts a vacation with an old school friend. 368

PLAYING CARDS. (See also Cards.) If you dream of playing cards, you will have a falling out with the one you love best. This interpretation holds whether you win or lose; but if you dream of winning, you will have good fortune with regard to money affairs. 797

PLAYMATE. You will receive an important and interesting communication in regard to property if you dream of an old playmate of childhood. 653

PLEDGE. If you make a pledge in a dream, you will have to sacrifice one of your treasured possessions to help out a relative. 571

PLOT. Bad luck in a variety of ways will follow if you dream of being a party to a plot to injure another. If you discover a plot against yourself you will be able to pay your debts and save money. 284

PLOW. To use a plow drawn by horses or mules foretells slow but sure progress in business and love. A tractor plow augurs a lucky turn in real estate. 138

PLUM. Eating a fresh plum in a dream and having the juice trickle down your chin indicates that you will be appointed to a position of honor. Canned plums augur a disappointment. Plum pudding is a sign of danger from gossip. 672

PLUMBING. Bright new chromium plated plumbing seen and used in a dream forecasts leisure and the means to take a short pleasure trip. Old leaky plumbing portends great irritation from nagging relatives. 431

PNEUMONIA. There will be difficult times ahead if you dream of having this disease, but you can make your own destiny by avoiding any course of which your better judgment would disapprove. It is a particular warning to guard your health. 258

POCKET. A dream of being surprised at what you find in your pocket is a promise of an easy-going mate who will bear with you in your peculiarities and shortcomings. A dream of having a hole in a coat pocket predicts loss of prestige among your neighborhood group. 631

POCKETBOOK. If a man dreams of looking through a woman's pocketbook and finding a great variety of articles, he will be confronted with a problem he cannot solve. For anyone to dream of having a pocketbook full of money means that an increase in salary is on the way. 002

POEM. To dream of writing a poem that pleases you is a sign that you will be approached by a motion-picture concern to do special character parts. Reading another's poem in a dream portends popularity among church members. 257

POET. If you dream of being on friendly terms with a poet, one of your friends will ask you for a loan or will suggest coming to live with you. A poet with long hair signifies unusual experiences. 179

POINTER. Good news may be confidently expected after a dream of seeing a pointer in the hunting field. 394

POISON. A dream of taking poison portends that someone will ridicule you for your strange views on behavior. To dream of poisoning an animal signifies distressing events in your family life. 040

POISON IVY. Suffering in a dream from contact with poison ivy is a forerunner of misunderstandings with a very good friend of the opposite sex. 724

POKER. A game of poker played in a dream foretells pleasant relaxation with good friends. The augury is much the same whether you win or lose. Using a fire poker to chase an animal or robber is a sign that you will have to explain an ill-advised action. 518

POLAR BEAR. Seen in a zoo, a polar bear portends misery from the loss of treasured possessions, but if you dream of seeing it in its native habitat of ice and snow, it is an omen of improved living conditions for yourself and family. 477

POLECAT. (See Skunk.) 060

POLICE. It is good luck to dream of the police unless you are trying to escape from them. To stop and ask directions from a traffic officer portends a visit to wealthy friends. To be stopped by a traffic officer for some minor infraction of the law predicts that you will apologize to some friend. 794

POLICE DOG. To dream of being attacked by a police dog is a forerunner of being called upon to contribute to a cause in which you do not believe. A friendly police dog is a good augury for people who enjoy outdoor sports. 681

POLITENESS. (See Courtesy.) 121

POLITICS. Talking politics in your dream is a sign of success in business if the conversation is between members of the same sex and there is no bitterness in it. It is bad luck for a man to talk politics with a woman, or vice-versa. Listening to a political speech during a campaign betokens a row with your in-laws. Making a speech of this kind is a sign that you will receive a small sum of money. 416

POLKA. It is a prediction of good times in the company of quiet, well-bred people to dream of dancing the polka or of watching other people dance it. 840

POLO. You will be remembered in some wealthy person's will if you dream of playing polo or watching others play. 376

POLYGAMY. To dream of having several wives is a sure sign of worries and regrets. 849

POMEGRANATE. To pick and eat the seeds of a pomegranate in a dream augurs pleasant hours in the company of one of the opposite sex. 975

PONCHO. If you dream of putting a poncho over your head to keep off the rain or to keep you warm, the augury is of someone coming to your aid in time of great need. 072

POND. (See also Lake.) A clear pond in which there are swans portends wealth through industry. To see the reflections of trees and clouds in a pond indicates that you will develop a genius for addressing audiences. A muddy pond seen in a dream is a sign of a hilarious time with professional people. 351

PONY. (See Filly, Horse.) 552

POODLE. You will have amusing experiences in business if you dream of seeing a French poodle clipped according to the fashion for these dogs. 377

POOL. A pool in a garden in which are growing water lilies, lotus and other aquatic plants is a harbinger of contentment for lovers. To play pool in a dream predicts that you will acquire much skill in reading character. 804

POOP. To dream of standing on this raised deck in the stern of a vessel is a splendid augury in almost any circumstances. 176

POPCORN. Eating fresh, white crisp popcorn in a dream portends money, leisure and enjoyment of life. If it is limp and stale and full of unpopped kernels, you are likely to be disagreeably surprised by a letter that you will receive. 683

POPGUN. Shooting a toy gun in a dream and making only a loud pop warns you that someone will make a derogatory remark about your personality. Check up on your personal faults. 128

POPLAR. Bending before a stiff breeze, poplar trees in a dream are an indication of adventures with people who value neither their lives nor their reputations. Cutting down a poplar augurs temporary financial embarrassment. To plant one is a sign of good returns on a small investment. 210

POPPY. A short but passionate love affair is predicted by a dream of red poppies in a garden. California poppies in a field are an augury of sentimental delight. To dream of picking poppies betokens disappointment. 139

PORCELAIN. Fine, dainty porcelain, whether new or old, seen or used in a dream foretells meeting people of social importance under pleasant circumstances. To break a porcelain dish augurs making a good friend. 315

PORCH. Women who dream of sitting on a porch with young men will have a proposal within a short time, but they should not be too quick to accept it. Anyone who dreams of sleeping on a porch will have to explain the reason for what appears to be a definitely crazy act. 821

PORCUPINE. You will be advanced in your position if you dream of being stuck by quills on a porcupine, but you will have a serious argument with one of your friends. 756

PORK. In any form—fresh, salted or smoked—a dream of eating pork foretells that you will obtain a better job, either with the same employer or a different one. You will need it, however, for you will have added responsibilities. 981

PORT. Dreaming that you drink port wine foretells that you will entertain your friends with your sparkling conversation and behavior. Reaching a port in a sailing vessel or steamship augurs the successful completion of a pet project. 418

PORTER. To have a porter carry your luggage in a dream is an omen of going on a trip that will add to your success. To dream of drinking porters beer predicts better health. 483

PORTFOLIO. If you dream of carrying a portfolio, you will be asked for advice by an important and influential personage. This is a dream that suggests that you try to improve your mind through study and reading of the newspapers. 851

PORTHOLE. To dream of looking through the porthole of a ship and seeing another ship is a sign of approaching adventure in which you will meet a friend whom you have not see in years. 688

PORTRAIT. Having your portrait made in a dream, either by photography or painting, is a sign of disillusionment. To see another person posing for a portrait portends being invited to a select social gathering. 211

POSTAGE. (See Stamp.) 187

POSTCARD Writing a message on a postcard in a dream foretells being accused of an indiscretion. To dream of receiving a postcard written in fine handwriting that is hard to decipher is a prediction of being harassed by debt. 694

POSTERIOR. (See Buttocks.) 862

POSTMAN. To dream of receiving mail matter from a postman—letters, circulars or parcels—augurs the receipt of good news from an old friend. 126

POSTPONEMENT. To dream of the postponement of your wedding prophesies a long trip by airplane. Postponing an outdoor event on account of rain presages bad weather and a delayed vacation. 831

POT. Whether of crockery or metal, a pot in a dream forecasts an upset condition of mind from which you should make a determined effort to get away. To break a pot augurs grief through the lack of consideration of one of your friends. 555

POTATO. Peace of mind and a comfortable income are predicted by a dream of eating potatoes in any form. Hoeing in a potato field is a sign of a lucky business deal. 871

POTTER. To dream of a potter fashioning a vase on a revolving potter's wheel is an omen of meeting someone who will become a true friend and who will have a good influence over you. 691

POTTERY. Dreaming of fine pottery in shop or home portends the beginning of a new order of things in which you will be able to live the kind of life to which you have aspired. 816

POUT. Dreaming of a pretty girl with a pout on her face is a sign of having to break an engagement of long standing. 285

POVERTY. A dream of poverty is unlucky only if it is accompanied by dirt or degradation. Otherwise it is a forerunner of better times. 121

POWDER. A man who dreams of seeing his sweetheart or wife powdering her nose in a public place is warned against women who are both vain and lacking in the niceties of behavior. A woman who dreams of dropping face powder on the floor will have a series of minor accidents that will keep her in a state of turmoil. 974

PRAIRIE. Being alone on a great flat prairie in a dream is a prophecy of having a struggle with your conscience. 126

PRAISE. If you dream of being praised for your accomplishments, you will find a new and profitable interest in life. 106

PRANK. To dream of playing a prank on a friend is a sign of having to account for something you have left undone. If you are the victim of a prank and take it good-naturedly, you will be likely to have an honor conferred on you. If you show irritation in your dream, prepare for family troubles. 711

PRAYER. A dream of praying for Divine guidance or help augurs good fortune in both your spiritual and material condition. To listen to the prayer of another, especially a child, is a forerunner of making a friend who will remain faithful through life. 089

PREACHING. (See Sermon.) 749

PREDICTION. If you dream of making a prediction and of its coming true, you are likely to find that people will begin to ask your advice on all sorts of matters. 031

PREFACE. Reading a book's preface in a dream is a sign that you will shortly begin a new and successful project. 176

PREGNANCY. For a woman to dream that she is pregnant foretells that she will have the means to buy many new pretty clothes. If a man should have this dream, it augurs an adventure in which there will be considerable danger. 318

PRESCRIPTION. Having a prescription filled by a druggist in a dream is a sign that you will have an illness that will be the result of your own carelessness. 863

PRESENT. To receive a present in a dream foretells good luck in gambling; to give one, the receipt of money by mail. 319

PRESENTIMENT. Having a presentiment of death in a dream is a sign that you should take special care not to do anything involving risk. 654

PRESERVES. A woman who dreams of making preserves in her kitchen will be invited to become a member of a prominent woman's organization. Eating preserves is a fortunate dream for those connected with the grocery business. 371

PRESTIDIGITATOR. (See Magic.) 484

PREVARICATION. (See Lie.) 887

PRICK. Giving your finger a prick in a dream is a portent of what will appear to be supernatural happenings. If blood is drawn, there will be general misunderstandings and matters that will cause you perturbation. 163

PRICKLY HEAT. A dream of having prickly heat forecasts a major operation for yourself or one of your friends. 980

PRIEST. Whatever the denomination, a priest in a dream is usually a good sign. 986

PRIMA DONNA. To dream of meeting socially a prima donna of the dramatic or operatic stage prophesies a succession of adventures with a glittering circle of people. To see her perform on the stage predicts an escapade that will make you a little ashamed of yourself. 214

PRIMER. To dream of seeing a child reading out of a primer is a sign that you will take up the study of a new language. If you dream that the child is yourself, you will have happy adventures. 918

PRIMROSE. A dream of sending a primrose plant to a person of the opposite sex is a forerunner of a love affair that is not likely to turn out happily. 212

PRINCE. A woman, young or old, spinster or wife, who dreams of meeting a prince at a social function will find that she will have increasing influence in her community, but she should guard against arousing jealousy among other women. 565

PRINCESS. The interpretation for this dream is for a man, and is a parallel to that in the preceding. 899

PRINTING. A person who dreams of being in the printing business or trade will be received in the best society and much respected for being well-informed on most subjects. It is a fortunate dream for those who aspire to write magazine articles and books. 147

PRISON. (See Jail.) 201

PRIVACY. A dream of having your privacy invaded by a person of the opposite sex predicts a happening that will be upsetting but amusing. 799

PRIVET HEDGE. (See Hedge.) 349

PRIZE. To dream of being awarded a prize in any kind of a contest indicates that you will be successful in your work. If you give someone a prize in a dream, you will be left a small legacy by a friend who has passed on. 835

PRIZE-FIGHTER. For a young woman to dream of being wooed by a prize-fighter is a prophecy of quarrels with her suitor. If she dreams of seeing him go down for the count in the prize ring, it means that she will be married within a month. If a man dreams of being a prize-fighter, he will have a raise in salary before long. 593

PROCESSION. (See Parade.) 050

PRODIGAL. If you dream of the Biblical story of the Prodigal Son, you will have an opportunity to forgive an enemy and thereby make a friend. 723

PRODIGY. A dream of a very young person who is accomplished far beyond his or her years—such as a violinist, pianist, or other kind of musician or artist—points toward your being bored by the people with whom you mingle every day. 434

PROFANITY. Hearing profanity from a man in a dream portends a drop in the value of your securities and real estate holdings. If the swearing is done by a woman, you are going to have an embarrassing experience with one of the opposite sex, and if you are not careful it will develop into something quite serious. 669

PROFIT. If you dream of making a business deal and thereby turning a profit, you are warned to stick to your plans during the following few weeks. 017

PROHIBITION. To dream that prohibition is in force in your country or state is a sign that you will be punched by an officer of the law. 244

PROMISSORY NOTE. If in a dream you have a note coming due and have no resources with which to meet it, you are warned against over-extravagance in spending. To dream of meeting a note when it is due augurs success in business and a good income. 157

PROPAGANDA. Trying to influence public opinion in favor of or against certain things is a dream that predicts a lack of trust on the part of your acquaintances. If is appears to be in wartime, you will be falsely accused of irregularities in the conduct of your business. 048

PROPELLER. It is a sign that you will fail in work that has been given you to do if you dream of being on a boat that has lost its propeller. 628

PROPOSAL. A single young woman or widow who dreams of having a proposal from an eligible man will be given much attention by men older than they will admit. A man who dreams of proposing will have increased power of making money; but if he is rejected he will spend everything he gets. 660

PROSTITUTE. If the prostitute of whom you dream is an object to inspire sympathy, the augury is of success as a worker for the downtrodden. If she is brazen and unscrupulous, you will suffer a short illness. 410

PRUDE. (See also Plum.) Dried prunes eaten in a dream signify a change of address. Stewed prunes predict better health than you have enjoyed for years. 730

PTOMAINE POISONING. To dream of suffering from ptomaine poisoning is a direct warning against gluttony, especially in restaurants and other public eating places. 393

PUBLISHER. For a man or woman to dream of meeting a publisher is a sign that unless he or she is very careful, there will be a loss of money sustained. To dream of signing a contract with a publisher is an augury of great wealth. 421

PUDDING. Eating pudding in a dream is an indication that you will have a prosperous but uneventful life. If it is plum pudding, however, there will be many ups and downs. 830

PUDDLE. It is a sign that you will have a disagreeable experience if you dream of being splashed by muddy water from a puddle. 838

PULLMAN CAR. Riding in a Pullman car in a dream is a forerunner of prosperity and time for travel to places you have never seen. The augury is similar whether the Pullman is a chair car, sleeper, diner or observation car. 715

PULPIT. You will be suspected of double-dealing if you dream of delivering a sermon from a pulpit. 825

PULSE. To dream of feeling the wrist pulse of a sick woman warns of being too confidential with people whom you have met recently. If in a dream your own pulse quickens either at emotion or danger, you will find that there will be a new interest in your life. 559

PUMP. Drawing water from a pump in a dream is a sign of a successful career in banking. To push a pump handle back and forth without getting any water predicts disappointment in a business deal. To find a pump frozen up means that you will have to work hard for little money. To prime a pump portends temporary prosperity. 474

PUMPERNICKEL. Eating pumpernickel in a dream foretells the ability to buy a new automobile and new and fashionable clothes. 983

PUMPKIN. You will have a smooth and happy family life if in your dream you eat pumpkin in any form. To see yellow pumpkins at harvest time in a cornfield predicts a season of plenty and comfort. 075

PUN. To dream of making a pun that amuses you but offends others foretells the loss of a friend. 314.

PUNCTURE. If you dream of being without a spare tire and having a puncture, you will go a long time in your automobile without having an accident. Trying to repair a puncture in a dream is a prophecy of an argument with husband, wife or sweetheart. 981

PUPPY. It is a good portent for married people to dream of having one or more puppies playing on the floor. To dream of a dead puppy foretells sorrow. 995

PURGE. (See also Laxative.) To dream of a purge in the sense of killing politically undesirable people by a despotic government points toward a situation in which you will be called upon to save a relative or friend from disgrace. 893

PURSE. (See Pocketbook.) 302

PUS. Dreaming of a wound from which pus is issuing foretells an accident from which you are likely to carry scars for the rest of your life. 643

PUSHBUTTON. Pressing a pushbutton in a dream and hearing a bell ring in the deep recesses of the house portends a surprise that will probably be pleasant. 775

PYTHON. To dream of this large boa-like serpent is a sign that someone will try to intimidate you. Hold your ground and you will win out. 911

QUACK. To dream of finding out that you have asked the advice of a quack doctor is a portent of better health. 358

QUAGMIRE. (See Mire.) 911

QUAIL. If you get a covey of quail to take flight suddenly in a dream, you are likely to have a surprising and altogether agreeable experience. To dream of eating quail predicts an increase in your income and greater comforts in your daily life. 273

QUAKER. Peace and comfort will be your daily lot if you dream of associating with Quakers. 097

QUARANTINE. Being held in quarantine in a dream augurs misery unless you can show a clean bill of health. 830

QUARREL. For a girl to dream of quarreling with her suitor is an omen of an early marriage. A man who dreams of quarreling with a woman will come off second best in an argument with his boss. A dream of quarreling with your neighbors portends travel by bus. A family quarrel foretells that you will move to other living quarters. 163

QUARRY. If you dream of working in a quarry, getting out pieces of rock, you will have to work hard for a meager living. 709

QUARTETTE. To dream of singing in a quartette denotes a lessening of influence with people whom you formerly controlled. 170

QUARTZ. To find a beautiful piece of quartz in a dream is an augury that someone will try to cheat you. You must be alert to everything that is going on or you will lose money. 921

QUAY. You will go on a vacation trip to foreign shores if you dream of seeing ships lying alongside a quay. 834

QUEEN. If a woman dreams that she is a queen and inspires awe and reverence among her subjects, she is in great danger of being asked for money that she owes. To dream of kneeling before a queen is an omen of promotion to a better job; but if you kiss her hand you will be the victim of office or church politics. Seeing a queen go by in a carriage or automobile signifies honor, happiness and prosperity. 440

QUEST. (See Searchlight.) 798

QUESTION. In general, it is good luck to ask questions in a dream; but if someone questions you and you are unable to answer, the augury is not propitious. 213

QUESTIONNAIRE. Petty irritations are foretold by a dream of replying to a long list of questions in a questionnaire. 090

QUICK. You will hear disparaging remarks about yourself if you dream of cutting a fingernail or toenail down to the quick. 075

QUICKSAND. A dream of sinking in quicksand is a sharp warning against prying into the affairs of other people. To help another out of quicksand foretells increasing income. 536

QUIET. If you dream of being in an absolutely quiet place, you are likely to undergo some nervous shock. A sudden change from a noisy to a quiet place is a portent of a trip. 668

QUILL. Plucking a quill from a bird of any kind foretells the writing of an important letter that will bring you luck. 770

QUILT. To dream of covering yourself with a patchwork quilt predicts a reunion with several members of your family. A down quilt is a sign that you will soon be able to afford more luxury. 696

QUINCE. Someone will accuse you of being stupid if you dream of eating ripe quinces. Jelly made from this fruit portends meeting a person whom you will not understand. 988

QUININE. Taking this medicine in a dream is a sign to engaged couples that their ardor will cool sooner or later. If the bitter taste is apparent, there will be a sharp quarrel and a broken engagement. 085

QUINTUPLETS. It is a favorable augury to dream of seeing a group of quintuplets of any age or sex. An early marriage is predicted to lovers and a happy home life to those who are married. It is a portent of obstacles overcome for a woman to dream of giving birth to quintuplets. 804

QUIP. You will meet a new and interesting person if you dream of making a clever quip. To hear one made signifies that you will be invited to a gay party. 560

QUIVER. You must make up your mind to avoid alcoholic liquors if you dream of a quivering face. A quiver full of arrows is a portent that if you pay a little more attention to your job, your salary will be raised. 156

QUIZ. If you dream of answering questions in a quiz, the augury is good or bad according to whether you give the right or wrong answers. 875

QUOITS. Young people who dream of playing quoits will have delightful love affairs. To get a "ringer" in a dream predicts an early marriage and a long honeymoon. 897

QUOTATION. Hearing well-known quotations in your dream—such as lines from Shakespeare, maxims from the Bible and similar sources—predicts success in literature, art, music and the drama.

R

RABBI. If you are of the Jewish faith and dream of consulting a rabbi, you will be prsperous in business. If you are of another faith, you will make a new friend who will help you toward the goal you have set for yourself. 818

RABBIT. Many rabbits seen in a dream signify that you will have several children who will be a credit to you. To go rabbit hunting predicts meeting an interesting person of the opposite sex on a trip by bus, train or plane. To wear a rabbit fur coat is a sign that you will be able to wear mink.

RABIES. If in a dream a mad dog attacks you and you get rabies, it is an indication that you have an unsuspected enemy who is talking behind your back. 416

RACCOON. Raccoons seen in their native haunts foretell the purchase of a new saddle horse. To go on a 'coon hunt is a sign of good crops for the farmer and good business in general. To wear a raccoon coat is a sign that you will go further with your education. 833

RACE. To watch a race being run—on foot, horseback, in an automobile or airplane—is a fortunate augury if you win money as the result. Lovers will come together in a happy marriage, and important business deals will be consummated. If you dream of running in a footrace, you will have a new position offered to you whether you win or lose. To dream of hating any race other than your own augurs bad luck in your business or social life. 244

RACKET. Hearing a loud racket in your dreams is a sign that you will be criticized for talking out of turn. To dream of playing tennis with a racket portends an argument that will cause ill feelings. 409

RACKETEER. Be on your guard against false friends after a dream of being made a proposition by a racketeer. You will be tempted to do something against your better judgment. If you are threatened with physical harm by a racketeer, you are likely to suffer an illness. 670

RADIATOR. Dreaming of a radiator that is hissing and pounding with steam is a sign that there will be an attempt at blackmail. Be warned not to do anything to warrant it. A cold radiator betokens regret for thoughtlessness. If you dream of your car radiator boiling, there will be difficulties to smooth out in your love life. 055

RADIO. To dream of hearing a radio playing gently in your dream is a portent of peaceful days spent at home with your family, among your books and hobbies. A blaring radio that annoys others foretells an attack of rheumatism or arthritis. 0423

RADISH. If you eat a radish in your dream, you will be flattered by a designing person of the opposite sex. 738

RADIUM. Handling a particle of radium in your dream is a sign that you will acquire a large amount of money but that it will give you little happiness. If you dream that it burns you, you are warned against car accidents. 984

RAFFLE. Winning a raffled article in a dream foretells luck in bingo. 761

RAFT. To dream of floating on a raft on a slow-moving, sluggish river indicates that your indolence is causing you to fall behind in the procession of life. If in your dream you build a raft and launch it on swift, bright waters, you will have reason to feel encouraged about the future. 877

RAG. Dirty rags in a corner indicate the probability of illness. To fold clean rags and put them away for use in cleaning is a dream that portends a prosperous season. Ragged clothes worn in a dream are a sign that you are on the verge of receiving a legacy. 001

RAGE. If you dream that you fall into a rage and are so angry that you are ready to go to any lengths to seek revenge on one or more individuals, it is a sign that you will be snubbed by someone whose favor you would like to enjoy. To dream of trying to pacify another person who is in a rage foretells that you will have hard luck in the work you are doing. 972

RAID. To dream of being in a city that is being raided by enemy airplanes portends the loss of property. If you dream of making a raid, you will make a small sum of money outside your regular income. 475

RAILROAD. Riding on a railroad in a dream foretells that you will find a new and pleasant hobby. To dream of seeing a streamlined railroad train whiz by you indicates that someone will help you get out of a tight place. 012

RAIN. To be out in the rain and drenched to the skin in your dream foretells a cool reception from the person you love. To watch the rain from indoors or some other sheltered spot predicts a disappointment in business. 312

RAINBOW. You may chase rainbows even in your dreams. You may search for the pot of gold at the end of the rainbow, and the interpretation is ever the same—trouble of various kinds, followed by the greatest happiness that you have ever known. 846

RAISIN. To eat raisins in a dream foretells that you will develop strength of character that will stand you in good stead when you are tempted to go wrong. 582

RAKE. To dream of using a rake on the lawn or in the garden is an omen that you and your family are due for a good time together. To step on a rake and have the handle come up and hit you is a sign of an approaching agreeable surprise. 923

RAM. If you dream of being chased or butted by a ram, it is time that you thought of giving up loose companions with whom you have been associating. 920

RANCH. If you dream of owning and living on a western ranch, you will make many new friends in the show business and newspaper circles. Being a guest at a dude ranch in a dream is a sign of getting into trouble through repeating an accusation that you have heard. 750

RANGER. A fit of homesickness is portended by a dream of seeing forest rangers at work. 562

RANSOM. To be held for ransom in a dream portends the receipt of a large sum of money from someone who has wronged you and wishes to make amends. 698

RAPE. A dream of rape in any form is a warning to anyone to avoid the appearance of evil. 623

RASPBERRY. Seen on the bush in a dream, raspberries foretell a day of leisure; eaten from a dish, they are an omen of a day of pleasure. 851

RAT. Sickness of an epidemic nature is foretold by a dream of rats. It is a warning to avoid crowds and to guard your health. 675

RATTLE. You will sit at the head of your own table if you dream of a baby's rattle. A rattle in your automobile that is hard to locate predicts worry for the safety of your relatives. 727

RATTLESNAKE. A warning against people whom you do not trust is contained in a dream of encountering a rattlesnake; you will likely suffer a severe illness if it bites you. 379

RAT TRAP. To set a rat trap in a dream foretells release from a menace that you have feared. To dream of catching a rat in a trap is an omen of better fortune. 519

RAVEN. (See Crow.) 565

RAVIOLI. Eating ravioli in an Italian restaurant foretells that you will meet a family of foreigners who are in some way connected with army or navy life. 200

RAZOR. If you dream of using the old type of razor with an unguarded blade for shaving, it presages a meeting with an old-fashioned girl. To shave with a safety razor in a dream portends winning esteem from your employer through your close attention to work. If you cut yourself with either type of razor, you will have to answer for a misdeed that you did not expect to be discovered. To dream of fighting and slashing with a razor portends years of poverty. 867

READING. Reading aloud from a magazine or newspaper in a dream is a portent of meeting a rich man who will help you to succeed. Reading a book foretells comfort. Reading in a dream is always a good sign, unless it is bad news. Reading books foretells peace of mind in the home life. 087

REAL ESTATE. A dream concerning the purchase or sale of real estate predicts an inheritance of both money and securities. 137

RECEPTION. To attend a reception, large or small, in a dream indicates that you will be asked to make a speech before a church or school gathering. To dream of giving a reception is a portent of being received into the social group that is of greatest interest to you. 548

RECIPE. Exchanging recipes in a dream is a sign that you will receive a valuable gift in return for a favor you have done. 785

RECORD. If you dream of playing records on a record player, indicates that you will reach a position of honor. To keep a record of your daily movements, expenses, etc., predicts good fortune, but if you lock them up in a chest or closet, you will unearth a family skeleton. 368

RED. If red is the outstanding color in your dream, it will have a disturbing influence. 941

RED CROSS. To dream of seeing Red Cross nurses in action during a war or other disaster is a forerunner of your being called upon to relieve the distress of one of your family or friends. 570

REDHEAD. If a man dreams of a red-headed girl he will be in danger from indiscreet actions. A woman who dreams of a red-headed man will have a quarrel. 587

REFORMATORY. A dream of being sent to a reformatory for either boys or girls is a warning to avoid low companions. 293

REFRIGERATOR. Putting food away in a refrigerator is a sign that you will be prosperous and that you will give many popular parties. To take food out of one portends a visitor who will stay a long time. 225

REFUGEE. Dreaming of refugees from a war-torn country predicts a national disaster. If you harbor one or more of them in your home, someone will criticize you unjustly for a deed that was misunderstood. 324

REGIMENT. To see a regiment marching by in your dream is a sign that you will be asked to take an active interest in civic and state affairs. This is a good luck dream if you will make it so. 621

REINDEER. What you had believed to be worthless securities will prove to be valuable if you dream of seeing reindeer either in the open country or hitched to Santa Claus's sleigh. 759

RELIEF. To dream of being on relief is a sure sign that easier and happier days are just ahead of you. 777

RELIGION. If you seem to be deeply religious in your dream and get a spiritual uplift from it, you will take a growing interest in all kinds of church and social work. 612

RENT. Someone will shortly invite you out to lunch or dinner at an excellent restaurant if you dream of being unable to pay rent. If you dream of trying to collect rent from someone else, you will have a long visit from a single aunt. 416

REPTILE. (See Alligator, Asp, Boa, Python, Rattlesnake.) 346

RESERVOIR. To dream of approaching a reservoir that is protected by a fringe of evergreen trees and shrubs is an omen that you will be able to buy a new outfit of clothes. 862

RESOLUTION. In a dream if you make good resolutions and then break them it portends mental torture for someone you love. 008

RESORT. Summer or winter resorts visited in a dream indicate that you will have a passing fancy for one of the opposite sex, an amusing flirtation, and a sharp rebuke. 623

RESTAURANT. To dream of eating alone in a cheap restaurant, studying the prices of the foods rather than the foods themselves is a prediction that you and your mate will have a comfortable little house in the country. If you are with others, and "going Dutch," you will suffer some kind of embarrassment. 098

RETIREMENT. If you dream of retiring from business, you will have your salary raised, but it is a warning that you will have to increase your working speed to keep up. 223

REUNION. Family, school or college reunions in a dream signify that you will have cooperation of a kind that will help you to further your ambitions. 459

REVEILLE. To dream of hearing reveille played by the bugler in a camp at daybreak means that you have a chance to go way ahead of your fellow-workers if you get started now. 700

REVENGE. Any dream of having revenge on an enemy is a bad sign, especially for women and girls. It portends accidents and illness. 448

REVOLUTION. You will have to rearrange all your affairs if your dream centers about a revolution in which there is blood and carnage, but if the revolution is bloodless, there will simply be a change in your position. 432

REVOLVER. Shooting a revolver in a dream warns you not to yield to blind jealousy, for if you do, it will warp your whole future and make you and others very unhappy. 505

REVOLVING DOOR. To dream of being caught in a revolving door having to push and fight your way out is a sign that until you take stock of your resources your luck will be at a standstill. 722

REVUE. If you dream of being in the cast or the cHorus of a theatrical revue, it is an indication that you should follow your interest in acting, dancing and singing. You will be successful, but it will be hard work. 404

REWARD. To offer a reward of any kind in a dream means that you are unlikely to win your next lawsuit. If you are rewarded for some act of honesty, kindness or heroism, it predicts a surprisingly good streak of luck. 671

RHEUMATISM. If you dream of having rheumatism, it is a warning not to fall down on any promises you have made. 587

RHINESTONE. Worn on yourself or admired on others, rhinestones in a dream foretell that someone whom you asked for a reference will not give you a good one. 740

RHINOCEROS. You will be snowed under with bills if you dream of seeing a rhinoceros in a jungle. Seen in a menagerie or zoo it portends that a person of the opposite sex will seek your company. 096

RHUBARB. Eaten or picked from the garden in your dream, rhubarb foretells better health. Taken as a medicine, it is an omen of a move to new quarters. 313

RIBBON. Ribbons worn by a girl in a dream augur catching a new boy friend. To dream of losing a ribbon hatband is a forerunner of an accident through carelessness. 208

RICE. Boiled rice served in a dream portends a visit to a bazaar or fair held for charity. Seeing rice growing in paddies is a forerunner of a long trip to strange and unfamiliar lands. If you throw rice at a dream wedding and it goes on the bride and groom, you will hear good news about one of your own family. 512

RICHES. (SeeMoney.) 741

RIDDLE. Riddles asked and answered in a dream are an omen of a lukewarm love affair that will go on for a long time. 985

RIDE. To ride a horse in your dream signifies that you will reap the reward of another's labor. To ride in any vehicle is a sign that you will have news of a distant friend. 189

RIFLE. (See Arms, Gun, Pistol, Revolver.) 937

RIGGING. To dream of busying yourself about the rigging of a boat means that you will engage in some sort of transaction with a person of a different race. 340

RING. If someone of the opposite sex places a ring upon your finger in a dream, you will have some very disquieting moments in your love life. If you find a ring, you will find another object of your affection. To lose one foretells good luck in business. 051

RINK. Skating on an ice rink in a dream portends a party with happy-go-lucky friends. Roller skating rinks imply a disappointment of a minor kind. 934

RIOT. To dream of being in a riot is a warning against luxurious excesses and sensual indulgence. Beware of being too free with persons of the opposite sex. 854

RIVAL. To have a hated rival in your dream and proceed to do him or her harm foretells that you are in great danger through loss of temper. It is a warning to be on your guard against hasty actions. 454

RIVER. Sitting on the bank of a river in a dream and watching boats of all kinds is a portent that you are headed in the right general direction and that if you will try to correct your faults, you will succeed handsomely. 541

ROAD. To dream of seeing a long straight road ahead with little traffic on it foretells good luck and smooth going. If the road twists and turns and you have difficulty in driving, you will encounter many discouragements before you meet with the success you will have. 804

ROAST. To carve a large roast in your dream points toward a celebration to which you will be invited. 794

ROBBERY. If you dream that a robbery is committed in your home and you lose something that you have treasured, it is a sign that someone will give you a present that will give you great satisfaction. To dream of a robber tying you up predicts a visit to a good show. 462

ROBIN. Hearing a robin sing in a dream promises a new opportunity to make good in every way. Robins pulling worms out of the ground or building nests portend that your income will be sufficient to meet your daily needs. 281

ROCKER. To sit in a rocking chair and rock back and forth in your dream foretells that you will not need to worry for a long time. To rock an empty rocking chair is a portent of misfortune to yourself and your family. 912

ROCKET. (See Fireworks.) 230

RODEO. To dream of watching cowboys and cowgirls whooping it up in a rodeo is a sign that you will be invited to a reunion of your classmates and that you will celebrate with wine and song. 653

ROGUES' GALLERY. Looking through a rogues' gallery in a dream and finding there a picture of yourself portends a narrow escape from being involved in a public scandal. To see a photograph of a friend or relative is a portent of censure from someone whose authority you respect. 110

ROLLING PIN. Using a rolling pin in a dream for the purpose of thinning pastry dough is an omen of pleasant times with your family. If you throw a rolling pin at someone you will regret a display of temper. 114

ROLLS. (See Bread.) 858

ROLLS ROYCE. If you dream of riding in a Rolls Royce automobile, you will have the best opportunity that has ever been offered you. Take it, and make your fortune. 307

ROMAN CANDLE. (See Fireworks.) 061

ROMANCE. (See Love.) 704

ROOF. To climb on a roof in your dream implies that you will have a better understanding with your family and friends. To see a roof on fire is an omen of living in dread of an unlikely catastrophe. To dream of nailing shingles on a roof predicts new sources of income. 773

ROOM. To dream of opening a door and going into a room is a warning not to trifle with the affections of one of the opposite sex. If the room is furnished, the omen is that someone will be jealous of you; if unfurnished, you are likely to be sued. If you dream of occupying a small room and being slowly suffocated, you will have a narrow escape from a major catastrophe. 974

ROOSTER. (See also Cock-crow.) Dreaming of seeing a rooster lording it over his harem in a barnyard is a good sign for men, but it denotes hard work and much responsibility for women. 910

ROPE. Handling a coil of rope in a dream indicates that you will find a good friend for whom you will be willing to make sacrifices. 445.

ROSARY. Counting the beads of a rosary in a dream is a forerunner of great peace of mind and easier living conditions than formerly. 435

ROSE. Roses of any color in a dream portend love between a man and a woman. Faded roses imply the loss of a dear friend. Artificial roses are an omen of deceit on the part of someone you had trusted. 886

ROUGE. (See also Cosmetics, Lipstick, etc.) To notice rouge on the cheek of a young girl covering her natural beauty and coloring is a sign that you will be criticized for narrow-mindedness regarding things that do not concern you. If you see an elderly woman who is heavily rouged, you will develop a more optimistic viewpoint toward life in general. Dreaming of women applying rouge to their faces in public places is a sign that an adventuress will come into your life and make trouble for you. 396

ROULETTE. A woman who dreams of playing roulette at a fashionable gaming resort will doubtless fall in love with a playboy and live to regret it. A man who spins the wheel in a dream will be lucky in gambling. 839

ROYALTY. (See King, Prince, Queen.) 049

RUBBER. In any form, rubber in a dream foretells that by taking proper precautions you will enjoy good health and freedom from worry. Wearing rubbers and sloshing through water is an omen that you should protect your interests with proper insurance. 901

RUBBISH. To dream of seeing piles of rubbish indoors or out is an omen that you will have a visitor and will have to do housecleaning in anticipation. 752

RUBY. If a girl dreams of wearing one or more rubies, she will soon have many ardent suitors. 9859

RUFFLES. A dream of ruffles on a dress or on dainty curtains is a sign that your attitude toward your friends is narrow and biased. You are warned to act more sensibly. 024

RUG. If you dream of walking on large, luxurious velvety Oriental rugs, you will inherit a fortune when you least expect it. But you will have to make a dollar go a long way if your dream is of rugs that are worn and full of holes. 763

RUIN. To dream of standing in the midst of ruin, desolation and suffering, presages the receipt of bad news by mail or telegram. 697

S

SABBATH. If you dream of keeping the Sabbath according to the tenets of your religion, you will be invited to participate in an important public ceremony. If you dream of making the Sabbath a day of revelry, you will be likely to be charged with a serious offense. 419

SABLE. Rich sables worn or admired in a dream portend the coming of a mysterious woman into your life. 554

SABOTAGE. Being concerned in sabotage, or the wrecking of machinery and other property belonging to your employer, is a dream that predicts a disastrous collision. 467

SACHET. You will meet a sweet, motherly woman to whom you may go for comfort and advice if you dream of putting sachet bags away with your clothing or linens. 547

SADDLE. If you ride horseback in a dream and feel that the saddle is slipping or otherwise uncomfortable, it is a sign that you are not paying careful enough attention to your work. 501

SAFETY RAZOR. (See Razor.) 650

SAFFRON. If you dream of eating saffron, you should guard against yielding to momentary sex urges that are bound to get you into trouble if followed through. This is a warning dream. 517

SAGE. Dreaming of desert sagebrush portends homesickness for friends and things that are no more. To dream of the odor after rain is a sign of good luck and good times to come. 369

SAILOR. A dream of sailors ashore is a warning to boys and girls that they will lose their sweethearts. Sailors aboard ship portend adventure away from home. 274

SAINT. You will have a sin to confess if you dream of seeing or talking with a saint. 027

SALAD. Appetizing salads eaten in your dream foretell that you will go to a party where you will not know anyone. You will be ill at ease until you force yourself to unbend. 491

SALARY. If you dream that your salary is raised and you immediately begin to spend money recklessly, it predicts a cut instead of a raise in salary. If you dream of asking to have your salary raised and it is refused, you will receive added money from an outside source. If the request is granted, you must be careful not to loaf on the job. 455

SALE. (See also Auction.) To attend a bargain sale in your dream and to be pushed and mauled by frenzied women is a sign that you will be given some old family silverware and other heirlooms. The sale of any of your personal belongings augurs a better income in the future. 237

SALMON. To dream of eating canned salmon is a sign that you will have an adventurous career somewhere east of Suez. Fresh salmon portends lovers' quarrels and reconciliation. If you dream of fishing for salmon, you will make new friends in an unconventional manner. 674

SALOON. If you dream of drinking at a bar or table in a saloon, and the atmosphere is decent and reasonably quiet, you will be asked by someone in your neighborhood to join a church or lodge. If the saloon is peopled by noisy, drunken characters, you will find it necessary to go with a relative to a gathering of tiresome people. 754

SALT. Sprinkling salt on food in a dream portends a mild attack of food poisoning. 051

SALVATION ARMY. To stop and listen to a meeting of the Salvation Army in a dream is a portent of you doing a good deed for someone less fortunate than yourself. 056

SAMPLE. To dream of receiving samples of food from your grocer is a sign of having to pay a bill that you incurred unwillingly. 175

SAND. A dream of sand in your spinach, on the seashore, or in an hour-glass predicts that you will be annoyed by a presumptuous person who will try to use you to advance his or her own interests. 724

SANDALS. To wear sandals in a dream predicts, if they are comfortable, a romance by moonlight. If they chafe your feet, the augury is of an altercation with someone to whom you owe a small amount of money. 702

SANDBAGS. A dream of using sandbags as a defense against bombs or as a bulwark against a flood foretells that you will have a burglary in the house where you live. 769

SANDWICH. To dream of eating a sandwich is a prophecy of an opportunity to better your condition. Indoors, eating sandwiches at a lunch counter warns against casual conversations with people you do not know. A toasted sandwich foretells an adventure that you may wish to forget. Sandwiches at a picnic portend a love affair that is liable to backfire. Be on your guard. 307

SANITARIUM. If you dream of being a patient in a sanitarium, it is a warning to take better care of your health and to avoid being alarmed too easily. 693

SAPPHIRE. You will regret a hasty action if you dream of wearing sapphires set in either a ring or a brooch. If you see them but are not wearing them, you will be introduced to a person of rank. 291

SARDINE. To dream of opening a sardine can is an omen of distress of mind. Eating sardines portends that you will be defamed by someone who is jealous of your mental attainments. 628

SATAN. (See Devil.) 369

SAUERKRAUT. Good sauerkraut eaten in a dream is a forerunner of an invitation to listen to a fine musical program. Drinking sauerkraut juice predicts good health. 964

SAUSAGE. You are likely to be accused of stealing another's love if you dream of eating sausage. To see a variety of sausages hanging in a meat store or delicatessen shop augurs a fortunate turn in business. 681

SAW. It is a sign that you will change your political beliefs if you dream of using a handsaw in a factory or the home. To dream of a buzz saw in operation is a portent of approaching danger to your reputation and your credit. Using a hacksaw to cut metal predicts that you will have to devote more time to the job you are doing, but with extra pay. 982

SAXOPHONE. Heard in a dream, a saxophone is a forerunner of a gay dancing party with much liquor flowing. To dream of playing it is an omen of a quarrel with someone living in your immediate vicinity. Good luck is predicted by a dream of losing a saxophone. 303

SCAFFOLD. A hangman's scaffold seen in a dream is an omen of a dreadful happening close to home. It can be averted only by your walking the straight and narrow path for a long time to come. Wooden or iron scaffolding erected in connection with building operations predicts new business opportunities. 374

SCALES. To weigh food upon scales is a sign that you will have plenty to eat. To dream of weighing yourself presages disappointment and worry. To scrape the scales off a fish in a dream portends the discovery of a plot to discredit you. 024

SCALLOPS. Dreaming of having a plate of freshly cooked scallops served to you forecasts a change to a more desirable place of abode. Raw scallops predict a vacation by the sea. 797

SCANDAL. To dream of being mixed up in a scandal implies that you should clear your conscience of something that has been bothering you. Otherwise you will have much regret. To dream of talking scandalously about other people predicts that you will be accused of dishonesty. 674

SCAR. It is a sign of difficulty in meeting the wishes of your employer if you dream of seeing a woman whose face is disfigured with a prominent scar. If the scar is on your own face or body, you will try to hide something of which you are ashamed. 428

SCARF. Wearing a bright scarf in your dream foretells the best of luck in a heartfelt love affair. 507

SCENARIO. If you dream of writing a movie scenario, you are likely to be successful in a writing or acting career. 534

SCENERY. Beautiful natural scenery, whether on land or at sea, is a good augury, and if you enjoy it with a person of the opposite sex, your friends will soon have reason to buy wedding gifts. Theatrical scenery presages missing a good time through a minor illness. 355

SCHOOL. To dream of being young and going to school predicts an enjoyable encounter with an old friend who lives a long distance from you. If the school burns in your dream, you will have a temporary streak of luck, during which you should save as much money as possible. 330

SCIENTIST. If you dream of being a great scientist and making a tremendous discovery of benefit to all mankind, you will be called upon to join a group of amateur actors. If you see a scientist in a laboratory doing experiments with intricate apparatus, the augury is of meeting a high official who will look with favor upon you. 734

SCISSORS. Cutting with a pair of scissors in a dream indicates that you will be the victim of a humorous prank. To dream of using a left-handed pair of scissors foretells that you will make a discovery of interest. 240

SCOLDING. Dreaming of being scolded by a parent or employer is a warning against being too sure of yourself in arguments. You will profit by a suggestion from a younger person. 779

SCORE. If you dream of keeping the score for any outdoor game and there is a dispute as to the manner in which you keep it, you will be closely watched by a jealous mate. 746

SCORPION. To dream of a scorpion is a sign of warning against over-confidence in yourself. Enough is plenty. Try to take other people's advice occasionally if you value your peace of mind. 248

SCOTTISH TERRIER. To own a Scottish terrier and play with it in your dream, is a sign that you will be invited by a charming spinster to a cocktail party. 507

SCOUT. (See also Boy Scout.) It is a sign that you will go on a diet to reduce your weight if you dream of scouting in the wilderness or in a battle area. 453

SCRAPBOOK. To busy yourself with a scrapbook in a dream and paste in it clippings and pictures of subjects in which you are interested is a sign that points two ways: you will be a success in whatever you attempt, and you will have a loving mate. 553

SCRAPBOOK. You will be fortunate financially and in your family life if you dream of keeping a scrapbook. 667

SCREAM. A bloodcurdling scream heard predicts that you will be afraid of having a family skeleton revealed. But you should remember that you are not responsible for anything your forebears have said or done. If you dream of screaming, it is a sign that you will join a movement for the betterment of the aged and infirm. 349

SCREWBALL. If you dream of calling someone a screwball, you are likely to find that you will not have good luck in your business. 611

SCULPTOR. To admire the work of a sculptor in your dream signifies that you will have a temptation to meddle with someone's personal affairs. Therefore it is a warning to mind your own. To dream of seeing a sculptor at work presages embarking on a new and interesting enterprise. 765

SEA. (See Ocean.) 470

SEAHORSE. To dream of seeing a tiny seahorse grow to a gigantic size augurs traveling in a motor caravan. A dream of harnessing a seahorse predicts pleasant adventures. 329

SEAL. A fishing trip is predicted by a dream of many seals disporting themselves on a rock. To kill a seal is an augury of hard going in business. A sealskin coat worn in a dream foretells prosperity. 108

SEANCE. To attend a spiritualistic seance in a dream and be conscious of being skeptical of it is a portent that you will turn down someone's offer of help and live to regret it. 830

SEARCHLIGHT. To dream of being in the direct beam from a powerful searchlight is an omen that you will get your heart's desire, but you will have to go through fire and water for it. To see many searchlight beams playing in the sky indicates coming danger from your enemies. Be prepared. 867

SEAWEED. Dreaming of seaweed that is tangled about you while you are trying to swim denotes that a very strong-willed person will try to persuade you to do something against your better judgment. 276

SECRET. Intrigue among people whom you have trusted is foretold by hearing a secret in a dream. If you repeat a secret that has been told you in strict confidence, you will be annoyed by malicious gossip. 962

SECRETARY. To dream that you are a beautiful young secretary and that the boss is in love with you is a sign that you are going to have trouble in getting along. For a man to dream of kissing his secretary augurs criticism from his relatives. To dream of being elected secretary of a corporation or other organization portends an increase in salary. 506

SEDUCTION. (See Rape.) 351

SENATOR. For a man to dream that he is a senator in Washington indicates that someone among his acquaintances will ask him for a favor. A woman will achieve social prominence if she dreams of having a senator make love to her. 143

SERENADE. A woman who dreams of being serenaded by a young man will have a proposal within a month. If she throws him a flower from her window, it foretells a happy marriage and lovely children. 274

SEWING. Look to the future and provide for it if you dream of anyone sewing. If it is you who sew, an opportunity for advancement will come shortly. 210

SEX. Few dreams there are that have no connection with sex, for all living things are created male and female. Therefore as such, it has little significance. Dreaming of the biological functions of sex in the manner in which they should be used portends a long and happy life. 014

SHAKING HANDS. A dream of shaking hands with a firm hearty grasp augurs new friends, but if the grasp is weak and flabby, the omen is of failure in some important enterprise. 554

SHAME. If you dream of being shamed, you have every reason for looking forward to the respect of your friends and your employer. To shame another in a dream portends a motor accident on a highway. 524

SHAMPOO. Having a shampoo either at home or at a hair-dresser's is a sign that you will be admired by a stranger who will find some way of meeting you socially. To dream of giving a shampoo to another indicates that you will receive good news. 681

SHAMROCK. You will receive three party invitations for the same date if you dream of seeing the green shamrock of Saint Patrick. 799

SHAVING. (See also Razor.) To dream of seeing a woman shaving her face augurs an experience that you will not understand for a long time. If she is shaving under her arms, there is the probability of your being taken on a trip by a wealthy friend. For a man to dream of shaving means that he will have to keep an appointment. 434

SHAWL. To dream of wearing a shawl over your head is a warning against being careless in your manners. A shawl over your shoulders is an indication that you will have difficulty in cashing a large check. 820

SHEARS. (See Scissors.) 715

SHEEP. Counting sheep in a dream is a portent of petty irritations and temporary setbacks. If you dream of shearing the wool from sheep, you will be moderately prosperous. 273

SHEET. Putting clean sheets on a bed in a dream is a portent of more ease and comfort than you have had before. To dream of being tangled in bedsheets is a sign of worry over a love affair. To escape from a high window by tying bedsheets together augurs a business difficulty from which you will emerge after a period of unrest. 523

SHELL. Gathering sea-shells in a dream is an omen of going to a spiritualist meeting. To crack the shell of a coconut or any other variety of nut, augurs success in an undertaking. A shell used as ammunition for a gun of any size predicts an appointment with a dentist. 783

SHERBET. Eating sherbet at a dinner party in a dream foretells a situation with a person of the opposite sex in which you will need to exercise great restraint. To spill sherbet on your dress or suit is an omen of being distrusted by someone you like. 266

SHERIFF. If you dream of having the sheriff on your trail, someone whom you have offended will demand an apology. It is a sign of bitter wrangling with your relatives if you dream of seeing a sheriff make an arrest. 274

SHERRY. To drink sherry in your dream denotes a new association with a high grade group of people. 620

SHIP. To dream of ships, powered either by sail or steam, is an augury of an adventure that will be productive of profit and satisfaction. To be on a ship that is wrecked is a portent of having to struggle to save your good name. To build a model of a ship in a dream foretells that you will love someone madly and marry within the year. 963

SHIRT. To put on a clean shirt in a dream is a sign of good luck, but if there is a button missing, you will have trouble with members of your family. To lose a shirt augurs a long period of grief. 782

SHOE. New shoes worn in your dream portend short journeys. Shoes that are old and comfortable are a phophecy of home relaxations and good friends. To dream of losing one of your shoes prophesies new activities that will come to naught. To throw an old shoe at a wedding is a sign that you will have family worriees. 902

SHOEMAKER. To dream of a shoemaker working at his last is an omen of finding someone who will be able to finance a business deal for you. 025

SHOP. (See Store.) 454

SHORE. If you walk along the seashore in a dream and watch the tide come in, you will be called a hero or heroine for some worthy action. If the tide is going out, you will make money through some transaction involving food or real estate. 089

SHORTHAND. (See also Secretary.) If in a dream your employer dictates a letter and you take it down in shorthand, you will receive an advance in salary; but if you dream that you cannot read your own notes, the prophecy is definitely inauspicious. 956

SHOVEL. An increase of responsibility is augured by the use of a shovel in a dream of any kind. 180

SHRIMP. A woman who dreams of eating cooked shrimps will soon step out with a new suitor who will be able to entertain her royally. For others, the dream portends pleasant adventures with highly respectable people. 589

SIGNATURE. Putting your signature to a legal paper in a dream means that you will work at a desk for a small salary. To sign a check in a dream foretells moderate prosperity, but many worries. 254

SILK. A dream of wearing silk next to the skin is a fortunate augury for women of all ages, for it portends all the necessities of life and many of the luxuries. To wear silk gowns in a dream predicts that your neighbors will gossip about you on account of something they do not understand. For a man to dream of wearing silk underwear or pajamas is a sign that he will be singled out for promotion by his employer. A dream of raw silk or a bolt of silk yardage prophesies election to a position of honor and trust. 874

SILO. Taking ensilage out of a silo in a dream is a sign that you must avoid overindulgencee in whiskey, gin and other hard liquors. A silo on fire is a warning against waiting too long before paying your bills. 153

SILVER. To dream of possessing a large quantity of table silver and having to work hard to keep it bright augurs a long visit from critical relatives. Silver money in a dream is an omen of plenty but with great responsibility. 255

SIN. (See Adultery, Robbery, etc.) 309

SINGING. To dream of singing a solo before a large audience implies a desire for solitude, and you are likely to go away for a vacation in a small place where you are not known. To join in the singing of a chorus or congregation indicates good companionship and merry times with your friends. 828

SISTER. It is an ill portent to dream that your sister is in any kind of difficulty. To dream of hating a sister is a sign that some stupid person will tell you lies about a friend. 043

SKATING. (See also Ice, Rink.) Good times are predicted by a dream of either ice or roller skating. To fall while skating is a sign of being asked to contribute to a fund for underprivileged children. 104

SKELETON. A dream of a human skeleton found in a closet or chest is a sign that you will be ridiculed for being afraid of what might happen. Seen in an anatomical display, it augurs new and interesting friends who are of a scientific disposition. 684

SKIDDING. If in a dream you are driving a car that skids, you are in danger of making a grave error of judgment that has great possibilities for danger to yourself and your family. To get out of a skid is a sign that you will make a favorable business turn. 009

SKIRT. If a woman dreams that her skirt is either too short or too long in a dream, it is a sign that she will be unhappy over something that is relatively unimportant. For a man to dream of seeing a woman wearing a skirt that shows practically all of her legs is a portent that there will be a rise in his worldly fortunes. 781

SKULL. (See also Skeleton.) To dream of handling a skull is a portent of success in either literary work or dramatic acting. If in digging you unearth a skull, you are likely to have an adventure that will at first puzzle you and then give you delight. 374

SKUNK. To smell or see a skunk in a dream is a sign that you will not receive an invitation to a party you expected to attend. To kill a skunk augurs sadness through homesickness. 632

SKY. A dream of a colorful sky either at sunset or sunrise portends a hectic love affair that will come to nothing. A sky that is leaden and gray is a prediction of making a good friend who will stick by you through thick and thin. 391

SLANG. To dream of hearing a precise and dignified person using picturesque slang is a portent of attending a gathering of substantial and likeable people. If your dream is of slang that you cannot understand, there will be a deep and fascinating mystery in your life. 036

SLAUGHTER HOUSE. To dream of working in a slaughter house portends criticism of a serious nature from your employer. 696

SLED. Sliding downhill on a sled in a dream is an omen of happy times with young people. If the sled overturns and you are thrown off in the snow, you will be called upon to take a comedy part in an amateur theatrical performance. 622

SLIP. For a woman to dream of making a slip portends an early marriage and a trousseau of many silken underthings. 345

SMALLPOX. If you dream of having smallpox, you are slated for an experience that will be serious but not fatal. It is a sign that you will make many new friends if you dream of taking care of a smallpox patient. 461

SMOKE. (See also Cigar, Pipe.) To dream of smelling smoke and not know where it is coming from augurs worry for a long period. To see smoke coming from a fire or a chimney is a sign of an increase in income. 319

SMUGGLER. A dream in which you or another person is trying to smuggle articles into your country predicts that you will be called upon to explain something that you would rather keep hidden. 387

SNAIL. Eating snails in a dream is an omen of happiness in love and married life. To gather them prophesies success to those who work with their hands. 288

SNAKE. (See Adder, Asp, Rattlesnake.) 421

SNEEZE. Sneezing in a dream foretells good health and a satisfactory income. To hear others sneeze portends danger through infection. 796

SNOW. Dreaming of a snowstorm and walking through deep drifts means that you will work long and hard upon a project but that you will eventually make it a big success. A wet snow that sticks to the branches of trees is a sign that you will make money on your investments. Shoveling snow is an augury of having words with a person who has the power to do you either good or harm. 982

SNOWSHOES. Young people who dream of traveling on snowshoes may look forward to a complete understanding with their sweethearts. To dream of putting on snowshoes is a portent of being rewarded for a good deed. 159

SNUFF. (See also Sneeze.) It is a sign of a healthy and contented old age if you dream of taking snuff. 350

SOAP. Scented soap used in a dream portends moonlight and roses with the one you love. Soap-flakes, kitchen or laundry soap indicates that you will have to struggle before you will achieve competence. Any antiseptic soap is a sign that you will be ill at ease in company. 285

SOCKS. (See Stockings.) 091

SODA. Drinking an ice-cream soda in a dream foretells that you will meet an outstanding celebrity in the motion picture world. 625

SOFA. To dream of sitting on a sofa with your sweetheart and making earnest love denotes that you will be called upon to make a hurried business trip that will help you toward success. If you dream of having a slipcover made for a sofa, you are likely to have visitors with children. A sofa with a broken spring is a sign of distress. 021

SOLITAIRE. Playing solitaire in a dream predicts that you will engage in some work that will tire you both physically and mentally. If you dream of winning, you will receive a large amount of money that you did not expect. 932

SON. A man who dreams of his son or a woman who dreams of her son is sure to achieve happiness through his or her own efforts. 916

SORE. It is a sign of unpleasant times ahead if you dream of having sores on your body. If you dream of sores on another person or on an animal, you are likely to receive disquieting news. 627

SOUP. To dream of hearing a person make a noise while eating soup foretells that you will receive an invitation to a dinner party. 830

SPAGHETTI. Dreaming of difficulty in eating spaghetti, getting it on your chin and clothes, is a portent of good times in the company of your friends. 472

SPANIEL. Any type of spaniel in a dream is an augury of pleasant home associations. To dream of seeing a spaniel getting his ears in his food predicts a humorous experience with a school teacher. 966

SPARROW. To dream of sparrows indicates that you will have to get along with little money and have unpopular children. It is a lucky omen to dream of chasing these birds away. 425

SPATS. A man who dreams of wearing spats is likely to have an offer of a new and better position. To wear only one spat is a sign of losing your job. 382

SPEECH. Making a speech in a dream augurs success in business and social life. 153

SPEEDBOAT. Driving a speedboat through the water in a dream is a portent of accomplishing an important job to the satisfaction of your employer. 113

SPELLING BEE. If you dream of taking part in a spelling bee, you will receive an invitation to compete for a valuable prize. To dream of misspelling a simple word is a sign of a minor disgrace. 483

SPHINX. Bathed in moonlight, the sphinx seen in a dream is a portent of meeting someone whom you like immensely but do not understand. 384

SPICE. Pungent aromatic spices used in a dream are a forerunner of a trip that will lead toward far eastern countries. Hearing spicy conversation foretells danger from unscrupulous people of the opposite sex. 920

SPIDER. Encouragement is predicted by a dream of seeing a spider in his web, for it is an omen that through industry and skill you will achieve the end for which you have been working. 989

SPINACH. Good health and enjoyment of life is foretold by a dream of eating spinach as long as you find no grit in it. But if you bite on a grain of sand, the augury is of meeting a group of thoroughly detestable people. 656

SPIRE. To dream of seeing a church spire outlined against the sky is an augury of the blessings of friendship and love. If the spire leans away from the perpendicular, it means that you will have many difficulties before you finally achieve the end toward which you have been working. 273

SPIRIT. You should take warning against certain people who will try to deceive you if you dream of seeing or talking to the spirit of someone who has passed on. 129

SPIT. To dream of seeing meat being roasted on a spit is a sign of being invited to be a guest at a dinner. If you see someone spit in your dream, you are likely to be offended by a friend. 172

SPITE. If you dream of an act being committed for spite, you will have occasion to censure one of your friends. To be spiteful in a dream augurs physical pain. 629

SPLINTER. It is a sign of an acrimonious dispute with relatives if you dream of getting a splinter in any part of your body. To remove a splinter from anyone else forecasts the loss of an important letter or document. 148

SPONGE. To wash your body with a sponge predicts a sea voyage; to wash an automobile is a forerunner of being commended for good work that you have done. Squeezing the water out of a sponge is a portent of greater earning power. Trying to squeeze water out of a dry sponge is a dream that warns against gambling at cards or in lotteries. 868

SPOOL. If in a dream you step on a spool lying on the floor, and fall down, you are warned against indiscreet relations with a person of the opposite sex. To unwind thread from a spool predicts embarking on a new enterprise that is almost certain to bring you profit. 644

SPOON. To dream of eating with a spoon something that ordinarily would be eaten with a fork—such as meat, potatoes, salad, etc.—is a sign that you will get yourself talked about for your informal behavior. To lose a silver spoon in a dream predicts a loss of money through an unlucky business deal. 191

SPORTSMANSHIP. Any display of sportsmanship is a good portent. You will be much sought after by people of refinement and influence. 525

SPOTLIGHT. (See also Searchlight.) A dream of being on a stage and having a spotlight thrown on you indicates that you will be singled out of a large group to receive an award or other honor. 742

SPRAIN. If you dream of spraining an ankle, wrist, your back or other part of your body, you will be approached by a committee who will ask you to run for office. 315

SPRAY. A spray from a hose, atomizer or other source in a dream is an indication of good times with your friends. 270

SPRING. A dream of springtime, with budding trees, blossoming flowers and birds singing is a favorable omen to lovers and to those starting a new business. 577

SPRUCE. Better health is the portent of a dream in which spruce trees figure. 383

SPUR. Spurs in a dream predict that you will be nagged by someone who has some sort of authority over you. 581

SPY. To dream that you are a spy in the service of your country augurs being elected to an honorary position that you do not want. If you dream of being spied on, you are warned to be more circumspect in your behavior. 340

SQUALL. A sudden short storm at sea in a dream predicts a coming difficulty that you can overcome if you use good sense. 223

SQUASH. A good opportunity will be given you to make money if you dream of preparing or eating squash. 569

SQUINT. Eyes that squint in a dream portend concern over the condition of a sick relative or friend. 866

SQUIRREL. Feeding nuts to a squirrel in a dream is an augury of pleasant times in the company of your friends. A squirrel in a cage, running on a revolving wheel, predicts a hopeless love affair. To see squirrels chasing each other among the branches of a tree is an omen of trouble through unpaid bills. 224

STADIUM. To dream of watching at a football game or other athletic contest in a stadium foretells a round of parties with friendly and worthwhile people. 172

STAG. An antlered stag seen in a dream is an omen of exciting adventures outside of your everyday experience. If the animal is brought to bay by staghounds, your adventures will be dangerous as well. 496

STAGE. (See also Actor.) If you dream that you are on the stage, you may regard it as a distinct sign of encouragement to continue in any efforts along dramatic or literary lines. It is a good omen for those who write poetry. 851

STAGECOACH. Being a passenger in a dream stagecoach drawn by horses is a portent of a stirring love affair that will depend on its innocence for its success. To dream of driving a stagecoach prophesies an adventure that will be something to tell your grandchildren about. 824

STAGGER. If you walk with a stagger in a dream, it is a warning against being influenced by flattery. To see another person staggering augurs a cry for help from one of your friends. 443

STAIN. If a woman dreams of staining her dress, she is warned not to accept the attentions of men much older that she is. To dream of a stain on one's family name is a sign of honors in store for you. 947

STAIR. To fall upstairs in a dream augurs peace of mind for the unmarrried, but a short period of trouble for married people. To fall downstairs is a sign that you will be drawn into a conspiracy unless you have the good sense to keep out of it. To sweep or scrub a flight of stairs is a prophecy of improved living conditions. 326

STAKE. To dream of driving a stake into the ground for a tent or other purpose predicts starting a new and probably successful enterprise. If you dream of being present while someone is being burned at the stake, you will have an opportunity to assert yourself in no uncertain terms to a person who tries to bully you. 968

STALL. Dreaming of putting a horse into a stall indicates that you will win approval for your work from your employer. If you dream that someone ties you in a stall, you will win a prize in a lottery. 067

STAMP. To put a stamp on a letter in a dream is a prophecy that you will receive money and commendation for a job well done. To buy stamps at the post-office is an omen of better business. Collecting postage stamps of all countries in a dream is a prophecy of meeting high-grade people socially and being able to advance yourself through knowing them. If you dream of finding a rare stamp on an old envelope that you had forgotten, you will have good luck financially for a year or more. 892

STAR. To dream of a certain bright star predicts that through the help of a friend of the opposite sex you will be able to achieve an ambition of long standing. 367

STARCH. Using starch in a dream is a portent of carrying out a project that will net you a round sum. If you dream of eating starch, you will get into trouble through being too sure of yourself. 859

STARE. If a person of the opposite sex stares at you in a dream, you are likely to have to make an abject apology for a mistake you have made. 925

STARFISH. Finding a starfish on the shore in a dream is a prophecy of meeting an influential person who, if properly approached, will help you to an excellent position. 840

STARVATION. Dreaming of being starved is an ill omen. You are warned to curtail your expenses and save as much money as possible. It is a sign that you will have many unhappy days if you dream of seeing other people starving. 212

STATEROOM. Going into a stateroom aboard ship portends an adventure that may or may not be to your advantage, according to whether you are alone or in company with one of the opposite sex. 261

STATIC. To dream of hearing static on your radio is a prophecy of being called to account for something irregular about your behavior. 678

STATIONERY. Buying stationery in a dream—paper, typewriter ribbons, pencils, pens, ink, etc.—is a sign that you will be increasingly successful in your business. 431

STATUE. Carving a statue in a dream is a sign of a new opportunity to advance yourself in your career. To look at statues in a museum foretells meeting an interesting group of people who will stimulate you to do better work. 452

STEAK. To dream of broiling a steak presages popularity in your community. You will be asked to join a select club or society that you have wished to be associated with. If you dream of eating steak you are likely to have an offer to go with a new concern that will pay you an excellent salary. 550

STEALING. If you dream of stealing, you are warned to go slowly in making investments. To dream of being caught is good luck. 734

STEAM. The sound of escaping steam in a dream is a sign that you will have an altercation with a person who has some authority over you. To turn off the steam indicates that you will succeed in accomplishing a task that you had thought was impossible. If you dream that you are burned by steam, you should be on the lookout for evidences of underhanded work against you. 845

STEAMROLLER. Operating a steamroller in a dream augurs success in any enterprise that you have embarked on. If you dream that a steamroller runs over you, look out for those who wish you ill. 176

STEAMSHIP. (See Ship.) 076

STEEL. If you dream of steel being used for a constructive or worthy purpose, the augury is of increased value to the community and corresponding reward for your labors. If it is used for destructive purposes, such as guns, swords, etc., you are warned against evilly disposed persons. 821

STEEPLE. Women who dream of church steeples will have exciting experiences with young men whom they do not know but who wish to make their acquaintance. A dream of a broken steeple is an augury of thwarted ambitions. 844

STEEPLECHASE. Horses in a race in which they jump hurdles are an omen of much social excitement involving theatres, night clubs and cocktail parties. If any of the horses fall with their riders, the portent is of having to foot the bill at the next party. 084

STENCH. A foul odor in a dream foretells much grief over an innocent mistake. It is a warning against making jokes at the expense of your friends. 128

STENOGRAPHER. (See also Secretary.) If a man dreams of making love to his stenographer, he will have to answer to either his wife or his employer for something he has forgotten. A young woman who dreams of being a stenographer is likely to be married within the year. 810

STETHOSCOPE. To dream of a doctor listening to your chest with a stethoscope presages an accomplishment of which your family and friends will be proud. 640

STEW. Eating stew in a dream portends a reunion with old friends. To dream of making stew is an indication that there will be a birth in the family of one of your near relatives. 275

STILETTO. If you should happen to stab someone with a stiletto in a dream, you are quite likely to make a rash statement that will get you into serious trouble. Guard your tongue lest you hurt yourself as well as others. 120

STILTS. Walking on stilts in a dream is a warning against pride, for pride goeth before a fall. If you dream of falling, it is a good sign because it will make the warning more potent. 569

STINK. (See Stench.) 715

STOCK FARM. If you dream of being on a stock farm and having charge of the care and breeding of animals, you may look forward to a successful business career. 065

STOCKING. Putting on one's stockings in a dream portends the beginning of an adventure that is likely to lead to a profitable contract for services. To find a hole in your stocking is a sign that you will have to explain an absence from duty. To mend stockings is an omen of hard work that will give you satisfaction but no financial reward. If you dream of hanging up a stocking at Christmas, you will have many friends but not much money. 688

STOMACH. To dream of having a belly-ache and calling it a stomach-ache is a sign that you will be embarrassed by the revelations of a friend. Beware of showing jealousy of anyone if you dream of having a sour stomach; it will react on you unfavorably. 366

STORAGE BATTERY. Bad luck will follow you for a long time if you dream that your storage battery goes dead while you are driving in traffic. 104

STORE. One may expect an increase in income if he or she dreams of working in a store. If the dream is of being the proprietor, the augury is better. 229

STORM. To dream of being caught in a storm, either rain or snow, portends a season of discontent from which you will emerge only when you have found that you can control your own destiny. 925

STORY. To dream of reading a story portends happy days. To dream of writing one is a sign of heartaches. 625

STOVE. (See Furnace.) 477

STRAIT-JACKET. Struggling to free yourself from a strait-jacket in a dream foretells a time during which you will have difficulty in getting your debts paid. If you release yourself, or if someone else releases you, the outcome will be propitious. 158

STRAWBERRY. Picking strawberries in a dream is a prophecy of a luxurious vacation that will be paid for by a wealthy friend. Eating strawberries prophesies happy days in the company of your favorite companion. 382

STRIKE. To dream of going on strike against unfair treatment by your employer is a sign that you will make progress in the work that you are engaged in. 871

STRING. A dream of saving string taken from packages predicts that you will be laughed at for being fussy or prim. 192

STRING BEAN. Eating string beans in a dream foretells gay and unrestrained parties where you will meet many people who are engaged in artistic pursuits. To prepare string beans for the table is a sign of receiving word that will cause you to seek another position. 724

STRIP TEASE. You had better watch your conduct if you dream of being at a performance where a young woman does a strip tease act, for it portends disgrace through an indiscretion that can and should be avoided. 941

STUDIO. Any dream transpiring in a studio predicts association with artists, writers, actors and musicians. 881

STUNT. To dream of being among a group of people who are doing stunts is a portent of a joyous reunion with people you have known since childhood. 540

STUTTER. If in your dream you talk with a person who stutters, and you have difficulty in following him or her, you will have trouble with a relative who is critical of you and your actions. 426

SUBMARINE. Being on a submarine in a dream predicts having to explain your absence from a gathering at which you were supposed to be present. To dream of firing a torpedo from a submarine portends an occurence in connection with a friend of the opposite sex that will have a profound influence on your life. 726

SUBWAY. Dreaming of riding on a crowded subway foretells a succession of irritating incidents that will be likely to cause you no end of trouble unless you keep a stiff upper lip. A wreck in a subway is a sure portent of disaster. 615

SUFFOCATION. You are warned to avoid large gatherings of people if you dream of being suffocated. Keep out in the open air as much as you can. 411

SUITCASE. To pack a suitcase in a dream does not augur a trip as might be supposed. It portends a visit from a tiresome busybody or a relative who will stay a long time. 642

SUITOR. A young woman who dreams of her suitor will be happy with him if the dream is a pleasant one; otherwise the engagement will be broken. 634

SUNDAE. To dream of eating a luscious and drippy sundae is a portent to women that their men friends are thinking of them. It is a good sign if one dreams of spilling a sundae on clothing, but a sign of sorrow if the ice cream is bad. 209

SUN DIAL. It is a distinctly pleasant dream if there is a sun dial in it, especially if it is in a garden with blossoming flowers. If you can tell time by the dial, your best hopes will come true. 184

SUNFLOWER. Wearing a sunflower in your buttonhole or as a corsage predicts that you are in danger of making a spectacle of yourself by some unusual action. Guard against being too informal. To eat sunflower seeds is a portent that you will meet old friends when you least expect to. 049

SUNRISE. If you dream of seeing the sunrise, you are likely to have success in the work that you are doing. A red sunrise portends a struggle through which you will emerge triumphant. 400

SUNSET. Gorgeous colors in the sky at sunset are a prophecy of a new opportunity to make good with your wife, husband, sweetheart or employer. 630

SURF. A dream of watching surf beat upon the seashore is a sign that you will receive encouragement. This may be in a love affair or in your work. 934

SURGEON. To dream of being a surgeon and performing delicate operations prophesies that you will change your occupation to one that is connected with the newspaper business. If you dream of being operated on by a surgeon, the augury is of an improvement in health. 266

SUSPENDERS. A woman who dreams of her lover wearing suspenders will be disillusioned through his lack of manners. If a man dreams of losing his suspenders, he will win a prize in a public contest. 654

SWAMP. Being lost in a swamp in a dream is an augury of bad luck in financial matters. It also predicts family squabbles. 194

SWAN. Graceful white swans gliding over smooth waters in a dream foretell a happy married life for all women. Swans flying portend healthy children and a satisfactory income. 640

SWASTIKA. A dream of this symbol of good luck is a forerunner of eventual riches and in the meantime a well-ordered life among people with culture and a sense of humor. 184

SWEARING. (See Profanity.) 044

SWEAT. To dream of sweating, either in winter or summer, predicts a comfortable living through hard work. If the sweat gets into your eyes, you will worry for the health of your loved ones. 774

SWEATER. Wearing a sweater in a dream portends harsh criticism for a deed that you did not intend to be harmful. 012

SWEETHEART. A pleasant dream of your sweetheart is always a good augury, but if you dream of a quarrel, the omen is of having to make amends for an unintentional wrong. 146

SWIMMING. The best of luck in fortune and friends may be expected if you dream of swimming in the nude. If you wear a bathing suit, you will be chastised for failing to recognize someone whom you have recently met. To dream of teaching another how to swim is a prophecy of an increase in income. 822

SWINE. (See Pig.) 527

SWISS CHEESE. (See Cheese.) 153

SWITCHBOARD. To dream of working at a telephone switchboard is a portent of making a new acquaintance who will take a keen interest in you. Give him or her a chance. 152

SWORD. Wearing a sword in a dream is a presage of being called upon to fill a higher position either in your community or office. To fight a duel with a sword foretells a quarrel with someone whose good will you should cultivate instead. 797

SWORDFISH. To angle for swordfish in a dream predicts that you will struggle to attain an object which is hardly worth fighting for. If the battle is a tiring one, you will be laughed at for your pains. To eat swordfish in a dream foretells a vacation at the beach. 026

SYNAGOGUE. To dream of seeing people going into a synagogue predicts prosperity for those engaged in mercantilism. Attending a service in a synagogue is a forerunner of progress of an intellectual nature. 475

SYRUP. Using syrup on food in a dream is a prophecy of delight in the company of young people. You will be able to further their love affairs and make them and yourself happier thereby. If you get your hands sticky the portent is so much the better. 456

TABERNACLE. (See Church.) 745

TABLE. Sitting at a table has many meanings in a dream. A library table with a lamp and books on it portends a promotion in your work through home study. A dining-table is an omen of convivial times ahead. A card table augurs a new opportunity to make money. A kitchen table predicts hard work at a small salary. 009

TAIL. If you dream that you have a tail, it is a prophecy of having to apologize for the actions of one of your relatives. To pull the tail of a cat or dog in a dream is an omen of sickness. 114

TAILOR. To be measured for a suit by a tailor in a dream foretells an answer to a letter that you have written concerning a position. A dream of seeing a tailor sitting cross-legged at his work signifies travel on another continent. 741

TAMBOURINE. A dancing girl with a tambourine in a dream is a sign of having to explain an absence from home to one of your family. It is a warning to be discreet. Trying to play a tambourine augurs hearing a rumor that will cause you concern. 247

TANGERINE. Eating a tangerine in a dream is a sign of better health and good friends. 627

TANGLE. To dream of tangled threads, either actual or in your personal affairs, augurs a distressing situation tht will cause you much embarrassment. 327

TANTRUM. If you dream of seeing one of the opposite sex in a tantrum, and you are at your wits' end to know what to do, you will get into a predicament through carelessness in your speech. 130

TAPESTRY. To dream of being in a room hung with tapestry is a prophecy of having to deal with a plot against your reputation. Hanging worn tapestry portends mental distress. 729

TARANTULA. Guard against menaces to your health and your personal safety if you dream of a tarantula. If this large spider bites you, the augury is of a ghastly experience. 170

TART. (See Pastry.) 795

TATTOOING. Being tattooed in a dream is an augury of travel on sea and land. To dream of seeing odd designs on a person's body predicts hearing a story that you cannot repeat. 402

TAVERN. (See Hotel.) 243

TAX. If you dream of being oppressed with taxes, you are likely to have a new opportunity to make money. 783

TEA. Drinking tea in a dream, iced or hot, is a presage of pleasure among your church or club friends. To pour tea from a pot predicts that you will have a visitor. 545

TEACHER. If you dream of meeting a former schoolteacher socially, it is a sign that you will be asked to contribute to a charitable fund. To dream of being a teacher portends headaches, both physical and mental. 693

TEAR. To shed tears in a dream augurs happiness to come within a very short time. To see others shed them and to try to give comfort means that you will be made happy by a kind act from someone else. 380

TEAR GAS. A dream of seeing a crowd dispersed with tear gas predicts that you will be greatly concerned over the fate of one of your friends. 789

TEASING. (See also Strip Tease.) If you dream of being teased by someone of the opposite sex, you are likely to have trouble in making one of your actions understood by your friends. 818

TELEGRAM. To dream of receiving a telegram depends for its meaning on the nature of the message it contains. If it is good news, the augury is of money; otherwise it means that you will get into hot water through tax evasions. 669

TELEPATHY. If you dream of receiving a message through the medium of telepathy, or through transference, you will receive good news by mail. 295

TELEPHONE. The ringing of a telephone in a dream portends trouble and sickness. To dream of using a telephone is a sign that you will meet an old friend unexpectedly after several years. If in a dream you try to use a dead telephone you will receive news of a serious illness of one you love. 716

TELEVISION. To dream of seeing an important public event on television—an inauguration, coronation, Olympic games, etc.—portends greater activity and more profits in your business. It is bad luck to dream of seeing a hanging or electrocution on television. 240

TEMPLE. (See Church.) 136

TEMPTATION. Dreaming of being tempted by one of the opposite sex has a good or bad augury according to the extent of the temptation and whether or not you yield to it. The dream is a warning not to get into a situation where you will be tempted. 398

TENNIS. (See also Racket.) Watching a tennis game in a dream is a portent of increasing activity in business. To play tennis, whether you win or lose, augurs social advancement. 761

TENT. (See also Camp.) To pitch a tent in a dream is a prognostication of relief from personal and business worries. To dream of being in a tent when it is blown down by a storm is a forerunner of disaster. 104

TERRIER. Beware of letting yourself get into a nervous condition after a dream of any kind of a terrier. This is a warning. 314

TERROR. To dream of being in the midst of any terorizing experience foretells that you should be on your guard against those who are trying to get your means of support away from you. 975

TESTAMENT. (See Bible.) 462

TEXTBOOK. Studying a textbook in a dream predicts that you will have an opportunity to fill a higher position than the one you occupy. 563

THANKSGIVING. Giving thanks to God in a dream augurs contentment. Dreaming of eating a Thanksgiving dinner, with turkey, cranberry sauce and all the rest of the fixings, is a portent of a happier and more prosperous life. 048

THEATRE. If a performance is going on, a dream of a theatre predicts happy hours in the company of people who are energetic in the pursuit of pleasure. A dark theatre portends a period of boredom. 657

THERMOMETER. To be surprised in a dream by looking at the thermometer is a sign that you will be embarrassed in public by finding something unbuttoned or a hole in a garment. 375

THIEF. Seeing a thief caught in a dream foretells that you will be given a vacation with pay. If you dream that you are called a thief, the augury is of having to exercise great economy in your daily life. 801

THIMBLE. To dream of losing a thimble predicts a slight injury. For a man to dream of giving a thimble to a woman as a present prophesies that he will have a love affair that will come to a happy climax. 514

THIRST. Being thirsty in a dream is a prophecy of an invitation to visit relatives in another part of the country To quench your thirst at a well or spring augurs the receipt of money for a service rendered. To drink alcoholic liquors when you are thirsty for water is a presage of accident. 767

THORN. To catch your clothing or person on a thorn in a dream is a signal that you are heading for trouble through the company you have been keeping. If you see a bird or animal impaled on a thorn, you will suffer for an error in judgment. 973

THREAD. (See also Spool.) To dream of picking a thread off someone else's clothing portends getting into a slight difficulty of a humorous nature. Harassing experiences are predicted by a dream of trying to thread a needle. 071

THRIFT. To dream of exercising thrift in your buying is a sign that you are in danger of committing some extravagance. Putting money away in a bank predicts receiving a remittance by air mail. 506

THROAT. For a man to dream of a woman's throat is a sign that he will be irritated by a woman's caprice. If a woman dreams of a man's throat including his Adam's apple, she is warned to pay more attention to her personal appearance. 410

THRONE. (See also King, Queen.) To dream of sitting as a ruler on a throne prophesies that if you are not more willing to take chances, you will lose out in the race for fame and fortune. 173

THUG. (See Gangster.) 593

THUMB. A sore thumb in a dream indicates coming prosperity. To "thumb" rides on a highway is a warning to watch your conduct. 532

THUMBNAIL. (See Fingernail.) 947

THUNDER. (See also Lightning.) If thunder rolls and growls in your dream, be warned of treachery from acquaintances whom you have suspected of double dealing. If it cracks, booms, and crashes, it presages the solution of pressing problems. 622

TIARA. (See also Crown.) For a woman to dream of wearing a jeweled tiara on her head foretells being upset by the jealousy of her female friends. 522

TICKLE. You are warned against indiscreet behavior with a person of the opposite sex if you dream of tickling anyone or being tickled. 138

TIDAL WAVE. A dream of the devastating effects of a tidal wave portends death in your own family or that of one of your close friends. 058

TIDE. An incoming tide in a dream predicts increased financial resources; an ebbing tide is a sign of added worry. 880

TIGER. To be attacked by a tiger in a dream is a portent of a family quarrel that will have far-reaching results. If you succeed in killing the tiger or making it go away, the outcome will be in your favor. 329

TIRE. To dream of changing an automobile tire on a country road is an augury of having to meet a bill that you thought was outlawed. To have a tire blow out when you are driving is a portent of danger from jealous business associates. To buy a new tire augurs peace of mind. If you dream of losing your spare tire you will have family outcries. 026

TOAD. If you dream of stepping on a toad, you will castrate a plot to harm you. To pick a toad up in a dream predicts that you will suffer a slight but annoying incident. 739

TOADSTOOL. (See also Mushroom.) To dream of picking a toadstool and eating it raw is a sign of impending disaster. To hand it to another person augurs an enmity that you will have to combat. 774

TOAST. Making toast in a dream is a fortunate augury unless you allow it to burn, in which case it predicts great annoyances. To eat toast is a sign of being invited to a dinner party with a group of old friends. To butter toast in a dream is a portent of increased expenses. 716

TOBACCO. (See also Cigar, Cigarette, Pipe.) To smoke tobacco in a dream augurs content. To chew tobacco is a sign of trouble with one of the opposite sex. 984

TOMATO. Eating tomatoes, either fresh or canned, in a dream foretells having an offer made to you that will entail considerable enjoyable travel. To drink tomato juice predicts travel by airplane. 908

TOMB. A dream of entering a tomb signifies that your enemies will fail to do you harm. Being locked in a tomb augurs disease. 138

TONGUE. To eat tongue in a dream predicts being invited to go on a picnic in the country. To dream of seeing a person stick out his or her tongue at another is a sign that your personal affairs will be discussed in an unkindly manner by your close neighbors. 327

TOOL. To dream of using tools of any kind is a sign of a raise in your weekly salary. If you dream of losing a tool and hunting high and low for it, you will have an opportunity to advance yourself by not losing your temper. 263

TOOTH. An aching tooth in a dream portends family squabbles and upset business conditions. To dream of having a tooth filled by a dentist is a sign that you will soon hear agreeable news. Having a tooth extracted signalizes a good opportunity to make investments or a change in your business. 628

TOOTHPICK. Bad luck will follow you for many days if you dream of picking your teeth with a toothpick. Be on your guard against false friends. 681

TORCH. Carrying a torch in a dream forecasts a love affair under strange circumstances. You are likely to be discomfited by the way it turns out. 961

TORPEDO. (See also Bomb, Mine.) To dream of being on a submarine or warship and helping to launch a torpedo is a sign that you will have to fight against competition that will try to ruin you. If you dream of being on a ship that is torpedoed, you are likely to receive distressing news. 313

TORNIQUET. To dream of stopping the flow of blood by applying a tourniquet to one of the limbs predicts a stroke of good luck through an old friend. 993

TOTEM POLE. These Alaskan Indian memorials seen in a dream foretell meeting a distant relative whom you have never seen before. It will result in a happy association. 394

TOWEL. To dry your hands and face on a cloth towel in a dream predicts prosperity and good health, but if the towel is of paper, the augury is the reverse. If you are disappointed by finding that the towel is wet and soggy, you are due to receive disquieting news. To strike another person with a wet towel in a dream, portends danger of losing your position. 432

TOWER. To dream of seeing a tall tower from a far distance augurs wasted effort in a love affair. Looking at the top of a tower from its base is a sign that you are in danger of being swindled by an unscrupulous person. 288

TOY. To dream of playing with toys forecasts new friends; children to young married people. If you make a child happy by giving it a toy, you will be greatly beloved by your family and friends. 391

TRAFFIC. Watching the traffic in the city or on the highway is a dream that augurs a new and vexing problem connected with your business. To drive through traffic successfully predicts the solution of business and family problems, but a traffic jam foretells serious difficulties. 076

TRAIN. Travel by train in a dream means that you will accomplish more both for your employer and yourself if you will give greater attention to your work. 608

TRAPEZE. If a young woman dreams that she is a trapeze performer, swinging high over the heads of an audience in a circus tent or theatre, she will meet a handsome and agreeable man who will eventually propose marriage. To dream of falling from a trapeze is an omen of making a grave mistake; therefore it is a warning to use caution. 086

TRAVEL. By whatever means—car, train, bus, steamship, airplane, or even foot—travel for pleasure or rest in a dream foretells that you will have a sudden and large increase in your income. 723

TRAY. Carrying a tray loaded with dishes is a dream that portends good fortune, but if you drop the tray and break dishes, you will get into trouble. 402

TREACHERY. (See also Traitor.) A dream of treachery from one you had considered friendly is a forerunner of losing a sum of money through the failure of a business. 948

TREASURE. Finding treasure in a dream predicts travel and adventure that will bring you pleasure but not much money. Digging for treasure is an omen of good health; diving under the sea for it is an augury of receiving a gift. 747

TREE. To plant a tree in a dream is a fortunate omen for those who are in love; it augurs a June wedding, a blissful honeymoon, and a serene and happy married life. Beautiful trees in the forest or elsewhere have an auspicious influence on the interpretation of any dream. To cut down a tree is an omen of misfortune in love. 480

TRIAL. If you dream of being on trial in a courtroom, you will be confronted with a problem that will have to be approached with the greatest care lest you do or say the wrong thing. It is a warning to be cautious in all your dealings with professional people. 711

TRICK. (See also Magician.) Dreaming of a trick that you cannot explain is a portent of a day's excursion full of interesting and innocent amusements. If you dream of doing tricks to amuse one or more persons, you will receive an invitation to join a church organization. 202

TRIP. (See Travel.) 371

TRIPE. Prepared in any way, tripe is a good augury for business and health, but it is a warning to exercise great discretion in matters of the heart. 029

TRIPLETS. (See also Quintuplets.) A dream of baby triplets being wheeled in a wide carriage predicts that you will have good luck at cards. A woman who dreams of giving birth to triplets will have many admirers. 102

TROPHY. If you dream of winning a trophy in any athletic contest, you will profit greatly in buying and selling. 512

TROUSSEAU. A young single woman who dreams of getting together a trousseau may look forward to happy hours in the company of her lover. For a widow to dream of a trousseau augurs a marriage for companionship. 796

TRUCK. A good living and a dignified place in the community is foretold by a dream of being a truck driver. To dream of running a truck over an embankment forecasts an attack on you by a thug. 104

TRUMPET. Blowing a trumpet in a dream predicts a surprise in which you will be gratified by the result of something you have accomplished. If you dream of an angel blowing a trumpet, you will suffer from rheumatism. 808

TRUNK. To dream of packing a trunk foretells travel; unpacking a trunk is a sign of a change of address. If you dream of carrying a heavy trunk on your back, you will have to assume a new responsibility. 405

TUB. (See also Bathtub.) Trees or other large plants growing in tubs are a dream sign that you will be invited to a large and brilliant social gathering. Packing butter or other food in a tub foretells a visit from a cousin, uncle or aunt. 403

TUBERCULOSIS. A warning is contained in this dream to take better care of your health. It is not necessarily a prediction that you will contract the disease. 719

TUGBOAT. Dreaming of a tugboat towing a steamship or a long line of barges predicts that you will have to work longer hours but at a higher wage. To dream of being a passenger or one of the crew of a tugboat is a sign that you will be involved in labor troubles. 383

TULIP. If you dream of a row of bright-colored tulip blossoms in a garden, you will be kissed by a handsome person of the opposite sex. To gather tulips implies a round of gayety. To plant tulip bulbs foreshadows disappointment. 306

TUNNEL. To dream of going through a dark tunnel predicts a period of difficult going before you finally achieve your heart's desire. 962

TURKEY. (See also Thanksgiving.) A flock of gobbling turkeys seen in a dream foretells a position in which you will have to go to many public meetings. To kill a turkey is a portent of good luck; to dress one is an omen of plenty. 120

TWINE. (See String.) 380

TYPEWRITER. If you dream of using a typewriter, the augury is of advancement as long as it does not get out of order. If the ribbon sticks or the keys jam, you may look for disquieting news. It is bad luck to dream of writing love letters on a typewriter. 170

TYPIST. (See Secretary, Stenographer.) 299

UKULELE. To hear a ukulele strummed in your dreams foretells an avowal of love from an old friend whom you have not suspected of being sentimental. To play a ukulele and have a string break is a sign of having a short period of hard luck. 116

ULCER. (See Sore.) 951

ULTRA VIOLET RAYS. If you dream of lying beneath a sun lamp, basking in the health-giving ultra violet rays, you will be compelled to take a deferred vacation, but the postponement will be to your advantage. 709

UMBRELLA. To dream of carrying an umbrella in a downpour is a sign that you will meet with reverses. To be burdened with an umbrella when the sun shines presages startling news that will have a definite effect in changing your plans for the future. 009

UMPIRE. If you dream that you are umpiring a game of baseball and a heated argument occurs regarding your decision, it denotes a rift at home. Family differences will be the means of your having to leave for another address. To citicize the umpire harshly at a game foretells a season during which you will be under the close scrutiny of a critical relative who may have money to leave to you. 303

UNDERTAKER. To see a solemn, unctuous undertaker in your dream augurs that someone will try and cheat you of your birthright. Guard, therefore, both birth and marriage certificates and keep your personal papers under lock and key. 440

UNDERTOW. If you dream of swimming and of being drawn seaward by the undertow, it indicates that you will share in the sorrows of another. 594

UNDRESSING. To dream of seeing a person of the opposite sex undressing is a warning to go very slowly in placing your trust in any new person you may meet. 813

UNIFORM. To dream of wearing a smart military or naval or police uniform is a sign that you will be honored for a kind or heroic deed for women or children. 900

UNIVERSITY. If you attend a university in your dream, the portent is of a bright outlook in business and a strong political pull. 061

UPHOLSTERY. To dream of heavily upholstered furniture in your home is a sign that you will inherit a number of shares of stock that have as yet never paid a dividend. 192

URN. If in a dream an urn is filled with fresh plants or flowers, the augury is of calm happiness, but if the urn is empty or the flowers are faded, there will be sad times for you ahead. A funeral urn holding the ashes of the dead is a dream that presages a voyage to strange but interesting lands. 701

V

VACATION. To dream of taking a vacation at the expense of your employer is a portent of increased earning capacity, but if it is at your own expense you will be able to retire in a few years. 056

VACCINATION. If you dream of being vaccinated, you are on the way to making a great success in the work that you like best. 366

VACUUM CLEANER. Using a vacuum cleaner in a dream and walking with it from room to room foretells success with projects concerned with persons of the opposite sex. If a fuse blows out while you are at work, you must guard your conduct while in their company. 010

VAGABOND. To dream of being a rollicking, devil-may-care vagabond portends a season of relaxation during which you will not be bothered by care or worry. 034

VALENTINE. If you receive a valentine decorated with lace and perfumed, you will kiss someone of the opposite sex. 912

VALET. To dream of having a valet lay out your clothes, shave you and keep you in fit condition for social events is a sign that you will be asked to take a position of high honor in your community. 872

VAMPIRE. You will have many disquieting experiences if you dream of being attacked by a vampire bat, but if you are able to kill it, you will have a season of good fortune, especially with persons of the opposite sex. 910

VAN. If you dream of having your household goods piled into a moving van, you will soon make a change in your position and your address that will be for the better. If you dream of riding in a van you will have a chance to make a large amount of money. 206

VANILLA. Smacking your lips over any food flavored with vanilla in a dream is a sign that you will have a party given for you on the occasion of a birthday or anniversary. 378

VARNISH. To dream of putting varnish on a piece of furniture or a floor indicates that you will try to excuse a flagrant mistake that you have made. It is therefore a warning against making errors that could have been avoided. 418

VASE. If you dream of filling a vase with flowers, you are likely to find that friends will come to your rescue when you most need their help. 391

VAUDEVILLE. A dream of vaudeville is a sign that you will have friends that are true but of the type known as screw-ball. To dream that you are a vaudeville actor portends many friends of a professional type. 630

VAULT. To dream of being entombed in a subterranean vault denotes a nerve-wracking lawsuit and much litigation. 791

VEGETABLE. Eating vegetables in a dream is a sign that you will have to pay for a pleasure that is long past. To dream of raising vegetables in a garden portends good health and pleasure with your family. 923

VEIL. If you wear a veil in your dream you will be able to defy fate. Seeing a bride who is wearing a veil means you will transgress but you will not have to repent. 324

VEIN. To dream of cutting a vein is a sign of distressing news from an old friend. 143

VELVET. Wearing velvet in a dream indicates that you will do a deed that you will have to live down. If you make a velvet dress, you will meet a handsome man who will court you with great ardor. 551

VENEER. If you dream of seeing a piece of furniture with the veneer coming off, you will be surprised at the behavior of one whom you believed to be your friend. 553

VENETIAN BLINDS. After a dream of Venetian blinds you must behave with great circumspection unless you are willing to take the consequences of ill-advised acts. 509

VENISON. Eating venison in a dream predicts that you will go to a party without an escort and be critized for an act that is considered a breach of etiquette. 725

VENTRILOQUIST. to be amused by a ventriloquist in a dream is a sign that someone whom you do not like will make uncomplimentary remarks about you. 224

VERANDA. (See Porch.) 467

VERMIN. Suffering from vermin in a dream predicts disappointment in some project you had believed to be favorable. 551

VERTIGO. Dreaming of a sudden attack of vertigo is a warning to unmarried persons against designing people of the opposite sex. 207

VEST. If your vest is unbuttoned in your dream you will make a glutton of yourself. If you dream of wearing a vest in a loud and striking pattern it is a sign that you will be critized for drinking too much. 258

VETERAN. To dream of seeing a veteran of a war marching in line or selling poppies on the street is an augury of trying to explain why duties have been unfulfilled. 075

VETERINARIAN. To watch a veterinarian skillfully administer help to some unfortunate animal is a sign that you will have a slight accident such as a fall or a jar. 340

VICAR. If you dream of a vicar in the pursuit of his duties you are likely to be invited to a party where women will dominate. 406

VINE. To dream of seeing an old building covered with vines foretells that a bearded man will enter your life and bring great happiness. 204

VINEGAR. You will have to account for being away from your accustomed haunts if you dream of tasting vinegar. To put vinegar into a salad dressing portends good fortune in family life. 788

VINEYARD. Dreaming of a vineyard laden with ripe fruit indicates that you will have a good year in which to try experiments. If the vineyard is stripped of its vintage, you are warned to look before you leap—do not try to engage in new businesses that are hazardous. 811

VIOLET. Pleasant company is promised by a dream of picking violets. For a woman to dream of wearing a corsage of violets is a prophecy of social advancement. 529

VIOLIN. If you dream of playing a violin, you will be critized for having queer ideas about life and religion, but you will be loved for your generosity and your friendliness. 680

VIRGIN. If a woman dreams of being a virgin, she will have many good friends of the male sex. For a married woman to dream of being a virgin is a sign that she will have disquieting episodes in her life. 421

VISION. You will have strange premonitions if you dream of having visions. If they are pleasant you are due for a happy surprise; otherwise you will be harassed by debt. 788

VISITOR. To dream of having a visitor is a sign of receiving a gift of silver. If you dream of being a visitor at the house of a relative or friend, it is a sign that you will be a guest at a house party. 270

VOLCANO. If you see an active volcano in your dream belching forth molten lava, it predicts an experience with a neighbor that will give you some concern but will be harmless. 207

VOMIT. It is a prognostication of better conditions in your business and home life if you dream of vomiting. 495

VOODOOISM. A dream of voodooism is a sign that you will be subject to nervous disorders. If you dream of being a party to voodoo rites you will have difficulty in your business life. 599

VOTE. A dream of voting indicates that you will be likely to express yourself in public when it would have been better if you had kept silent. 993

VOW. If you take a solemn vow in a dream, it foretells a happy solution of any problem that you may have concerning your love life. 534

VOYAGE. To dream of going on a voyage to countries that you have seen before portends living again the scenes and events of your childhood. It is one of the happiest auguries that you could have. 607

WAFFLE. Eating waffles in a dream portends having to break an engagement with a person of the opposite sex. To cook them is a sign of being called upon to entertain a small child who will annoy you considerably. 431

WAGON. Riding in a wagon in a dream foretells that you will attend an auction. Young women who dream of riding in a hay-wagon will have offers of matrimony. 226

WAITER. Tipping a waiter or waitress in a dream is an augury of losing a piece of jewelry. To dream of having a waiter spill soup or other food on your clothing portends being misunderstood by your best friend. If you are kept waiting a long time for your food in a dream, you will have trouble with your landlord. 608

WAND. To wave a fairy wand in a dream and achieve the fulfillment of a wish signifies that you will play an important part in amateur theatricals. 099

WAR. (See Arms, Army, Battle, Submarine, Torpedo, etc.) 069

WARDEN. If you see the warden of a prison in your dream, it foretells that you will be under a nurse's care for a few days. 262

WAREHOUSE. It is a good omen to dream of being in a warehouse that is crowded with stocks of various kinds. You will not need to worry about the future. 195

WASHING. If you dream of washing clothes in a tub, it presages that you will be called upon to act as peacemaker between quarreling lovers. Washing clothes in a machine portends a vacation with pay. To dream of washing your body is a sign of success in a new venture. If you wash a baby in a dream, you will find happiness in your home. 637

WATCH. Wearing a fine watch in your dream is a sign that some influential person is keeping his eye on you. An old-fashioned watch foretells that you will be made the guardian of a young person. 553

WATER. (See also Brook, Ocean, Pond, etc.) A dream of drinking cold water is a lucky omen for man, woman, or child; but throwing it on anyone portends that you will be unpopular. If you dream of hot water in any form, it predicts a season of great trouble, both socially and in business. 815

WATERFALL. To see beautiful waterfall in your dream is a sign that you will be introduced to a handsome and gracious man or woman who will be exceedingly kind to you. 449

WATERMELON. Eating watermelon in a dream points toward a cruise in southern waters. If you dream of snapping the seeds at another person, you will find a small sum of money. A watermelon on the vine portends a moonlight tryst at which you should be on your guard. 064

WAVE. To dream of seeing high waves dashing on the shore predicts the futility of your love affair. 661

WAX. (See also Beeswax.) Lighted wax candles in a dream foretell that you will meet small, dainty women. To walk on waxed floors is a sign that you will fail to keep an important appointment. 354

WEALTH. If you dream of possessing great wealth, you will have a financial upset that may have beneficial results. 809

WEAVING. To watch a weaver at his or her loom foretells that you will make much progress in your chosen work. To dream of weaving portends a peaceful and prosperous life. 031

WEB. (See also Spider.) Beware of getting mixed up with any kind of intrigue after a dream of a spider spinning its web. 145

WEDDING. To dream of going to your own wedding is a forerunner of happiness in love; another's wedding predicts meeting new friends. Eating wedding cake portends long life with a loving partner. 208

WEEDS. Weeds in a flower garden warn you to protect your good name by denying a scandalous act that has been attributed to you. 165

WEIGHING. To dream of weighing yourself and finding that you are overweight or underweight is a sign that you will be gossiped about by your neighbors. 321

WHALE. If you dream of getting a whale on a fishline, you can make up your mind that there will be an improvement in your relations with your acquaintances. 029

WHARF. If you dream of tying a boat to a wharf, you will buy a piece of jewelry for one of the opposite sex. Standing on a wharf and watching a boat leave predicts sadness. 876

WHEAT. A dream of seeing a wheatfield ready for reaping foretells prosperity and well-being. Wheat in sheaves is a sign of accomplishing an arduous task. 805

WHEEL. To dram of seeing wheels turning portends hard labor that will be productive of good results. Adventure is predicted by a dream of having a wheel come off your car while driving. An old wheel by the side of the road foretells disappointment. 754

WHEELBARROW. Pushing a loaded wheelbarrow in a dream is a forerunner of a delightful companionship with one of the opposite sex. To draw a wheelbarrow predicts a sad happening to one of your friends. Seeing a wheel-barrow upside down is a sign that you will bear a heavy burden. 803

WHIP. (See also Flogging.) To whip an animal in a dream foretells that someone will take pleasure in making you uncomfortable. 431

WHISKERS. To wear whiskers in a dream predicts For a woman to dream of being kissed by a man wearing whiskers is a sign that she will be made love to by a beardless youth. 954

WHISKEY. To drink whiskey in a dream denotes a busy season in business but no great profit from it. 822

WHISTLE. If in a dream you whistle a tune you will find that you can buy something that you have always wanted. To whistle for a taxicab is an omen of prosperity; for a policeman, poverty. 215

WIDOW. For a man or woman to dream of being a widower or widow is a sign that money will arrive in the mail. 244

WIG. To dream that you wear a wig foretells having a new and better position offered you. If the wig is blown off or otherwise removed in public, you will have to answer an embarrassing question. 817

WIGWAM. If in a dream you enter an Indian wigwam and feel at home, you will be given a handsome present of considerable value. 870

WIND. To hear the wind howling in a dream is a portent of woe. If at the same time you feel it in your face, it indicates that you will be required to do work that you despise. 506

WINDOW. Opening a window in a dream foretells better health. Closing a window is a portent of having a visitor. To enter a house through a window indicates that someone will libel you. To break a pane of glass in a window augurs a period of poor health. 944

WINE. If you dream of drinking wine, you are likely to meet a clergyman who will appeal to your imagination. Be on your guard against giving away a secret if you dream of becoming intoxicated on wine. 210

WING. A bird with a broken wing in a dream means that you are going to have trouble in attaining the goal you have set for yourself. To dream of seeing an airplane wing crumple while in the air presages having to atone for an old sin. 258

WINK. To dream of winking at a comely person of the opposite sex is a sure forerunner of distress. It is a warning to use discretion every day of your life. 652

WISHBONE. Making a wish and breaking a wishbone with a person of the opposite sex foretells the receipt of a sizable legacy. 544

WISTARIA. An arbor covered with wistaria in bloom is a dream that predicts happiness to lovers and married folk. 872

WITCH. Dreaming of witches riding broomsticks forecasts a good time in the company of your friends. 404

WOLF. To be pursued by wolves in a dream is an augury of having to borrow money temporarily on which to live. If you are able to kill them or scare them away, you will overcome your obstacles. 429

WOODPILE. It is a fortunate augury for a man to dream of working on a woodpile, especially if the day is sunny. Women who have this dream are likely to have a short illness. 570

WORSHIPER. To dream of seeing one or more people at worship in church predicts that you will meet people who will work for your advancement. 409

WREATH. Hanging a wreath of flowers or holly is a dream that foretells being invited to attend a dinner or other celebration as the guest of honor. 306

WRECK. To be a witness of an automobile, airplane, train or shipwreck predicts a round of disturbances in business and in love. To be injured in a wreck is a warning to drive with caution. 385

WRESTLER. A dream of wrestlers in action portends that you will win the next bet you make. 668

WRITER. To dream of being a writer of books, magazine articles, poetry and the like is a sign that you will accumulate a library of good books and enjoy life. 952

X-RAYS. To dream of having an X-ray taken of your teeth or other part of the body is a forerunner of a mysterious occurrence in the life of one of your friends. If you dream of looking at your own bones by means of the X-ray, you will be called to account for an indiscretion you have committed. 906

XYLOPHONE. Playing a xylophone or hearing one played in a dream is a portent of taking part in a pageant of historical interest. If the xylophone is played out of tune, it foretells an accident. 241

YACHT. Being entertained on a yacht in a dream is a sure sign of improvement in your financial condition. If the water is rough and you are seasick, you may look forward to a lucky stroke in business. To talk with people of the opposite sex on a yacht foretells a happy love life. 360

YAM. Eating yams in a dream predicts an increase in your weight. It is therefore a warning to fat people. 179

YARDSTICK. To measure anything with a yardstick in a dream is a portent of being criticized for your conduct. To break a yardstick augurs good luck for salespeople. 081

YARN. If you dream of winding yarn off a hank into a ball, you will increase the number of your friends. Using yarn for knitting or crocheting forecasts marriage to single women. 746

YAWL. Sailing a yawl in a dream predicts progress as long as the sea is calm; if not, you will suffer a setback both in love and business affairs. 226

YEAST. Eating yeast in a dream is a sign that you are slated to receive a high honor. Mixing it for use in bread or biscuits predicts receiving the adoration of your beloved. 020

YELL. To emit a yell in your dream presages being discovered in an unworthy plot. To hear the yell of another is a prediction of being able to help an old friend. 853

YODEL. It is a lucky sign, particularly for those who are in love, to hear a singer yodeling in the open air. It points to marriage and happiness. 456

YOKE. To wear a yoke of any kind in a dream portends hard labor under an exacting taskmaster. To dream of seeing a yoke of oxen is an omen of a new address quite distant from your present place of abode. 604

YOUTH. For an elderly person to dream of his or her youth is a portent of continuing ease and comfort. 962

YUCCA. Dreaming of a yucca plant in full bloom predicts love and matrimony to young people, love and comfort to the married, and an appreciation of spiritual values to all. 323

YULE LOG. To dream of cutting and bringing in a yule log at Christmas time foretells true friends and much simple comfort. 953

ZEBRA. If you dream of one of these striped, horse-like animals, you are likely to visit good friends who live in the country. A dead zebra portends that one of your acquaintances is in danger of having to serve a prison sentence. 298

ZEPHYR. A dream of a warm, gentle breeze, or zephyr, is a forerunner of peace through a loving family and moderate prosperity. 139

ZERO. Dreaming of zero temperature and of suffering from the cold is a prophecy of having a present of a new dress or suit of clothes. 521

ZIPPER. To dream of fastening one's clothes with a zipper is a sign that you will preserve your dignity in the face of great provocation to do otherwise. If you dream of a zipper getting stuck, you will be chagrined by the actions of one of your friends. 047

ZITHER. Playing the zither in a dream foretells peace of mind and a host of friends. 378

ZOO. You will travel to far-off places if you dream of looking at animals in a zoo. If you take a child to the zoo, you will make a great deal of money. 968